Making the Miscellany

Making the Miscellany

Poetry, Print, and the History of the Book
in Early Modern England

Megan Heffernan

PUBLISHED IN COOPERATION WITH
FOLGER SHAKESPEARE LIBRARY

PENN

UNIVERSITY OF PENNSYLVANIA PRESS

PHILADELPHIA

Published by
University of Pennsylvania Press
Philadelphia, Pennsylvania 19104-4112
www.upenn.edu/pennpress

Printed in the United States of America on acid-free paper
10 9 8 7 6 5 4 3 2 1

A Cataloging-in-Publication record is available from the
Library of Congress
ISBN 978-0-8122-5280-4

CONTENTS

NOTE ON TRANSCRIPTIONS

I quote early modern texts in their original spelling, with the exception of *i/j* and *u/v*, which have been silently modernized. I also expand abbreviations, change long *s* to short, and give *vv* as *w*.

Making the Miscellany

Introduction

Delight in Disorder: The Miscellany as History

> A wilde civility:
> Doe more bewitch me, then when Art
> Is too precise in every part.
>
> *—Robert Herrick, "Delight in Disorder"*

In 1578, the printer and bookseller Richard Jones published a collection of poems called *A gorgious Gallery, of gallant Inventions*. With this imagery of the "gallery," or a large and open room, the volume title launched an elaborate architectural figure that served to unite the multiple parts of the compilation.[1] As the title page continued, the "divers dayntie devises," the immaterial poems, were initially "framed and fashioned," or planned and made, "by divers worthy workmen"[2] (see Figure 1). These "sundrie formes" were then "joyned together and builded up by T. P.," the book's first compiler.[3] *A gorgious Gallery* created a hybrid material and conceptual form to teach readers how to perceive the multiple kinds of poetic labor that went into its production. It was a bid to please future readers, promising to "recreate eche modest minde withal."[4] The clunky alliteration in the title-page blurbs even picked up on and amplified the style of several of the compiled poems, showing off the alert reading that went into making the book. From the proliferating metaphors to the vertical hierarchy of textual agents to the riot of typography, the title page sold *A gorgious Gallery* as a physical expression of the efforts of a whole network of workmen poets, compilers, and readers.

The volume's investment in multiple kinds of framing was not lost on the young poet Anthony Munday, who Jones commissioned to write an

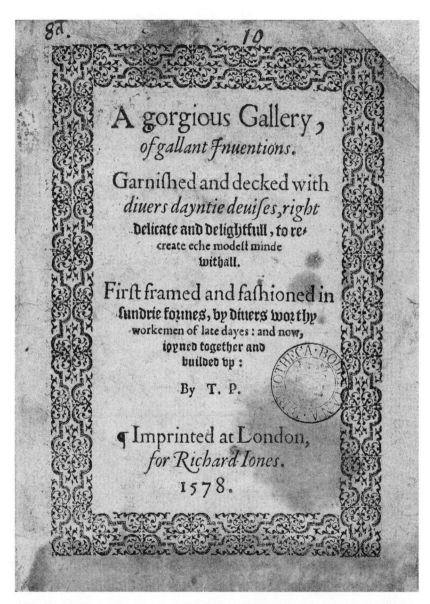

Figure 1. Title page from *A gorgious Gallery, of gallant Inventions* (London: Richard Jones, 1578), sig. A1r, Mal. 464a. By permission of the Bodleian Libraries, The University of Oxford.

introductory poem. Addressed to "all yong Gentilmen, in commendacion of this Gallery and workemen therof," the verse expands on the process of transforming the fleeting poetic inventions into a more durable structure.[5] Munday was a savvy witness to the print trade, and his origin story for *A gorgious Gallery, of gallant Inventions* offers an insightful account of the production and reception of poetry compilations.[6] He first describes "this Gallery of delightes" as a set of "buyldings brave, imbost of variant hue" that had been "devisde by worthy wights."[7] Later, we learn that a single perceptive reader was responsible for identifying the continuities that spanned this work:

> (Perusde) least in oblivion it should ly:
> A willing minde, eche part togeather sought,
> And termde (the whole) *A gorgious Gallerye*.[8]

Munday depicts compiling for print not just as a material practice but, more significantly, as a conceptual skill. This savvy reader was most likely the publisher, Richard Jones, who was responsible for articulating the connections between the diverse poems. The success of the book depended on Jones persuading buyers that he had added value to its contents. As a testament to his willing mind, the compilation expressed a dynamic, responsive poetics by reimagining the gathered work as a larger (if parenthetical) "whole." Like the playful typographic enclosure of these parentheses, the physical design of *A gorgious Gallery* sought to contain the discrete poems, imposing external boundaries that would define the conceptual form of gathered work.

A gorgious Gallery, of gallant Inventions is an exceptional case of an altogether common approach to textual organization in early modern England. For decades, professional compilers engaged in the dynamic transactions between poetry and print, and, like Jones, they incorporated an experimental poetics of compiling into the material design of their books. In 1557, the publisher Richard Tottel took the unprecedented step of adding a title to each of the nearly three hundred poems in his *Songes and Sonettes*. These were lengthy headings like, "The lover compareth his state to a ship in perilous storme tossed on the sea," and they were at least partially attentive to poetic form and content.[9] Across the 1570s, there was a crop of poetry books with floral titles: Thomas Howell's *The Arbor of Amitie* (1568), Isabella Whitney's *A Sweet Nosgay, or Pleasant Posye* (1573), Timothy Kendall's *Flowers of Epigrammes* (1577), N. B.'s *A Smale handfull of fragrant Flowers* (1575), and H. C.'s *The Forrest of Fancy* (1579).[10] Like *A gorgious Gallery*, these figurative titles imagined a larger material form for the perishable poems. In the 1590s, the printers and publishers chasing Philip Sidney's success launched a fad for sonnet books in which each lyric was set on its own page and surrounded by ornamental borders. In all these cases, printed compilations were cast as imaginative creations that entwined poems with the arrangement of the codex.

Making the Miscellany is about the poetic design of early modern printed books. It considers how volumes of compiled poems, which have always existed in practice, responded to media change in sixteenth- and seventeenth-century England. My focus is not only the material organization of printed poetry, but also how those conventions and innovations of arrangement contributed to vernacular poetic craft, the consolidation of individual authorship, and centuries of literary history. I argue that the design of printed compilations contains a largely unstudied and undertheorized archive of poetic form. In an evolving system of textual transmission, compilers were actively experimenting with how to contain individual poems within larger volumes. By paying attention to how they navigated and shaped the exchanges between poems and their organization, we can begin to witness the basic power of imaginative writing over the material text. *Making the Miscellany* is also a study of how this history of textual design has been told by the distinct disciplines of bibliography or book history and literary studies, each of which has handled—and obscured—the formal qualities of early modern poetry compilations and the practices that produced them. Revisiting these editorial and critical approaches, this book recovers a moment when compilers, poets, and readers were alert to a poetics of organization that exceeded the limits of the individual poem.

For the makers of early modern books, the material arrangement of poems was an act of creation. Before a later semantic division between the activities of composing and compiling, multiple textual agents contributed to the process of turning discrete poems into larger volumes. "'Compiling,' in fact, *was* production" Jeffrey Todd Knight has shown, because the division "between ideas and material practice—between making works and making books" was "a later imposition."[11] For the users of early modern books, this fluid approach to textual organization made material context a meaningful guide for interpretation, particularly in the case of print. Sixteenth-century publishers and booksellers "imagined, mustered, and/or assembled" the "heterogeneous arrangement that is the Elizabethan book" by adding textual features including title-page blurbs, dedications, and various kinds of finding aids, from tables of contents to indexes.[12] In turn, material production influenced future acts of writing. "Literary possibility" was fueled, Adam Smyth observes, "by the nature and conditions of its medium," because poets "wrote with an often-acute sense" of the forms and formats in which their work would circulate.[13] Writers and compilers alike were participants in a media landscape in which the imprecise boundaries between literary and textual craft were profoundly generative.

Habits of contextual poetic reading have been most fully treated by scholars at work on early modern manuscripts, because scribal organization holds a history of active reception. Manuscript verse collectors had the "distinctive ability," Joshua Eckhardt explains, to "cultivate relationships between texts" when they put poems "in new contexts, changing their frames of reference and, so, their referential capabilities."[14] This accounting for the significance of physical context develops Arthur F. Marotti's foundational work on social textuality, which identified a continuity between the practices of poetic writing, compiling, and reading.[15] Recently, Lara M. Crowley has offered "the social nature of texts" and the "systematically material manuscript contexts" as an illustration of "interpretive responses by those participating in literary exchange."[16] Attending to the production and use of early poetry compilations can help recover a much broader range of interpretive approaches, correcting the traditional sense that transmission was a detriment or even a threat to authorial poetic craft.

To this robust and growing interest in physical context, my book adds a specifically formal attention to the points of contact between poems within printed compilations. I identify and explain a range of fine-grained approaches to compiling in the design features that both materially and conceptually linked the discrete texts within larger volumes. The printed poetry book was an opportunity for multiple agents of the book trade—named printers and publishers, certainly, but also unknowable compositors and even the manuscript compilers who supplied them—to contribute to a burgeoning vernacular poetic culture. In premodern England, poetry developed through "ad hoc, improvisatory, and unregulated" social practices, that is, "tactics" that were "responsive and adaptive," not "proscribed and determinate."[17] Early modern poetry was more "a doing" than a thing, in Colleen Rosenfeld's formulation, a "quality of action" that was "inseparable from the process in which" it was made.[18] This process-oriented poetics continued into the compiled forms of books. Printed compilations reveled in the active and emergent relations between gathered poems, using the social dynamics of transmission to guide production.

Because textual design was responding to multiple, explicitly formal qualities of gathered poetry, it can offer a way to theorize how different kinds of readers approached their compiled books. In the chapters that follow, I explore the poetics of these material contexts by considering compiling's complementary textual practice: organization. Malcolm B. Parkes has outlined the thirteenth-century development of scholastic manuscripts as the dual evolution of the activities of *compilatio* and *ordinatio*. Where *compilatio* was the gathering up and large-scale arrangement of multiple component texts, *ordinatio* was the secondary addition of features like paraphs, rubrication, division into chapters and paragraphs, and other visual finding aids that help in moving through the multiple pieces within a given volume.[19] In both medieval and early modern textual studies, *compilatio* has figured centrally in arguments for the intellectual practices that can be identified within the structures of material gathering, often in the ad hoc formations of amateur scribes.[20] My attention to *ordinatio*, or the practices of ordering and organizing poems, shows the savvy reading of professional compilers who were invested in explaining how to think across the diverse components within their books. In the development of strategies for textual organization, in other words, we can watch the emergence of a new conceptual category for compiled poetry, tracing a genre in active formation.

The very ability to recognize an unwieldy mixture of contents is an often-telling sign of a cultural split between the moment of textual production and a later reception. Mixed texts have always existed in practice, perhaps appearing even more frequently in earlier periods when vernacular poetry was sparse and "difficulties of textual supply" meant that compilations would "always approach miscellaneity as a limit."[21] The textual formations that were once utterly familiar now appear strange or disorderly. As Arthur Bahr puts it, a compilation "whose contents and organization appear miscellaneous today may have appeared coherent or at least unproblematic to its original audience." In current usage, "terms like miscellaneity" are often expressions "of the distance between the past and the present."[22] The sixteenth-century compilations that have, for modern readers, been known as "miscellanies" and "anthologies" did not carry this designation when they were first compiled, ordered, printed, sold, and read because the genre was largely unremarkable to contemporary audiences. The early modern framework for understanding compiled volumes "was notoriously slippery," as Angus Vine reminds us. "There were not clear-cut distinctions" between "heterogeneous compilations" precisely because "it is their very mixedness that distinguishes them."[23]

The vocabulary through which we now approach early modern poetry books is the expression of a desire for textual coherence that was just coming into focus in an era with a flourishing culture of compiling. Since the eighteenth century, mixed volumes have been known as miscellanies or anthologies: nonauthorial compilations with varying degrees of order. Yet these textual genres—and even these terms, which now seem like natural descriptions—were only beginning to be available in early modern England. In 1601, Philemon Holland faltered over the word "anthology" in his translation of Pliny's *The Historie of the World*: but none of them all, so farre as ever I could find, wrote any Treatise concerning flowers."[24] Either lacking the English for "Anthologicon" or fearing it was beyond his readers, Holland quashed Pliny's bookish joke by preserving the original Latin and then giving an overly literal gloss, "Of flower gathering," in the margin.[25] This English reluctance to adopt the classicizing vocabulary of the "anthology" was short-lived. By 1625 Holland's son Abraham used the inkhorn term to complain about the degraded state of current poetry, which he derided as a mere "Packe of *Epigrams*," such "undigested mish-mash" that would "make / Th' Authors of th'Anthologie to quake."[26] Abraham Holland's observation about the "undigested" packets of poems, an early reference to the *Greek Anthology*, was noting the absence of classical protocols of textual gathering and arrangement.[27] The son here signaled the palpable lack of poetic organization with a language that the father had been unable to translate just two decades earlier.

The development of a native terminology for compiled books reflects the shifting sense of the relationship between the diverse texts within a single volume. For this reason, *Making the Miscellany* opts for the formally and bibliographically descriptive "compilation," because it is recognizably ahistorical, and therefore more obvious as my own critical term, not a contemporary one. As Joshua Eckhardt and Daniel Starza Smith have explained, it was not until the early decades of the seventeenth century that the "English noun 'miscellany,'" from the Latin root *miscere*, to mix, "gradually came to refer not only to the miscellaneous parts or contents of a volume, but also to the volume itself."[28] The designation of "miscellany" was essentially anachronistic, in Smyth's account, since the "difference between early modern and contemporary meanings of the term is a striking reflection of twenty-first century preoccupations with authorship."[29] The retrospective understanding of early modern poetry books as miscellanies proleptically anticipates a moment when authorial agency—and especially its absence—would become the primary frame through which to read compilations.

One "miscellany" in particular has occupied an outsized position in English literary history. In 1557, the publisher Richard Tottel experimented with a new kind of poetry book, *Songes and Sonettes written by the ryght honorable Lorde Henry Haward late Earle of Surrey, and other*, a small quarto of lyrics by nearly contemporary English poets.[30] Appearing in a moment before England had established a tradition of printing short vernacular poems, Tottel's risky venture paid off.[31] The first edition of *Songes and Sonettes* sold out in less than two months and went through ten further editions over three decades.[32] While this book would be a point of reference for early modern English poets—and for generations of literary historians—our current sense of the singular importance of *Songes and Sonettes* depends on a modern reappraisal of it as a "miscellany." Tottel did not use the term in 1557, nor would it even be applied to *Songes and Sonettes* until 1781, when the early literary historian Thomas Warton called it the "first printed miscellany of English poetry."[33] Yet by the early twentieth century, Hyder Rollins would write that "Tottel's *Miscellany* is one of the most important single volumes in the history of English literature" and "the beginning of modern English verse may be said to date from its publication."[34] *Songes and Sonettes* was hailed as the impetus for a profound transformation in Elizabethan writing, "a wellspring for the poetry that followed," because it disseminated advances in style and form to future generations of poets.[35] This sense of the long influence of Tottel's book in fact depended on its modern status as a "miscellany." The modern designation made it possible to recategorize a large set of poetry books according to their neglect of authorship, thus reading for a quality that was not yet in sight in 1557.

As a genre, the poetry miscellany holds a history of how we have come to read the past through modern eyes, collapsing the distance between our own moment and earlier textual epistemes. This leap is, at base, the result of a literary critical history that filtered out the much more complex, uneven landscape of poetic composition and compilation in early modern England. Far from a definitive break with older paradigms of material production and use, the recognition signaled by the English adoption of "anthology" and "miscellany" was just one episode in the ongoing development of textual design that started before these words entered the language and continues today. This much more experimental culture of textual organization has been lost to modern readers because we assume that poetic mixture and disorder were a meaningless accident, not the telling residue of an evolving conceptual category for the compiled book.

The opportunity for a new mode of poetic historiography is not without its challenges. Laura Estill argues astutely that twenty-first-century scholars "are conditioned to read miscellanies" and compiled texts "in a particular way," one informed by a retrospective sense of a literary canon. The result is that "we cannot mimic the kind of early modern reading that accepts these texts without seeking to sort or categorize their contents . . . anew."[36] Estill is right that we always bring our own methods to bear on our studies of the textual past. The history of reading is a recursive loop that turns later modes of interpretation back onto earlier periods.[37] But if we take the poetry compilation seriously on its own terms, the very qualities that now seem the most miscellaneous might also offer a new approach to the history of the genre. It matters that, when publishers in the 1570s, like Richard Jones, did not quite have a name for the kind of poetry books they were selling, they instead used elaborate architectural imagery and figures of floral gathering to explain the imaginative structure of their compilations. Poetry was a resource for thinking through and even ameliorating material disjunctions.

For this reason, a critical attention to the influence of poetic form, style, and genre on textual design can help recover older ways of reading that have been obscured by our presumptions of miscellaneity. Early modern printed books were valued precisely because they were multiple, varied, and often pushing the limits of already available textual genres. Their organization and design could accommodate sensitive responses to diverse kinds of poetry because their conceptual form was still unfixed. The commercial success of *Songes and Sonettes* is a case in point. Where literary historians and editors like Rollins emphasized the simple fact of the book's phenomenally successful publication, early modern readers at first approached the book as dynamically engaged with the form and contents of vernacular poetry. It was this aspect of *Songes and Sonettes* that was picked up by later amateur and professional compilers who were seeking new ways to understand the poetry volumes that were proliferating during the sixteenth and seventeenth centuries. The design of printed poetry reflects how compiling booksellers promoted their efforts in putting together books with varying degrees of order.

By reading for the poetic discourse secreted away within the organizational features that linked discrete poems, *Making the Miscellany* develops a history of form that has not often entered into studies of the material text. My book identifies, in the arrangement of compiled poetry, a vital archive for how early modern readers and writers were beginning to think about writing from their own moment. To that extent, what follows is both a history and a historiography of the early printed poetry book, because it aims to recover how we have arrived at our current methods for understanding past expressions of poetic form. In aspects of textual design, including poem and volume titles, *mise-en-page*, and the sections of poems grouped by genre, we can begin to see how professional compilers used the affordances of print to adjust the horizons of interpretation by making it possible to recognize continuities and read at a scale greater than the single poem. What an attention to the broadest coordinates of compiled poetry ultimately yields is a formal history of the book that can account for the poetics of compilations made by multiple agents—named poets and stationers, certainly, but also the numerous figures whose identities have been obscured by the print trade.

Treating poetry as a resource for a history of these mixed forms, my argument takes a cue from Robert Herrick's poem, "Delight in Disorder," which describes his mistress's wanton clothes. Herrick depicts the "sweet disorder" of her "dresse" in garments playfully in congress with each other: "A Lawne" tossed "Into a fine distraction," "An erring Lace" that "Enthralls the Crimson Stomacher," "A winning wave" that whirls the "tempestuous petticote," and "A carelesse shooe-string" that all proclaim the "wilde civility" of the louche clothes.[38] Herrick's objectifying gaze travels down the body of the fully clothed mistress, who is herself never mentioned. The poet is enchanted by the disheveled variety of her garments, which "Doe more bewitch me, then when Art / Is too precise in every part."[39] Using the clothes to insinuate the character of the woman, this poem revels in the allure of wandering, misplaced objects, identifying or even manufacturing a significance in the points of contact between unruly things.

For Herrick, and for early modern readers more generally, disorder was a delight because it was the expression of an active, evolving, and changeable form. In *The Art of English Poesy* (1589), George Puttenham praised the "tolerable disorder" of the parenthesis, a figure of speech in which "ye will seem" to "graft in the midst of your tale an unnecessary parcel of speech."[40] "Disorder" here signals a disruption of the conventional placement of words, "a deliberate rearranging of the order, not an absence thereof."[41] It was form *in potentia*, a legible trace of other possible figurations. As an early modern critical term, "disorder" offers a corrective to our retrospective focus on bounded, contained poetic forms. Drawing on an array of "materially inflected" critical approaches, the most recent histories of form have approached it as "as an action or a series of actions," in contrast to both New Critical and New Historical accounts of "unifying" or "containing" poetic structures.[42] Instead of a consistent object, early modern poetic form was more a "verb" than a "noun."[43] In moments of disorder, form was the more poetic for this disclosure of an active and ongoing practice of composition. A legible disarray was, in Jenny C. Mann's formulation, the "working out of a vernacular mode of figuration" within a new discourse of English writing.[44]

This poetic sense of "disorder" cropped up frequently as a description for the organization of early modern poetry books. The term was not pejorative, as it might now seem, but was rather a much simpler observation about the lack of any set sequence or organization, often because the final state of the compilation reflected the process of making it. Poets and compilers alike approached the open, modular design of the printed book as a tool that could serve both their own expressive purposes and the desires of readers. In *A Hundreth sundrie Flowres* (1573), George Gascoigne invented a feigned editor who comments on the jumbled arrangement of poems in the volume. One poem heading explains the final state of the book as a result of how the compiler received the "doings which have come to my hands, in such disordred order, as I can best set them down."[45] The pairing of "order" and "disorder" is illuminating because, rather than disparaging the prominent disarray of *A Hundreth sundrie Flowres*, Gascoigne identified the placement of poems as the result of how the compiler received them, reflecting the chronology of transmission.

For readers seeking poetic variety, disorder was actually promoted as a benefit because it allowed any single book to be approached from multiple different perspectives. The compiler of *The Forrest of Fancy* (1579) praises the book of diverse poems and prose epistles for its "disordered placing of every perticuler parcel thereof," which "being rudely and dispersedly divided," would be "fit for every degree, & agreable to their diverse affections."[46] The arrangement of *The Forrest of Fancy* was loose, associative, and available to insinuations—like the wanton, disorderly dress of Herrick's nearly invisible beloved. The arrangement of the book could promise to accommodate "diverse affections" because it was open to whatever interpretation readers wanted to draw from it. Similarly, in *Sundry Christian Passions Contained in two hundred Sonnets* (1593), Henry Lok writes of his religious sonnets that he was "perswaded their disorder doth best fit the nature of mankind," offering a kind of verisimilitude in what he calls the "preposterous placing" of the work.[47] The poems in these printed compilations could be combined, dissolved, and drawn together again in endlessly flexible configurations that were expressive of multiple different meanings.

By considering poetry as it was arranged before the age of the miscellany, *Making the Miscellany* advances a set of field-specific claims about the relationship between individual poems and the larger forms they take when gathered for print. It argues, first, that poetry books initially promoted not the skill of authors but, rather, of compilers, who were often professional agents of the book trade trying to attract readers. Second, this investment in compiling for print meant that poems were gathered and arranged with an eye to explaining the connections between them, which might be based on a shared topic, style, authorship, or even a disorderly material bundling. This study thus turns the resources of book history toward a disciplinary argument about the textual objects that ought to feature in a more capacious approach to literary history. I recover the material substrates for a collaborative cultural investment in the workings of poetic form within work that is now often read quite simply as the origins of English lyric authorship.

The chapters that follow treat both canonical and lesser-known books of poems. I focus on volumes from publishers including Richard Jones and John Marriot; from poets who collaborated with stationers, like George Gascoigne and Henry Lok; and from authors like Philip Sidney, John Donne, and William Shakespeare who seem not to have participated in gathering most of their secular poetry for print. These interrelated case studies situate poetry books within broader practices of textual production and reception, in particular the history of reading devotional texts and manuscript poetry. By showing that the design of compiled volumes was responding to fashions of writing and publishing that changed during the sixteenth and seventeenth centuries, this study unfolds an account of the granular development of English vernacular poetry that has not been available from a critical perspective that treats disorder as the limit of meaning. This long experimental moment witnessed the invention of the poetry miscellany as a conceptual category that was consolidated alongside a new investment in authorial collections. In both practice and theory, poetic authorship and miscellaneity were constituted mutually by the habits, actions, and desires of compilers, not the poets who wrote the poems.

The development of the poetry compilation in early modern England was not linear. At any given moment, multiple different kinds of books were competing for buyers, editions were reprinted for decades, and poets who were wary of print publication shared their work in manuscripts. Instead of treating *Songes and Sonettes* as a clarion call for printing English poetry, *Making the Miscellany* charts the unforeseeable, fitful, and contingent influence of Tottel's unprecedented book. The opening two chapters focus on poetry compilations printed by the stationers who were the first to publish roughly contemporary English poetry. They survey nonauthorial books from 1557 to 1608, many of which have been treated as heirs to *Songes and Sonettes*, to show how printers and booksellers were much more invested in imitating books printed in their own moment than in following Tottel's example. The next three chapters take up different models for compilations devoted to the work of individual poets: feigned multiauthor collections, formally homogeneous sonnet books, and the posthumous memorialization of celebrity authors who wrote in multiple styles. I trace how compiled volumes were actively responding to the historical and poetic context of the moment in which they were made. By arguing for a much broader range of approaches to the organization and design of gathered poetry, the arc of this study recovers the significance of poetic form for press agents who have been excluded from traditional literary histories.

The first chapter closely examines *Songes and Sonettes*, both as it was published and revised in the sixteenth century and as it was reimagined by modern editors. The chapter opens by showing how Richard Tottel created a market for a new kind of collection by using innovative textual features to organize discrete poems into a legible body of work. Tottel's printing house added a heading above every poem in *Songes and Sonettes*, predicting the lyric scenario with descriptions like "The lover thinkes no paine to[o] great, wherby he may obtain his ladie."[48] These lengthy titles were revolutionary in 1557. Headings for individual poems were not typical in either manuscript poetry compilations or the printed books that preceded *Songes and Sonettes*. I argue that Tottel's experiment with how features added in the print shop might intersect with poetic content contributed to the runaway success of his compilation. By amplifying—and at times inventing—the continuities between discrete texts, *Songes and Sonettes* aligned the contingent arrangement of the printed book with an idea of the immaterial collection, creating the conditions for form and content to exceed the individual poem.

This investment in the occasional, thematic, and stylistic continuities between poems could not have been farther from the mixture of materials presumed by the genre of the miscellany, and so the chapter closes with a

history of how *Songes and Sonettes* came to be understood as a miscellany.
The volume's singular importance was consolidated by a nineteenth-century
editorial tradition that obscured the multiple agencies behind early printed
poetry. This retrofitting was accomplished by John Payne Collier, the notorious Shakespeare forger and erstwhile editor of *Seven English Poetical Miscellanies* (1865–1867), which included the book he titled, for the first time,
Tottel's Miscellany. Cash-strapped and brought low after the exposé of his
fraudulent dealings in rare books, Collier used the designation "poetical
miscellany" to minimize the real distinctions among an almost random clutch
of books that he was claiming as a recognizable tradition. By demonstrating
how Collier misread Tottel's approach to *Songes and Sonettes*, this chapter
shows how the genre of the miscellany carries presumptions about normative models of textual agency that hide the experimental poetics of early
modern volumes that do not align with our sense of categories like authorship, practices like compiling, and organizational structures like poem titles
and parcels.

My second chapter traces an alternative, less continuous history of the
poetry books published in the second half of the sixteenth century in order
to resist the literary history of authorship that has been preserved along
with Collier's terminology. The relationship between *Songes and Sonettes*
and six further decades of publications, including *The Paradyse of daynty
devises* (1576), *The Phoenix Nest* (1593), *Englands Helicon* (1600), and *A Poetical Rapsody* (1602), was not a continuous genealogy. Rather, I argue that
these were interrelated sets of collections that each took shape around the
topics and styles that held currency in their own moment; they reflect a
culture of experimental compiling that was driven by the priorities and
proclivities of stationers including Richard Jones and Nicholas Ling. In
books with titles that cast the collected poems as motley assemblages of
immaterial conceits, like *A Handefull of Pleasant Delites* (1584) and *A gorgious Gallery, of gallant Inventions* (1576), Jones wrote poetic invention into
commercial textual features and cast the book itself a vital and active response to the gathered work.[49] His aim was to combat the ravages of commonplacing readers who were wont to pillage his books for choice sentences
and fragments, making books that could not be torn apart. This strategy
became particularly significant in *Englands Helicon* (1600), Ling's volume
from the turn of the seventeenth century that retrospectively lent both a
form and a format to poetry from the 1590s and thereby made it possible for
English writers and readers to comprehend a national poetic tradition. The

history that comes into focus is explicitly not one of authorship but rather of the printed book as an active influence on the genres, modes, and styles of compiled poems.

Chapter 3 reads the exchanges between poems and textual arrangement in two editions of George Gascoigne's poetry in order to rethink the material basis for poetic authorship. While Gascoigne first published his work in *A Hundreth sundrie Flowres* (1573), a collection that pretended to draw material from multiple poets, just two years later he reissued all of the writing under his own name as *The Posies of George Gascoigne Esquire* (1575). This quick revision has been treated as a paradigmatic instance of the "stigma of print," but I argue that Gascoigne's inventive arrangement for his work was a poetic response to the essential disorder of early printed books.[50] Other compilations from the 1570s taught Gascoigne to slip fictional narratives of compiling into poem titles, attributions, and marginalia, which were all typically within the purview of agents of the print shop. By imagining an organization for *A Hundreth sundrie Flowres*, Gascoigne crafted a layered, additive structure that, rather than taming the diversity of his work, preserved a sense of the discord between the pieces of writing. Beyond drawing aspects of lyric content outward into the organizational features, as was common in earlier printed compilations, Gascoigne also reversed that tactic, for instance, meditating on the merits of an aphoristic attribution to the poem "Despysed things may live," which was itself a paratactic series of aphorisms. The effect of these dynamic interactions between poetic and organizational features was to align the practices of writing and compiling to support bald hints about Gascoigne's outsized role in the production of his books. He wove traces of his efforts in compiling into the continuous narratives that ordered discrete texts within the volume. This network of clues encouraged an inferential attention to the imaginative contours of the book, placing authorial identity in service of the textual object, not the other way around.

The fourth chapter considers the increasing division of labor between poets and compiling publishers. I contend that the brief moment in the 1590s in which sonnet books dominated the market for printed poetry was the condition that made earlier and later collections palpably miscellaneous by obscuring the poetic sensibilities of compiling stationers. While Philip Sidney's sonnets were set without titles or headings in the unauthorized quartos of *Astrophel and Stella* (1591), in the sonnet books that quickly followed his example, publishers developed novel approaches to lyric arrangement. Most particularly, they added headings with a numeral and a designation of genre

above every poem, like "Sonnet II" in Samuel Daniel's *Delia* (1592). I show
these numbers to be a new kind of title that helped in distinguishing between
the iterative form. The repetitive sonnets demanded an indexical organization, one in which the numbers did not reflect a progressive authorial sequence but rather provided an explanation of the arrangement of a given
book. These nonverbal conventions occluded the expansive, active poetics of
compiling so visible a few decades earlier and, ultimately, imposed a new division between writing and arranging poems. It was this split, which required
the interventions of publishers and compositors, that paradoxically entangled
the emotions of poets with the order of their books by hiding the distributed
agency of compiling behind an expanded author function that could claim to
precede and direct the arrangement of any particular volume.

Chapter 5 reads the new kinds of authorial collections that came into
being alongside the miscellany by dissolving the poetics of compiling. It
shows how printed books began to express the thematic, generic, and occasional connections within and across an authorial corpus, even when those
immaterial links defied material arrangement. The posthumous *Poems,
By J. D. with Elegies on the Authors Death* (1633, 1635) printed work that John
Donne had deliberately never gathered himself but that had circulated extensively in personal manuscripts. This flexible manuscript corpus was carried into the printed book, which was both revised by the bookseller John
Marriot and annotated by readers who were trying to articulate the connections between Donne's diverse poems. This chapter concludes by following
the afterlife of Marriot's new kind of compilation in a sudden rush of books
called *Poems*, a volume title rarely used before the 1630s. One of these was
Poems: Written by Wil. Shake-speare, Gent., which John Benson published in
1640 as a late reissue of *Shake-speares Sonnets*, first published by Thomas
Thorpe in 1609. Benson radically altered the form of Shakespeare's lyrics by
collapsing individual sonnets together as stanzas within longer and titled
poems. Yet far from an act of destruction, I take this new format as a sensitive and timely reading of the outmoded sonnet book in light of three decades of experiments in compiling poetry. At the same time that the newly
created "poems" followed the local order of the 1609 *Sonnets*, Benson's volume and poem titles, his layout of the pages, and the form of the lyrics
themselves were all fashioned after Donne's *Poems*. This flexible model of
authorship demanded a new way to express the immaterial connections between poems, which could be lifted out of the context of any particular
compilation.

Making the Miscellany closes with a coda on the modes of historiography that have been hidden by the presumed timelessness of the miscellany as a genre. Briefly surveying early eighteenth-century editions of Shakespeare's poetry, it lays out the debate raging between 1709 and 1711 over whether editors should follow the arrangement of Benson's *Poems* or Thorpe's *Sonnets*. At the same time, in search of a language for how their new editions were distinct from seventeenth-century collections, both camps referred to their books as Shakespeare's "miscellanies." Miscellaneity here was a measure of historical distance, a marker of a nascent and perhaps not wholly conscious desire to suss out the temporality of poetic organization. As Shakespeare's poetry was reframed for a new moment in literary history, it was once again read through later presumptions about how material design ought to reflect the poetic craft of early modern England's preeminent author. Reading this forgotten archive of literary history, *Making the Miscellany* shows how the poetry compilation not only reflects this dynamic process of historicizing poetic form but also fuels it, remaking Shakespeare's books for subsequent generations of readers.

CHAPTER I

Plain Parcels

The Poetics of Compiling in
Tottel's *Songes and Sonettes*

The legal printer Richard Tottel has long been known for changing the fate of English poetry. According to Thomas Warton, who wrote the first modern literary history in the late eighteenth century, Tottel salvaged "many admirable specimens of antient genius" when he "collected at a critical period, and preserved in a printed volume" poems that had previously "mouldered in manuscript."[1] This auspicious volume was *Songes and Sonettes written by the ryght honorable Lorde Henry Haward late Earle of Surrey, and other* (1557), or as Warton called it, "The first printed *Miscellany* of English poetry."[2] Without Tottel's publication, Warton surmised, poems by Surrey, Thomas Wyatt, and dozens of unknown writers "would never have reached the present age," because "their detached and fugitive state of existence, their want of length," not to mention "the capriciousness of taste," made manuscript copies vulnerable to "the general depredations of time, inattention, and other accidents."[3] For Warton, *Songes and Sonettes* was a defense against the loss of cultural origins. The legacy of the otherwise perishable poems was ensured by the durable format of the printed book, which became a foundation for the future development of verse in early modern England.

Generations of literary historians have accepted Warton's sense of the simultaneous progress of poetry and print. "As the first printed anthology," Hyder Rollins wrote in 1928, "Tottel's *Miscellany*" was "of the greatest historical importance: the beginning of modern English verse may be said to date from its publication."[4] One reason that *Songes and Sonettes* has been understood as an origin point is that it had a long run in print, reaching eleven editions over thirty years.[5] "Tottel's *Miscellany*" was "a goldmine to its publishers," C. S. Lewis observed, crediting the volume's commercial success with the transformation of English poetry. "The grand function of the Drab Age poets" writing in the mid-sixteenth century "was to build a firm metrical highway out of the late medieval swamp" of native English verse. Lewis continued, "in Tottel we can discover traces of one or two uncompleted highways," provisional routes on this march forward into poetic modernity.[6] *Songes and Sonettes*, in other words, was one of the conduits of the innovative Petrarchan style of Surrey and Wyatt for later writers, including Philip Sidney, Edmund Spenser, and Shakespeare. As Arthur F. Marotti writes, "The story of the literary institutionalizing of English lyric poetry in print culture really begins in 1557 with *Songes and Sonettes*," because the book created a new reading public for writing that had circulated privately in manuscript.[7]

But this sense of development or progress requires the benefit of hindsight. It was only from the long vantage point of Warton or Rollins that *Songes and Sonettes* could be taken as a new kind of compilation with an explicit investment in the literary status of English poetry.[8] From the perspective of the summer of 1557, when Tottel published the compilation in two distinct editions in less than two months, there was no reason to predict that *Songes and Sonettes* would become so successful.[9] Most of the nearly three hundred poems in the volume were written by members of Henry VIII's court, poets who held little currency late in Mary I's reign.[10] Equally, printed compilations of new vernacular poetry were rare in England.[11] Within this uncertain landscape, Tottel was experimenting with how to make a book of poems that could appeal to his customer base of London law students. He needed to draw on modes of organization and design that would have been legible to readers of manuscript poetry.

This chapter reconsiders the basis for the literary history that has identified *Songes and Sonettes* as a singular origin point for modern English poetry. The volume's significant development was not immediately a sense of the skill of native poets, nor of the elevated status of vernacular writing. *Songes and Sonettes* rather promoted the value that individual poems might gain by being included within a larger collection of writing. England was relatively late in producing compilations devoted exclusively to lyric poetry, and in the absence of an established tradition of anthologizing, the organization of gathered texts was idiosyncratic and experimental.[12] Further chapters in this book explore how the conceptual categories—the textual genres—through which English readers and writers understood compiled poetry remained in flux well into the seventeenth century. Here, I begin by showing how *Songes and*

Sonettes created a material arrangement that was an intuitive response to poetic form and content. Tottel's major innovation was to compose titles for poems that had circulated without such features in manuscript. These headings were often miniature narratives that summarized the events in each lyric, like "The lover having enjoyed his love, humbly thanketh the god of love: and avowing his hart onely to her faithfully promiseth utterly to forsake all other."[13] With such ponderous detail, Tottel's titles began to draw out the themes, tropes, and styles that surfaced repeatedly throughout *Songes and Sonettes*. The features that arranged the printed book made it possible to read across the discrete forms of the poems and thus to approach the larger compilation as a context for interpretation.

By treating textual design as an active response to gathered writing, this chapter recovers the evolving poetics of compiling for print. While no accounts of making *Songes and Sonettes* have survived, we can take the placement of poems, the layout of pages, the introduction of organizational features, and the revision of copy as evidence for how Tottel and his print house were engaged with the work they were gathering and arranging for publication.[14] In both the first quarto and the revisions that led to the second edition, the design of the volume was attuned to the potential fissures and connections between the discrete poems, as well as to the future readings that these formations enabled.[15] An uneven care is evident in how poems were grouped by author, genre, and topic. There were slight clusters on common themes and longer sections devoted to the work of Surrey, Wyatt, and Nicholas Grimald. But the arrangement of *Songes and Sonettes* was also ad hoc and incomplete; it broke down in multiple places that remained uncorrected in nine further editions. I read this imperfect design as an indication of how agents of the print trade were negotiating a dynamic interaction between the material ordering of the book and multiple aspects of poetic form. Lyric meter, lineation, length, and mode all actively informed the production of *Songes and Sonettes*, even as those formal features were themselves altered by the exigencies of setting type and laying out pages.

Songes and Sonettes thus holds a history of the poetry collection as a genre in active formation. Far from heralding the modern origins of English poetry, this compilation was a speculative experiment in how writing might travel from manuscript to print—and back again to manuscript, when generations of readers reused its poems. To the extent that *Songes and Sonettes* was an origin point, it was profoundly "liminal," as Jeffrey Todd Knight has described other sixteenth-century printed books that "evoke a mode of textual organization usually associated with the premodern, with manuscripts" in both their material framing and their creative composition.[16] Tottel's publication is a valuable illustration of how early modern poetry was understood before it was classified as "literature," an interpretive category that licensed certain modes of reading even as it restricted others. Recent studies have accordingly begun to qualify narratives of the formal progress of printed "verse miscellanies," returning our attention to the social formations created when "the space of the book functions as a meeting-place for various readerships."[17] For *Songes and Sonettes* in particular, scholarship on the manuscript and print sources available to Tottel has identified the political climate of 1557 as an impetus for several of the volume's idiosyncrasies, including the novel poem titles.[18] Recent accounts of the bibliography and print history of *Songes and Sonettes* have likewise recovered the editorial labor Tottel invested in his work, showing how his compiling was poetically conscientious.[19]

Building on the growing consensus around Tottel's active investment in his publications, this chapter pursues a broader conversation about the status of printed poetry compilations in mid-sixteenth-century England. Even as the care given to *Songes and Sonettes* has become apparent, we have not fully considered the conceptual categories through which the volume was understood by its first makers and users. At least since Warton, the innovative compilation has been treated as a "miscellany" or an "anthology," and it continues to be read through those terms today.[20] But while this vocabulary seems naturally descriptive, it was not applied to *Songes and Sonettes* in early modern England, including during the thirty years in which it was being published. As late as 1623, Slender in Shakespeare's *The Merry Wives of Windsor* calls the book by the title under which it was sold, "my book of *Songs and Sonnets*."[21]

Both the vocabulary and the genre of the volume of compiled poetry were still evolving in early modern England. This long experimental moment was an opportunity for poets, readers, and compilers to test out approaches to gathering diverse texts for print. Before ideals of literary writing began to separate theory from practice and practical craft from creative invention, *Songes and Sonettes* was a testament to the poetics that influenced the activities of the print house.[22] As such, it urges a critical method that can reunite modes of poetic and textual interpretation in a formal history of the book. In the pages that follow, I begin to offer that history, first by showing how the material organization of *Songes and Sonettes* was responding to aspects of poetic form that have long been considered beyond the purview of early modern printers and publishers. To that extent, the compilation was part of a media landscape that was significantly more in flux than the established genre of the miscellany would suggest. I then turn to the afterlife of *Songes and Sonettes* in sixteenth-century England and beyond in order to explain how these dynamic exchanges between poetic and textual craft were displaced by a literary history oriented to the singular agency of authors. It was this loss of the original poetic materiality that would make the book into *Tottel's Miscellany*.

Plain Design

The poetics of *Songes and Sonettes* developed out of the process of compiling for print. Richard Tottel earned his fortunes with a lucrative patent for common-law books, first granted for seven years under Edward VI in 1553 and then renewed for another seven years under Mary in 1556.[23] Alongside this steady business supplying Tudor London's burgeoning legal class, Tottel began to publish more speculative handbooks and English translations of classical and continental works, including John Lydgate's translation of Boccaccio's *A Treatise Excellent and Compe[n]dious, shewing [. . .] The Falles of Sondry Most Notable Princes and Princesses* (1554) and Thomas Tusser's *A Hundreth Good Pointes of Husbandrie* (1557). But *Songes and Sonettes* departed from these publications in ways that suggest the real anomaly of the small quarto, both in Tottel's list and in the printing of English poetry more generally.[24] Other poetry publications were filled with extensive organizational features: multiple prefatory addresses, tables of contents, marginalia, and other finding aids for navigating the contents. By contrast, the pages in *Songes and Sonettes* were almost bare, adding only titles above each of the poems. The effect of this sparse page layout was to wash away prior traces of circulation. Unlike books that explained their origins, the design of this compilation made it possible for poems to stand as their own context for interpretation.

A veritable storehouse of poetry, the organization of *Songes and Sonettes* was strikingly inconsistent. The first quarto contained 270 poems that were divided into six sections, with the first four comprising most of the volume: thirty-six poems by Surrey, ninety by Wyatt, forty by Grimald, and ninety-four by unnamed poets. The final two sections are brief runs of four poems by Surrey and six by Wyatt, likely added after the volume was already in

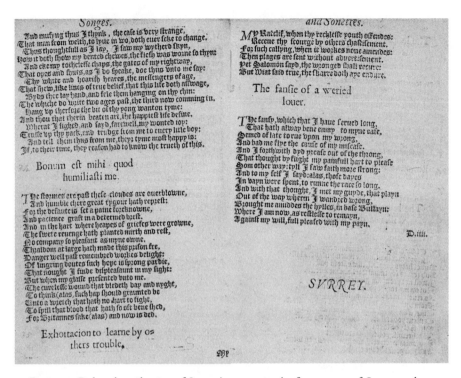

Figure 2. Delayed attribution of Surrey's poems in the first quarto of *Songes and Sonettes* (London: Richard Tottel, June 1557), sig. A1v, Arch. G.f. 12 (1). By permission of the Bodleian Libraries, The University of Oxford.

press. In a bid to promote the most aristocratic poet, the full title was *Songes and Sonettes written by the ryght honorable Lorde Henry Haward late Earle of Surrey, and other.* Yet while Surrey is named in the volume title, and "the depewitted sir Thomas Wyat the elder" is mentioned in the prefatory note, the arrangement of the poems did not consistently promote the agency of individual poets.[25] Surrey's poems are not attributed until the end of his section. His name appears in a much larger italic type below the final poem— and even below the signature mark—in the otherwise blank bottom half of the page (see Figure 2).[26] The work of Wyatt, the other poet identified in the preface, is signed in the same way. But if the names of the two most prominent writers were literally an afterthought, the other sections begin with headings that announce the poems that follow: "Songes written by Nicholas Grimald" and "Uncertain Auctours." The extra clutches of poems at the end of the volume are similarly introduced as "Other Songes and Sonettes written by the earle of Surrey" and by "sir Thomas wiat."[27] Together with the redundant final sections, the piecemeal attribution suggests that the need for treating authorship as a basis for textual organization only became apparent well into the process of compiling, after the first pages had already been set, and no one found it necessary to revise the earlier portions.

Anonymity was not the norm in published poetry compilations from this moment. In editions of medieval English writing still being printed in the mid-sixteenth century, the identities of poets actively guided textual arrangement. Volumes of work by John Skelton and Geoffrey Chaucer attempted to stitch poems together with abundant organizational features, including woodcuts of the poet, tables that laid out sections and subsections, and volume titles that advertised the composite nature of each book. Henry Tab's *Here After Foloweth Certayne Bokes, Co[m]pyled by Mayster Skelton* (1545?) was a multitext volume that consistently referred to the recently deceased poet laureate.[28] Divisional titles like "Skelton Laureate agaynst the Scottes" and "*Prologus Skeltonidis Laureati super* ware the Hawke" appeared above each of the six poems in Tab's compilation, using headings to make textual organization into an expression of an origin in Skelton's hand.[29] Robert Toye's *The Workes of Geffray Chaucer Newly Printed* (1550) similarly included a lengthy prologue about Chaucer's place in a tradition of English poetry and then a detailed list of contents, promising readers: "In this table ye maye fynde any thynge that ye woll have in this volume by the folio, as foloweth."[30] Tools for navigation were crucial in the large Chaucer folio. The transitions between the distinct texts were explained with combined incipits and explicits, such as "Here endeth the legende of Dido quene of Cartage: And here foloweth the legende of Hypsiphile and Medea."[31] These tiny narratives of textual order were possible because Chaucer's authorship pertained to all the volume's components.

Compilations of new poetry also helped readers navigate gathered texts by explaining their origins and their organization in the hands of their authors. In 1550, Thomas Berthelet published *An Hundred Epigrammes Invented and Made by John Heywood*, a subtitle that cleverly puns on the dual senses of "invention" as both discovery and creation.[32] Heywood would expand on that doubled poetic activity in *A Fourth Hundred of Epygrams, Invented and Made by John Heywood* (1560), where he remarked "none do I touche here: by name, but onely one, / which is my selfe" and "I, for myrth, myrly dyd make it."[33] "Making" is the English for *poesis*, vernacularizing an act of artistic creation that was at once imaginative and material.[34] Heywood thus blurs the distinction between writing and compiling. Was he "making" poems or a book of poems? Tottel's editions similarly picked up on this question of how a poet's agency might extend to the design of printed books. In 1557, the same year as *Songes and Sonettes*, Tottel published Thomas Tusser's *A Hundreth Good Pointes of Husbandrie*, a manual of versified advice on farming. The volume opens with a poem to the patron William Paget, Lord Privy Seal, defending the value of Tusser's "homely gyft." This poem is also an acrostic in which "THOMAS TUSSER MADE ME" is spelled out by the first letters of each line, running vertically along the left margin.[35] With a typographic arrangement that verges on ornamentation—and that could not have been implemented by the poet farmer himself—"making" once again collapses the otherwise very real distance between the composition of the single poem and the multiple acts of compiling that produce the homely book.

Where other midcentury compilations stretched the limits of a poet's textual agency, *Songes and Sonettes* by contrast gave extraordinarily few signs of who was responsible for the book. In addition to the uneven attributions to Surrey and Wyatt, the preface "The Printer to the Reader" was a model of impersonal speech, leaving no clues about how these poems arrived in Tottel's print shop. *Songes and Sonettes* was instead advancing a model of publication that had proven successful for classical and continental poets.[36] As the preface claimed, "the workes of divers Latines, Italians, and other doe prove sufficiently" that "our tong" is able "to do as praiseworthely as the rest."[37] Tottel urges his potential buyers to excuse his publication of poems that had been circulating privately: "Thinke it not evill doon, to publish, to the honor of the Englishe tong, and for profit of the studious of Englishe eloquence, those workes which the ungentle horders up of such treasure have heretofore envied thee."[38] With this claim for general eloquence, Tottel shifted attention away from how poems had been gathered. *Songes and Sonettes* lacked all the usual expressions of the publisher's influence over the compilation, containing no defenses of the author, no pleas for patronage, no accounts of the manuscript origins of the poems, and no marginal glosses identifying sources or intertexts. The compilation instead shared responsibility with a new community of readers. Later in the preface, Tottel feared that "some may mislike the stateliness of stile removed from the rude skil of common eares," and invoked the goodwill of his readers: "I ask help of the learned to defend their learned frendes, the authors of this work."[39] This request for help transfers textual agency from the people who made the compilation—both the poets and the printers—to the readers who willingly buy the book.

The anonymous origins and sparse organizational features in *Songes and Sonettes* have most often been explained by histories that posit Tottel's motives as political, commercial, and aesthetic. Jason Powell has recovered new evidence about the network that was circulating Wyatt's poetry in manuscript, which included Wyatt's heirs and their relatives who were in frequent trouble with the law.[40] Tottel may well have been avoiding his own legal troubles by omitting references to this circle. The reluctance to engage politics in *Songes and Sonettes* has more generally been understood as a response to the turmoil of the English Reformation. The compilation's "long period of writing, circulation, and publication" was, Stephen Hamrick observes, "congruent" with England's confessional strife between the 1530s and the late 1550s.[41] Protracted reception cannot, however, account for Tottel's interests as a publisher during the summer of 1557 when he printed *Songes and Sonettes*—and then hastily rearranged and reprinted it two months later. Accordingly, J. Christopher Warner has questioned the view that Tottel was suppressing religious content, showing instead that "censorship" was mostly a matter of selecting uncontroversial poems.[42] Warner offers the Italian and French collections that continental publishers had been issuing for decades as a source for Tottel's investment in attributions. In particular, he identifies the multivolume series *Rime diverse di molti eccellentiss auttori* launched in 1545 by Gabriel Giolito as a model for arranging poems into authorial sections.[43] *Rime diverse* sorted lyrics into clusters by author, with several of the anonymous poems being marked "D'Incerto Autore," a clear precedent for the "Uncertain Auctours" heading in *Songes and Sonettes*.[44]

Accounts of the idiosyncratic and at times opaque arrangement of *Songes and Sonettes* have focused largely on the intent *behind* Tottel's publication. To that extent, textual studies have extended the purview of the literary histories that treated the book as an origin point by positing potential explanations for commercial practices that we no longer understand. This chapter takes a different approach to questions of textual agency. Shifting our attention from the *causes* of the plain design of *Songes and Sonettes* to its *effects*, I find another kind of evidence in the compilation's material and poetic arrangement. My argument offers a poetic history of the book that theorizes the compilation as it stands instead of imagining any alternative form it might take. *Songes and Sonettes* was at its most innovative in the use of textual features to situate poems within the compilation. Unlike the headings in Heywood's *Epigrammes* or Skelton's *Certayne Bokes*, which tether texts to the figure of the poet, Tottel added titles that drew on the imaginative scenarios within the poems. These titles, I am suggesting, are the result of an active, instrumental reading practice that was invested in how clutches of poems might fit together. They reflect an intent *in the process* of compiling *Songes and Sonettes*. I thus follow Tottel's lead in drawing together the agencies of production and reception. The material connections between poems—as well as the pronounced gaps and fault lines at multiple points in the compilation—echoed their contents in ways that would have been available to readers.

The use of titles that could express poetic fictions was revolutionary in 1557. Manuscripts from the period, including those circulating the work of Wyatt and Surrey, tended not to provide headings for individual poems.[45] Nor were titles used consistently in two earlier experiments in printing multiauthor poetry compilations, *The Court of Venus* (1538?) and *A Boke of Balettes* (1549?).[46] But in *Songes and Sonettes*, every poem is preceded by a heading that is set in a large roman type, looming over the smaller, black letter text of the poems. These titles typically reflect poetic content, "what can be deduced from reading each poem," not the circumstances that inspired them.[47] Like the preface, the headings downplayed authorship, the social occasions of composition, and how this work was compiled. Rather than positing origins, Tottel's textual design promoted the present and future reception of *Songes and Sonettes*.

To be sure, individual titles did frequently skew the readings of poems. The first poem is Surrey's complaint of a lost love, which was called "Descripcion of the restlesse state of a lover, with sute to his ladie, to rue on his diyng hart."[48] Beyond relating the speaker's current suffering, the title predicts the effect the poet hopes to achieve by the conclusion of the long, fifty-five-line poem. He ultimately compels his cruel beloved to "rue" his waning life and "Printe in your harte some parcell of my tene."[49] The poet further threatens to expose the mistress if she does not acknowledge her own ruthlessness: "Rue on my life: or els your cruell wronge / Shall well appere, and by my death be sene."[50] The title thus picks up on and tames the poem's scenario, diminishing the speaker's manipulative shaming of the addressee. Yet while this heading is extensive, spanning four lines, it is a profoundly uneven synopsis. Only in the last six lines does the speaker address his beloved: "For I, alas, in silence all to[o] long," have "plaine[d] my fill / Unto my selfe."[51] Before this plaintive turn to a public audience, the bulk of the poem—forty-nine lines— consists of the private complaint of a lover who has wallowed alone in his erotic disappointment. The title thus compresses the lament, transforming the memory of prolonged suffering into a warning about the even more harmful conclusion to come.

Whatever the title's inaccuracies, the imperfect summary in "Descripcion of the restlesse state of a lover" had the effect of affiliating Surrey's poem with work elsewhere in the compilation. By amplifying—and at times inventing—continuities between discrete poems, the textual features in *Songes and Sonettes* created a common context for reading. Many headings softened the disparity between poetic scenarios with attributions to anonymous, seemingly interchangeable lovers:

> The lover comforteth himselfe with the worthinesse of his love,
> The lover complaineth himself forsaken,
> The lover shewing of the continuall paines that abide within his
>   brest determineth to die because he can not have redresse,
> The lover praieth his service to be accepted and his defaultes
>   pardoned.[52]

Like the foreshortened erotic suffering in Surrey's first poem, these headings generate a sameness of tone and content by promoting the Petrarchan clichés that surfaced repeatedly across *Songes and Sonettes*. They identify the speakers as stock lovers, making it possible for readers to recognize and engage the similarities between poems by Surrey, Wyatt, and the anonymous poets. By prompting readers to project themselves into the world of each poem, the compilation added tools through which the generic and fictional lyric personae take priority over the identities of the authors. *Songes and Sonettes* encouraged a textual use that was responsive to the imaginative writing.

Put more strongly, poetic content seemed to determine aspects of material design and arrangement, allowing poems to fall into position without a discussion of origins either in the process of compiling or in the hand of a known author. This evolving, fluid design was profoundly uneven. The layout of pages sometimes divided headings from poems. One example appears at the end of Surrey's section, where the title "Exhortacion to learne by others trouble" is given at the bottom of one verso page, but the poem, which begins "My Ratclif, when thy rechlesse youth offendes," does not appear until the top of the next recto (see Figure 2). The "heading" here is even further expanded by the setting that splits "o-thers" across two lines, an improbable and unnecessary hyphen that allows the already large type to occupy even more space on the page. Such expansive spacing was characteristic of headings throughout the compilation. The result was a conflict between the physical and the conceptual organization of *Songes and Sonettes*, since the attempt to promote the titles visually also had the effect of separating them from the poems they were meant to introduce.

This uneven *mise-en-page* is a telling sign of the multiple conventions of poetry compiling that were still being worked out in 1557. The splitting apart of poems and titles does not seem to have particularly troubled either Tottel or anyone else in his shop, since these ruptures occurred frequently in *Songes and Sonettes* and were not usually corrected in later editions. If the palpable absence of most organizational features produced an unwieldy abundance of poems, that attenuated structure was also an opportunity for the dynamic, even poetic arrangement of the printed compilation. Because the volume lacked editorial explanations for how to move through the distinct texts, the context for reading and interpretation was generated anew in each encounter with the gathered poems. The counterintuitive—and likely unintended— effect of the sparse textual frames in *Songes and Sonettes* was to open the material design of the printed book to poetic fictions.

Poetic Parcels

The arrangement of *Songes and Sonettes* expressed a complex relation between the forms of individual poems and the larger compilation. As the uneven titles and attributions demonstrate, Tottel was working at the point of intersection between poems, exploring how the book's contents might be drawn together or pried apart in open and flexible formations. Far from an "organic" or "coherent" structure, *Songes and Sonettes* testifies to "the dynamism of form" activated by the process of compiling.[53] We can watch this fluid structure develop across the multiple editions, which experimented with how best to fit poetic texts together within the printed book. In particular, the revisions between the first and second quartos refined the order, placement, and headings of poems. Like the volume's plain design, these revisions encouraged readers to seek the meaning created by the local organization of *Songes and Sonettes*, identifying the profound continuities between poems as one of the benefits of the printed compilation.

Tottel's book proposed that compiling increases the value of lyrics that were at first discrete and self-contained pieces of writing. His preface opens with the announcement that "to have wel written in verse, yea & in small parcelles, deserveth great praise."[54] It is not surprising that lithe, tightly crafted verses are praised in a book called *Songes and Sonettes* because these are the two forms most associated with the master lyricist Petrarch, whose work was beginning to influence vernacular poetry in England.[55] But more than just praising small poems, Tottel was emphasizing their position within a larger field of writing. "Parcel" had multiple meanings in this moment. The term was above all a relational description; it measured and defined one component against another.[56] We can get a sense of this relational structure in the legal usage of "parcel," which was used to refer to a portion of land held apart from surrounding plots.[57] "Parcel" could also mean a package to be sent, identifying poems with the bundles in which they circulated. The praise for verse "in small parcelles" thus widens the ambit of individual poems, affiliating them materially with their near neighbors and conceptually with the process of compiling that delivers them to readers.

In early printed books, "parcel" was also used more specifically to describe an internal division or a short section within a larger volume. The term was at first a relic of how print shops received copy, "the discrete bundles of sheets in which the individual works" arrived for printing.[58] But "parcel" developed from a material description into a term for how those original packets of texts influenced the organization and arrangement of compilations. In 1560, the printer-publisher John Day used the word to explain the relation between Anne Vaughan Lock's translation of *Sermons of John Calvin* and *A Meditation of a Penitent Sinner*, her run of sonnets published in the same volume. The divisional title page between the two texts includes the disclaimer: "I have added this meditation folowyng unto the end of this boke, not as a parcell of maister Calvines worke, but for that it well agreeth with the same argument, and was delivered me by my friend with whom I knew I might be so bolde to use & publishe it as pleased me."[59] "Parcell" here is a relational structure that bridges Lock's translation of Calvin and her own verse meditations. Past acts of compiling are transformed into guides for future reading when Day explains both the continuities of the "argument" and the divisions between distinct texts within the single book.

Like Day's description of the material divisions within his book, Tottel's "small parcelles" suggest how *Songes and Sonettes* both divides and joins its component texts. The design of the compilation stitched extant writing together into new material and conceptual forms that exceed the original limits of any individual poem. Tottel's titles helped produce these dynamic clusters by announcing both the scenarios that unfold within poems and, in a few key places, their position in relation to other pieces. One example of such doubly contextual headings appears above two of Wyatt's poems, "Of his love that pricked her finger with a nedle" and "Of the same."[60] In the first poem, the speaker gleefully relates Cupid's retribution on a beloved who "hath done me the wrong." The cruel mistress sits embroidering, and with each thrust of the needle, she viciously "wisht my hart the samplar." But Cupid turns this injury back on her hand: "Made her own weapon do her finger blede: / To fele, if pricking wer so good in dede."[61] Following this justly painful and erotic punishment, the second poem repeats and intensifies the scene:

> she cruell more, and more,
> Wished eche stitche, as she did sit, and sow,
> Had prickt my hart, for to encrease my sore.[62]

In a final twist, the concluding couplet of the second poem inverts the rhyme words used at the end of the first: "For as she thought, this is his hart in dede: / She pricked hard: and made her self to blede."[63] As a doubled erotic scenario, this pair of poems at once embraces and resists the formal breaks that characterize the experience of reading multiple short texts together. At the end of the first poem, the tidy couplet and the intervening white space separate the two lyrics both verbally and visually. But the title "Of the same" unexpectedly stretches elements of form and content across those signals of conclusion, thrusting the reader back into the experience of the first poem.

This pair of poems, in other words, was one of the "small parcelles" that Tottel found so worthy of praise in his preface. The titles that draw together the two accounts of vindictive stitching—structuring both the material and the formal relation between the discrete texts—were added in the process of arranging *Songes and Sonettes* for print. Both of these embroidery poems appeared in the Egerton manuscript, an important witness to the circulation of Wyatt's poetry before his death in 1542.[64] But in the manuscript, these accounts of the vindictive needle were unrelated by either proximity or textual frames, since Egerton gives the two poems without headings, separated by more than a dozen pages, and in the reverse order.[65] The two stitching poems were simply repeated treatments of a common theme. By contrast, the arrangement fashioned through the new titles in *Songes and Sonettes* established a slight sequence with a necessary order. "Of the same" only makes sense as a guide for reading if the poem appears second, as an extension of the scene of sadistic stitching.

By reordering the two poems and titling them as a pair, the printed *Songes and Sonettes* draws the small forms into a parcel that extends and amplifies the account of suffering in love. "Of the same," opens with a question, "What man hath hard such cruelty before?"[66] When placed second, as it is in *Songes and Sonettes*, this response functions as both commentary *on* the previous poem and inspiration *for* a second investigation of this mistress's cruelty. Contemporary readers observed this dynamic arrangement of the stitching poems. In a copy of the 1565 edition of *Songes and Sonettes*, now held at the Huntington Library, a contemporary hand has added trefoils next to the first line of each.[67] These symbols could very well be traces of a reception that was attuned to the formal continuities created by the textual apparatus of *Songes and Sonettes*. The process of compiling for print made it possible for each lyric to heighten the significance of the other.

As an expression of the active reading of the publishers and printers who added these titles, Tottel's small parcels are artifacts of the multiple negotiations between poetic form and the material arrangement of *Songes and Sonettes*. This evolving design, in other words, allows us to witness a poetic compiling that was itself a formal practice. Ben Burton and Elizabeth Scott-Baumann have argued recently for an approach to early modern form that exceeds traditional presumptions of unity and constraint. "Form is as useful as a verb as a noun," they write, urging us to "think of it as an action or a series of actions" instead of a consistent object.[68] *Songes and Sonettes* is a powerful illustration of form as an active process in which Tottel and his printers were the agents of an evolving "force" that layered multiple historical and aesthetic relationships.[69] Their compiling was a practice that affiliated the discordant energies of poetic and material craft—and of political and literary influence—within parcels that jostled unevenly but productively within *Songes and Sonettes*.

In emphasizing the parcel as a primary unit of meaning, I am offering an account of form that is specific to printed poetry compilations from this moment in the mid-sixteenth century. The study of *Songes and Sonettes* has been advanced in recent years by a new attention to the "whole book," a concept first developed by medievalists who approach the "single manuscript as a historical artifact" that "came into being at the crossroads of a variety of social and professional expertises, demands, and intentions."[70] Most influentially, Paul A. Marquis has used this method to read *Songes and Sonettes* as a carefully constructed "anthology," particularly in the revised second quarto.

When "one progresses through *Songes and Sonettes* from the first to the last poem," he observes, a "formal integrity" comes into focus for "the compilation as a whole," proposing that the overarching order of the volume demonstrates a coherent arc.[71] While a necessary corrective to presumptions of miscellaneity, attention to the integrity of the whole book passes over the more intermediate workings of form that are specific to the parcel, the unit of textual and poetic composition that Tottel himself praised. Neither the opening preface nor the poem headings establish an overarching structure for *Songes and Sonettes*, but the publisher's titles did encourage readers to move between proximate poems. Even if the whole book was not itself coherent, the parceled design of *Songes and Sonettes* served as a cue for a textually—and a contextually—aware interpretation.

We can get a sense of Tottel's investment in the poetics of the parcel in the substantial revisions between the first and second editions of *Songes and Sonettes*. The immediate success of the compilation must have come as a surprise. The first edition was published on June 5, 1557, and sold out so quickly that a substantially revised *Songes and Sonettes* was set and printed eight weeks later, by July 31, 1557. The second edition significantly adjusted the material and the poetic design of the compilation. Where the first quarto had seven loosely authorial sections, the second edition moved poems into five with a new order. The late poems by Wyatt and Surrey were consolidated into their primary runs. In Grimald's case, all but ten of his lyrics were cut, and those that remained were moved to the end of *Songes and Sonettes*. Thirty-nine poems were also added to the "Uncertain Auctours" section.[72] After the poems, a new index gave the first few feet of each opening line and the corresponding page number under alphabetical headings. This was the arrangement of *Songes and Sonettes* that would have been known to most sixteenth-century readers. The order and organization of the second quarto was retained in all subsequent editions, even preserving the division of copy across pages—and the splintering of poems from their headings—when the format was downsized to an octavo in 1559. The compilation was published at least nine more times, more than any other book of nonreligious verse. By 1587, there were possibly 4,000 to 6,000 copies in circulation.[73]

As the movement of poems suggests, the revised *Songes and Sonettes* continued to experiment with how texts were both divided and united by the design of the book. In particular, the reordering of the poems by "Uncertain Auctours" shows how the compilation took advantage of the parcel as a relational structure that drew on aspects of both material and poetic forms.[74] One pair of poems added in the revisions, "The complaint of the hot woer" and "The answer," shows a consistent investment in the parcel's potential to sponsor contextual interpretation. The first of these poems compares the speaker's love to a "kinde of coale" that smolders without burning: "in the fire will wast away, / and outward cast no flame" (no. 237, lines 1, 3–4). His suffering is caused by an unresponsive mistress, whose chill only heightens his affections:

> As this is wonder for to se,
> > Cold water warme the fire,
> So hath your coldnesse caused me,
> > To burne in my desire.
> > > (no. 237, lines 13–16)

This lament is followed by "The answer" given in the voice of the frosty mistress. She first disparages the rote simile as "Your borrowd meane" and a "mone, of fume withouten flame," and then attacks the character of a poet who relies on such exhausted expressions: "Being set from smithy smokying coale: ye seme so by the same" (no. 238, lines 1, 2). Ultimately, "The answer" refutes the first speaker's complaint by reminding that cold water strengthens freshly forged steel: "the water trough may serve" through "worke of smithes both hand and hed a cunnyng key to make" (no. 238, lines 24, 25). Both the argument and the imagery of the two poems are yoked together through this direct, second-person response to "The complaint of a hot woer."

The tidy joining of a complaint with its answer was part of a much larger parcel of responses. From this initial set, an extended chain of paired poems unspools over ten pages.[75] In total, twelve pieces are linked by their headings into six thematic and dialogic pairs:

1. "The complaint of a hot woer" and "The answer"
2. "An epitaph made by W.G. lying on his death bed, to be set upon his owne tombe" and "An answer"
3. "An epitaph of maister Henry williams" and "An other of the same"
4. "Against women, either good or bad" and "An answer"
5. "Against a gentilwoman by whom he was refused" and "The answere"
6. "The lover dredding to move his sute for dout of deniall, accuseth all women of disdaine and ficklenesse" and "An answere" (nos. 237–48, pp. 188–95)

The second pair of two epitaphs, perhaps for William Grey, was present in the first edition in roughly the same position late in the "Uncertain Auctours" section. But the third set was also created in the revisions that led to the second quarto. While "An epitaph of maister Henry Williams" appeared in the first edition, it stood alone and without any related poems. In the second quarto, a paired parcel was fashioned by adding "An other of the same," which continued the themes of a young life too soon cut short by death.[76] Both poems lament the premature loss of a man in his prime, with the first bewailing "death" and "his dredfull dart," which "cut the lives line in twaine / of Henry, sonne to sir John Williams Knight," known for his "manly hart and prowes none could staine" (no. 241, lines 20, 22–23, 24). "An other of the same" repeated this story, though from the more general perspective of an anonymous corpse luridly begging the reader, "Stay gentle frend that passest by, / And learne the lore that leadeth all." Although "hopefull youth had hight me health," the grisly speaker could not thwart death: "But yet for all that here I lye" (no. 242, lines 1–2, 9, 12). "An other of the same" thus repeats a common theme, though from an even grimmer perspective. It contributed to a textual arrangement that was a sensitive expression of a poetics of lament.

Within the longer unfurling parcel of twelve poems, this third pair is clearly an outlier. Rather than refuting the topic, "An other of the same" duplicates the scene of mourning, and those two memorial poems do not take up the apparent viciousness of women that dominates the rest of the parcel. Yet the *mise-en-page* of this long chain of response poems downplays those differences, encouraging an attention to the iterative pairs by diminishing the particularities of the single poems (see Figure 3).[77] "An other of the same" and "An answer" are each vertically aligned in the center of the page and set as mirror images across the gutter. The effect is to visually affiliate those two poems, pulling "An other of the same" into the ambit of the responses. This is a parcel composed of smaller nesting parcels, interlacing poems with a textual apparatus that becomes a guide for how to move across the compilation. The reader's attention is drawn outward to the longer chain of poems, skipping backward and forward to encompass the questions and responses.

This commitment to clustering pairs of poems in *Songes and Sonettes* is borne out by the final set within the longer parcel, which was also produced by the revisions for the second quarto. Both "The lover dredding to move his sute for dout of deniall, accuseth all women of disdaine and

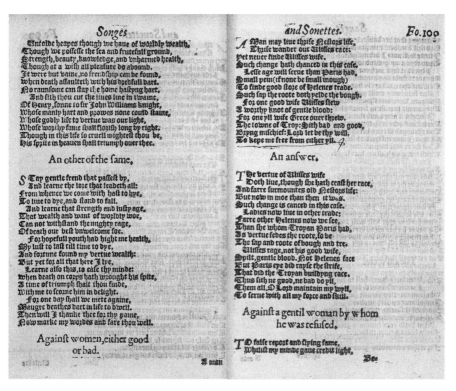

Figure 3. An extended parcel of response poems in the revised *Songes and Sonettes* (London: Richard Tottel, 1557), sigs. Bb3v–Bb4r, PFORZ 506 PFZ. By permission of the Harry Ransom Center, University of Texas.

ficklenesse" and its response were present in the first edition, but they were not placed at all near one another. Instead, that final "An answer" originally appeared at the very end of the "Uncertain Auctours" section, separated from its partner by thirty-seven pages and eighty-three intervening poems. This deficient placement was signaled by the original heading for the response: "An answere to a song before imprinted beginnyng. To walke on doutfull grounde."[78] That poem was first headed "Not to trust to much but beware by others calamaties," but in the second edition was retitled "The lover dredding to move his sute for dout of deniall, accuseth all women of disdaine and ficklenesse."[79] The new heading significantly expanded the first, transforming a pat aphorism into the speech of (yet another) apprehensive lover. With this flurry of revisions, the second quarto of *Songes and Sonettes* was sustaining a thematic connection that was in danger of being lost in the first edition's separation of the poems. The new material arrangement heightened the rationale for reading each piece in relation to another.

By fostering such intertwined networks of reading and interpretation, the design of *Songes and Sonettes* generated complex affiliations between poems and, in doing so, created a guide for readers to navigate the physical space of the book. The larger compilation was not an extended sequence or a continuous whole, but rather an unfolding assemblage composed of fluid and shifting parcels. *Songes and Sonettes* was an active form that developed out of the local links between poems drawn together by the material arrangement—and then rearrangement—of the printed book.

Compiled Forms and Fictions of Identity

Even if *Songes and Sonettes* developed a mode of textual arrangement that responded dynamically to the gathered material, it did not always transmit poems accurately and frequently lost or misrepresented details of form and content. With the rote anonymous lovers in the headings, the compilation consistently flattened out differences of source and occasion. This abstraction of poems was intensified by the revisions that produced the second edition. While many of Nicholas Grimald's poems first identified their subjects by name or initials, thirty of the most occasional poems were cut from the revised second quarto. For instance, both "An Epitaph of the ladye Margaret Lee, 1555" and the incredibly personal "A funerall song, upon the deceas of Annes his Moother," which narrated Grimald's own childhood, disappeared from the version of *Songes and Sonettes* read by most Elizabethans.[80] Tottel had real motives for suppressing biographical details in the poems he published.[81] But beyond disguising authorship, this strategic blandness had a pronounced effect on the poetics of material design this chapter is considering as a signal innovation of the collection. The volume's sparse arrangement and fluid, relational parcels allowed later readers to draw their interpretations from the textual features that actively remade the compiled poems. By removing occasional detail, *Songes and Sonettes* facilitated a mode of reading that was more focused on the fictions within poems than the situations that inspired them.

We know from extant manuscripts that Wyatt's work was especially subject to alteration in *Songes and Sonettes*, which changed the occasions, meters, and even genres of several of his poems. These pervasive adjustments may well have been an attempt to align Wyatt's idiosyncratic prosody with the regular verse forms popularized a decade previously in Thomas Sternhold's and John Hopkins's phenomenally successful *Certayne Psalmes chosen out of the Psalter of David, and drawen into Englishe Metre* (1549).[82] One of Wyatt's poems, called "The lover suspected of change praieth that it be not beleved against him" in *Songes and Sonettes* (p. 56), appears as well in the Blage manuscript.[83] There the poem was an account of political intrigue, far from the erotic infidelity implied by the printed heading. It was an acrostic with the first letter of every line spelling out "Anne Stanhope":

> Accusyd thoo I be without desert,
> Noone can hit prove, yet ye beleve hit treue;
> Nor never yet, sens that ye had my hart,
> Intendid I to be false or untrewe.[84]

Anne was the wife of Sir Michael Stanhope, one of Edward Seymour's conspirators who was executed for treason in 1552.[85] The speaker here confronts the public reputation she has gained as a result of her husband's treachery. She denies the baseless accusations that swirl around her by directly refuting the doubting listener, the second person "ye" who suspiciously presumes her intentions to be untrue. "Hart" is a token of the speaker's political allegiances, not her faithfulness in love, and indeed Anne was known for the piety with which she raised her children after her husband's execution.[86]

This fraught study of political intrigue vanished when the poem was printed in *Songes and Sonettes*. The new heading, "The lover suspected of change praieth that it be not beleved against him," transforms Lady Stanhope into a conventional male lover, shifting the language of fidelity from a political scenario to an erotic one. What is more, "Sith" and "For" are added as the beginning of lines two and three (see Figure 4).[87] These adjustments to "Accusyd thoo I be" express a practice of compiling that was attuned to poetics, though not in the ways that a modern desire for fidelity to Wyatt's voice might expect. The verbal additions and substitutions to this poem were "movements in the direction of regularity" that were characteristic of how Wyatt's poetry was handled throughout *Songes and Sonettes*.[88] The added words were likely meant to even out the meter, turning each opening foot into a regular iamb, but they dampened the more conversational rhythm of the poem that prevailed in the manuscript tradition.

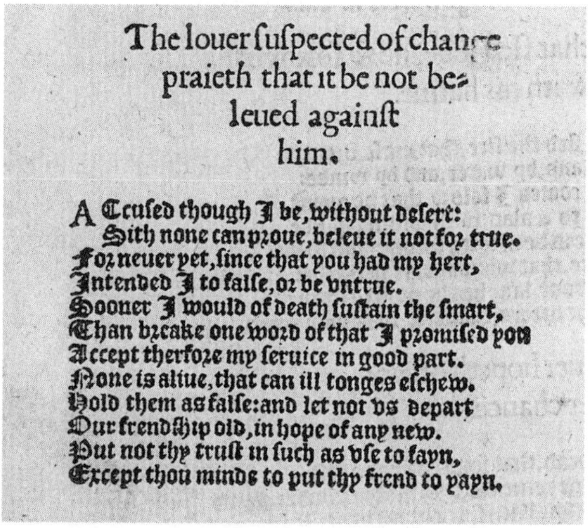

The louer fufpected of chan~e
praieth that it be not be=
leued againft
him.

A Ccufed though I be, without defert:
  Sith none can proue, beleue it not for true.
For neuer yet, fince that you had my hert,
Intended I to falfe, or be vntrue.
Sooner I would of death fuftain the fmart,
Than breake one word of that I promifed you
Accept therfore my feruice in good part.
None is aliue, that can ill tonges efchew.
Hold them as falfe: and let not vs depart
Our frendfhip old, in hope of any new.
Put not thy truft in fuch as vfe to fayn,
Except thou minds to put thy frend to payn.

Figure 4. Anne Stanhope's vanishing acrostic in the revised *Songes and Sonettes* (London: Richard Tottel, 1557), sig. HIv, PFORZ 506 PFZ. By permission of the Harry Ransom Center, University of Texas.

The added words also had the effect of disguising the acrostic that spells out Anne's first name. It is not clear that these adjustments were primarily meant to efface the identity of the speaker, scandalous though she might have been in 1557. The lines that remain preserve the most controversial part of her name, "A . . . Stanhope." Instead, the revisions that produce "The lover suspected of change" are a testament to the pressure that the plain design of the printed book placed on the formal composition of individual poems. In the same fashion as the slightly obtuse poem titles, the newly iambic lines were the expression of a compiled poetics that made it possible to read across the gathered writing by flattening out the particularity of any one poem. With metrical regularity supplanting origins, poetry took priority over history.

Indeed, the adjustments that made Wyatt's work hew closer to a regular form and meter contributed to the broader project of textual parceling in *Songes and Sonettes*. Three of Wyatt's poems in the compilation were originally rondeaux, a fifteen-line French form in which a refrain twice repeats the opening feet, once after the eighth line and once after the fourteenth.[89] In the Egerton manuscript, the poem that begins "What vaileth trouth or by it to take payn" gives lines seven to nine as:

True meanyng hert is had in disdayn
Against deceipt & dowblenes
    What vaileth trouth.[90]

Yet the setting of *Songes and Sonettes* drastically remade this structure, filling out Wyatt's half lines in the first repetition and removing them in the second. Those same lines become:

True meaning hart is had in *hie* disdain.
Against deceit, and *cloked* doublenesse,
What vaileth troth, *or parfit stedfastnesse*.
(no. 75, lines 7–9; emphasis added)

The introduction of "hie" and "cloked" served a dual purpose. First, the new words created even pentameter lines, smoothing out Wyatt's awkward iambs. They also intensified his imagery, rendering "disdain" even more haughty and "doublenesse" further obscure. The refrain, meanwhile, had the effect of lessening the uneasiness of the speaker's inquiry into the causes of deceit by completing the line with "parfit stedfastnesse." In the Egerton manuscript, the rondeau unevenly loops back to "What vaileth trouth," the question that opens the poem—and the question that remains unanswered at its end. In *Songes and Sonettes*, the new half line replaces the more metaphysical desire for a deep truth with a simple performance of faithful commitment.

Here and elsewhere in the compilation, the effect of these changes was to draw Wyatt's rondeaux closer to the more common English form of the sonnet, fashioning a new poem with fourteen even pentameter lines, although it never fully achieves the rhyme scheme of the sonnet. The balancing of Wyatt's restless, uneven questions thus matched, on the level of the foot, the broader approach to textual and poetic design in *Songes and Sonettes*. Just as the collection diminished the formal and occasional variety of the poems it contained, Wyatt's conversational openness was reined in by adjustments to the meter and even the genre of his work. His poems were reimagined to meet the emerging expectations of English Petrarchism, which *Songes and Sonettes* posited as a profoundly regular style.

Such alterations to poetic form were the condition that made the fictions that spanned the compilation legible for readers. Evidence of active reading has been washed away in many of the remaining copies of *Songes and Sonettes*, leaving clean pages to meet the demands of modern book collectors.[91] But copious annotations from multiple readers do remain in a copy of the 1587 edition now at the Bodleian.[92] The earliest hand frequently questioned verbal variants, including in the headings. In the first of Wyatt's stitching poems, for instance, the heading mistakenly identifies the malevolent embroiderer as pricking "his finger," an error introduced in the 1585 *Songes and Sonettes* and maintained in this edition. This reader responds by supplying "hir" in the margin.[93] Just a page earlier, the same hand amends the heading of another of Wyatt's poems, "The Lovers sorrowful state maketh him write sorrowfull songs, but such his love may chaunge the same" (see Figure 5).[94] This annotator extended the already lengthy title, so that the second half would read "but such *as* his love may change the same. *& it semeth hir name was Souch. or Chaunce.*"[95] The addition was a savvy development of the work performed by headings across *Songes and Sonettes*, which consistently transform poetic speakers into stock lovers and mistresses. By supplying an identity for the beloved, the reader continued the game of abstraction in the titles, following the verbal play with the mistress's shifting moods. Stereotypes of female inconstancy were turned *back* into a name.

In supplying this allegorical identity for the mistress, the annotator of this 1587 *Songes and Sonettes* was responding to multiple features introduced by how the poem was laid out for print. The final stanza coyly turns a lover's melancholy lament into the inspiration for the song:

> And if I have (Such) chance
> Perchance or it be long,
> For (Such) a plesant chance,
> To sing some pleasant song.[96]

The use of parentheses here, Hyder Rollins explains, was a way for the compositor to indicate a proper noun, typographically signaling that the mistress's name was "Such" by setting it off from the text that surrounded it.[97] This emphatic setting was the typographic expression of the fiction of anonymous and interchangeable lovers produced by the process of compiling the poems for print. The parentheses allowed "Such" to signify in two ways at the same time, both supplying an allegorical name for the mistress and completing the metrical diction of Wyatt's lines. The annotator then extrapolated on this doubling in his or her expansion of the heading. The note picked up on the play with potential identities at the end of the poem and added a third

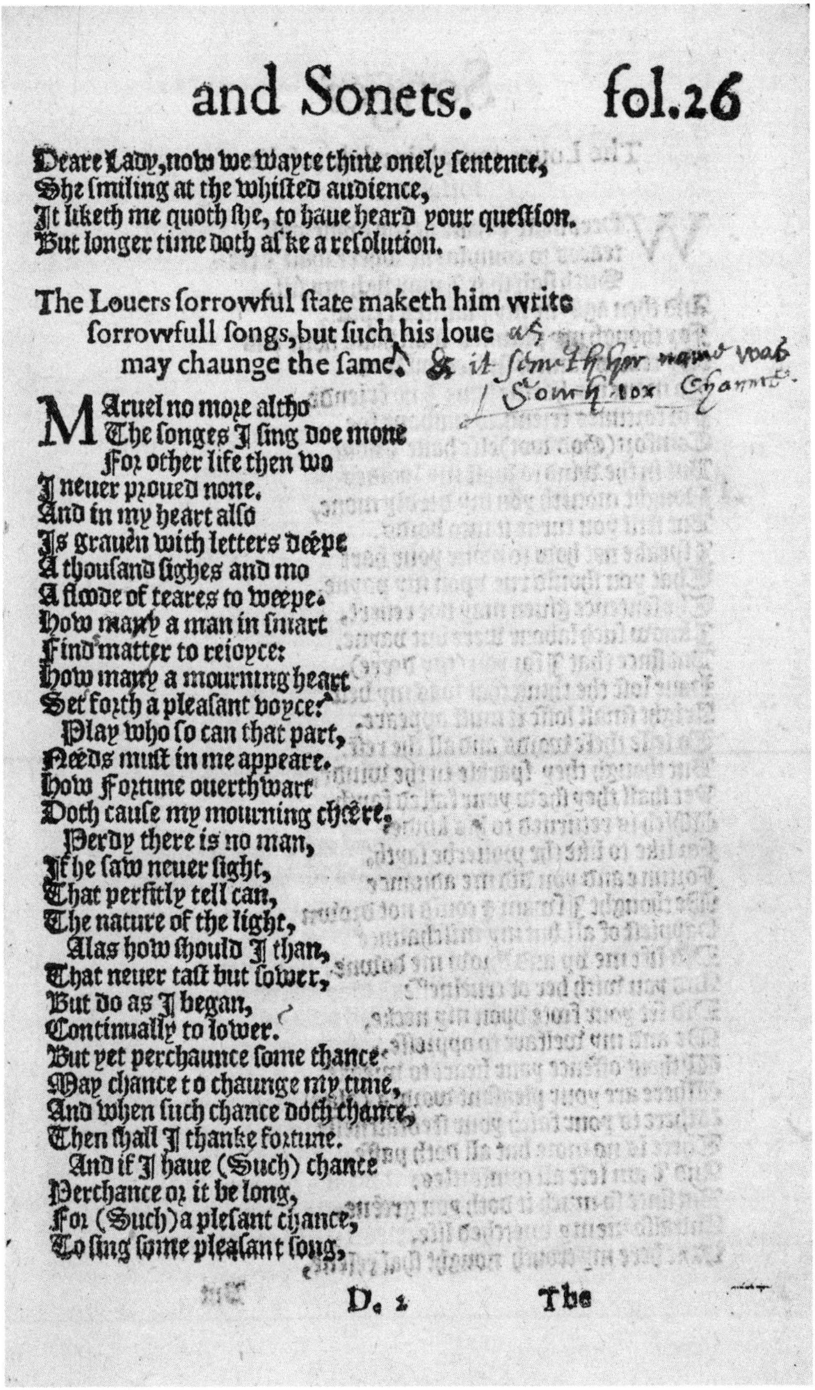

Deare Lady,now we wayte thine onely sentence,
She smiling at the whisted audience,
It liketh me quoth she, to haue heard your question.
But longer time doth aske a resolution.

The Louers sorrowful state maketh him write
   sorrowfull songs,but such his loue *as*
   may chaunge the same. *& it semeth her name was / Soth for Charite.*

Maruel no more altho
   The songes I sing doe mone
     For other life then wo
I neuer proued none.
And in my heart also
Is grauen with letters deepe
A thousand sighes and mo
A sloode of teares to weepe.
How many a man in smart
Find matter to reioyce:
How many a mourning heart
Set forth a pleasant voyce?
   Play who so can that part,
Needs must in me appeare,
How Fortune ouerthwart
Doth cause my mourning cheere.
   Perdy there is no man,
If he saw neuer sight,
That perfitly tell can,
The nature of the light,
   Alas how should I than,
That neuer tast but sower,
But do as I began,
Continually to lower.
But yet perchaunce some chance,
May chance to chaunge my tune,
And when such chance doth chance,
Then shall I thanke fortune.
   And if I haue (Such) chance
Perchance or it be long,
For (Such)a plesant chance,
To sing some pleasant song.

Figure 5. A reader's allegorical naming of the characters in the heading of Wyatt's "Marvel no more," in *Songes and Sonettes* (London: Robert Robinson, 1587), sig. D3r, 8° H 43 Art. Seld. By permission of the Bodleian Libraries, The University of Oxford.

(and even more capricious) name for the mistress, who might be either "Souch or Chaunce."

To be sure, this engaged reading of typography misunderstood the handling of identity in *Songes and Sonettes*. With an overly literal investment in the strategies of titling, the annotating reader supplied a name for a figure who had been rendered anonymous by the plain design of the compilation. At the same time, this expansion of the title according to the fictions established by the material setting was a testament to how effectively *Songes and Sonettes* steered readers to the evidence *within* poems. Even in the 1587 edition, which was published thirty years after the first quarto, this reader was taking the headings and other aspects of typography as a guide for how to make sense of Wyatt's playful opacity within the textual environment of this book.

The Time of the Compilation

What was the effect of this contextually aware compiling on the long circulation of *Songes and Sonettes* in early modern England? How did contemporary readers—and future writers—respond to its plain, parceled poetics? One reason that *Songes and Sonettes* has been identified as an origin point for vernacular poetry is that it was actively republished until 1587. As Rollins put it, the "influence" of *Songes and Sonettes* "was more or less constant throughout the pre-Shakespearean period."[98] Elizabeth Pomeroy equally identified the book as an impetus for the flourishing of nonauthorial poetry compilations across the later sixteenth century.[99] Yet this orthodoxy is harder to accept when we take account of a tight clustering of publication dates. *Songes and Sonettes* was indeed reprinted for three decades, but demand slowed considerably by 1567. The first eight editions came out in ten years, and Tottel then published the collection only once more, in 1574.[100] After another decade without a new edition, in 1584 he turned his rights to *Songes and Sonettes* over to the Stationers' Company for relief of the poor.[101] The two final editions were published by John Windet in 1585 and Robert Robinson in 1587.

The narrow range of publication dates for most editions of *Songes and Sonettes*—as well as the multiple publishers who took over the title—suggests that we need a new explanation for "Tottel's" impact on English literature. The compilation was most profitable from late 1557 to 1559, years that witnessed the major political and religious upheaval between the end of Mary I's reign and the beginning of Elizabeth I's. In downplaying the identities of the poets and their social worlds, the arrangement of *Songes and Sonettes* may have initially been a response to this distinct political climate because the general anonymity of the headings and the plain parceled poetics were unlikely to alienate readers of any faith. But this design also contributed to the longevity of *Songes and Sonettes* both in its moment of publication and across the sixteenth and seventeenth centuries. The absence of textual features that might explain the social and political origins of the work promoted the significance that could be gleaned from reading poems—and from reading them together. *Songes and Sonettes* could appeal to buyers for decades, even after the occasions of composition were lost, because the design of the book lifted poems out of the context that inspired them.

When poems from *Songes and Sonettes* began to circulate independently, they continued to carry traces of the time they had spent in the compilation, either in murky attributions that testify to the volume's lack of interest in authorship or even in the basic texture of the verse. In 1600, Nicholas Ling compiled *Englands Helicon*, a new collection of 150 pastoral poems, most of which had been printed previously. Two of these poems appeared first among the "Uncertain Auctours" section in *Songes and Sonettes* as "Harpalus complaint of Phillidaies love bestowed on Corin, who loved her not and denied him that loved her" and "The complaint of Thestilis amid the desert wodde" (pp. 105, 129). Somewhat unusually, *Englands Helicon* reprinted both the poems and their titles from *Songes and Sonettes*, thereby transporting the textual apparatus innovated in 1557 into a much later book. Decades of textual transmission were preserving precisely the features of the book that were the product not of composition but of compiling. Whatever this apparent fidelity, *Englands Helicon* also misread aspects of its source. The two poems from *Songes and Sonettes* were attributed to "L. T. Howard, E. of Surrie," mistakenly taking the volume title's naming of the first poet and stretching it across to the rest of the work.[102]

The enduring visibility of *Songes and Sonettes* made the book a touchstone for the development of English poetic style, which developed not as a matter of individual skill but rather through the protracted influence of the compilation. Shakespeare treated it as a handbook for love and poetry, albeit one showing its advanced age. When Slender in *The Merry Wives of Windsor* (1623) is left speechless at the sight of his beloved, he does not reach for Petrarch, Wyatt, or any other single poet but instead begs for Tottel's whole volume: "I had rather than forty shillings I had my book of *Songs and Sonnets* here."[103] The inept suitor's yearning for Tottel's old book is a joke that depends on a dual consciousness of the compilation, which allows it to be liked by one kind of reader and mocked by another for precisely the same qualities.[104] The reference was not in the first quarto of *Merry Wives* from 1599 but appeared only in the 1623 First Folio, when the outmoded style of *Songes and Sonettes* would have been even more legible to readers of Shakespeare's printed plays. By layering temporally dissonant perspectives, the knowing reference to Tottel's book became a tiny meditation on English poetic history.

While Shakespeare used *Songes and Sonettes* as fodder for his jokes in *Merry Wives*, his readers would continue to have the poetry book in sight for over a century after it was first published in 1557. In one copy of the First Folio, now held at the Free Library of Philadelphia, a reader has noted the source for the gravedigger's song in *Hamlet*: "Among Surreis Sonnets fol. 72."[105] This annotation is the trace of an extensive reading practice that moves precipitously across textual genres and across the years.[106] The reader was observing that when the gravedigger sings:

> In youth when I did love, did love,
> Me thought it was very sweete,
> To contract O the time for my behove,
> O, me thought there was nothing meet![107]

He is lending a new voice to the poem headed "The aged lover renounceth love" in *Songes and Sonettes*:

> I lothe that I did love,
> In youth that I thought swete:
> As time requires for my behove,
> Me thinks they are not mete.
> (no. 182, lines 1–4)

The aged gravedigger was appropriating a long-expired farewell to love while he was harvesting the skulls of an earlier generation of courtly entertainers. In recognizing and cross-referencing the older poem, this annotating reader was observing Shakespeare's magpie quotation of work written five decades before the play. He was also somewhat too literally applying the information conveyed in the material design of *Songes and Sonettes*. Like the attribution in *Englands Helicon*, this annotation misidentifies the gravedigger's song with Surrey, even though the poem was anonymous in Tottel's publication and was elsewhere assigned to Thomas Vaux.[108] In the same fashion as the compilation itself, a century of work by poets, playwrights, and compiling stationers was flattened into an untimely and artificial present tense.

This anachronic patchwork of poetic circulation was enabled by the plain design of *Songes and Sonettes*. The compilation set poems loose from their origins, scoured away all traces of an occasional temporality, and made it possible to read the gathered writing in multiple different ways. A copy of the third edition, now at the Harry Ransom Center at the University of Texas, shows how the book was available to readers with widely divergent interests. This volume was annotated in two hands, one that wrote in a clear secretary script and the other in a looping italic that may have been later or was perhaps a woman's hand. The first reader left notes of the classical sources that poets were referencing, like "Out of Horace," which was written between the heading "Praise of meane and constant estate," and the first line of Surrey's poem that began "Of thy life, Thomas, this compasse wel mark."[109] Elsewhere, this hand added "Translated out of Martial" and "Qui notas nimis omnibus ignotus moritur sibi. Senec," the conclusion of a Senecan commonplace about a notorious man who dies before he gains self-knowledge.[110] There are also numerous marks of attention—underlinings, brackets, flourishes—that could well have been in the same hand. Overall, this was a reader who turned to *Songes and Sonettes*, a book marketed as a compilation of love lyrics, for snippets of wisdom that could be included in a rather sententious commonplace book.

The other annotating hand in this copy of *Songes and Sonettes* took an approach that could not be more distinct from a performance of classical knowledge. In six places, the second reader supplied the vernacular music to which poems might be sung, adding notes of the tunes that fit the meter and rhyme of particular poems. "To the tune of As I went to Walsingham" was supplied for an anonymous poem in four-line tetrameter stanzas, "Harpalus complaint of Phillidaes love bestowed on Corin" (see Figure 6).[111] "As I went to Walsingham" can be dated to the early 1590s; it was included in a manuscript of lute music from around 1591, registered as *Frauncis New Jigge* in October 1595, and mentioned by Thomas Nashe in his *Have with You to Saffron-Walden* (1596).[112] Together with the style of the transitional italic hand, this annotation suggests that this copy of *Songes and Sonettes*, which was printed between 1557 and 1559, was being actively read for at least four decades.

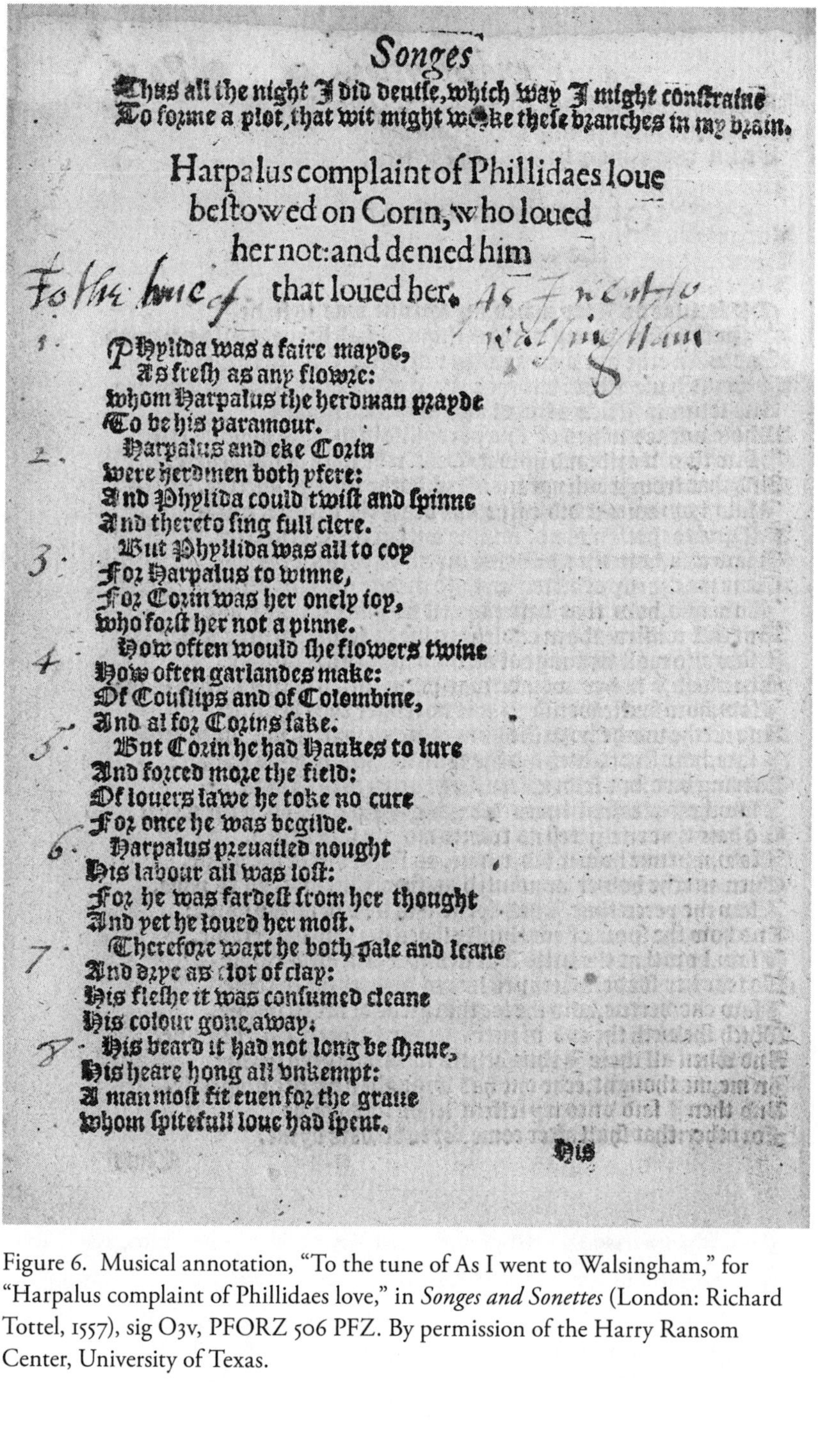

Thus all the night I did deuise, which way I might constraine
To forme a plot, that wit might make these branches in my brain.

Harpalus complaint of Phillidaes loue bestowed on Corin, who loued her not: and denied him *To the loue of* that loued her. *As I went to Walsingham*

1. Phyllida was a faire mayde,
   As fresh as any flowre:
   whom Harpalus the herdman prayde
   To be his paramour.

2. Harpalus and eke Corin
   were herdmen both yfere:
   And Phyllida could twist and spinne
   And thereto sing full clere.

3. But Phyllida was all to coy
   For Harpalus to winne,
   For Corin was her onely ioy,
   who forst her not a pinne.

4. How often would she flowers twine
   How often garlandes make:
   Of Couslips and of Colombine,
   And al for Corins sake.

5. But Corin he had Haukes to lure
   And forced more the field:
   Of louers lawe he toke no cure
   For once he was begilde.

6. Harpalus preuailed nought
   His labour all was lost:
   For he was fardest from her thought
   And yet he loued her most.

7. Therefore waxt he both pale and leane
   And drye as clot of clay:
   His fleshe it was consumed cleane
   His colour gone away.

8. His beard it had not long be shaue,
   His heare hong all vnkempt:
   A man most fit euen for the graue
   whom spitefull loue had spent.

His

Figure 6. Musical annotation, "To the tune of As I went to Walsingham," for "Harpalus complaint of Phillidaes love," in *Songes and Sonettes* (London: Richard Tottel, 1557), sig O3v, PFORZ 506 PFZ. By permission of the Harry Ransom Center, University of Texas.

If *Songes and Sonettes* was an origin point for the development of English literary writing, it was a source that was itself profoundly ahistorical and blind to the circumstances of its own production. Where the commonplacing reader had approached this volume of English poetry as a source of classical wisdom, reaching back across time for the echoes of authors like Horace and Martial, the annotations from this reader interested in contemporary music were evidence of how *Songes and Sonettes* could also be understood through the latest cultural developments. The "Walsingham" marginalia appeared next to a poem that itself circulated widely in early modern England. Recall that "Harpalus complaint of Phillidaes love bestowed on Corin" was one of the poems from *Songes and Sonettes* included in *Englands Helicon*. In this long circulation, we can witness the impact of Tottel's experimental compilation. The plain design of *Songes and Sonettes* made the poetry available to multiple kinds of appropriative reuse. By turning the poems into their own hermeneutic context, freeing them from their occasional origins, the compilation allowed generations of readers to apply the perspectives of their own moment to the much older book.

Forgetting the Poetics of Compiling

If *Songes and Sonettes* testified to a broad network of poetic circulation in early modern England, one that persisted for decades, that vibrant culture would become less visible across the centuries that followed. When the compilation began to be identified as the origin for modern English poetry, *Songes and Sonettes* also started to be understood as a miscellany that mixed the work of multiple writers. These two developments were of course related. With the assumption that gathered poetry should express the agency of individual poets, modern literary histories retrospectively applied ideals of authorship to an earlier moment in which the genre of the compilation was still emerging. By way of conclusion, I offer here two signal examples of how *Songes and Sonettes* started to be read through the conceptual category of the miscellany. The first was Thomas Warton's new periodization of English poetry, and the second was the "orthodox" textual history of the book finally consolidated by John Payne Collier, who edited the first quarto of *Songes and Sonettes* for his reprint series of *Seven English Poetical Miscellanies*. In each moment, the plain design of the sixteenth-century printed book was conscripted by a modern desire to privilege poetic composition over compiling. It was this occlusion of the process of making *Songes and Sonettes* that led editors to retitle it *Tottel's Miscellany*, the name by which it is commonly known today. Readers lost sight of the poetics that had been created by the flexible arrangement of parcels, casting aside the material and conceptual affiliations between poems.

Thomas Warton developed an innovative new approach to the history of imaginative writing. His *The History of English Poetry* (1774–1781) is best known for establishing a concern with periodization that was "foundational for an emergent discipline of English."[113] The birth of the discipline of English literature depended on the introduction of a sense of the present that was divided from the past.[114] In tracing the forward progress of poetic style, Warton was reconstructing the agency of individual authors, distinguishing poets from the unnamable makers and users of printed books. He was also keen to identify *Songes and Sonettes* as an origin point, "the first printed poetical miscellany in the English language."[115] Lashing poets into a chronological order had the effect of privileging the moment of composition—and of suppressing the long circulation of poems across the sixteenth and seventeenth centuries. It was for this reason, I want to suggest, that "miscellany" came to seem like a natural description for books that early modern readers never really approached through the vocabulary and ideology of authorial agency.

The material history of the compiled poetry was occluded by an investment in authorship. It is important to note that Warton did not identify the entirety of *Songes and Sonettes* as a miscellany. His reference to "the first printed poetical miscellany" was describing only the poems of "uncertain authors" that "are annexed" at the end of the book.[116] In this division according to the principles of authorship advanced by the compilation's sections, which had been illegible to many early modern readers, Warton treated *Songes and Sonettes* as a hybrid of authorial collection and nonauthorial miscellany. He complained, for instance, of the poet Michael Drayton's praise for *Songes and Sonettes* that he "seems to have blended all the several collections of which Tottel's volume consists," objecting to how Drayton failed to see the distinction between the poetry attributed to Wyatt and Surrey and to anonymous poets.[117]

Warton's sense of an awkward medley of textual genres within a single volume was a fitting emblem of the transitional period in which he was writing. His investment in authorship would have a profound effect on the future development of bibliography and textual studies. The modern historiography of English printing had begun a few decades earlier, with Joseph Ames's *Typographical Antiquities*, a catalog of printers that was first published in 1749 and then considerably expanded by William Herbert between 1785 and 1790.

The details of this chronology matter because, in updating Ames's catalog, Herbert drew on Warton's developments in the emerging field of literary history. In the first edition, Ames identified Richard Tottel as an important stationer, known for holding a license for law books and for his experiments in printing vernacular poetry, including Lydgate's translation of Boccaccio. But *Songes and Sonettes* was nowhere on Ames's list of Tottel's books, likely because the remaining copies were relatively unknown.[118] When Herbert expanded *Typographical Antiquities* between 1785 and 1790—just a few years after Warton's *History of English Poetry*—he added "'Songes and Sonnettes of Henry earle of Surrey,' & others" to Tottel's list, along with the observation that this book was "Frequently printed, and yet very scarce."[119] Crucially, Herbert cited Warton as the source for his discovery of *Songes and Sonettes*, even providing the page numbers for all the moments in which the poetry book was mentioned in *The History of English Poetry*.

Herbert was thus reading Ames's catalog of printers through Warton's squeamishness about the mixture of poets in *Songes and Sonettes*. In this moment when the disciplines of literature and bibliography were each carving out their own domains, the first forays into a history of print were cross-pollinated with a desire for a chronological, developmental model of authorship. It was this accounting for the patchy record of early modern print through the anachronistic expectations of literary history that changed the very categories through which printed poetry could be understood. An emerging sense of the historicity of imaginative writing disguised a fuller awareness of past practices of making and using early modern books. Reading the textual past through the genre categories of literary history made it possible to reimagine compilations like *Songes and Sonettes* as miscellanies.

No one did more to consolidate this history of the poetry miscellany than John Payne Collier, the erstwhile Shakespeare forger who was the first editor to adopt *Tottel's Miscellany* as a title. Collier included the compilation in a small run of "poetical miscellanies" that he issued by subscription between 1865 and 1867, and his title became common when Edward Arber adopted it for his more affordable edition of *Tottel's Miscellany* in 1870. Collier's edition was the culmination of his long personal history with rare books. When he embarked on this project, he was a prominent antiquarian who had suffered a public disgrace for forging marginalia in a copy of Shakespeare's Second Folio.[120] Within this hostile climate, Collier was attempting to regain his status as an expert on rare books, and he turned repeatedly to *Tottel's Miscellany* in his campaign to rehabilitate his public reputation. His 1865 *A Bibliographical and Critical Account of the Rarest Books in the English Language* opens with the announcement of "my latest discovery" of "'Tottel's Miscellany,' 1557," which he calls "the oldest and most interesting in our language."[121] *Songes and Sonettes* was known before 1865, of course. This self-declared "discovery" was the Bodleian's unique copy of the first quarto, but Collier was characteristically overstating his own acumen when he complained that *Songes and Sonettes* "has always, during the last three centuries, been reprinted by Dr. Sewell, Bishop Percy, Dr. Nott, and their followers, from the second instead of the first edition."[122] Previous editors were aware of the Bodleian's unique copy, even if it had not yet been issued as a single volume.[123] Neglecting these recent editions helped Collier market his own reprint of *Tottel's Miscellany*, the first part of which was published within three weeks of his catalog.[124] *A Bibliographical and Critical Account*'s entry for *Songes and Sonettes* slips in an announcement for a forthcoming edition made "from the first authentic impression" that "is about to be reproduced in, as nearly as possible, its original form."[125]

With this preference for the apparent authenticity of the first quarto, the history of *Songes and Sonettes* was remade according to modern ideals of chronology and authorship, precisely the categories of social and contextual meaning that had been largely absent from the early printing of the book. Collier was keen to turn his apparent expertise into claims for the value of his edition of *Tottel's Miscellany*. In a notice issued between the second and third installments, Collier defended its price of thirty shillings, because "the whole undertaking has been somewhat enhanced by the unusual cost of an exact transcript, observing all the errors of the press, and the old mistakes of punctuation."[126] Collier acquired new copy for his editions either by transcribing it himself or by asking librarians to send him transcripts, which he then marked up for his printer. A nineteenth-century manuscript copy of *Songes and Sonettes*, now at the Folger Shakespeare Library, includes bracketed notes in Collier's hand that dictate the page layout, typography, and contents of the forthcoming volume: "Let a new page begin here," "Sm[all] caps Ital[ics]," and "I cannot send more copy until I have been to Oxford," presumably to acquire or vet further transcriptions.[127] The aim of this significant investment was to restore the traces of authorship that, according to Collier, had been obscured by the early printing of the work. He claims that his choice to follow the text of the first quarto allows his edition of *Tottel's Miscellany* to "represent[t] the true language of the various poets, and the manner in which the pieces were originally arranged, without the corruptions which were multiplied in every reprint."[128]

This promise of a faithful reprint of the first edition of *Songes and Son-ettes* would misrepresent the bibliography of the compilation by championing an "original arrangement" that was in fact hardly read in its own moment. Despite a general distaste for Collier's fraud and forgery, histories of English poetry continued to follow his insistence on the value of the first quarto of *Songes and Sonettes*. After 1865, the first quarto remained the standard copy text of *Tottel's Miscellany* for more than a century, until new editions by Paul A. Marquis in 2007 and Amanda Holton and Tom MacFaul in 2011.[129] At the same time, the first quarto was not readily available outside of a printed facsimile of the Bodleian's unique copy.[130] It was not included in the UMI microfilms of *Early English Books* begun in the 1930s, was never available on *Early English Books Online*, and no digital facsimile exists today. The twentieth-century media history of *Songes and Sonettes* thus continued to elide the poetics of compiling that had first guided the order and arrangement of the printed book.

Across this long moment, the literary histories that treated *Songes and Sonettes* as an origin for English poetry were relying on a bibliographic history that had little to do with how the compilation was experienced in early modern England. To the extent that *Songes and Sonettes* was an origin point, it offered an innovative response to poetic form and content within the material design of the compilation. But the evidence of this history has been all but impossible to see from within the categories for understanding textual genre that would eventually grow out of Tottel's experimental publication. The material dimensions of textual organization came to seem distinct from the composition of poems.

In subsequent chapters, I examine the development of this compiled poetics within books printed in early modern England. To make their dynamic craft legible for readers, compilers used increasingly elaborate performances of gathering and arranging discrete poems. Tottel's plain parcels gave way to extensive narratives of compiling, fanciful figures for embodied books, and poem headings with multiple systems of numbering. Yet although this flourishing book design followed from the experimental poetics within the apparatus of *Songes and Sonettes*, the development of the poetry compilation was not in any simple way a progress or trajectory. To return to Warton, if *Songes and Sonettes* preserved "many admirable specimens of antient genius," that act of salvage was itself influenced by the imaginative writing that was being gathered up. The tendency for compilations to respond actively to poetic form and content meant that each book was a local response to the work it contained.

CHAPTER 2

Stationers' Figures

Mixed Forms and Material Poetics

Professional stationers from the later sixteenth century were increasingly attuned to the forms and fictions created by their poetry compilations. In the years after Richard Tottel's *Songes and Sonettes* (1557), printed books began to demonstrate more inventive techniques for arranging poems. Headings incorporated alliterative and rhyming verses, attributions identified fictional characters as authors, and prefatory addresses were voiced by speaking books. Such imaginative approaches to textual design were a testament to how agents of the book trade could be sensitive readers. Like Tottel's plain parcels, these features were attempts to appeal to book buyers, and they were largely unconcerned with the influence or control of authors. Publishers and booksellers invested time and money in explaining the points of contact between discrete poems, in smoothing out the juxtapositions of discordant styles, and in positing broader figures for the gathered writing. They used the affordances of print to establish a new, mixed form for the book of poems.

This chapter considers the development of English poetry compilations in the years after 1574, when Tottel published his final edition of *Songes and Sonettes*. By tracing the evolution of textual design, it shows how strategies of material arrangement were transformed into figures that could imaginatively articulate the formal connections between poems. Publishers conspicuously mixed material and poetic forms as a way to fashion larger, composite structures within their books. During the 1570s, volume titles used elaborate horticultural metaphors to call attention to their abundance of poems. Later in the century, professional compilers moved away from imagery of gathering to promote a conceptual organization that amplified a common style or mode for all the work. Across these decades, stationers including Richard Jones,

Henry Disle, and Nicholas Ling were explicit about their active interventions
in the organization of poems. They laid the process of compiling bare as a
way to promote the value of the volumes they were selling. In this moment
when books of all kinds were approached as fodder for future writing, available to being broken down and commonplaced, stationers were experimenting with how to make a textual design that could be useful to—but still
withstand the ravages of—willful readers.[1] By announcing the hybrid material and poetic design of their compilations, publishers made a claim for attending to the entirety of these books, or at least for readers to buy them
before pillaging their choice lines.

That sixteenth-century publishers and booksellers could be sensitive readers of poetry has traditionally been unrecognized because their motives have
more often been ascribed to the commercial market of print. As the twentieth-
century editor Hyder Rollins observed, "Elizabethan printers" were known
for their "trickery in misleading the public with puffing title-pages."[2] Such
"trickery," Rollins surmised, was the result of attempts to follow Tottel's
successful model of poetic publication.[3] Later Elizabethan compilations
have been considered Tottel's heirs since at least 1781, when the early literary
historian Thomas Warton observed that *Songes and Sonettes* "seems to have
given birth to two favorite and celebrated collections of the same kind."[4] Here,
Warton was referring to *The Paradyse of daynty devises* (1576) and *Englands
Helicon* (1600). The rather modest pair of miscellanies that Warton saw emerging in the wake of Tottel's compilation would swell in number across the
centuries to the point where, in 1973, Elizabeth Pomeroy tallied the "progeny" of *Songes and Sonettes* as at least "twenty multiple-author collections" of
which "one was being printed or reprinted in nearly every year in Elizabeth's
reign."[5]

This sense of Tottel's prolific descendants is a result of the outsized significance that *Songes and Sonettes* has held in histories of English poetry. As I
show in my first chapter, this genealogy was most fully articulated by John
Payne Collier, editor of the series *Seven English Poetical Miscellanies*, who was
the first to use the title *Tottel's Miscellany* in 1865. Collier adopted the term
"miscellany" to minimize the real distinctions between an almost random
clutch of books, to which he gave modernized titles: *Tottel's Miscellany* (1557),
Paradise of Dainty Devices (1578), *Gorgeous Gallery of Gallant Inventions* (1578),
Phoenix Nest (1593), *England's Helicon* (1600), *England's Parnassus* (1600), and
Davison's Poetical Rhapsody (1602). The only features shared by all these books
were that they had no single author and that their publishers promoted their

interventions in the gathering and arranging of the diverse poems. For Collier and the literary historians who accepted his corpus, the designation of "miscellany" worked to affiliate a largely unrelated set of poetry compilations that had been published across more than five decades.

One of my larger arguments in this book is that a modern focus on miscellaneity has occluded the formal history of printed poetry compilations. By affiliating collections simply because they mixed the work of multiple authors, we have overlooked how early printed books were dynamic and local responses to poetic culture. Returning to several compilations from Collier's series, this chapter offers an alternative to his genealogical account of Tottel's influence. Rather than a continuous tradition, the sporadic publication dates of Elizabethan poetry books propose that we read them as interrelated clusters that took shape around topics and styles fashionable in distinct moments. Recognizing the unevenness of this history can help recover a different, more creative legacy of *Songes and Sonettes*. When we take material context as a measure of interpretation, the resonances between gathered texts can shed light on how writing was understood by the individuals who made these books.[6] The very categories through which compiled poetry was read and understood were being reformed across the sixteenth century because textual formations are the expression of a hermeneutic practice, a historically conditioned mode of reading, not a universal genre.

Early modern publishers and printers used the resources of poetry—alliteration, meter, rhyme, imaginative figures—to span the gaps between the discrete texts gathered together within their volumes. This intertwining of form, content, and organization means that we need to rethink a reflexive critical tendency—one implicit in Rollins's editorial work, for instance—to distinguish between literary and textual histories. The profoundly mixed form of the premodern compilation is an invitation to expand the practical limits of poetic craft. Writing of an earlier moment, Eleanor Johnson has shown that the medieval *prosimetrum*—a genre that mingled prose and verse—enabled "a literary encounter with the aesthetics of the mixed form."[7] Heterogeneity exposes the seams of composition, giving readers purchase on an aesthetic making that was an active process. The "palimpsestic" mixture of forms supported a "theory and a practice of literature" that "became available for complex meditations on the nature of the literary experience itself."[8] The same is true of the early printed book, which was not so much "a single stable object" as "a coming together or an alignment of separate component pieces, each possessed of particular conventions and histories" and "each the product of distinct kinds of labour."[9] This layering of multiple histories of production, transmission, and use was particularly visible in poetry books from the sixteenth century, when the genre of the compilation was still being consolidated. By reading the mixed design of these books as a response to poetic style and genre, this chapter shows how poems could actively influence the material forms of early print. Textual features hold an archive of a poetic theory written by the professional compilers who were also the earliest critics of this work.

Cultivating Figures of Disorder

During the last decades of the sixteenth century, agents of the London book trade innovated a new model for the English poetry compilation by turning strategies for promoting their books to creative ends. Professional compilers drew on the resources of poetic form in their active responses to the challenges—and the opportunities—of gathering imaginative writing into the form of a book. Where the title of *Songes and Sonettes written by the ryght honorable Lorde Henry Haward late Earle of Surrey, and other* had simply listed poetic contents, later volumes started to offer justifications for reading the gathered poems together. With elaborate titles, title pages, and prefatory addresses, stationers announced both the original variety of the gathered poems and their new arrangement within the larger compilations.[10] These organizational features consistently deployed images of horticulture and cultivation—activities of husbandry that were ubiquitous tropes for poetic craft.[11] More than a metaphor, these tropes were figures that turned textual design into "an instrument of making," allowing "artifice" that was "at once eccentric and typical" to become a "reproducible" form.[12] When used in the arrangement of printed books, the imaginative resources of the floral imagery exposed and lent value to the process of thinking across poems, calling out the formal, thematic, and stylistic continuities that affiliated the gatherings of discrete texts. By explaining the significance of the larger compilation, the elaborate figures served the interests of publishers, which were distinct from how writers and readers might approach their books as storehouses of fragments ripe for a piecemeal reuse.

Sixteenth-century poetry books featured titles with a shared language and grammar of compiling. The etymology of the anthology as a gathering of flowers, from the Greek *anthos*, was first taken at face value in collections of

aphorisms and proverbs.[13] Individual *sententiae*, known as the flowers of rhetoric, were gathered into garden plots and bouquets in books like *Garden of
Wysdom wherin ye maye gather moste pleasaunt flowres* (1539), a translation of
Erasmus's *Adages* compiled by the reformer Richard Taverner, and *The Floures
of Philosophie, with the pleasures of poetrie annexed to them* (1572), a gathering
of Senecan sayings put together by the natural scientist Hugh Plat. Picking
up on such literal tropes, poetry compilations developed the legacies of humanist reading and citation into ever more fanciful assemblages.[14] Volumes
from individual poets were given titles like *The Arbor of Amitie* (1568) by
Thomas Howell, *A Hundreth sundrie Flowres bounde up in one small Poesie*
(1573) by George Gascoigne, *Flowers of Epigrammes* (1577) by Timothy Kendall, *The Forrest of Fancy* (1579) by H. C., and *A Banquet of Daintie Conceits*
(1588) by Anthony Munday. The figures of arrangement in each title depict
the compilations as groupings that could shelter and preserve the perishable
or immaterial poems.

These imaginative titles were responding to a contemporary sense of the
relationship between writing individual poems and gathering them into a
larger compilation. In sixteenth-century English, "poesie" was both a traditional designation for poetry or a poetic composition and a novel term for a
bouquet, a bundle of individual flowers.[15] With the inclusion of horticultural
imagery in their volume titles, professional compilers were doubling down on
this semantic play between part and whole.[16] Speculating on the larger form
that ephemeral writing might take, they wrote two-part titles hinged on the
preposition "of." The printer and publisher Richard Jones was at the center of
this trend. Over three decades, Jones either printed or published poetry collections including Isabella Whitney's *A Sweet Nosgay, or Pleasant Posye* (1573);
the nonauthorial *A gorgious Gallery, of gallant Inventions* (1578) and *A Handefull of Pleasant Delites* (1584); N. B.'s *A Smale handfull of fragrant Flowers*
(1575); and Nicholas Breton's *Brittons Bowre of Delights* (1591) and his *The arbor of Amorous Devises* (1597). These agricultural and arboreal tropes further
developed the stock imagery of floral gathering, depicting the books as
human assemblages that maintain the original diversity of the compiled poems.[17] Jones's figurative titles cast the structure devised by the compiler as
relatively unconcerned with poets' own gathering and arranging of their
work. The book itself, in its physical form and its layout, was an imaginative
response to the poems it contained.

In identifying this traffic between composition and compiling, I mean
to respond to the modern sense that textual design was poetically insensitive.

Much of this criticism has its roots in early twentieth-century ideals of poetic form as bounded, unified, and determined solely by the author. This ideal was so hermetic that the mixed forms of miscellanies and anthologies apparently threatened to obscure or even damage its coherence. In 1946, T. S. Eliot warned against the "dangers" of collections that distract readers with a busy mixture of poems, "for there are poetry-lovers who can be called anthology-addicts, and cannot read poetry in any other way."[18] But for the early modern makers and users of compiled poetry, the mixed form of these books was an opportunity, not a liability. How could the titles that transform the etymology of the anthology into aestheticized figures—complete with a common syntax and frequent alliteration—be anything but poetic? The floral volume titles in fact suggest that sixteenth-century publishers were engaging with a much more capacious and active sense of poetic form. Colleen Rosenfeld has shown that early modern poetry was more "a doing" than a thing, observing that form was a dynamic "quality of action" that was "inseparable from the process in which" it was made. Poetry was "a noun that is always acting like a verb."[19] This process-oriented aesthetics was prominent in the mixed construction of early printed poetry books. By deploying formal resources in their material design, compilations reveled in the active and emergent figures as a means of expressing the evolving relations between poems.

With their elaborate imagery of cultivation, stationers promoted their books as composite structures that grew out of the formal and imaginative dimensions of the diverse poems. *The Forrest of Fancy*, published by Thomas Purfoot in 1579, offers a particularly strong illustration of how agents of the London book trade used the resources of poetic form to explain compilations that strained the practical limits of organization. This nearly anonymous collection of forty-four poems and twenty-one prose epistles was only attributed—and only on the final page—to H. C., whose identity is still uncertain.[20] In the absence of evidence for the control of any one poet, I want to consider how this compilation was more invested in understanding the connections between the diverse pieces of writing than in identifying an origin or source in the hand of a known author. The figures of cultivation in the textual frames emphasized the labor that went into making the compilation, contributing to a conceit for the book as a whole by acknowledging how *The Forrest of Fancy* unevenly joined together distinct kinds of writing. If the author was literally an afterthought, the compilation was itself offered to readers as an experiment in how the affordances of print might draw out and amplify qualities that the figurative poet-farmer explored in his own writing.

The front matter in *The Forrest of Fancy* admits that it is tricky to know
what kind of book this is. It opens with an address entitled "The Booke speaketh to the buyers," a slight verse in which the compilation promotes itself to
readers:

> What kind of thing I am,
>   my shape doth shew the same:
> No Forrest, though my father pleasde,
>   to tearme me by that name.[21]

Beginning with a riddle of obscured identity, the prosopopoeic book next
quibbles with the title imposed upon it by the publisher, whose power to assign a name is akin to paternity.[22] The prefatory verse frets that the publisher
might be overexerting his will on the contents. The uneasiness about this
particular name acknowledges that, like the book itself, readers might be
skeptical about a compilation described as a forest, an image that is both a
horticultural trope and a reference to classical collections such as Statius's
Silvae.

Cast as an animated and speaking object, *The Forrest of Fancy* toys with
the imprecise line between the ideal and physical dimensions of poetry. Admitting that the forest conflicts with "my shape," the loquacious book pushes
back against the physical figure in the title and claims instead to be just an
amalgam of thoughts:

> But Fancy fits me well,
>   For I am fully fraught,
> With Fancies such as may correct
>   but not corrupt the thought.[23]

With this qualification, the thinking book accepts the second part of the
volume title, the immaterial fancies that together make up the volume. *The
Forrest of Fancy* markets itself as loaded or equipped—"fully fraught"—with
ideas that promise to improve the reader:

> In me my friend thou mayst,
>   (though thou be yong or olde)
> Ritche, poore, of high or low degree,
>   thy duety here beholde.[24]

The Forrest of Fancy holds something for everyone. It contains a "store" of "foolish trifles" for the young and "seemely sightes" for the "auncient syres," as well as lessons for lovers and commiseration for men with "fickle friends."[25] What unites this varied work is the future utility that readers might derive from such poems, as well as their inclusion in this handy volume. "Purchase me withall," the book begs, "What foole a Forrest would forsake, / that sees the price so small?"[26]

This sales pitch for *The Forrest of Fancy* mixed poems together with the material features added by Purfoot, the paternalistic publisher whose act of compiling drew the immaterial fancies into a physical book available for readers to buy. In the sixteenth century, this dual composition was known as "framing," a polysemous term that, Rayna Kalas has explained, meant both "an idea made manifest" and "the manipulation of matter according to human design."[27] Kalas focuses on the materiality of language, demonstrating that a poet's skill was understood not just as an act of imaginative composition but also as *techne*, or a physical craft. Frame "was used to describe the engendering of any kind of matter," from the skeletal structure of a building to "the concoction of fluids," and it "referred to mixing as well as joining."[28] Extending Kalas's observations about poetic discourse to the larger structure of the compilations in which these texts traveled, I want to consider the mixed forms of books like *The Forrest of Fancy* as the result of a similarly hybrid framing. If early modern language mingled thoughts and things, publishers expanded on that dual mode of poetic creation when they included aspects of form and content in the textual features that mixed and joined immaterial poems into physical compilations. *The Forrest of Fancy* describes its origins as an act of framing. In the words of "The Booke speaketh to the buyers":

> What follies fond we frame,
>   our foolish fancy to:
> Here mayst thou see, and so discearne,
>   what best beseemes to do.[29]

As an expression of the conceptual (and alliterative) work of fitting follies together with fancies, "frame" names a process of mediation that was itself inherently poetic, since it took advantage of the resources of form to fashion a new relation between the multiple immaterial thoughts. At the same time, the deictic "Here" calls readers' attention to the book as the technology necessary for this framing, situating this act of creation within the physical context of *The Forrest of Fancy*.[30]

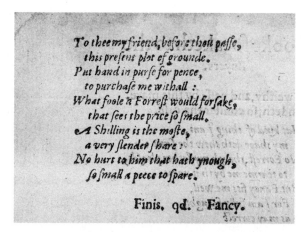

To thee my friend, before thou passe,
  this present plot of grounde.
Put hand in purse for pence,
  to purchase me withall :
What foole a Forrest would forsake,
  that sees the price so small.
A Shilling is the moste,
  a very slender share :
No hurt to him that hath ynough,
  so small a peece to spare.

                    Finis, qd. Fancy.

Figure 7. "The Booke speaketh to the buyers," attributed to
the voice of "Fancy," in H. C., *The Forrest of Fancy* (London:
Thomas Purfoot, 1579), sig. A2v, Mal. 283. By permission of
the Bodleian Libraries, The University of Oxford.

These multiple points of intersection between poems and the material
design of early printed books reflect the distributed agency of compiling, a
collaborative textual practice that became a kind of poetic making. The prefatory address is subscribed "Finis. qd. Fancy" (see Figure 7), an attribution
that playfully aligns the scenario in the introduction with the volume title.[31]
By insisting that "Fancy" is the speaker who lends a voice to the talking
book, this subscription unsettles the status of individual poems as the primary site of imaginative writing. Stepping out of the poem and into the material organization of the book, the jabbering "Fancy" loosens the limits of
form and allows the conceit that spans the compilation to travel within the
organizational features Purfoot added in publication.

After this opening verse, *The Forrest of Fancy* included multiple further prefaces that all elaborate on the process of making the compilation. Each draws together the work of multiple textual agents by picking up on and developing the
horticultural metaphors in the volume title. In "The Authour to the Reader," the
nearly anonymous poet H. C. adopts the guise of a farmer cultivating his fields:

My selfe I count to be the Husbandman,
For in this booke, as in a ground most fit,
To sow the seedes of my unwi[e]ldy wit.[32]

Yet although he "plow[s]," "sow[s]," and "reapes" the "good seedes" of his fertile mind in the ground of his book, this farmer-poet cannot bring in his crop alone. With his "corne" lying "scattered on the ground," he is helpless,

> Till at the last he thrashers doth provide,
> Who from the corne the straw and stubble take,
> And on a heape the graine togither rake.[33]

The "thrashers" here supplement the process of poetic invention, separating the grain from the chaff, or clearing away the remaining traces of composition. In the elaborate figure of textual production conveyed by this horticultural imagery, the infusion of fresh labor corresponds to the interventions by the compiling publishers. By sweeping the winnowed poetry into a jumbled "heape," the acts of gathering and arranging turn the poet's work into the compiled form in which it is available to readers.

The poet-farmer's discussion of the haphazard pile of his newly threshed grain captures the productive disarray of the texts within this book, maintaining a sense of their great variety. The multiple prefatory addresses in *The Forrest of Fancy* go on to narrate the long path that poems took from the poet's pen to a published book. The front matter concludes with "The Epistle to the Reader," which is unsigned but reads like the defense of a bookseller's collaboration with the poet, complete with a modesty *topos* for "presuming thus boldly to *publish* a thing of so small valew."[34] This compiler had a savvy sense of what readers wanted, observing, "So variable are the minds of men" and "so diverse their opinions" that "one will peruse pleasant Histories, and other poeticall devises, this man merry tales, and the other like toyes: that man devine and morrall matter, every one severally, according to his severall affection."[35] To meet the desires of such capricious readers, the single book would attempt to contain every possible kind of writing. It "gathered togither in one small volume diverse devises, as well in prose as meeter, of sundry sortes, and severall matter," and it preserved the basic variety of the "diversly framed" work.[36] Living up to the imagery of cultivation, the compiler offered a frame that was an expression of the process of gathering. He praised "the disordered placing of every perticuler parcel thereof, being rudely and dispersedly divided" because that variety was designed to be "fit for every degree, & agreable to their diverse affections."[37]

The "rude" and "dispersed" state of this book works to materialize the haphazard, unfolding process of poetic compiling as the development of prior actions of composing. As my first chapter showed, the "parcel" was a publisher's term for an internal division or a short section of a longer text and could refer to the packets in which copy arrived at the print house.[38] In praising "the disordered placing of every perticuler parcel," this address paradoxically registers the larger poetic structure of *The Forrest of Fancy*. "Disorder," like "framing," was an early modern term for an active, materially engaged poetic craft. In *The Art of English Poesy* (1589), George Puttenham used the word to illustrate figures of speech that altered the conventional placement of words in "a deliberate rearranging of the order, not an absence thereof."[39] Puttenham praised figures that worked through "tolerable disorder," like parenthesis, which "is when ye will seem" to "graft in the midst of your tale an unnecessary parcel of speech."[40] "Disorder" here exposed an active, evolving, and potentially changeable form; it was the index of multiple other possible formations. Early modern texts in which disorder rose to the surface were meditations on the conditions of poetic craft, Jenny C. Mann observes, because "misplaced words" expressed the "working out of a vernacular mode of figuration."[41]

In *The Forrest of Fancy*, the compiler's praise for the disorderly placement of poetic parcels thus signaled the surprising value of the larger form of the book. Readers could recognize—and critique—how well the arrangement of the compilation expressed the manifest diversity of the gathered writing. Reading across the front matter, the accumulative nature of the poetry book comes into focus as an accommodation of the multiple agencies within the compilation, from the physical and ideal form of the speaking book to the author-farmer with his crew of compiling threshers to the publishing bookseller who meets his customers' desires for variety. Throughout, the figures of cultivation bear witness to a material design that was palpably jumbled, but that was the more poetic for this disorder. *The Forrest of Fancy* used the imaginative resources of form to project a structure that exceeded the divisions between the gathered texts, and the shoddy organization was itself a tool for sensitively remaking the poet's craft within the context of this book.

Compilations as Potential Forms

To what end did compilations present an identity and a form that was in excess of the labors of poets? What was at stake in calling attention to the process of cultivating a book of poems? Between the 1570s and the 1590s, Richard Jones was both the printer and the bookseller for dozens of poetry volumes that ostentatiously performed the practice of compiling for potential buyers. By claiming a specific value for how printed compilations were put together, Jones showed his books to be the product of an alert reading that amounted to a kind of poetic making. He had an interest in building a market for new poetry books, attracting readers who might otherwise borrow a used copy of Tottel's *Songes and Sonettes* or transcribe their friends' manuscripts. Where Purfoot offered an unruly jumble of poems, perhaps suggesting that the figurative trees could be perused separately from the forest, Jones anticipated the habits of destructive readers by offering both a material and a conceptual design that attempted to resist the omnipresent threat of fragmentation. Such elaborate framing was, of course, more of a performance than an actual solution. Readers would always break texts down to their choicest parts. But if Jones overcompensated with his elaborate figures, his ambitious textual design speaks to a publisher's desire for compilations that were too valued to be torn apart. What Jones imagined was a book *in potentia* that could never be destroyed because it was always in the process of coming into being.

In 1575, Jones printed *A Smale handfull of fragrant Flowers*, a very slight octavo of only sixteen pages, or a single sheet, for sale in his own shop. The compilation was attributed to N. B. on the title page, but elsewhere in the book, there was little concern with who that poet might be.[42] Advertised on the title page as "selected and gathered out of the lovely garden of sacred scriptures," *A Smale handfull* was composed of just three poems but contained abundant prefatory material. The volume opens with a prose address from N. B. "To the right honourable and vertuous Lady, the Lady Sheffeeld," which begs the patroness "to accept the simple gift of a yong and unskilful husbandman," promising "the s[c]ent wherof I trust, being gathered in so fruitful a time, wil so revive your senses."[43] The contents of this bouquet belie the inexperience of the modest farmer-poet, who claims the labor of gathering the poems to be more valuable than his writing of them. The horticultural tropes continue in the next dedication, a poem "in the prayse of this handful of flowres" in which a "little Bée" flits about collecting the sweetest nectar for "fayre Ladies al."[44] This poem announces that "virgins, wives, and widowes" will alike be pleased by "suche a honeycombe" because "although this booke be small, / The flowres thereof may wel delyght."[45] Conflating multiple stages in the apian metaphor of textual consumption and production, this introduction values the compilers who bring the poems to fruition. It replaces any sense of the anonymous poet's control over his work with the uses to which it will be put by a whole circuit of past compilers and future readers.

With this broad appeal, *A Smale handfull* was both extending and adjusting humanist reading practices that were traditionally more invested in the fragmentary contents of books than in their design as a whole. Sixteenth-century poetry collections were, as Mary Thomas Crane puts it, "an exercise in gathering," and far from an expression of individual authorship, these books valued "the collection and framing of already existing matter that could in turn be gathered by the reader."[46] But if poetry compilations exposed the circumstances of their own production in an ongoing cycle of textual reuse, their design attempted to mitigate the omnipresent threat of disintegration. Stationers like Jones pushed back against the future destruction of their books with claims for their unique value *as* compilations. *A Smale handfull of fragrant Flowers* begged readers to attend to the entirety of the slight posy.[47] This is another volume that incorporates an address from a speaking book beseeching the potential buyer:

> Since I poore booke am put into thy hand,
>   although the tome or volume little bee,
> Yet Reader deare that I be throughly scand
>   with zelous minde I begge and crave of thee.[48]

A Smale handfull is here given a body and a voice, as well as a mind that can predict how the "volume little" might be used in the future. With this demand for careful study, *A Smale handfull* initiated a hermeneutic process in which the fruits of poetic cultivation should be understood within the ambit of the compilation. The adverbial clause "with zelous minde" hovers ambiguously between a particular condition of reading and the book's own consciousness. "First reade," the embodied book begs, and only "then chuse such fruits as lyke thee best."[49] Buyers were encouraged to purchase the book before they tore it apart.

Begging for a thorough consumption of its very slight form, *A Smale handfull of fragrant Flowers* was protecting itself from readers who might be tempted to follow the example of the nectar-seeking bee that flits selectively from poem to poem. We can witness this attempt to ward off destruction in the book's craving to be "*throughly* scand." This ambiguous spelling has two potential meanings: to be read *thoroughly* but also, we discover in the lines that follow, to be read *through*. The stanza closes with the book requesting that the prospective reader "Ne seeme to judge or sentence thyne to frame, / Before *throughout* thou do peruse the same."[50] Most literally, "peruse" means to "read through" and, in an older etymology, it even carried the meaning of "use up" or "consume entirely."[51] Before the modern sense of a hasty skimming, "peruse" connoted a thoroughness and completion that required an attention to the physical form of the book. The spelling "throughly" may be the work of the compositor, of course, but given the subsequent command to read "throughout," the ambiguous spelling is just possibly a further exhortation to attend to the entirety of this tiny book, rejecting both hasty judgments and the destructive selection of choice sentences.

Jones's compilations frequently mingled the influence of multiple and distinct textual agents, ultimately turning practices of material framing into a rationale for thinking across diverse poems. Here I return to *A gorgious Gallery, of gallant Inventions* (1578), which was considered briefly in the opening of this study, because this book illustrates how Jones took his figures of compiling to something of an extreme. Printed by William How for sale in Jones's shop, *A gorgious Gallery* was a quarto containing ninety very diverse poems: lyrics by lamenting lovers, moralizing precepts guarding against worldly vice, poems in praise of friendship, and the prosimetric "History of Pyramus and Thisbie."[52] While some of the items in *A gorgious Gallery* were subscribed with the initials of their authors, most were not, and the compilation was overall invested in advancing a larger, figurative identity for the book itself.

Jones sustained this conceit with the title's figuration of the gallery as an architectural frame for the "gallant Inventions" it shelters. At this moment, a "gallery" was a covered space designed for walking indoors and only secondarily for displaying art.[53] It was also a space that occasioned the writing and copying of poetry, as in George Gascoigne's "The Adventures of Master F. J.," where the protagonist was "walking in the Gallery" when he "there in passion complyed these verses."[54] According to its title page, *A gorgious Gallery* was "Garnished and decked with divers dayntie devises," casting poems as the ornaments that embellished the built structure (see Introduction, Figure 1).[55] Jones pushed these images of construction to their limit, claiming that the poems were "First framed and fashioned in sundrie formes, by diverse worthy workmen of late dayes" and "now, joyned together and builded up: By T. P."[56] With this announcement of the significant labor that went into writing and compiling the poems—all of which were, in and of themselves, acts of "framing"—Jones called attention to the poetic craft that stood behind the printed book. The imagery of a process of construction shared by multiple textual agents illuminated how aspects of poetic form were mobilized in the physical design of the compilation.

Jones used the architectural figure of the "Gallery" to help explain how he was now printing multiple earlier compilations within a single volume. The "T. P." named on the title page was probably Thomas Proctor, who was an apprentice to the stationer John Allde, and one of several compilers whose work was incorporated into *A gorgious Gallery, of gallant Inventions*.[57] About two-thirds of the way through the book, the running title was swapped out for the heading "Pretie pamphlets, by T. Proctor," which introduces the fifty-two poems that follow. The first of these was titled "Proctors Precepts," and ten more were subscribed "T. P."[58] With this alliterative riffing on Proctor's name, Jones cast *A gorgious Gallery, of gallant Inventions* as a shelter for several smaller compilations. Pamphlets were short printed texts that risked being read to pieces because they were too slight to merit the cost of their own bindings.[59] By incorporating the fleeting material form of Proctor's "Pretie pamphlets" into the organizational features of *A gorgious Gallery*, Jones shed light on his recursive process of textual gathering and arrangement. He preserved—and only partially subsumed—multiple instances of compiling within the design of his book.

With this long process of gathering, *A gorgious Gallery, of gallant Inventions* could claim to have a value in excess of the individual poems, many of which buyers could have found elsewhere. But beyond the contents, Jones proposed that the material and conceptual organization of the book was worthy of careful attention. The volume's front matter included two prefatory poems that explicitly praised the larger figure imaginatively projected by the gathered work. In an address to "the curious company of Sycophantes," Owen Roydon wards off the future destruction of the book by chastising lazy readers inclined to seek out fragments, disparaging them as "drowsie Drones" who "rudely read and rashly put to foyle / What worthy workes, so ever they doo finde."[60] This is a scene of cultivation in which the value of the harvest depends on the stewardship of the resources for the collective good of all readers. Roydon inverted the traditional apian metaphor, turning the imagery of nectar-seeking bees into an attack on excerpting readers who greedily deplete the precious store of honey. He rails at the droning "Sicophantes" who "never cease to swell" when they "the Hony combes doo eate" and leave the more industrious bees to "starve for want of meate."[61] The verse even includes an apotropaic defense against such destructive consumption:

(Depart from hence) that cursed kinde of crew,
And let this Booke, embrace his earned meede:
Which was set forth (for others) not for you.[62]

Dispatching a whole crew of drowsy readers, Roydon makes it possible for this personified book to receive future esteem or praise. The volume's "earned meede," or payment, was a further riff on the apian imagery of the honey wine, "mead," subverting the very terms through which the figure of the compiling bee typically determined value.

The ostentatiously mixed metaphors in the design of *A gorgious Gallery, of gallant Inventions* encouraged a sense of the compiled poetry as itself a figure that was continually in the process of coming into being. The gathered poems could take on multiple potential forms because the connections between them were active and evolving, remade when each thorough reader perused the book. *A gorgious Gallery* claims to merit this care because its industrious crew of book builders fashioned a durable compilation that will outlive the natural designs of husbandry. Unlike the earlier bouquets, and maybe even the forests, which leave the gathered work open to the elements, this gallery offers a sturdier and more enduring shelter for poems. The other prefatory verse, "A. M. Unto all yong Gentilmen, in commendacion of this Gallery and workmen therof," more directly engages the architectural conceit of the book fashioned by multiple workmen-poets.[63] This introductory poem was probably written by Anthony Munday, another of Allde's apprentices, who would go on to become a prominent poet. It conjures the figurative space of *A gorgious Gallery*, commanding potential buyers to picture it for themelves: "See Gallaunts, see, this Gallery of delightes, / With buyldings brave, imbost of variant hue."[64] Using *enargeia* to establish the vivid, varied details of the poetic delights, Munday relates how this textualized architecture was the product of multiple hands, "devisde by worthy wights," and came into being gradually: "(Which) as time servde, unto perfection grew."[65] These protracted efforts of writing and compiling, the "studies toyle" that "fraught / This peerelesse peece," were oriented to the future, undertaken "In hope to please your longing mindes therwith."[66] With this structure designed to satisfy readers, Munday imagined *A gorgious Gallery* as a book that can stave off the cannibalizing drones in Roydon's dystopian beehive. The compilation could promise an enduring form because it exists in the minds of readers, where it would be safe from being plundered by lazy bees.

This optimistic construction depended on the labor of the compilers who, in putting together the volume, created a figure that could sensitively accommodate the gathered work. Midway through his commendatory poem, Munday introduces a new kind of reader who is alert to the continuities that span this book-to-be:

> Which workemanship, by worthy workemen wrought,
> (Perusde) least in oblivion it should ly:
> A willing minde, eche part togeather sought,
> And termde (the whole) *A gorgious Gallerye.*[67]

Discerning the skill of the workmen-poets, the owner of this "willing mind" turned his private perusal into a future and public life for this writing. He rescued their poetry from obscurity by seeking out each distinct part, and he established a collective identity for the diverse work by lending it a name. Punning on the dual meanings of poetic "invention" as both discovery and imaginative composition, the speaker predicts that his audience will "Such fyne Inventions finde," as "will you binde / To yeelde them prayse."[68] The compiler's alert reading compels future book buyers to recognize the merit of *A gorgious Gallery, of gallant Inventions.* His "willing mind" teaches how to see the volume not as a container for individual poems, which would continually be in peril of becoming fragments, but rather as a "(whole)" fashioned to meet their desires.

This parenthetical naming of *A gorgious Gallery, of gallant Inventions* epitomizes in miniature the expansive network of compiling for print. The curved brackets that set off "(the whole)" simultaneously evoke the broadest coordinates of the compilation and propose that the ambitious figure of the "Gallery" was dependent on the external support of the printed book.[69] The parenthesis was "both a rhetorical figure and a typographic arrangement" in early modern England.[70] Like Puttenham's account of the "figure of tolerable disorder," the parenthetical framing of "(the whole)" conjures the possibility of other arrangements. It projects the multiple potential forms that the gathered poems might take through Jones's material and conceptual figuration of the printed *Gallery.* Matthew Zarnowiecki has identified how early modern poets and compilers were "conscious of the new medium of print and the new poetic objects being created in this medium," exploring the impact of "media in the poetic works themselves."[71] The compilations considered in this chapter very clearly demonstrate that the opposite was also true: the medium of print actively accommodated—even amplified—poetic form as a function of the design of the book. Through sensitive readings of the poems they had gathered and arranged, Jones and other stationers were using the devices of print to stretch the boundaries of poetic craft, profoundly entangling aesthetic and material forms.

A gorgious Gallery, of gallant Inventions came together through the efforts of a long chain of compilers. Munday's introductory poem was an ode of praise for the willing minds of Roydon, Proctor, and especially Jones, the publisher who was likely responsible for the naming of the book. This reading with an eye to the future was a genesis story, an etiology that used both the imaginative and the material creation of the book of compiled poems to explain its final state. Munday's commendatory verse was at once a fanciful, figurative history of the circumstances of print publication in 1578 London and a wager that exposing the production of *A gorgious Gallery* would entice buyers with a compilation that was fashioned with their interests in mind. For this reason, the literary history of English poetry requires a critical reading of the figures imaginatively created and sustained by print.

From Compiled Figures to a Common Style

Jones's gamble in *A gorgious Gallery, of gallant Inventions* did not pay off. The compilation was never reprinted and, with the exception of ballads in *A Handefull of Pleasant Delites* in 1584, the printer-publisher largely turned away from poetry for over a decade. This gap in the publication of compiled poems was certainly not unique to Jones. From the perspective of literary history, this moment has been understood as a period of transition between older "plain" styles of poetry and the renovation of English verse through new continental influences at the end of the sixteenth century.[72] But we should also read the scarcity of English poetry in the 1580s as a transitional moment in the history of literary printing. From this moment on, the poetry books that thrived did so by rejecting the overt figures of compiling promoted in *A gorgious Gallery, A Smale handfull of fragrant Flowers*, and *The Forrest of Fancy*. Expressions of the mind of the compiler fell away, and the influence of poets—and even of poems themselves—became more legible within the arrangement of printed books.

The Paradyse of daynty devises (1576) was a multiauthor compilation that Jones printed three times in three years for the bookseller Henry Disle.[73] It would go on to nine total editions by 1606.[74] The title page prominently combined the work of multiple compilers, promising that *The Paradyse* was "aptly furnished, with sundry pithie and learned inventions: devised and written for the most part, by M. Edwards."[75] This deviser "for the most part" was Richard Edwards, the dramatist and poet who served as master of the Children of the Chapel Royal and who had died ten years earlier in 1566. Edwards's personal manuscript was probably expanded by Disle, who wrote the prefatory address explaining that this compilation had been "penned by divers learned Gentlemen, and collected togeather, through the travell of one" who has "not long since departed this lyfe."[76] Across the first five editions of *The Paradyse of daynty devises*, the order and organization of poems were adjusted at multiple points as items were added and removed.[77] The shifting arrangement shows, first, how agents of the book trade were invested in updating their volumes, revising even when it would have been simpler to reprint. Second, as a palpable disorder crept into the design of *The Paradyse*, the multiple editions also show that its compilers were not especially interested in projecting a larger conceptual form or figure for the collected poems. The "paradise" created by the publishers and printers who worked on the book was instead a consistent— and consistently godly—poetic style. Where older compilations had worked to explain the points of connection between diverse poems, *The Paradyse of daynty devises* began with stylistically similar poems and then wrote that common approach into the features that materially organized the work. Elaborate performances and explanations of compiling were no longer necessary because the poems themselves made the case for their inclusion in the book.

Outside of its inclusion in a tradition of Elizabethan miscellanies, *The Paradyse of daynty devises* has not been significant for literary history. The consistent moralizing tone of the compilation has been characterized as a hallmark of the "drab verse" that was common in mid-sixteenth-century England. "Drab" was C. S. Lewis's coinage for the workmanlike poems from "a period in which, for good or ill, poetry has little richness of either sound or images."[78] While Lewis averred that the term was not itself "pejorative," he admitted that the period had more bad poetry than good and aligns *The Paradyse* with the worst of it. The "poulter's [measure] and 'sentences' and verse knick-knacks," as well as the "gnomic deluge" of the moralizing poems, were all so distasteful for Lewis that, he concluded, "the popularity of [the] collection" across three decades "is shocking."[79] Whatever Lewis's distaste for midcentury verse, when *The Paradyse of daynty devises* is considered from the perspective of the compilation—that is, when we read it through the organizational features that repeatedly echo the moralizing style of the poems—the flood of proverbs seems less like a failure to achieve metrical variety. The repetitive gnomic knickknacks in both the poems and the organizational apparatus were rather an experiment in a different way to present the gathered poems as a body of work, writing the moralizing forms into the material arrangement of the book.

For this reason, the multiple exchanges between the contents and the apparatus of *The Paradyse* complicate textual histories that have distinguished between poetic and material making. Gérard Genette launched one such approach with his theory of the "paratext" as a "threshold" that allowed readers to move between "the inside and the outside" of a text.[80] Beginning from a structuralist investment in intertextuality, Genette focused on the discursive interactions between the authorial text and the cultural systems that informed that body of work, largely overlooking the interventions of nonauthorial agents and the development of textual practices across time. While the field of book history has accepted Genette's taxonomy of the paratext, it has rejected his almost exclusive focus on language. Helen Smith and Louise Wilson have argued for a more "embodied" sense of the early modern book as "an object which is handled by particular readers, and whose physicality is constructed through the processes and operations of the printing house."[81] *The Paradyse of daynty devises* blurs those boundaries even further, urging a mixed history in which poetic style and material design are difficult to pull apart. Textual features like poem titles and attributions were not a liminal space of transit between the "inside and the outside" of the compilation, but actually collapsed that distance.[82] At the same time, the embodied physicality of the codex could not fully explain the poetics that ran throughout the organizational structures developed in the process of printing, which demonstrate a careful attention to linguistic elements within the poems.

The Paradyse of daynty devises developed a modular approach to material design. With poems that were movable, compiling was an active process that could fashion a broader conceit for the volume, even when it stretched the physical connections between the poems. While headings in the first two-thirds of *The Paradyse* included both thematic titles and continuous numbers, these devices were not markers of the poetic sequence but rather of quantity, the tally of poems within the book. Three proximate poems demonstrate how the numbered headings counted the aggregate total of verses:

42. "Amantium irae amoris redintigratia [*sic*] est" ["The fallyng out of faith-
    full frendes, is the renuyng of love"]
43. "Thinke to dye"
44. "Beyng asked the occasion of his white head, he aunswereth thus"[83]

Each of these poems is uttered by a separate speaker, and each takes up a
distinct topic: a mother reassuring her child about the reconciliation of strife,
a pious Christian anticipating the salvation he has earned, an elderly man
explaining the cares that have aged him. Such variety is characteristic of *The
Paradyse of dainty devises* as a whole. The compilation is one in which readers
pivot from scene to scene and speaker to speaker while they move between
poems without any narrative continuity. At the same time, this slight cluster
also captures the compilers' consistent investment in activating the common
speech that is a basic characteristic of moralizing proverbs. The speaker in
poem 42 relates how he recorded the mother's lullaby: "tooke I paper, penne
and ynke, this proverbe for to write, / In regester for to remaine."[84] And poems 43 and 44 each incorporate stock wisdom: "The life is long, whiche loth-
somely doeth laste" and "Where wretched woe doeth weave her webbe, /
There care the clewe, can catche and caste."[85] All three poems turn aphoristic
sayings into poetic speech, either by writing a scenario that could lend a context to a proverb or by using a maxim as the condensed expression of a common conceit.

Yet the arrangement of *The Paradyse of dainty devises* does not facilitate
tracing continuities between the scores of stylistically similar poems, nor
does it explain the circumstances that produced such a material disorder. The
organizational features were slightly haphazard in every edition, with numbered headings that are missing or out of order, inconsistent attributions, and
poems left without titles or headings. This disarray was increased by the multiple rounds of revisions. Across the editions, new poems were added because
they were explicitly in dialogue with earlier work, but there was little material
intervention to signal those thematic continuities. One poem by the original
compiler Richard Edwards, headed "2. M. Edwards MAY," prompted at least
two responses during the life of *The Paradyse*.[86] Besides moving this poem to
number 6, the 1578 edition added "29. A replie to M. Edwards MAY," an
anonymous verse in which the poet relates the inspiration he found in his
source: "I Read a maying rime of late delighted much my eare / It may delight as many moe, as it shall read or heare."[87] This addition sketches the
influence of *The Paradyse of dainty devises*, weaving scenes of the book's

reception into the evolving body of the text. But the arrangement of poems did not take advantage of this opportunity to narrate the collection's impact. As the numbered headings suggest, the response was not placed near its source, and without an index or table of contents, readers were not given tools to perceive the affiliations between poems scattered across the book.

Early modern readers did not need such help, of course. This chapter has discussed multiple occasions in which compilers resisted readers' tendency to disintegrate poetry books. But the lost opportunity to situate Edwards's "May" among its responses is illuminating because it reveals the priorities that guided a compiling in which poems were independent building blocks that could be shifted without concern for disrupting the rest of the compilation. *The Paradyse* did not emphasize the material connections between the component parts of the book because physical design was made irrelevant by the common moralizing ethos. The scattering of shared topics across the volume continued through the final round of revisions in 1585, when "Maister Edwards his I may not" was added at the back of the collection, in the portion without numbered headings.[88] This reply, which was written as if by Edwards himself, was a kind of protracted response that allowed the poet to speak back to his own work nearly twenty years after his death. Where his first poem sang the praises of the fertile month of May, the speaker now bemoans the neglect of the beloved who rejected him: "I sorrow in May, since I may not, in May obtaine my love."[89] But without an explicit instruction to link these responses—which were separated by almost seventy poems—that circuit of reading and writing was not made legible by the design of *The Paradyse of daynty devises*, even when authorship might have encouraged it.

If the organizational features in *The Paradyse of daynty devises* were not concerned with explaining the potential connections between poems, they nevertheless contributed to the moralizing tone of the volume as a whole by working to draw out a common style. The alliterative form and moralizing ethos of the poems seeped into the textual frames of *The Paradyse of daynty devises*, as if the compilers Disle and Edwards—or perhaps the printer Jones—had their ears tuned to the work they were gathering and organizing for future readers. Several headings anticipated both the form and the content of the poems that they introduce. Many picked up on common verbal qualities, like "Faire woordes make fooles faine," which revels in the alliteration and assonance that were characteristic of midcentury poetry.[90] Other titles were themselves proverbs in verse, like the rhyming tetrameter couplet, "Mans flitting life, fyndes surest stay, / Where sacred Vertue beareth sway,"

which was even set with line breaks.[91] This exhortation to lead a virtuous life
was the heading for a poem that relates how even the sturdiest objects and
the strongest beings succumb to the destructive forces of their worlds:

> The Marble stone, is pearst at length,
> With little droppes, of drislyng rayne;
> . . . .
> The greatest Fishe in deepest Brooke,
> Is soone deceived with subtil hooke.[92]

This litany of failure extends to "man him selfe," who doth "fade at length,
and fall away" without the support offered by the "state of Vertue," which
"never slides."[93] The rhymed and metrical heading above this series of com-
monplaces predicts the lesson that unfolds across the three stanzas of the
poem. It is a moralizing rubric in praise of a virtuous life that, by echoing the
homogeneous tone of the collection, further affiliates the poetic writing with
the apparatus of the printed book. The heading collapses the semantic and
formal distance between the poet's composition and the compilers' sense of
how to gather and organize that work.

In addition to a common style, the book's organizational features participated in the imaginative framing of the scenarios within the poems. The
majority of verses were subscribed with an attribution that gave either part or
all of the poet's name, like "M. Edwardes," "W. H.," "F. Kindlemarsh." But
several taglines resisted disclosing the identity of the author, giving instead
the aphoristic motto "My Lucke is losse."[94] A common saying that was conscripted as a marker of authorial identity, "My Lucke is losse" simultaneously
offers two readings of the verses it follows, casting them as both personal expressions and universalizing moral lessons that arc away from any single poetic scenario. This intertwining of individual and common speech likewise
motivated the attributions for two poems that were only included in the 1580
edition of *The Paradyse*. Headed "A Complaint" and "A Replye," this pair was
subscribed with the identities of their poetic speakers, "Troylus" and "Cressida" (see Figure 8).[95] In the same fashion as the aphoristic "My Lucke is
losse," these attributions evoke common knowledge of the Trojan lovers, slot-
ting the identities of those fictional characters into the position that the design of the book usually reserved for named poets.

Lending voices to the infamous lovers, this pair abstracts the legendary
narrative into a generalized warning about the perils of unfaithful women.

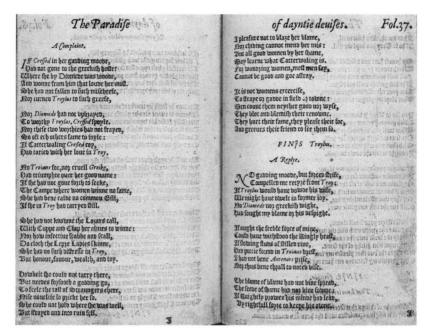

Figure 8. "A Complaint" and "A Replye" with attributions to the Troilus and Cressida legend, in *The Paradyse of daintie Devises* (London: Henry Disle, 1580), sigs. K3v–K4r, STC 7518. By permission of the Folger Shakespeare Library.

Each poem traffics in gendered stereotypes, like Troylus's accusation that "all good women by her shame, / May learne what Catterwaling is," which is met with Cressida's abnegating plea for forgiveness: "My heavie hart and dolefull case, / Which craves your pitie not your spight."[96] The material arrangement of the 1580 edition of *The Paradyse of daynty devises* thus bolstered the lessons readers were meant to take from these moralizing poems. When the conventional wisdom is borne out by the attributions to Troylus and Cressida, the compilation further generalizes that message, closing the distance between the camps of the Trojan war and Tudor London where poets like Francis Kinwelmarsh and William Hunnis ply their trade—and where readers might purchase Disle's book.

The organizational poetics of books like *The Paradyse of daynty devises* grew out of the exigencies of compiling poetry for print: the habits of titling, attributing, and arranging that helped publishers promote their volumes of gathered poems to buyers. But in the process of transmitting and then re-transmitting this work, the organizational features that were at first external supplements became essential guides for poetic reading and interpretation. In the case of *The Paradyse of daynty devises*, we have evidence of how readers treated the headings as integral to the bodies of poems. A slim poetry manuscript owned by John Leche, now held at the Folger Shakespeare Library, was copied out of multiple books printed in the 1560s and 1570s.[97] While the first six poems were transcribed without headings, as was common in contemporary poetry manuscripts, the scribe's method changed for the remaining twenty-two poems, all of which were sourced from the 1576 edition of *The Paradyse of daynty devises*. In addition to the poem texts, Leche copied the headings from *The Paradyse*, including the moralizing verses like "Who wyll aspire to dignitie / By learning must advanced be" and "Though Triumph after bloudy warres, the greatest brags do beare: / Yet Triumph of a conquered minde, the crowne of Fame shall weare."[98] In handling *The Paradyse* differently from other sources, Leche carried the design of the printed book forward into the new context of the manuscript, even while he was tearing his source apart.

This manuscript copy of poems from *The Paradyse* was, admittedly, the result of a slightly unschooled reading. Besides being copied in secretary and italic hands that were slightly too careful, several pages in Leche's manuscript have real problems with spacing, with insufficient room marked out for titles and poems that break off abruptly before concluding.[99] Yet this inept transcription was also the expression of an unlikely fidelity to the material arrangement of the printed book, and it helps in identifying the 1576 first edition of *The Paradyse of daynty devises* as the scribe's exemplar. The most stunning instance of fidelity to the source appears in the poem title "Finding worldly ioyes but vanities, he wysheth death," or, as this scribe wrote, "worlaly ioyes," with the ascender on the *d* separating from the lobe and becoming a separate *a* and *l*.[100] The scribe was slavishly following the 1576 edition of *The Paradyse*, where the compositor made the same mistake (see Figures 9 and 10).[101] The "worlaly ioyes" heading captured the scribe's indiscriminate reading of the printed compilation, his sense that the title should be approached in the same fashion as the body of the poem. As a kind of textual care that betrays, perhaps, a degree of illiteracy, this blunder was the trace of an indiscriminate reading practice that flattened out the distinction between poem texts and the frames that gathered them together. The copying reader found meaning in the textual features that Disle and Edwards introduced when they incorporated the moralizing poems into a compilation with a consistent mode.

Finding worlaly ioyes but vanities, he wysheth death: 21.

Forlorne in filthy froward fate, wherein a thousand cares I finde;
By whome I doo lament my state, annoide with fond afflicted minde;
A wretche in woe, and dare not crie:
I liue, and yet I wishe to dye:

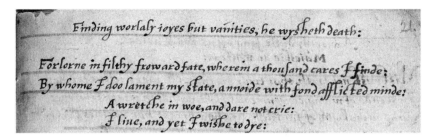

Figure 9. Transcription of the compositor's error, "worlaly ioyes" in John Leche's poetry manuscript, fol. 21r, V.a.149. By permission of the Folger Shakespeare Library.

23. Finding worlaly ioyes but vanities, he wysheth death.

FOrlorne in filthy froward fate, wherein a thousand cares I finde,
By whom I doo lament my state, annoide with fond afflicted minde:
A wretche in woe, and dare not crie,
I liue, and yet I wishe to dye.

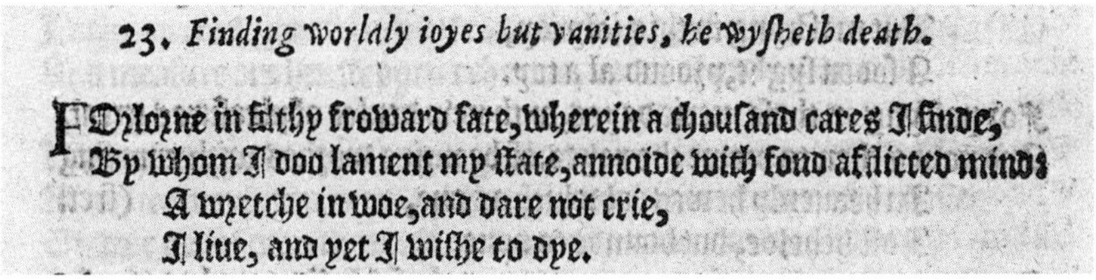

Figure 10. Leche's source, *The Paradyse of daynty devises* (London: Henry Disle, 1576), sig. C3r, RB 13658. By permission of the Huntington Library, San Marino, California.

Ultimately, Leche's manuscript helps us see how sixteenth-century readers valued continuities of poetic style and topic. Learning from *The Paradyse*'s consistently moralizing contents, this scribe affiliated that compilation's poems with didactic writing from other volumes all published within the span of a few years. His overly careful copying of the book's textual apparatus was, in its way, the expression of a desire for as much moral advice as he could glean, extracting it not only from poems but even from the features of the material text that were themselves poetic readings. In the longer history of printing English poetry, *The Paradyse of daynty devises* charts a new way forward for a poetically engaged textual design. Instead of positing either a fanciful figure or an abundant variety, the compilation was depicted as distinct from the material clusters or parcels in which compilers first received work. The conceit of *The Paradyse of daynty devises* was distributed on to each individual poem—and even to each heading and attribution—such that it was possible to change the order and arrangement of the compilation without disturbing the common ethos. The material connections between poems were irrelevant because they so obviously belonged together. The result was a compilation that could be endlessly reimagined, even while aspects of its design were carried over in later print editions and manuscript copies. With this shift away from an earlier, more literal approach to the process of making the book, the conceptual category for understanding the compilation began to be uncoupled from material order and arrangement.

Compiling and the Fictions of Literary History

The poetics of compiling for print has remained difficult for modern readers to see because, unlike Leche, we have assumed that publishers and printers were insensitive to the contents of their volumes. Far from taking the design and organization of collected poetry as an expanded field of interpretation, the influence of professional stationers has been seen as damaging to authorial craft. As Hyder Rollins observed of *Englands Helicon* (1600), "by far the majority of the poems are printed with unauthorized changes from originals."[102] Literary histories have traditionally thought across discrete lyrics only when licensed by authorship or common sources, and this focus on the workings of form within single poems has elided a more dynamic history in which professional compilers understood the points of exchange between poems and books as integral to an emerging tradition of English writing. Yet books like *The Paradyse of daynty devises* and *A gorgious Gallery, of gallant Inventions* suggest that compilations hold a history of how poetic form and content were understood by their earliest readers. The organizational apparatus of printed poetry books was increasingly an opportunity for professional compilers to introduce a metacritical perspective, making a claim for the value of a particular kind of poetry.

This chapter concludes with poetry published at the end of the sixteenth century, a moment in which the contents, arrangement, and design of lyric compilations moved beyond performances of material gathering. Volumes like *The Phoenix Nest* (1593) began to advertise a new kind of compilation, promising readers access to "the most rare and refined workes of Noble men, woorthy Knights, gallant Gentlemen, Masters of Arts and brave Schollers."[103] Transcending the labor of figurative craftsmen or farmers, this esteem for contemporary and elite poets has been identified as "a decisive shift in the format of the printed poetry" compilation.[104] *The Phoenix Nest* created a sense of the book as a social formation, a "literary gathering" that contributed to a textual "unity that is defined communally," as Michelle O'Callaghan puts it.[105] Publishers and booksellers from this moment exchanged figurative titles for imagery that attempted to lend a harmony to the gathered writing. In *A Poetical Rapsody* (1602), compiled by the poet Francis Davison, the title referred to the stitching together of Homeric songs.[106]

Above all, late sixteenth-century compilations were experimenting with a strategic anonymity, not as a way to disguise the influence of named authors but rather to incorporate a whole culture of shifting poetic fashions within their conceptual and material framing. *Englands Helicon*, for instance, was a response to the outsize influence of Philip Sidney's posthumously published work. In the 1590s, Sidney inspired a broad turn to pastoral writing. As William Scott observed, "Sir Philip Sidney amendeth" the long pastoral tradition reaching from Theocritus to Virgil to Spenser, and "leaves all behind him in the pastoral kind."[107] In *Englands Helicon*, Sidney was placed in dialogue with his heirs, creating a collective of shepherds that amplified the prominent fictions of the pastoral mode.[108] Eclogues were "personating poems," Scott explained, in which "the poet speaks little or nothing in his own person," but rather through "dissembled actions."[109] When the powerful response to Sidney's work was gathered within a new compilation, his influence on English poetry was felt as an extension of the fictions within his writing. *Englands Helicon* was composed entirely of pastorals, 150 eclogues that recount the mournful plaints of multiple Coridons, Sylvanuses, and Cynthias, directed at dozens of flocks of sheep. Besides Sidney's own poems, *Englands Helicon* contained work by living and deceased poets including Edmund Spenser, William Shakespeare, Thomas Lodge, Anthony Munday, Robert Greene, Fulke Greville, Michael Drayton, and Thomas Watson. Most of this work had been published previously, for instance in Spenser's *The Shepherds Calender* (1579), Watson's *The Hekatompathia, or Passionate Centurie of Love* (1582), and *The Passionate Pilgrim* (1599), which was attributed to Shakespeare on the title page. But several of the poems by Munday had, as far as we know, not yet seen print and were likely commissioned for *Englands Helicon*.

The circuit of textual transmission that delivered poems from these diverse publications to *Englands Helicon* illustrates how agents of the book trade contributed to the rising status of English vernacular poetry. The forms and fictions of pastoral informed both the commercial choices and the material practices that went into printing the compiled poems. As a result, the volume began to sketch a literary history that was written neither by poets nor by critics but rather by stationers invested in the organizational potentials of poetic genre. *Englands Helicon* was published by the bookseller John Flasket, who worked with John Bodenham, the London grocer behind an unprecedented attempt to elevate English writing to the status of classical authorities. Collaborating with a group of stationers and poets, Bodenham funded a series of printed commonplace books that elevated the status of contemporary poets and playwrights: *Politeuphuia, Wits Common-wealth* (1597); *Palladis Tamia, Wits Treasury* (1598); *Wits Theater of the little World* (1599); *Bel-vedére, or The Garden of the Muses* (1600), and *Englands Parnassus, or the Choysest Flowers of Our Moderne Poets* (1600).[110] *Englands Helicon* was part of the same project. It opens with a verse dedication from "A. B." "To His Loving Kinde Friend, Maister John Bodenham," which describes "thy *Helicon*" as an attempt "to make compleate" the work started in "*Wits Common-wealth*, the first fruites of thy paines," then continued in "*Wits Theater*, thy second Sonne" and "the *Muses Garden*," a "Nosegay, as was never sweeter."[111]

Instead of excerpting choice sentences, as Bodenham's commonplace books had, *Englands Helicon* gathered whole poems. It also privileged a consistent pastoral mode over the formal and thematic variety encouraged by the earlier tropes of floral gathering. The project was probably led by Nicholas Ling, whose transposed initials appear under a prefatory note promoting the value of the compiled book.[112] He declares, "The travaile that hath beene taken in gathering" poems "from so many handes" and "hath wearied some howres" "might in part have perished" had they not been "digested into this meane volume."[113] Ling imagines *Englands Helicon* as a storehouse that preserves not only the gathered poems but also the process of compiling, "digesting" that labor along with the contents of the book. He is particularly concerned with defending his "travail" from charges of theft, because so many of the poems had been published previously: "If any Stationer shall finde faulte, that his Coppies are robd by any thing in this Collection, let me ask him this question, Why more in this, then in any Divine or humaine Authour: From whence a man (writing of that argument) shal gather any saying, sentence, similie, or example, his name put to it who is the Authour of the same."[114] Ling here presents compiling as a kind of writing. Stationers, he says, are just like authors who should know that their choice sentences may be subject to the threats of excerpting readers. The rest of this defense explains the juxtaposition of the multiple kinds of textual agency within *Englands Helicon*, assuaging the patrons, poets, and princes who might find themselves awkwardly rubbing shoulders in this book that flattens out the hierarchies of poetic production.

Overall, *Englands Helicon* was concerned with smoothing over the juxtapositions between the poems that had been gathered from multiple sources. Bodenham's circle of compilers scoured extant publications to find enough material for their collection, drawing from songbooks like Thomas Morley's *Madrigalls to Foure Voyces* (1594) and Nicholas Yonge's *Musica Transalpina* (1597); from prose narratives with inset poems like John Dickenson's *The Shepheards Complaint* (1596) and Bartholomew Yong's translation of Jorge de Montemayor's *Diana* (1598); from George Peele's play *The Araygnement of Paris* (1584); and even from *Speeches Delivered to Her Majestie this Last Progresse* (1592) issued by the Oxford stationer Joseph Barnes. Ling drew this writing into a new compiled form that amplified the shared mode of all the work by introducing strategic pastoral fictions in the organizational apparatus of *Englands Helicon*. Headings to poems by Sidney and Spenser included references to the poets' well-known personae, like "Astrophell the Sheepheard, his complaint to his flocke" and "Hobbinolls Dittie in prayse of Eliza Queene of the Sheepheards."[115] These titles condense the fictions of identity first articulated across *Astrophel and Stella* and *The Shepheardes Calendar*, contracting the broader context of publication into the dissembling pseudonyms that introduce single songs. When headings with these fictions appeared above multiple items in *Englands Helicon*, their common fantasy of the shepherd poet made it possible to read across poems that had not at first been intended to be considered together.

Most poems in the compilation were subscribed with poets' names, like "S. Phil. Sidney" and "Edm. Spencer," but that commitment to distinguishing between factual attributions and fictional titles faltered in a few places. Seven poems in *Englands Helicon* were subscribed "Sheepheard Tonie," and because two had been attributed to Anthony Munday previously, we think all of the comically rustic pseudonyms in *Englands Helicon* refer to him.[116] The tagline is the playful emblem of a poet who had worked closely with compiling stationers across his career.[117] With a nod to the pastoral fantasy that spans the compilation, Munday and Ling subverted the logic of attribution, treating the poet's name—and the space it was expected to occupy within the printed book—as an opportunity to deepen the reach of poetic fictions.

Elsewhere in *Englands Helicon*, anonymity disrupts the consistent naming of poets in order to amplify the fictions that span the compilation. "Ignoto"

appeared as the attribution for eighteen poems, filling what should be a position of identity with a placeholder that called attention to the compilers' lack
of knowledge about who wrote the poems. Strikingly, three of these "Igno-
tos" were belated additions to *Englands Helicon*, appearing on cancel slips
added after John Roberts's printing of the sheets. These extra layers of paper
changed two attributions to S. W. R. (Sir Walter Raleigh) and one to Fulke
Greville, effectively removing those prominent poets—who had real connections to Sidney—from the fictional community of singing shepherds.[118] The
belated imposition of anonymity echoes other points in *Englands Helicon* in
which the pastoral fiction takes priority over poets' identities. One short song
headed "Apollos Love-Song for faire Daphne" was subscribed with the occasion of Elizabeth I's 1592 progress to Bisham Abbey: "This Dittie was sung
before her Majestie, at the right honourable the Lord Chandos, at Sudley
Castell, at her last being there in prograce. The Author thereof unknowne."[119]
This song had first appeared in the 1592 *Speeches Delivered to Her Majestie this
Last Progresse*, a collection in which the publisher-compiler did not name the
performers of the pageant, but instead allowed the queen's own authority to
stand as the impetus for the elaborate spectacle. When the single song was
lifted from this context and reprinted in *Englands Helicon*, the collaborative
energy stands in for any named author.

Anonymous attributions are more common in the later pages of *Englands
Helicon*, perhaps because Bodenham's compilers were running out of sources.
Ling and his collaborators discovered that, if they wanted such a large collection of contemporary pastoral writing, they would need to intensify or even
invent traces of the mode in several more general poems. At multiple points,
they used the print apparatus to amplify the rural tone, adding new headings
and speech tags that transformed "lovers" and "ladies" into "shepherds" and
"nymphs." One poem, called "The Sheepheards allusion of his owne amorous
infelicitie, to the offence of Actaeon" in *Englands Helicon*, was preceded by
a much longer heading when it was printed two decades earlier in Thomas
Watson's *The Hekatompathia, or Passionate Centurie of Love* (1582).[120] The original title included an elaborate account of the poet's Ovidian inspiration:
"Actaeon for espying Diana as shee bathed her naked, was transformed into a
Hart, and sone after torne in pieces by his owne houndes, as Ovid describeth
at large in lib. 3 Metamorph."[121] An inset quotation of several lines of commentary on the Actaeon story by Silius Italicus follows, and then the heading
turns to Watson, explaining how he read his source: "The Author alluding in al
this Passion unto the fault of Actaeon, and to the hurte, which hee sustened,

setteth downe his owne amorous infelicitie; as Ovid did after his banish-
mente, when in another sense hee applied this fiction unto himselfe."[122] In
The Hekatompathia, the elaborate apparatus of citation contributed to the
poet's measure of his own work. Nestling his poem within both the story of
Actaeon and the long history of commentary on the *Metamorphoses*, this
heading helped Watson assume Ovid's mantel, just as the classical poet "in
another sense hee applied this fiction unto himselfe" when Ovid figured his
exile as a pastoral retreat. While these multiple feigned identities were no
doubt the basis for including the poem in *Englands Helicon*, the use of the far
simpler title, "The Sheepheards allusion of his own amorous infelicitie, to the
offence of Actaeon," dropped the story of how the classical source reached the
poet. A whole circuit of intertextual reading was hidden behind a title that
proposes the lamenting shepherd was directly inspired by the Ovidian myth.

This occlusion of textual origins—and of the narratives of writing and
reading they carried with them—was repeated throughout *Englands Helicon*.
Ling lifted several poems from *The Phoenix Nest*, another collective response
to the loss of Sidney, but that source was once again significantly refashioned
by the addition of textual features that imposed a new pastoral mode. A
poem that had first been called "A description of Love" was retitled in
Englands Helicon, becoming "The Sheepheards description of Love" (see Figures 11 and 12). The compilers took advantage of an implicit dialogue in the
stanzas that were arranged into questions and responses, inserting marginal
speech tags so as to assign lines to two speakers. Every stanza in the version
in *The Phoenix Nest* begins with an abstract question about the nature of love,
"Now what is Love, I praie thee tell?"[123] But in *Englands Helicon*, Melibeus
speaks directly to his friend Faustus: "Sheepheard, what's Love, I pray thee
tell?"[124] More than just adding a rustic air to the poem, the introduction of
new comically pastoral personae prompted several further adjustments to the
rhythm and structure. In the penultimate stanza, the metrically regular "Yet
what is Love, I pray thee say?" from *The Phoenix Nest* becomes the much
more uneven "Yet Sheepheard, what is Love, I pray?"[125] An audience is even
summoned by the fictions of this pastoral world. While listeners are not at
first named in the poem, in *Englands Helicon* Faustus speaks directly to the
audience, commanding, "Then Nimphs take vantage while ye may."[126]

These dynamic exchanges between poems and the textual features added
in the process of gathering and printing *Englands Helicon* speak to the outsize
influence of poetry books on the literary histories beginning to take shape at
the end of the sixteenth century. The sense of an emerging tradition of English

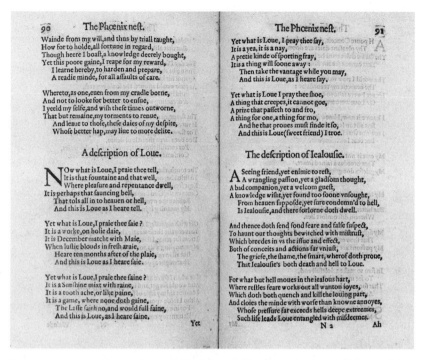

Figure 11. "A description of Love," *The Phoenix Nest* (London: John Jackson, 1593), sigs. N1v–N2r, STC 21516. By permission of the Folger Shakespeare Library.

verse—which Bodenham advanced in both his commonplace books and the remarkable commitment to pastoral in *Englands Helicon*—far exceeded the impact of any single poet, compiler, publisher, or bookseller. "The Sheepheards description of Love" offers a stunning illustration of how authorial identity was incidental to this cultural conversation about the status of vernacular writing. The poem was anonymous in *The Phoenix Nest*, but *Englands Helicon* introduced a complicated set of attributions. "The Sheepheards description of Love" was first subscribed "S. W. R.," for Sir Walter Raleigh, but one of the printed cancel slips reading "Ignoto" was pasted over the initials.[127] Such an erasure of identity was, on the one hand, part of a hyperdefensiveness about authorial attributions in *Englands Helicon*. Perhaps as a result of the painstaking (and costly) addition of the cancel slips, Ling wrote in his preface that no poem was "here placed by the Collector" "under any mans name, eyther at large, or in letters, but as it was delivered by some especiall coppy."[128]

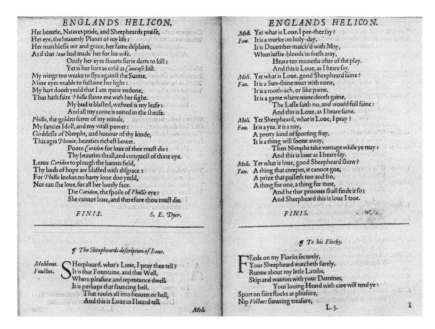

Figure 12. "The Sheepheards description of Love," with the "Ignoto" cancel slip mostly torn away to reveal the "S. W. R." underneath, *Englands Helicon* (London: John Flasket, 1600), sigs. L2v–L3r, STC 3191, copy 1. By permission of the Folger Shakespeare Library.

On the other hand, papering over Raleigh's "letters" was more than an admission of the care taken with naming poets. The cancel slip "Ignoto" was a material intervention in "The Sheepheards description of Love" in *Englands Helicon*. Like the new title, the speech tags, and even the naming of an audience of "Nimphs," this slip reflects the process through which the arrangement of the printed compilation actively refashioned the poem so that it could be read alongside the songs of other rustic shepherds. As a poem made and remade by the environment of each compilation it passed through, "The Sheepheards description of Love" is a relic of the process of transmission. The single poem condenses and preserves the active relationship between textual arrangement and poetic form. Both the belated attribution and the imposition of a pastoral mode quite literally show the role of authors to be secondary, or even irrelevant, to the poetic community coalescing in the pages of this book.

While literary historians have dismissed the poetic investments that inform the sporadic, contingent affiliations between poems in printed compilations, I have argued in this chapter that the textual features introduced in the process of publication hold an active and evolving formal history. Far from obscuring or disguising the identities of poets reluctant to seek publication, the careful labor of compiling shows how multiple, diverse agents of the book trade were invested in articulating figures for the compilations themselves. These forms were mixed, disorderly, and contingent on nonauthorial material craft. But it was through these very imperfections that compilations were able to project the outlines of a larger textual arrangement for readers. A careful attention to the poetic styles and forms that suffuse the design of late sixteenth-century poetry compilations can illuminate both the aesthetic priorities of early modern print and the corresponding impact of these books on the flourishing of Elizabethan poetry. Subsequent chapters follow the legacies of this impersonal poetic form into compilations that aspire to represent the skill of individual poets. In books with elaborate narrative organizations and repeated series of identical forms, we can witness a protracted experiment in fitting an idea of the book together with its material production. This process was consistently all the more poetic for encountering—and often surmounting but occasionally succumbing to—the practical challenges of compiling for print.

CHAPTER 3

Gascoigne's Inventions

Inference and Compiled Form

In the decades following *Songes and Sonettes* (1557), English stationers developed a poetics of compiling that reached ambitiously beyond the individual poem. I have focused so far on compilations with work from multiple and often anonymous poets in order to explain how the material design of early printed books could accommodate poetic form and content without privileging individual authorship. Participants in the book trade gathered and organized poetry with an eye to promoting the value of their collections, and their own skilled reading, not the identities of writers. In the midst of this experimental culture of compiling, poets also tried their hand at making their own books of poems, imaginatively taking over stationers' practices of arrangement as a way to redirect the collaborative energies of the print trade toward a new kind of textual agency. This chapter reads George Gascoigne's publication of his poetry in two distinct editions in the 1570s as a response to an earlier, more diffuse poetics of compiling for print. By using the innovative textual features from multiauthor compilations to organize his own work, Gascoigne promoted a sense of the book as itself a piece of imaginative writing, a motley and composite form with its own elaborate fiction of production.

A Hundreth sundrie Flowres bounde up in one small Poesie was published in 1573 by the bookseller and draper Richard Smith. The title of his volume plays with vernacular images for the anthology, a book traditionally figured as a compilation of flowers, describing the contents as "Gathered partely (by translation) in the fyne outlandish Gardins of Euripides, Ovid, Petrarke, Ariosto, and others: and partly by invention, out of our own fruitefull Orchardes in Englande."[1] Such conventional tropes locate value not in the singular order or totalizing design of the volume but rather in its wide-ranging sources, as well as its mixture of diverse items including drama, multiple different kinds of poems, and a prose romance inset with even more poems. These horticultural metaphors were further refined in 1575, when Smith republished the collection as *The Posies of George Gascoigne Esquire*. The sudden naming of Gascoigne as the sole writer was surprising. *A Hundreth* had minimized his influence both in the volume title and in the organizational features that multiplied the fictional compilers, editors, and printers responsible for the book. In 1573, the plays and a full third of the shorter poems were attributed to Gascoigne, and several other poems were signed with initials that slyly hinted at his authorship, like "G. G." and "A. O. G. N. C. S." (pp. 231, 253). But these local attributions cast Gascoigne as merely one among "sundry Gentlemen," neither the primary poet nor the compiler who gathered and organized the diverse work.

In the pages that follow, I explain how the authorial unity of *The Posies*, which seemingly came into focus when Gascoigne claimed the entirety of the compilation as his own in 1575, actually developed out of a more primary interest in the formal and imaginative poetics of textual design in *A Hundreth sundrie Flowres*. Despite the claim that the work had been "corrected" and "perfected" in *The Posies*, most of the dramatic and poetic writing was unchanged; it was primarily the framing devices that were updated in the new book. Such selective revisions in fact continued strategies of compiling in the first edition, where poem headings, prefatory letters, and prose links launch elaborate stories of gathering the diverse components for publication. Throughout *A Hundreth sundrie Flowres*, Gascoigne included traces of his own poetic invention within organizational features that were typically the purview of press agents. He developed multiple—and, at times, competing—narratives of textual origins as a way to project a conceptual order for a book that was materially composite. This imaginative play with the arrangement of *A Hundreth* demonstrates how the conceptual category of the poetry compilation was evolving rapidly during a moment of media change.

The revisions between *A Hundreth* and *The Posies* have been understood as a novel approach to poetic authorship that was occasioned by the innovations of print. In both compilations, Jane Griffiths explains, the multiple "fictional masks for Gascoigne" express a "simultaneous understanding and undermining of the 'language' of print."[2] From the perspective of arguments about print culture, the knowing manipulation of a textual idiom has constituted a savvy response to an earlier generation of compiling poems from multiple authors. Gascoigne "place[s] the *Flowres* in a direct line of descent from Tottel's Miscellany" and "produces himself as an author through his imaginative recursion on Tottel's book," as Rachel Stenner puts it.[3] Gascoigne has been understood as the poet who invented a knowing authorship by overcoming the paradigm of the miscellany. But despite such self-aware games, *A Hundreth sundrie Flowres* never mentions *Songes and Sonettes*, nor does it even refer to the poets within that publication. It is only in *The Posies* that "Sweete Surrey" and "Wiat" who "wrote of wondrous things" are mentioned in a new dedicatory poem ("The Printer in commendation of Gascoigne and his works," lines 3, 4). For a book that so baldly exposes the conditions of its own making, it is striking that *A Hundreth* claims a blindness to the English poetry publications that have been posited as its models. This chapter argues that, despite the prominent ruse of collaboration in 1573, print authorship and the corresponding logics of miscellaneity were not at first in sight for Gascoigne. Rather, *A Hundreth sundrie Flowres* appropriated the language and ethos of multiauthor poetry compilations as fodder for the projection of a larger, if still mixed form for his gathered writing. The book itself was the object of a poetics of compiling that spanned the material gaps between discrete poems.

In imagining a design for his compiled poetry, even in the first compilation from 1573, Gascoigne's skill consisted in directing a collective hermeneutics that drew on aspects of material arrangement. He accomplished this feat by harnessing an inferential mode of reading that was elemental to volumes like *A Hundreth*, which only partially obscured authors' names with coy initials.[4] By dropping frequent clues about his identity, Gascoigne taught the significance of the network of material, conceptual, and even aesthetic connections between the gathered poems, urging readers first to pay attention to the textual features that linked the diverse pieces of writing and then to think across the expanse of the compilation that contained multiple posies. Only in the 1575 edition, when the boundary between poem texts and organization was more rigidly enforced, did an investment in authorship take priority over a playful articulation of a fantasy of the book.

Gascoigne's publications challenge literary historical attempts to isolate the influence of individual poetic authors. Early printed poetry books were supple and paratactic compilations that unevenly layered the activities of poets, compilers, publishers, and printers. *A Hundreth sundrie Flowres* and *The Posies of George Gascoigne Esquire* suggest just how limiting it might be to attend to books as miscellaneous objects without also considering their imaginative projections of a piecemeal order that exceeded authorship. Through intensive readings of the features that organize gathered poetry, this chapter draws out several ways in which early modern poets responded to large-scale textual and poetic effects that we no longer remember how to see. What I am tracing is therefore a history of how the mixture of agencies in the printed poetry compilation began to take shelter under an author function that was a knowing fiction. Formal poetic agency rests not just with the poet, nor even with the compilers supposedly responsible for the volume, but also with the readers whose aesthetic engagement was conditioned by the volume's material parataxis.

Inventing the Compilation

A Hundreth sundrie Flowres showcases the diversity of its gathered writing in an unwieldy, barely tamed abundance. The stout quarto is composed of four main sections: (1) *Supposes* and *Jocasta*, a pair of Gascoigne's dramatic translations first performed for the legal community at Gray's Inn in the 1560s; (2) a new prose tale, "The Adventures of Master F. J."; (3) "The Devises of Sundrie Gentlemen," nearly eighty poems in a range of styles, some of them attributed to anonymous lovers and some to Gascoigne; and (4) "Dan Bartholomew of Bathe," a verse narrative that mixes the character's account of his thwarted love with a "Reporter's" retrospective synopsis of the story. The bibliographic relation of these sections is inconsistent. While there is a gap in the pagination and the register restarts after the plays, the narrator describes a continuous copy text between "F. J." and "The Devises," even though the compositor used a setting—narrowing the text into a V and giving a printer's flower—that signaled a conclusion.

These multiple inconsistencies were likely the result of a production schedule that was split unevenly between the printers Henry Bynneman and Henry Middleton while Gascoigne was abroad.[5] Nevertheless, several organizational features attempt to span these distinct components and thus to explain a continuous, if still compiled form for *A Hundreth sundrie Flowres*. The table of contents, running titles that set off each section, and lengthy poem titles in "The Devises" all worked to express a sporadic continuity between the diverse components. "The contents of this Booke" describes "The Adventures of Master F. J." as the background for an array of poetic genres, "a pleasant discourse . . . conteyning excellent letters, sonets, Lays, Ballets,

Rondlets, Verlayes and verses" (p. 2). And the prose tale concludes with the narrator explaining his part in compiling both F. J.'s adventures and the occasional poems by diverse authors that follow: "Henceforwardes I will trouble you no more with such barbarous style in prose, but will onely recite unto you sundry verses written by sundry gentlemen, adding nothing of my owne, but onely a tytle to every Poeme" (p. 216). In these explicit accounts of gathering and arranging the sundry pieces of this compilation, *A Hundreth sundrie Flowres* was working to soften the basic discontinuity of early printed books. By allowing imaginative writing to travel back and forth between poems and the features that joined them together both materially and conceptually, the compilation turns the labor of gathering and arrangement—precisely the textual practices that seem to threaten a poet's control—into an expression of Gascoigne's own imaginative design.

With this alertness to a broader organization, *A Hundreth sundrie Flowres* was participating in contemporary debates about poetic invention. In the mid-sixteenth century, "invention" did not refer primarily to a novel creation but rather to eloquence; it was the first part of rhetoric aimed at discovering ample subject matter.[6] One tool for cultivating this rhetorical skill was the commonplace book, a collection of short textual fragments and *sententiae*—often personal reading notes—arranged under headings so as to be available for future reuse.[7] To the extent that these notebooks digested existing sources, "invention" was unconcerned with either originality or any sense of a larger compilation. But Gascoigne later weighed this investment in textual recycling against a native fertility that aspired to a more imaginative production. One addition in *The Posies of George Gascoigne Esquire* in 1575 was "Certayne notes of Instruction," the first printed treatise on English poetics, in which he advises that all inventions ought to contain "*aliquid salis*," a certain salt or wit that proves the skill of an English poet seeking to adapt classical and continental poetic ideals (p. 454). "The first and most necessarie poynt" of "making a delectable poem," Gascoigne declares, is "to grounde it upon some fine invention," by which "I meane some good and fine devise, shewing the quicke capacitie of a writer" (p. 454). Invention works here both as organization and as wit—as finding and as imagining—two activities that diverged in later decades. Mary Thomas Crane in fact situates Gascoigne as a crucial figure in this split, noting that in his subtitle *Gathered partely (by translation) . . . and partly by invention*, the term that "previously used to mean something found or gathered, now shifts toward its modern meaning to bring in the possibility of imaginative creation."[8]

More than a definitive semantic shift, we ought to read these simultaneously available senses of invention as evidence of the developing relation
between individual poems and the larger forms that gathered writing might
take in early modern England. *A Hundreth sundrie Flowres* imagines a poetically sensitive compilation in which the discrete pieces of writing are joined
through a dynamic interaction with the physical book. In referencing the
material practice of binding, the volume title *A Hundreth sundrie Flowres
bounde up in one small Poesie* both explains the presence of the diverse works
and operates as a metaphor for the poetic connections between them.[9] As
Juliet Fleming has shown, "poesie" was used interchangeably with "posy," a
short poem "written in such a way that its material embodiment forms an
important part of its meaning."[10] Poems were thus conceptually and aesthetically entangled with the textual objects that drew them together.

Far from an innovative and poetic approach to compiling, *A Hundreth
sundrie Flowres* has more often been read as an example of the basic incoherence of the early printed book. As Crane explains, sixteenth-century textual
culture privileged fragments over volumes: "Texts were seen as containers,"
tools for gathering and arranging a "system of interchangeable fragments"
culled from other literature.[11] Authors did not ordinarily seek control over the
organization of their books. J. W. Saunders described the "stigma of print," a
bias against publication prompted by courtier poets who inspired a generation
of professional writers to deny their involvement with the print shop.[12] While
such accounts rightly describe the piecemeal composition of early printed
books, their exclusive focus on fragmentation has applied modern ideals of
authorial coherence to gathered volumes in which the agency of individual
writers was not the primary concern. The presumption of incoherence has
overlooked how sixteenth-century poets did—in their own way—push back
against a system of publication that dispersed their work widely. The paradigm of a distributed compilation actually became a way to articulate a different kind of order, of organization, and of collected meaning.

Sixteenth-century poetry books thus complicate easy distinctions between gathering and writing poems; between material formats and poetic
forms; and, perhaps most powerfully, between the production and the consumption of imaginative writing in a moment of media change. Colleen
Rosenfeld has shown how early modern writers and readers understood "poesy" as an activity, a "quality of action that shapes how a poem is made."
Recovering poets' investment in this process, Rosenfeld highlights the significant temporality of poetic craft: "When a poem points to the *poesie* out of

which it is made, it writes a history of composition that structures its imaginative domain."[13] With the single poem archiving the circumstances of its production, that history is never far removed from the materials that connect and preserve those fugitive traces of the literary imagination. Diverse and varied poems were collectively intertwined with the imaginative structure of the compilation, which came into focus through an inferential reading of the material disunity of the volume. This poetic orientation to the contingencies of print publication challenges histories of the book to account for the possibility of textual production, transmission, consumption, and imitation with an eye to the whole, even if that whole was unstable or just a fiction. By teaching readers to locate meaning in textual arrangement, the awkward mixture of agencies in Gascoigne's collected work helped sustain a sense of the book as itself a poetic composition.

In the case of *A Hundreth sundrie Flowres*, Gascoigne's engagement with contemporary books taught him to slip poetic fictions into material textual features such as prefaces, poem and volume titles, and aphoristic taglines that had traditionally been commercial and nonauthorial. Three letters describe the efforts of A. B., the printer; H. W., the publisher; and G. T., the friend who gathered the work and surreptitiously made it available for publication.[14] G. T. writes to H. W. of the disorder of "this written booke" containing "the workes of your friend and myne Master F. J. and diverse others" that "I had with long travayle confusedly gathered together" (p. 144). This story of extended compilation was, in theory, an opportunity for G. T. to impose an arrangement on the array of gathered works: "I thought it then *Opere precium*, to reduce them into some good order" (p. 144). The prose links in *A Hundreth* preserve the temporal experience of material gathering as a guide for interpretation. By associating the primary activity of writing with the secondary work of organizing the compilation, the design of the book wagers that the past labor of gathering poems and "reducing" their unwieldy abundance into some kind of organization will be legible in the future. But G. T.'s desire for order seems to have proven elusive, since the final arrangement of *A Hundreth sundrie Flowres* was profoundly confused. Although all three letters read as front matter, the two by H. W. and G. T. only appear *after* the plays, just before "The Adventures of Master F. J." A. B. even mentions that H. W.'s letter is "at the beginning of this worke" (p. 3), but it does not appear until nearly two hundred pages later.

A Hundreth sundrie Flowres is a riot of such contradictory explanations for how the book was made and, consequently, for how the overlapping poetic and material structures ought to be read. Adrian Weiss has reconstructed the division of the job among the print shops of Bynneman and Middleton in order to identify Gascoigne's delay in delivering copy as the factor that stretched the production schedule to more than eight months.[15] The result was the introduction of multiple discrepancies between the narrative of compilation in the organizational features and the final arrangement of the book. Supplementing Weiss's attention to the evidence of typeface, Kirk Melnikoff has read *A Hundreth sundrie Flowres* within the body of work published by Richard Smith, a draper and bookseller whose experience "working face-to-face with buyers selling books and other commodities" gave him a unique perspective on marketing books that would have appealed to browsing readers.[16] Where Weiss and others have identified Gascoigne as the author of all the prefatory letters, Melnikoff shows that, given Smith's own substantial investment in the idiosyncratic compilation, he was likely the author of the opening "Printer to the Reader," which was unsigned and did indeed appear at the beginning of the book. Of anyone, the printer should be aware of the order of the collection, and the basic, even improbable errors in the descriptions of compiling ultimately cast the imperfect organization of *A Hundreth* as a fiction. Smith, a semiprofessional bookseller, who never gave up his career as a draper, was thus an eager participant in the tales of compilation that Gascoigne had strewn across his collected work.

In appropriating the multiple agencies of printers, publishers, booksellers, and compilers, *A Hundreth sundrie Flowres* proposed that the makeup of the book might become a tool for grappling with the discontinuity that was a basic characteristic of compiled poetry. Gascoigne's fictions encouraged readers to seek out the explicitly poetic aspects of material organization. The false printer, A. B., observes and valorizes the indistinct boundaries between poetic forms and textual formats, noting how his "imprinting of this poeticall Poesie" gathers several "pleasant Pamphlets," the multiple component texts that never quite disappear within the new compilation (p. 3). This jumble has an effect in excess of recording production practices. In A. B.'s words, the volume has a "greater commoditie than common poesies" because it allows "the discrete reader" not to be "constreined to smell of the floures therein conteined all at once" but to "take any one flowre by itselfe" (pp. 3–4). Distinguishing "conteined" poems from "constreined" interpretation, the printer's letter articulates the value of disunity, promising that variety will teach readers to discern quality.

The productive limits of this interpretive process grew out of the awkward realities of how poesy was contained by the shifting, malleable compilation that never quite aligns with the organizational plan laid out in the prose links. *A Hundreth sundrie Flowers* displays what Michael Hetherington has called "a material hermeneutics" through which "meaning is not logically fixed but fluid and potential, awaiting the contingent circumstances in which it might be realised."[17] Through his coy fictions of compiling, Gascoigne projects the past temporality of writing forward for future readers, positing that knowledge of poetic origins will help in navigating this book. Meaning emerges from a doubled process of both reading the material composition of the printed book and recognizing in that organization the residue of a tangled poetic practice.

Because imaginative writing slips between individual poems and the broader design of *A Hundreth*, we can gain a sense of how Gascoigne developed an innovative approach to poetic invention by examining a single poem that repurposes discrete and static textual fragments as the basis for a strikingly dynamic scenario. "Despysed things may live" is a jangling string of aphorisms that rather literally amplified the posy "Spreta tamen vivunt" (p. 242). Most poems in "The Devises" are subscribed with such sententious taglines, proverbs like "Meritum petere grave," "Ever or Never," "Si fortunatus infoelix" that turn back to comment on a verse's mood or message by abstracting the scenario into a simple lesson.[18] "Despysed things" takes this mingling of material organization and poetic interpretation a step further by using the posy as a motive for composition. In the heading we learn that this poem grew out of an attempt to justify the motto: "This question being propounded by a Dame unto the writer therof, to wit, why he should write *Spreta tamen vivunt*, he aunswereth thus" (p. 242). The poem responds with couplets that are themselves aphorisms:

> Despysed things may live, although they pyne in payne:
> And things ofte trodden under foote, may once yit rise again.
> The stone that lieth full lowe, may clime at last full hye:
> And stand aloft on stately tow'rs, in sight of every eye.
> The cruell axe which felles the tree that grew full streight:
> Is worne with rust, when it renews, and springeth up on height.
>
> (lines 1–6)

This list stacks couplet on top of couplet, with each pair of lines narrating a transformation that disguises the agency of any human hand. Things suffering in pain simply "rise again"; lowly stones leap to the top of buildings; the rusty ax miraculously recovers to stand and mimic the tree it felled. With a paratactic syntax that disrupts any continuity of scenario, the opening of "Despysed things" depicts change as a tidy exchange of lowness for dignity. At the same time, the uneven lines of six and seven feet couch these transformations in a profoundly awkward rhythm that checks the transcendence of each nearly automatic renewal.

With these limited transformations, "Despysed things" suggests how a gathered, paratactic form might broadcast a writer's skill through a modest adjustment of his sources. Begun as a clatter of common speech, the poem develops into a lyric of erotic disappointment that grapples futilely with the limits of the aphorism. It takes a dark turn when the opening truisms become legible as self-consolations: "Thus much to please my self, unpleasantly I sing: / And shrich to ease my mourning minde, in spyte of envies sting" (lines 9–10). With this wail of loss, the speaker relates that he is "now set full light, who earst was dearely lov'd" (line 11). The lines that follow test whether platitudes might help in mending his broken heart:

> What resteth then for me? But thus to wade in wo:
> And hang in hope of better chaunce, when chaunge appointeth so.
> I see no sight on earth, but it to Chaunge enclines:
> As little clowds oft overcast, the brightest sunne that shines.
> No Flower is so fresh but frost can it deface:
> No man so sure in any seate but he may leese his place.
>
> (lines 15–20)

Abandoning control, the poet resigns himself to the vagaries that confront him and simply piles these common expressions of suffering into a discordant verse that relishes in disunity as an expression of change.

Yvor Winters praised Gascoigne for his sophisticated handling of plainness. His writing is "commonplace" poetry that "permits itself originality, that is the breath of life, only in the most restrained and refined of subtleties in diction and in cadence."[19] While Winters's account is persuasive for Gascoigne's best poems, like his "Woodsmanship," the yoking of individual inspiration to communal aphorisms is far more uneven in "Despysed things" and does not similarly instill "universals with their full value as experience," nor does it aspire to anything like a compassionate realization of feeling.[20] Wallowing in misery, the poet hangs his hope on the predictable workings of chance, which are sure to cloud the sun, scar fresh petals, and unseat the mighty. There is no whiff of life in this list of ruin to come. The bleak, nasty point of the poem is that universal expressions limit any basic commonness by trading in abstractions. Change does not place the speaker inside a shared experience of renewal but instead teaches how he might pass his pain on to others, as when he yearns "to see the time, when they that now are up: / May feele the whirle of fortunes wheele, and tast of sorrows cup" (lines 23–24).

In this slight play with the form and content of the posy, "Despysed things" shows how imaginative writing might repurpose textual features that were barely poetic. Gascoigne did not attempt to transcend aphoristic tag-lines; he rather demonstrated his skill by drawing his own work nearer to those impersonal forms, aligning his invention as closely as possible with the features that organized the compilation. The poem ends on a note of satisfaction:

> I now wish chaunge that sought no chaunge, but constant did
>   remain.
> And if such chaunge do chaunce, I vow to clap my hands,
> And laugh at them which laught at me: lo thus my fancy stands.
>
> (lines 28–30)

In each line, the speaker picks up and then quickly disarms the actions that had threatened him: changing, chancing, laughing. His subtle but unrestrained transformations revel in micro-adjustments of time, sound, and grammatical subject—attempts to find the slimmest margin that will allow him both to endure these threats and to prove that his "fancy stands." This simple poem is, like the larger compilation of *A Hundreth sundrie Flowres*, a paratactic form that derives invention from the textual features that connected Gascoigne's poems, bestowing new life on the "things" of the press while imagining a continuity between gathering and writing, seeing and reading, uncertain change and constant endurance.

Inferring Identities

When Gascoigne wrote with an eye to the poetics of organizational features, he not only fashioned a gathered form for *A Hundreth sundrie Flowres* but also situated that idea of the book within emerging social conventions of handpress-era publishing. Early modern poetry books preserved the labors of multiple writers and agents of the print trade, often defining their efforts against those of individual named authors. Richard Tottel announced the prominent, aristocratic identity of one of his poets in the title *Songes and Sonettes written by the ryght honorable Lorde Henry Haward late Earle of Surrey, and other*, but he only vaguely gestured to the "other[s]" included and, in the prefatory letter, emphasized his own role in releasing "those workes which the ungentle horders up of such tresure have heretofore envied" English readers.[21] In the decade after Tottel's compilation, books with the work of single named poets, like Barnabe Googe's *Eglogs, Epytaphes, and Sonettes* (1563) and George Turberville's *Epitaphes, Epigrams, Songs and Sonets* (1567) frequently included poems attributed to other men from the same social world, including Alexander Neville and Laurence Blundeston. Gascoigne was a participant in this collaborative network of writing and publishing. Neville also appears in *A Hundreth sundrie Flowres* as an addressee for poems composed while Gascoigne was at Gray's Inn, a center of legal education known for intensely communal writing.[22] Situating Gascoigne's poetry within this deeply social scene, Laurie Shannon describes his authorship as an experiment with the "creative dispensation between individuation and intersubjectivity and between solitary authorship and collaboration," one that treats both writing and personhood as essentially *"corporate* forms."[23]

Where the innovative use of the posy in "Despysed things" demonstrates Gascoigne's refashioning of material textual features, he was equally invested in appropriating the collaborative energy of early printed books. His treatment of the "corporate forms" of gathered writing was an opportunity to build sporadically continuous sequences within *A Hundreth sundrie Flowres*. Chains of poems unspool intermittently across "The Devises of Sundrie Gentlemen," with title after title describing, for instance, an unnamed poet writing to his "sayd friend," the "same friend," or "the same Gentlewoman" (pp. 220–22, 227). By referring to consistent recipients, these headings snare readers in an expanding, additive structure that gradually comes into focus as a haphazard sequence crafted out of *A Hundreth*'s organizational features. Like the small-format early printed book, these clusters of poems are contingent structures that could be drawn together, dissolved, and then refashioned in endlessly flexible arrangements. The nested forms of these sequences encouraged a habit of reading that was on the hunt for the shifting network of connections between individual poems. Gascoigne used this inferential engagement with the design of the book to close up a circuit of transmission that would typically point to other compilers but in *A Hundreth* repeatedly implicates his own hand.

Compilations like Gascoigne's, Tottel's, and Googe's have been understood as echoes of manuscript textuality within a poetic culture that had yet to recognize printed books as either generically or formally distinct. As Wendy Wall explains, *Songes and Sonettes* "stages a collision between poetry in its social environment and in its typographic form," while *A Hundreth sundrie Flowres* dwells on clandestine publication "as a means of emphasizing the manuscript features of the book."[24] Yet the abundant fictions of compiling explicitly for print also suggest that the manuscript references might be a knowing and coy disguise that actually highlights the distinct potentials of the two media. Alan Stewart reads Gascoigne's compilation as a challenge to the earnestness of many theories of print culture, describing the book as "a nostalgic manuscript fantasy that both insists on and denies its material form" and "positions itself on an *imagined* line between manuscript and print."[25] Extending my earlier argument about the fictions of publication in *A Hundreth*, I want here to consider how Gascoigne used the diffuse and scattered agencies of compiling for print to heighten the feigned intimacy of manuscript origins. His performance of authorial anonymity narrowed the account of textual production into a circuit so tight that it was implicitly personal. *A Hundreth sundrie Flowres* sustained a fantasy of self-collaboration in which Gascoigne could compile his own work as though it belonged to another poet.

Several half-hidden references to Gascoigne's poetic skill serve as clues to the meanings that travel, not in individual poems but throughout the compiled work. One brief sequence in "The Devises of Sundrie Gentlemen" takes the form of an extended riddle, a traditional poetic genre in which the mechanics of discovery are integral to the techniques of representation (see Figure 13). An expansive heading describes a dinner party where the "chief repast was by entreglancing of lookes" between a lady known for her "quick understanding" and a table of men: her brother, her husband, her former lover, and the poet who is now vying for her favors (pp. 230–31). The barely anonymous poet, "G. G. being stoong with hot affection could none otherwise relieve his passion but by gazing," is swept up in the tense scene of "watching," "winking," and "frowning" that stretches over nearly half a closely set quarto page (p. 231).[26] By contrast, the poem that follows, "His Riddle," condenses "this conceipt" into nine tightly laced lines that close with an exasperated sigh:

Thus every eye was pitched in his place.
And every eye which wrought eche others wo,
Said to itself, alas why lookt I so?
And every eye for jelouse love did pine,
And sigh'd and said, I would that eye were mine.

(lines 5–9)

The glances exchanged by the rolling, roving, yet ultimately stationary eyes trace a circuit of thwarted relations, where jealous looks measure the desire for connections that never quite materialize. All the eyes pine for an amorous possession that is held at bay both by the occasion, a scene of clandestine adultery, and by the epistemology of the riddle, which transforms the straight-forward narrative into a puzzle that asks readers to consider how all these eyes might desire the same object.

The knowing puzzles in "His Riddle" and the surrounding poems resist the modern expectation that textual origins ought to express authorship. When the game of erotic inference lures the reader into this awkwardly unfolding sequence, it is the organization of the gathered poems that is at stake, not the identity of the poet. Instead of disguising Gascoigne, the initials "G. G." teasingly call attention to his presence not only in the poem texts but even in the organization of the book. The riddle's partially hidden longing for the married beloved, "which was no sooner pronounced, but she could perfectly perceyve his intent" (p. 231) appears in the middle of a string of poems that is described in an earlier heading as "wrot in a booke of hirs as followeth" (p. 229). If the poet's "intent" is first obscured from prying eyes in the private manuscript, his desire is starkly legible to readers of the printed *A Hundreth sundrie Flowres*. The arrangement of the compilation expands the event by stretching it across multiple poems and organizational features. The rather inelegantly composed page opening urges a continuous movement through the clutch of poems, from the lady's answer—where the title and the poem are indecorously split between the bottom of one verso page and the top of the next recto—to the lengthy heading in which the occasion of composition substantially outweighs the riddle to follow. The loose, unfurling *mise-en-page* here prompts readers to seek out the local connections between poems and their headings. They are asked to infer the continuous poetic scenario, as well as how that imaginative framing lends a necessary order to this section of the printed book.

In other words, the compiled form of *A Hundreth sundrie Flowres* participates in the epistemology of the riddle, a type of poem that offers an

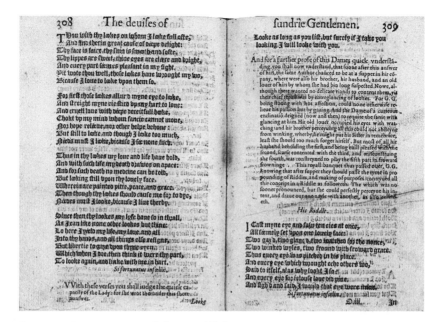

Figure 13. Page opening with "His Riddle" sequence, in George Gascoigne, *A Hundreth sundrie Flowres bounde up in one small Poesie* (London: Richard Smith, 1573), sigs. ²D2v–²D3r, STC 11635, copy 2. By permission of the Folger Shakespeare Library.

analogue for how early printed collections promoted a sporadically continuous reading. Riddles are, in Daniel Tiffany's account, hermeneutic puzzles that draw on a basic relation between lyric obscurity and poetic *techne*. They transmit an alternative literary history within the "enigmatic voice of certain highly wrought objects": speaking vessels, animated crosses, and melancholy inkhorns that unsettle the binaries of material cultural studies.[27] The "peculiar verbal disposition" of these puzzles recalls that matter is always known through language and "cannot be distinguished from the tropes and analogies that make it intelligible."[28] Sixteenth-century poetic riddles fashioned mental acts into things to be discovered by their readers. Tottel's *Songes and Sonettes* contained Wyatt's "A riddle of a gift geven by a Ladie," which teasingly remembers a kiss, "A Lady gave me a gift she had not, / And I received her gift which I toke not," and then uses that cryptic description of possession to make the audience complicit in the poet's wily tactics: "Conster what this is and tel not, / For I am fast sworne I may not" (Marquis ed., no. 120, lines 1–2, 7–8). The game of guessing at—but not naming—the kiss turns the physical gesture into an object of inference that is "wrought" by the language of the poem.

The duplicitous hermeneutics of such riddles was amplified by the organization of early printed books. Compilations like *A Hundreth sundrie Flowres* channeled the inferential thinking solicited by obscurity into an intensive reading practice that was attuned to material design. Their unwieldy mixture of contents asked readers to work through the relationship between poetic forms and material formats. Humphrey Gifford's *A Posie of Gilloflowers, Eche Differing from Other in Colour and Odour, Yet All Sweete* (1580) gathers diverse translations from French and Italian authors, as well as Gifford's own poems. One of his pieces is "Somewhat made of nothing, at a Gentlewomans request," in which the irritated speaker complains to his beloved who "would have me to make you some toy, / And yet will not tel me wherof I should write."[29] Unlike Wyatt's successful riddle of his lady's kiss, Gifford responds to these demands with a poem that revels in his failure to lend a physical shape to obscurity. Without her guidance, "Since nothing yea geve me," he can give her nothing in return. So he concludes with an almost talismanic invocation of the poem's emptiness: "now receive your nothing agayne, / Of nothing, but nothing, what else would yee have."[30]

The material design of the book actively informed how such wily puzzles could be read. *A Posie of Gilloflowers* concludes with a run of eighteen riddles of various lengths and in multiple different meters. Significantly, the solutions for these formally diverse puzzles are not supplied individually after each verse but collectively on the overleaf of the page with the last few clues. This organization prolongs the pleasure of speculating on or anticipating the identity of each speaking object. In the sixth riddle, readers find the clues "My beard it is gray, though not very old / The strong I make weepe, nor for heate, nor for cold" but must turn forward three leaves to discover that these human terms are being applied to an onion.[31] By using textual organization to heighten poetic obscurity, *A Posie of Gilloflowers* keys interpretation to the physical arrangement of this printed book.

A Posie of Gilloflowers also makes a specific claim for the value of this book as a compilation that mixes Gifford's writing with the work of other authors. Like the volume title of *A Hundreth sundrie Flowres*, the horticultural conceit of Gifford's *A Posie* privileges compiling as a practice that is at once material and aesthetic. He tells his patron John Stafford, "The thing I here present you with is, a posie of Gilloflowers collected out of the garden of mine own inventions."[32] Gillyflowers are hybrids, with red-and-white striped blossoms, and they were prized in early modern England as an emblem of how art might improve nature. In *The Art of English Poesy* (1589), George Puttenham treats the gillyflower as an illustration of judicious artifice, praising the "gardener" who "by his art will not only make an herb, or flower, or fruit come forth in his season without impediment, but also will embellish the same in virtue, shape, odor, and taste."[33] "Nature of herself," he concludes, "would never have done, as to make the single gillyflower, or marigold, or daisy, double."[34] The gardener, like the poet, can embellish the essential qualities of any single flower, making "things nature could not do without man's help and art."[35] Within Gifford's mixed bouquet of hybrid flowers, the compilation's doubled heterogeneity promises something to please every reader: "Though all the flowers herein contayned, carie one name, yet eche of them differs from other, both in colour and savour," and these apparent differences will be "the better to satisfie the diversitie of eyes that shall view them, and variety of noses that shall smell them."[36] By allowing readers to discern the variety of work, identifying the qualities that they find the most appealing, the compiled book heightens the inventiveness of any single poem.

An equally discerning mode of reading was encouraged by the printed form of Gascoigne's gathered writing. Like a riddle, or like the improbable mixture of art and nature in a hybrid flower, the great pleasure of *A Hundreth sundrie Flowres* is glimpsing the broader identity of the compilation come haltingly into focus. Across several hundred pages, the imaginative textual features, impromptu sequences, and partially hidden traces of Gascoigne's role in compiling the collection all help readers identify formal structures that were larger than the individual poem. Lorna Hutson has observed a related strategy of inference in Gascoigne's drama, showing that his 1566 translation of Ariosto's *Supposes* advanced a revolutionary "mimetic realism" by using "the pressure of sceptical enquiry" to heighten the rhetorical technique of *narratio*, or the narrative "emplotting of likelihoods" that strings discrete events together into a plausible sequence of actions.[37] For humanist-educated Elizabethans, Gascoigne's immediate audience at Gray's Inn, a mimetic reading of dramatic and poetic texts would have meant seeking "probable motives," inferring a backstory to explain events unfolding in the literary present.[38]

The savvy dramatization of the tools of legal reasoning and inference in *Supposes* found a broader expression within *A Hundreth sundrie Flowres*, the book in which the play was first published. In several sequences in "The

Devises of Sundrie Gentlemen," the social dynamics of the gathered writing prompt readers to identify Gascoigne's influence peeking through compiled textual structures that should exceed his agency as a poet. One intricately intertwined set of verses grew out of the world Gascoigne moved in as a law student during the 1560s: "I have herde master Gascoignes memorie commended by these verses following, the which were written uppon this occasion. He had (in the middest of his youth) determined to abandone all vaine delights and to retourne to Greyes Inne, there to undertake againe the study of the common lawes. And being required by five sundrie gentlemen to wrighte in verse somwhat worthy to be remembered, before he entred into their felowship, he compiled these five sundry sortes of meter upon five sundry theames whiche they delivered unto him" (p. 274). "Gascoignes memorie" leverages the poet's individual merit through a collaboration that initially seems to diminish his control over the volume.

With the surfeit of "sundry" motives for composition, all five poems in the sequence respond to themes set by named members of a literary clique: "the firste was at request of Francis Kinwelmarshe who delivered him this theame. *Audaces fortuna iuvat* [Fortune helps the bold]. And thereupon he wrote thys Sonnet following" (p. 274). Yet all five poems are also subscribed with "Sic tuli," a posy that is doubly idiosyncratic, since it is the only aphorism that appears nowhere else in *A Hundreth* and since it is oddly personal. This tagline most literally translates as "Thus I have borne," but the phrase is difficult to parse.[39] First, it can refer to so many different actions, and, what is more, it lacks the object that should accompany the transitive verb. What exactly has this poet carried, endured, or accomplished? By withholding a statement of the poet's labors, this boast of completion frames "Gascoignes memorie"—and especially the form that sequence takes within *A Hundreth sundrie Flowres*—into an object for readers to discover by moving through the gathered poems.

Rather than radiating outward into "The Devises," and then further out into *A Hundreth sundrie Flowres*, the extended occasion of "Gascoignes memorie" is confined by the claustrophobic organization of the compiled work. The fourth "poem" is itself composed of multiple sonnets: "Alexander Nevile delivered him this theame, *Sat cito, si sat bene* [Fast enough, if well enough], whereupon he compiled these seven Sonets in sequence, therein bewraying his owne *Nimis cito* [too fast] and therewith his *Vix bene* [hardly well], as foloweth" (p. 278).[40] These seven compiled sonnets, likely the first published corona in English, take up Neville's challenge in content as well as in pacing.[41] The poet's descent into profligacy is propelled by a surplus of haste:

> My wandring eye in haste, (yea poste post haste)
> Behelde the blazing badge of braverie,
> For wante wherof, I thought my selfe disgraste
>   (lines 34–36)

The interlocking corona, meanwhile, duplicates lines that narrate the poet's quick ruin, speeding across the breaks between quatorzains by passing the final line from one verse onward to the first line of the next: "Before myne eye to feede my greedie will," "And every yeare a worlde my wyll dyd deeme," "To prinke mee up, and make me higher plaste" (lines 14/15, 28/29, 42/43).

This hasty sequence captures, on the level of the line, a traffic in poetry that is internal, contained, and personal rather than digressive or collaborative. Across the seven poems, Gascoigne accepts Neville's lesson, but in terms that almost invert the theme of "Sat cito, si sat bene." He acknowledges: "So haste makes waste, and therefore nowe I say, / No haste but good, where wysdome makes the waye" (lines 83–84). What follows is a shift to an aphoristic mode of speech that seems appropriate for the theme, but which has been conspicuously absent thus far in the corona. The seventh sonnet steps back from the poet's life, giving "For proofe" of the proverb, a slow-moving snail that "clymes the loftie wall" a hasty soldier cannot scale and three abrasive sayings, including "The swiftest bitche brings foorth the blyndest whelpes" (lines 86, 89, 93). Gascoigne partially acquiesces to this collaborative speech, "With Nevyle then I fynde this proverbe true, / That Haste makes waste," but he also resists Neville's example by repeating his own formulation: "and therefore still I saye, / No haste but good, where wysedome makes the waye" (lines 96–98). The quick pace and closed circuit of transmission in the corona fold inward around the speaker, who completes the challenge through an extremely close, almost airless engagement with his own work.

If the multiple poems grouped under the heading's rubric of "Gascoignes memorie" transform the claustrophobic social world of Gray's Inn into an experiment in self-collaboration, the proliferation of agencies involved in printing A Hundreth sundrie Flowres also challenged Gascoigne's grasp on the nested lyrics. The corona's earlier sonnets all carry numerals denoting their place in the sequence, but in the final two poems the compositor omitted those markers, leaving a smaller blank space in the sixth and setting all lines

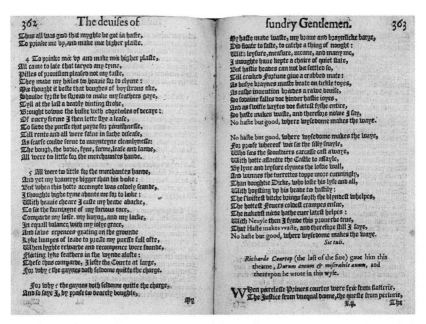

Figure 14. The conclusion of "seven Sonnets in a Sequence," with numbering that drops out in the final two poems, in George Gascoigne, *A Hundreth sundrie Flowres bounde up in one small Poesie* (London: Richard Smith, 1573), sigs. ²X1v–²X2r, STC 11635, copy 2. By permission of the Folger Shakespeare Library.

flush left in the seventh (see Figure 14).[42] To be sure, this vanishing numeration was not deliberately meaningful and was corrected in the 1575 *Posies*. But as is often the case with errors, this material accident speaks to the demands that the chain of sonnets placed on printing the complex network of writing in *A Hundreth sundrie Flowres*. As an innovative form that was at once written and compiled, the corona required the coordination of multiple facets of textual arrangement. The inconsistent numbering scheme betrays the shifting responsibility for the compiled volume, which did not rest fully with either Gascoigne or the multiple and anonymous agents of the book trade, but which nonetheless worked to enshrine the poet's public reputation through that protracted and collaborative act of reading.

As a record of this distributed agency, the faulty numbering scheme in "Gascoignes memorie" demonstrates how gathered writing pushed readers to infer meaning from the point where organizational features meet and intersect with the content of compiled poems. Inconsistencies in numbering were

A hundred good poyntes of Husbandrye.

62 Some burneth a load at a time in his hall,
some neuer leaue burning, till burnt they haue all.
Some making hauock without any wit,
make many poore foules without fier to fit.

63 From Christmas, till May be wel entered in,
al cattel war faint, and looke poorely and thin.
But when as theprime graffe, at first doth appeare,
then most is the daunger of all the whole yeare.

¶ Calues faire, that come betwene Christmas & Let
take huswife to rere, or else after repent.
Of such as fall betwene chaunge and the prime,
no rering, but fell, or go kill them in time.

¶ House Caife, and go suckle it twise on a day,
and after a while set it water and hay,
Stake ragged to rubbe on, no such as will bend,
then weane it (well tended) at fifty daies ende.

¶ The senior weaned, his yonger shall teach,
both how to drink water, and hay for to reach.
More stroke, more made on, whe ought they do aile,
more gentle ye make them for poke or to paile.

64 Long brome or good pasture, thine ews do require
warme barth and in saftie their Lambes do desire:
Looke often well to them for Foxes and Dogges,
for pittes and for brimbles, for vermine and hogges.

65 Geld bulcalfe & ram lambe, as sone as they fall,
for therin is lightly no daunger at all.
Some

A hundred good pointes of husbandry. fol 16

Some spareth the tone for to pleasure the eye,
to haue him shew great when the butcher shall buy.

¶ Sowes ready to farow, this time of the pere,
are for to be made on and counted full deare.
For now is the losse of a fare of thy Sowe,
more great than the losse of two calues of thy Cow,

¶ Of one Sow at once rere fewe aboue fiue,
and choose of the fairest and likest to thriue.
Vngelt of the best kepe a couple for store,
one Boare pig, one Sow pig, that sucketh before.

66 Geld vnder the dame within fortnight at least,
and saue both thy money and life of thy beast.
Geld later with Gelders as many one do,
and looke of a dozen to geld away two.

67 Thy Coltes for the saddle geld pong to be light,
for Cart do not so if thou iudgest aright.
For geld them but when they be lusty & fat,
for there is a point to be learned in that.

68 Geld Fillies but tittes, ere & nine daies of age,
they bye else of gelding, else many no rage.
But Fillies most likely, of bulke and of bone.
kepe such to bring Coltes, let their gelding alone.

69 For gaining a trifle, sell neuer thy store,
what ioy to acquaintance what pleasureth more?
More larger of body the better to brede,
more forwarde of growing, the better they spede.

Figure 15. Paraphs expanding a numbered sequence in Thomas Tusser, *A hundreth good pointes of husbandry, lately maried unto a hundreth good poynts of huswifery* (London: Richard Tottel, 1570), sig. L3r, RB 49623. By permission of the Huntington Library, San Marino, California.

frequent in early printed books. In the 1570 third edition of Thomas Tusser's *A hundreth good pointes of husbandry, lately maried unto a hundreth good poynts of huswifery* (1570), another of Richard Tottel's frequently published titles, uses a metaphor of marriage to mix together two distinct lists of household advice. Although the tasks for husbands are numbered consecutively, those for wives are marked with paraphs, or pilcrows, that are spliced into the annual calendar of household labor (see Figure 15).[43] Tusser, in fact, explains this intermittent numbering at the end of *A hundreth good pointes of husbandry*: "Note that those staves which be marked with this marke or Paraph (¶) before them, do appertaine to huswiferie, & are fitly intermixed with husbandrye for the apte tyme and use of them."[44] The paraphs thus signal both an expansion of time and a mixture of labor, complementing the husband's tasks with the wife's. What is left unstated, and therefore up to readers to infer, is the end of these "intermixed" sequences: the project of agrarian management that requires the collaborative efforts of the household.

Like Tusser's *A hundreth good pointes*, the numerical designation in the title of Gascoigne's *A Hundreth sundrie Flowres* does not offer an accurate tally of contents but rather an imprecise gesture of vastness that allows for flexibility in counting, sorting, and arranging the many different kinds of writing. Just as the paraphs intermix the distinct yet related labors of the husband and the wife, Gascoigne's poetic labor is nestled within several complementary formal and textual structures: within the "seven Sonets in sequence," within "Gascoignes memorie," within "The Devises of Sundrie Gentlemen," and ultimately within *A Hundreth sundrie Flowres*. All of these schemes should be the result of textual organization rather than the poetic imagination, but Gascoigne takes advantage of the fluid boundaries between these concentric forms to imply that his work as a writer stretches past individual poems and into the design of the gathered writing. As a larger paratactic form, *A Hundreth sundrie Flowres* developed simultaneously from knowing readers' sensitivity to the web of clues hiding within narratives of collaboration and from their willingness to grapple with meanings that are always slightly elusive, predicted but not fully worked through within the arrangement of the physical book.

Continuous Reading

Both the riddles of material coherence and the coy performances of compiling found an uneven expression in the final form of *A Hundreth sundrie Flowres*. The fictionalized accounts of publishing the compilation make clear that Gascoigne had imagined the book would open with "The Adventures of Master F. J.," then proceed directly to "The Devises of Sundrie Gentleman," and finally to "certayne devises of master Gascoyne," as his own poems are called in the table of contents (p. 2). G. T., the shadowy friend who first collected the "sundry copies of these sundry matters," explains how he "did with more labour gather them into some order, and so placed them in this register"—that is, a simple compiled volume—with the aim of representing how the author first put together his own work: "As neare as I could gesse, I have set in the first places those which Master F. J. did compyle" (pp. 144–45). Yet this *mise en abyme* of compiling unraveled futilely, never quite achieving Gascoigne's plan for a book that would be "a highly sophisticated, self-referential structure, the like of which had never been attempted before."[45] Gascoigne departed for the Netherlands in May 1572, and without his supervision, the order of the component texts was hopelessly scrambled in the process of compiling them for print. Their order remained opaque even after Gascoigne's addition of new prose links upon his return.[46]

The innovation of *A Hundreth sundrie Flowres* was the intricate set of narratives that crisscrossed the component texts and organizational features, remaining defiantly visible as a potential sequence even when the book was disordered by the protracted print schedule. With prose links that narrated stories of composition and compilation, poems were woven into an expanded occasion that was too intricate to be dissolved. In "The Devises of Sundrie Gentlemen," several poems were preceded by titles that extrapolate on the erotic scenarios within them, for instance, "He began to write by a gentle-woman who passed by him with hir armes set bragging by hir sides, and left it unfinished as followeth" (p. 226). With a reference to the "etc." that terminates the poem at least two lines early, this heading uses spontaneous poetic inspiration to excuse shoddy execution.[47] Such commentary is repeated in the titles across "The Devises," opening up a long scene of composition. In this case, the scenario extends into the next lyric: "Whiles he sat at the dore of his lodging, devysing these verses above rehearsed, the same Gentlewoman passed by agayne, and cast a longe looke towards him, whereby he left his former invention" (p. 227). Sourcing poetic inspiration from a series of related events, and consequently yoking poems to one other within the printed book, these narratives of composing construct a protracted temporality that guides both imaginative scenarios and aesthetic judgments.

These experiments with narrativizing textual organization were at their strongest in "The Adventures of Master F. J.," a prosimetric tale of an adulterous relationship that unfolds over several days at a country estate. Littered with inset lyrics, letters, and songs, as well as the diegetic quotation of continental romance sources, this prose romance inverts the relationship between poems and their organizational apparatus in "The Devises of Sundrie Gentlemen." By overshadowing lyric meditation with narrative exposition, "The Adventures of Master F. J." also mitigated against the multiple kinds of disintegration that elsewhere thwarted Gascoigne's plan for the broader organization of *A Hundreth sundrie Flowres*. This ingenious experiment in prose narration produced an order that could neither be dissolved by the haphazard arrangement of the printed book nor ignored by discontinuous reading.

Gascoigne's word for this kind of writing was "compyle," an early modern textual practice that encompassed both composing and collecting.[48] Scenes of compiling lent a necessary order to discrete poems within "The

Adventures of Master F. J." Partway through F. J.'s courtship of Elinor, he responds to her request for a new copy of a letter (because she had irately torn up his previous missive) with not one but three poems: "recompting hir words, he compyled these following which he termed *Terza sequenza*" (p. 149). The ensuing set of three English sonnets mixes aphorisms on the suffering of love into F. J.'s account of the origins of his own dangerous desire. The first quatorzain argues:

> What reason first persuades the foolish Fly
> (As soone as shee a candle can discerne)
> To play with flame, till shee bee burnt thereby?
> (lines 2–4)

By the third sonnet, F. J. has read his own experience through these truisms about the droning insect that cannot resist the lure of an incandescent candle:

> these dazled eyes of myne
> Did wincke for feare, when I first viewd thy face:
> But bold desire, did open them agayne,
> And bad mee looke till I had lookt to[o] long.
> (lines 3–6)

Across this slight sequence, F. J.'s recounting of his fearful yet witting passage from love to lust transgresses a fine line of propriety. His progressive descent into lust is expressed by the addition of taglines that link the poems together, with "And then" joining the first to the second, and "For when" transitioning between the second and the third (p. 150). These markers of temporal continuity draw the practice of "compiling" from the prose narrative into the poetic missive itself, showing one sonnet to follow from the other in the same way that F. J. responds to Elinor's request for a letter.

By stitching text together with context, this series of poems also impacts the course of the unfolding relationship. After F. J. "had wel sorted this sequence," he left the letter for Elinor to find, "And now the coles began to kindle, whereof (but ere whyle) she feigned hir self altogither ignorant" (p. 151). Like the corona in "Gascoignes memorie," F. J.'s sequenced sonnets reach beyond the poems themselves and into the material organization of the book. The set of poems documents the active influence of impersonal sayings over a community of susceptible readers within the fiction of the tale and, presumably, over the readers of *A Hundreth sundrie Flowres.*

In "The Adventures of Master F. J.," poetic and textual organization participate equally in the fiction of this love story by narrating the order of events that inspired the poems. But as intuitive as this sequential structure might be for us as modern readers of novels, it was an unusual arrangement in early modern poetry books. Other poet-compilers worried that the labor that went into structuring their books would be destroyed by readers. Isabella Whitney's *A Sweet Nosgay, or Pleasant Posye* was printed by Richard Jones in 1573, the same year as Gascoigne's *A Hundreth sundrie Flowres.* This diverse and varied collection included (1) versifications of Hugh Plat's *The Floures of Philosophie*; (2) letters to and from Whitney's family and friends; and (3) "The maner of her wyll," in which a woman leaving London imaginatively bequeaths the city to her readers. At the point of transition between the rhetorical flowers and the letters, Whitney relates her fears about how willful readers might potentially damage her collected writing:

> Good Reader now you tasted have
>   and smelt of all my flowers:
> The which to get some payne I tooke,
>   and travayled many houres.
> I must request you spoyle them not,
>   nor doo in péeces teare them.[49]

Whitney's admonishment not to root up her garden dwells on the sad truth of compiling: that the production of a new textual collection is just one step away from a future act of destruction. In her own repurposing of Plat's work, Whitney admits that she only "reposde one howre" with her source because she "leasure lackt," but she nonetheless managed to pilfer a small fragment of his work, "ere I parted thence: / A slip I tooke to smell unto."[50] Itself the product of recycling another writer's labor, *A Sweet Nosgay* could not be protected once Whitney released the compiled flowers for future acts of reading.

While Whitney lamented her lack of control over the broader design of her verses, Gascoigne took matters into his own hands. In "The Adventures of Master F. J.," he devised a textual structure that could not be separated from the order of poems. The prose narrative surrounds and protects the writing of the nearly anonymous lover. In response to one long poem, consisting of forty-two lines of rhyming couplets and a concluding "Lenvoie,"

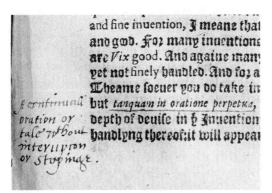

Figure 16. "Continuall oration or tale without interupcon or stopinge," a reader's explanation of prose, in George Gascoigne, *The Posies of George Gascoigne* Esquire (London: Richard Smith, 1575), sig. T2r, 821 G211575a. Rare Books and Manuscripts Library, University of Illinois, Urbana-Champaign.

the fictional compiler G. T. writes that although "These verses are more in number than do stand in contentation of some judgements," with "the occasion throughly considered, I can commend them with the rest" because they are "(as may well be termed) *continua oratio*, declaring a full discourse of his first love" (pp. 160–61). G. T. defends F. J.'s poem as a decorous response to his erotic suffering, which unfurls as ceaselessly as these prolix lines. With this identification of *continua oratio*—continuous or uninterrupted speech— the narrator was measuring how the discourse of love within the poem approaches the unbound form of the prose that surrounded it. In his later "Certayne notes of Instruction," Gascoigne warns aspiring poets against writing in prose, "*oratione perpetua*," because it lacks "depth of devise" and "will appeare to the skilfull Reader but a tale of a tubbe" (p. 455). "Continuall oration or tale without interupcon or stopinge," as one early modern reader glossed this passage, was associated with hasty stories (see Figure 16).[51] These were rushed speeches that allowed no pause or space for interjections from other speakers and that would not make sense if they were broken down or torn apart. In other words, the continuity of prose was a bulwark against later readers and compilers who might tear apart the textual organization invented by poets like Whitney and Gascoigne.

In using the affordances of prose to push back against the logics and structures of contemporary poetry books, "The Adventures of Master F. J." may have been picking up on changes to practices of Bible reading advocated by Christian humanist reformers during the early sixteenth century. Known as *lectio continua*, or continuous reading, these reforms promoted a sequential movement through scripture, working methodically through a single Bible text across multiple reading sessions. *Lectio continua* rejected the inherited rhythms of the liturgical calendar, which had traditionally interrupted this orderly progress with intervening saints' days and feast days.[52] In England, *The Booke of the Common Praier* (1549) laid out a new schedule for the annual reading of the "whole Bible," proscribing that it "shalbe doen in ordre, without breakyng one pece therof from another. For this cause be cut of Anthemes, Respondes, Invitatories, and suche like thynges, as did breake the continuall course of the readying of Scripture."[53] Like Whitney's fear of readers who might "in péeces teare" her compiled flowers, *The Booke of the Common Praier* resists the "breakyng" apart of the discrete texts gathered together within the Bible. Cutting out songs and intercessions from the daily service, the reformed calendar patches together an underlying order that had been obscured by Catholic worship practices. It insists that there will be no interruptions in the continual progress through the scriptures.

Gascoigne likewise approached narrative and textual continuity as a tool for joining the discrete pieces of "The Adventures of Master F. J." into a single tale. Following F. J.'s first dance with Elinor, she pretends to return his letter to him, "deliver[ing] unto him a paper, with these words. *For that I understand not (quoth she) th'intent of your letters, I pray you take them here againe*" (p. 146). Incensed with this apparent rebuff, F. J. "in great rage began to wreake his mallice on this poore paper, and the same did rend and teare in peeces" (p. 146). But in the midst of this biblioclastic destruction, F. J. realizes that the pages are not written in his own hand "and therewithall abashed" he attempts to mend the damage: "placing all the peeces therof, as orderly as he could, he found therin written these few lynes hereafter following," a prose letter Elinor had surreptitiously slipped him while seeming to reject his advances (p. 147). This act of reading across the torn pieces is materially reparative; it is a hermeneutic reconstruction of a textual order that has been interrupted by F. J.'s suspicious rage. Within the prosimetric structure of "The Adventures of Master F. J.," this narrative that patches the gaps in Elinor's letter demonstrates how an inferential reading for continuity might hold together compilations that could otherwise be sundered by destructive readers. The material form of the compiled letters is a bulwark against misreading—and hence losing—love.

By taking this revolutionary investment in textual order seriously, the prominent gaps in the tale, which appear at moments of sexual ecstasy and violence, come into focus as a deliberate slackening in Gascoigne's experiments with a continuous narrative sequence. When the lovesick F. J. takes to his bed, Elinor promises to come visit him in the night, propelling him "in[to] a traunce betwene hope and dispayre, trust and mistrust." When she arrives, Elinor's subsequent admission of her joy in the mutual "equalitie of our affections" pushes F. J. over the edge of his expectant ecstasy, and "Hee swooned under hir arme." But F. J.'s "happy traunce" does not last long (p. 196). Once he recovers sufficiently to admit his previous jealousy, his mood sours and devolves into a rageful battle: "Having now forgotten all former curtesies," F. J. "drewe upon his new professed enemie, and bare hir up with such a violence against the bolster, that before shee could prepare the warde, he thrust hir through both hands, and etc. wher by the Dame swoning for feare, was constreyned (for a time) to abandon hir body to the enemies curtesie" (p. 198). This violent attack passes F. J.'s swoon off to Elinor, who does not lose consciousness from an excess of joy but rather as a partial protection from the vicious "thrusts" of her sometime lover. The "and etc." in the midst of the account of the rape signals the breakdown of prose continuity at the instant in which the narrator, like Elinor, confronts the limits of any potential control over the ensuing actions. In contrast to F. J.'s reconstruction of the torn letter, this tiny gap in the narrative is the indelible trace of a violence that cannot be repaired, patched, mended, or read across. The "etc." both calls attention to and elides what it stands in for.[54] It signals the unspeakable. The penetration of Elinor's body is depicted as a forceful rupture—an imposition of discontinuity—in precisely the terms of textual destruction and disintegration that the prose tale elsewhere sought to counteract.

Where F. J.'s rape takes the form of a violence that is at once physical and narrative, the multiple interruptions in this scene are also explicitly related to Gascoigne's experiments with poetic agency. Elinor's fainting is "mimetic of her absence" from the remainder of "The Adventures of Master F. J.," as Margaret Simon puts it, since her lapse in consciousness "mimicks her silencing by G. T.'s cursory narration."[55] But Elinor's narrative absence paradoxically counteracts the expected absence of the female beloved in Petrarchan poetry. When Elinor rejects F. J.'s further advances, his only recourse is to poems that transform narrative into lyric laments in which her body remains stubbornly present. In one encounter, F. J. attempts to embrace the scornful Elinor, but is shamed by the knowing glances of the rest of the party: "The which F. J. perceyving, and disdayning hir ingratitude, was forced to depart, and in that fantasie complyed this Sonet" (p. 213). The quatorzain that follows begins "With hir in armes that had my hart in hold, / I stoode of late to plead for pittie so" (lines 1–2). Within the broader narrative context of "The

Adventures of Master F. J.," we as readers can interrogate the "fantasie" that motivates conventional hyperboles, like "I wept for woe: I pyn'd for deadly payne" (line 8). These woes become apparent as a blind desire for absolution that F. J. does not deserve and will never receive.

These swirling dynamics of absent and present agency are ultimately the condition that sustains the narrative fictions developed across *A Hundreth sundrie Flowres*, at least as Gascoigne first planned his book. At the conclusion of "The Adventures of Master F. J.," the narrator G. T. begins to retreat from the story he has spun, stopping short of full clarity: "I will cease, as one that had rather leave it unperfect than make it to[o] plaine" (p. 215). G. T.'s deliberate obfuscation is most prominent in how he names characters: "I have past it over with quod he, and quod she, after my homely manner of writing, using sundry names for one person, as the Dame, the Lady, Mistresse, etc." (p. 215). This hazy identification is intrinsic to G. T.'s narrative craft: "Neverthelesse for that I have seene good aucthors terme every gentlewoman a Lady, and every gentleman *domine*, I have thought it no greater faulte then pettie treason thus to entermyngle them, nothing doubting but you will easely, understand my meaning, and that is asmuch as I desire" (p. 216). G. T. defends his proliferating names, which not only multiply but also confuse the identities of figures in his story, because he trusts that readers will be able to untangle the web of fictions that he spins.

The fault of "intermingling" identities is so minimal that this prose narrative is immediately followed with "sundry verses written by sundry gentlemen." In the apparently multiauthor collection of "devises," the relation of prose to poetry is inverted, as narrative is compressed into the organizational headings. The ease with which one section of *A Hundreth sundrie Flowres* spills over into the next expresses this compiler's "desire" for inferential readers to discern and value the labor of his work in spinning this tale—and in constructing this book.

Suspicious Poesies

Along with the guise of collaboration, in 1575 the second edition of Gascoigne's collection excised the narratives of poetic and textual coherence from *A Hundreth sundrie Flowres bounde up in one small Poesie*. In the new title, imaginative "poesy" travels from the aggregate design of the book into the multiple, more independent subtexts in *The Posies of George Gascoigne*

Esquire. Overall, *The Posies* aspires to a stricter organization, claiming to sort the work according to moral value as bundles of "Flowers," "Hearbes," and "Weedes," sections that are both rhetorically and bibliographically distinct.[56] Three new letters sent from Gascoigne to "the reverende Divines," "al yong Gentlemen," and "the Readers generally" take the place of the missives from anonymous press agents in *A Hundreth* (pp. 359, 364, 369). New work is added, including a conclusion for "Dan Bartholomew of Bathe," "Dulce bellum inexpertis," "The Fruite of Fetters," and the poetics treatise "Certayne notes of Instruction." The larger, paratactic form of the book is no longer the object of a mobile network of inference because authorship is acknowledged rather than coyly withheld.

It is difficult to gauge whether Gascoigne understood this new compilation as a revision or as a reorganization. Although *The Posies* updated aspects of the textual features that had been integral to the imaginative framing of *A Hundreth sundrie Flowres*, including the titles and the prose links that had first connected the generically diverse work, both of the plays and most of the poems were unchanged. Only "The Adventures of Master F. J." was even partially rewritten to suppress the most salacious aspects of the tale by moving the setting to Italy and by specifying the identities of characters in "The pleasant Fable of Ferdinando Jeronimy and Leonora de Valasco."

From the perspective of a clandestine authorship, these gestures of revision have been taken as a response to public anxiety about the loose morals of the shadowy compiler of *A Hundreth sundrie Flowres*. Gascoigne claims to regret any offense, noting of his "Poesies" that "the same have been doubtfully construed and (therefore) scandalous," and he was probably correct in this assessment (p. 359). Just months after Gascoigne's death, George Whetstone published his *A Remembraunce of the wel imployed life, & godly end, of George Gaskoigne Esquire* (1577), in which Gascoigne's ghost returns to beg:

> Yea *Whetston* thou, hast knowen my hidden hart
> And therfore I conjure thee to defend:
> (When I am dead) my life and godly end.[57]

Like Whetstone, modern scholarship has read Gascoigne's repentance in *The Posies* as an overt shaping of his reputation. Richard Helgerson identifies a "moralizing" tendency that "was repeated in Gascoigne's work as well as in his projection of himself."[58]

But Gascoigne's motives for reissuing the compilation remain obscure. In the first place, we cannot gauge whether *A Hundreth* was actually censored because the Stationers' Register from the early 1570s has not survived. Second, and somewhat surprisingly, we do know that on August 2, 1576, "half a hundred copies of Gascoignes poesies" were called in, presumably seeking the 1575 revised collection.[59] Resisting biographical claims about a poet known for coy textual disguises, Cyndia Clegg and Gillian Austen have both argued that the second edition continues the imaginative strategies of *A Hundreth sundrie Flowres*.[60] Moral reform might well be another of Gascoigne's elaborate performances, especially since his reputation was largely unaffected by *The Posies'* recall.

If Gascoigne's repentance may have simply continued his earlier strategies of disguise, his hermeneutics of reform had a more pronounced effect on how the gathered writing was legible as a book. In contrast to *A Hundreth*'s riddling organization, which depended on provocative slips between textual agents, features, and forms, the 1575 compilation aspired to an openness and clarity that foreclosed inferential readings. Addressing his potential censors, Gascoigne praised the revised edition for delivering "the depth and secrets of some conceytes, which (being passed in clowdes and figurative speeches) might percase both be offensive to your gravitie and perillous to my credite" (p. 359). New textual features helped in disclosing and disarming the secretive conceits. Only seven marginal glosses appear in *A Hundreth sundrie Flowres*: four stage directions in *Supposes* and three descriptions of action in "Gascoignes devise of a maske for the right honorable Viscount Montacute." Glosses abound in *The Posies*, with thirty in the *Supposes* alone. Gascoigne adds, for instance, "The first supose and grownd of all the suposes," "An other supose," "A true supose" to caution readers who might otherwise be misled into believing the play's duplicitous characters (p. 9, n. 81; p. 12, n. 61; p. 41, n. 26). Lorna Hutson calls such glosses "government health warning[s]" that "pre-empt the reader's inferential work," shutting down misreadings "by flagging up every single moment of conjecture."[61] Across *The Posies*, the abundant glosses stabilize meanings that would otherwise be available to the vagaries of readers' inferences. In "Dulce bellum inexpertis," English translations are supplied for Dutch words: "At every porte it was (forsooth) (*) *belast*, / that I (†) *die groene Hopman* might not go out," and in the margin we find "(*) forbidden / (†) the Greene captaine" (p. 423). In "Dan Bartholmew of Bathe," glosses prevent attempts to discern hidden significance by noting that certain passages "are mistical and not to bee understoode but by Thaucthour him selfe" (p. 341, n. 161).

Such confusion between manifest and latent authorial meanings seems to have plagued *A Hundreth sundrie Flowres*, thwarting Gascoigne's experiment with a habit of imaginative writing that was entwined with the material organization of the book. Instead of tracing the myriad points of contact between the poems and commercial textual features, readers treated the inferential web of clues as an overly literal statement of the poet's identity, even misreading poems that Gascoigne signed with his own name. He complained, for instance, that readers of the 1573 edition, who "understande neyther the meaning of the Authour, nor the sense of the figurative speeches," were especially brutal to a poem called "Gascoignes araignement," which "(being written in jeast) have bene mistaken in sad earnest" (pp. 365–66). This flippant poem may have been misjudged because it treats the legal proceeding as a forum for arriving at deep knowledge about the character of the protagonist. It opens with a speaker called George being arraigned for an act of flattery that he swears he did not commit: "At Beauties barre as I did stande, / When false suspecte accused mee" (lines 1–2). The trial that follows repeatedly interrogates the basis for judging George's actions and motives. He first asks Dame Beautie to hear his case because she "Dothe knowe my guilte if any were," and, after a hasty conviction by a corrupt jury, begs her pardon because "You knowe if I have ben untrue, / It was in too muche praysing you" (lines 9, 35–36). This coy, perhaps even flattering appeal urges the sovereign to discern the hidden intentions of "the man that ment you good" (line 40). Beautie responds in kind, agreeing to George's plea "bicause I guesse / What thou doest meane henceforth to bee," a loyal slave or "bounden thrall" in her service for life (lines 43–44, 54). With this knowing yet unjust pardon, which substitutes one punishment for another, the poem turns the strategic reading of identity into an explanation for the continued enthrallment of a lover who happens to share Gascoigne's first name.

Where such knowing riddles led readers of *A Hundreth sundrie Flowres* to identify the poet with the fictional lovers, *The Posies* announces Gascoigne's desire to publish his work, but then uses that visible authorship of individual poems to detach him from the material organization of the compilation. Like many of the headings from *A Hundreth*, "Gascoignes araignement" was retitled in *The Posies*, dropping the redundant marker of authorship and becoming simply "The arraigment of a Lover" (p. 264). This generic title redirects the focus of speculation from Gascoigne by moving the inventive fictions that circulated within *A Hundreth*'s headings into the poetic scenarios. By confining imaginative writing to the individual poems, this authorial retreat from the material organization of the book curtails the potential for speculative inference—and for the meanings implied by those riddles to go awry.

We can measure the desire for a narrowed sphere of interpretation in a few revisions to the scene of judgment in the arraignment poem. In both *A Hundreth* and *The Posies*, justice is dispatched in the space of a stanza, with tidily end-stopped lines and a rollicking pace that nearly anticipates the decision of the sycophantic jury:

> Then crafte the cryer call'd a queste,
> Of whome was falshode formost feere,
> A packe of pickethankes were the rest,
> Whiche came false witnesse for to beare,
> The Jurie suche, the Judge unjust,
> Sentence was sayde I should be trus[sed].
> (lines 19–24)

This sentencing shows a jury swayed by false witness, in contrast to Dame Beautie's insightful "guesse" about what George "doest meane" with his actions. Yet *The Posies* attempts to moderate the jury's decision by bolstering the judge's power. In 1573, Dame Beautie summons the justice with a relational preposition, "Here is oure Justice well you wote," while in 1575 her beckoning "Here" becomes an allegorical figure, "Wyll is oure Justice well you wote" (line 15). A new gloss also appears in the margin, explaining "Wyll is dame bewties chiefe Justice of Oyre and terminer" (p. 265, n. 15; p. 264, n. 13). "Oyer and terminer," law French for "hear and determine," was an ad hoc commission that enabled assize justices to try indicted prisoners and to issue process against them while on circuit.[62] When Wyll enters the trial, Beautie not only hands the proceedings over to the most capricious of human faculties, she also grants him a commission that reflects the increasing pressure the central government was exercising on local jurisdictions in the mid-sixteenth century.[63]

The new chief justice consolidates the process of determining George's guilt, in theory bolstering the jury's finding. Yet Wyll's presence also betrays just how easily that collective decision-making might disintegrate without the oversight of a singular authority. Like the figure of the chief justice, *The Posies* plays with the balance between singular and distributed foundations for meaning. Wyll steps in as an external limit on the jury's collaborative finding of George's guilt in the same way that the marginal glosses imposed new strictures on readers' wayward inference. By using organizational features to sharpen readings of individual poems, *The Posies* localized meanings that had first spread across "The Devises of Sundrie Gentlemen," removing the tissue of connections that had joined imaginative writing to the material design of the compilation.

The adjustments to "Gascoignes araignement" thus show how, in the instant when Gascoigne apparently took authorial responsibility for his book, he publicly let go of the very devices of the press that seemed to point directly to him. Through the constraints placed on inferential reading, Gascoigne receded from the scene of judgment in the second printing of his work. Organizational features that, on the one hand, could not be more authorial because they identify Gascoigne as the writer with the sole responsibility for *The Posies*, on the other hand pull him out of the structure and design of the compilation. By consolidating an inferential process that had at first been distributed, these revisions tell a story of policing the wily riddles of compilation, of restricting the epistemological or discursive objects prompted by gathered volumes, and, ultimately, of how a poetic engagement with commercial textual features actually distanced writers from the material text. *The Posies* is an attenuated echo of a piecemeal, playful coherence that was actually much stronger in *A Hundreth* because it made imaginative use of the material affordances of the printed book.

The two states of Gascoigne's gathered work raise substantial questions about the impact of the printed book on the sixteenth-century history of English poetry. Complementing work on material textuality, Charlotte Scott and Sarah Wall-Randell have explained the early modern significance of the "metaphoric" and "immaterial" book in representations of reading onstage and within romance narratives.[64] *A Hundreth* and *The Posies* extend such insightful accounts by drawing the codex closer to its representation, showing both the substantial feedback loops between poetic form and material textual features and the strategies through which poets learned first to engage and then to hide the dynamic agencies that gave rise to this fiction of identity. Although Gascoigne's two volumes ultimately promote a model of authorship that eschewed the material text, nonauthorial devices were absorbed into every level of his poetry, from posies and poem headings to the aphoristic clause and the sequence of sonnets. In this way, even individual poems carry an occluded history of the book as a form available to the manipulations of ambitious writers. My subsequent chapters follow this hidden history into compilations from the turn of the seventeenth century. The legacy of this poetically sensitive compiling endures even within books in which individual authorship seems to transcend an outright concern for material design.

CHAPTER 4

These Ensuing Sonnets

Genre and Mediation After Sidney

During the 1590s, a new fashion for English sonnets changed the relationship between practices of writing and compiling poems. Earlier printed books had praised the poetics of contingent material forms, like the arrangement of "small parcels" in Richard Tottel's *Songes and Sonettes* (1557), or what the fictional narrator in George Gascoigne's *A Hundreth sundrie Flowres* (1573) described as the dynamic "doings which have come to my hands, in such disordred order, as I can best set them down."[1] These mixed genre compilations disclosed the processes of gathering poems from multiple sources, and they incorporated traces of that active fashioning into their arrangement. Compiled sonnets, by contrast, were the work of individual poets who claimed to transcend the material copying of their sources. England's preeminent sonneteer, Philip Sidney, mocked an earlier generation of poets as clumsy "Apes" who "from the ribs of old *Parnassus*" indiscriminately snatch "everie floure, not sweet perhaps."[2] Because sonnets were ideally free from such rote compiling, they have been understood as a turning point in the consolidation of English poetic authorship. From multiple critical perspectives, sonnets printed during the 1590s have been read as expressions of a willing engagement with the commercial press, an unprecedented depth of subjective experience, and a poetic order determined by the author's own hand.[3]

If compiled sonnets offered a new model of poetic craft, the textual agency of authors did not emerge spontaneously, nor was it separate from the material practices that made these books a print phenomenon at the end of the sixteenth century. These books could seem to express the influence of poets because they were designed by professional compilers who were sensitive to the workings of form and genre. Sonnet books were unique for gathering a single kind of poem. The print standards common to Elizabethan sonnets are discussed at length below, but I want to begin by noting their two most innovative features: the generic regularity of the gathered lyrics and the numbered headings that replaced the verbal titles common in earlier compilations. In England, the term "sonnet" originally referred to any short poem, but by the 1590s the genre finally hewed close to an ideal of fourteen pentameter lines, rhymed either in the Italian model of an octave and a sestet or the English form of three quatrains and a final couplet.[4] Printers and publishers responded to this aesthetic development with the innovative headings because they needed a new way to tell poems apart from one another. The narrative titles that, in earlier compilations, had evoked a variety of authors, scenarios, or occasions were no longer viable in books containing dozens or even hundreds of repetitive quatorzains—all uttered by the same speaker stalled in the same futile love. So compilers added numerals and a designation of genre, like "Sonnet II" in Samuel Daniel's *Delia* (1592), "Amour. 2" in Michael Drayton's *Ideas Mirrour* (1594), or (somewhat oddly for a fourteen-line sonnet) "Canzon. 2" in the anonymous *Zepheria* (1594). These headings distinguished between the visually identical poems by naming, for instance, the "second sonnet" in the book called *Delia*.

This novel approach to organization demonstrates how the poetry compilation—as both a material text and a conceptual category—was evolving in response to developments in vernacular writing. Sonnet books transformed the nature of the connections between the discrete texts gathered into the single compilation by lending a new priority to the genre expectations of the sonnet. My basic argument is that the innovative numbered headings tallied the quantity of a given kind of poem. Unlike the idealized gesture of vastness in volume titles like Gascoigne's *A Hundreth sundrie Flowres*, the simple numerals above each sonnet expressed a more abstract and granular arrangement. Stationers recognized and took advantage of the design potentials afforded by the repetition of the short sonnets, and they arranged each compilation as an iterative series of forms, not a progressive sequence. They charted a contingent order that could (and frequently did) change when books were republished with new contents. Attending to these real innovations in compiling for print, I argue that we need a new critical terminology for sonnets published during the 1590s, which never advocated any kind of order for the short poems—whether in sequences, narratives, or cycles. These compilations were published and read as "sonnet books" in which the printed codex created an abstract and modular organization.

It was this approach to textual design that was imitated by publishers and that ultimately began to occlude the active performance of compiling in earlier books. We can get a sense of this shift in the framing of *Shake-speares Sonnets* (1609), which the publisher Thomas Thorpe called "THESE.INSUING .SONNETS."[5] The same phrase had appeared in earlier sonnet books, most notably Henry Constable's *Diana* (1592), which describes "these insuing Sonnets" as abandoned by their author and "now by misfortune left as Orphans."[6] Thorpe's (perhaps knowing) echo of Smith shows how publishers contributed to the craze for sonnets even as they sought to distance themselves from the process of making books out of the poems that ensued.[7] The elaborate conventions that briefly dominated the market for English poetry were the work of publishers and printers who were imitating prior compilations. Yet this textual labor—which was explicitly poetic in its attention to aspects of form and genre—claimed to be in the service of a textual arrangement that valued the influence of authors.

These developments in compiling for print were propelled by the complex legacy of Philip Sidney's experiments in poetic mediation. The brief fashion for sonnet books was marked from beginning to end by the distinct formats in which Sidney's *Syr P. S. His Astrophel and Stella* was published.[8] His sonnets and songs were first printed posthumously in three slim quartos, twice in 1591 and then once more in 1597. Capitalizing on this success, nineteen distinct sonnet books were published in small formats during the mid-1590s, and several of these ran into multiple editions. In the quartos of *Astrophel and Stella* as well as the minor publications chasing their success, the modular arrangement of the sonnet book performed an "openness to divergent and sometimes dissonant perspectives," a media fluidity that Scott A. Trudell has identified as central to Sidney's poetry.[9] But this material openness was foreclosed in 1598, when *Astrophel and Stella* was revised and republished within *The Countesse of Pembrokes Arcadia*, a folio of Sidney's work corrected by his sister Mary Sidney Herbert. The 1598 revisions introduced a new system of numbering that uncoupled poetic order from textual format, instantly remaking the paradigm of gathered sonnets. No further sonnet books met all the design conventions of publications from the middle of the decade. For several early seventeenth-century sonnet compilations, including *Shake-speares Sonnets*, it was the revised *Astrophel and Stella* that was most in sight as a model.

But in the brief seven years between 1591 and 1598, before narratives of Sidney's poetic absence were consolidated as an authorial ideal, professional compilers explored alternative approaches to printing poetry. This chapter explains how early modern poetics of compiling became difficult to recognize—and to value—around the turn of the seventeenth century. Instead of following the rise of individual authorship, as a purely literary history might, I trace the media history of representing lyric emotions, the affects of desire and devotion that the repetitive form of sonnets was uniquely suited to explore. What comes into sight is the dynamic formation of textual agencies and genres that we now too often assume to be essential or timeless. The forms in which sonnets appeared in print in the 1590s obscured the process of gathering and organizing, but they nonetheless depended on a poetically sensitive material design. Sonnet books came to seem profoundly uncompiled because they promoted content before explanations of material arrangement. Without the elaborate headings required to link diverse and varied forms in earlier compilations, individual sonnets were brought into direct contact with one another, creating the conditions for fictions of poetic emotion to exceed the limits of the single sonnet. The work of this chapter is to offer a way of reading that makes the poetics of compiling visible, even when it was registered indirectly in books that occlude this practice. In the longer history of English poetry that I tell in this book, it was this shift in the esteem for compiling that made it possible to categorize earlier and later volumes as miscellanies.

Imitation and Compiling: Sidney's Kisses

English sonnets launched a new paradigm of poetic craft by changing contemporary approaches to compiling. Sonneteers shifted their inspiration from collaborative to personal sources. Philip Sidney's *Astrophil and Stella* famously opens with a speaker who, "faine in verse my love to show," seeks "fit words" to express his desire (1.1, 5). This first sonnet recounts the failure of a rhetorical tradition that achieves eloquence by imitating existing work. Poring over "inventions fine," the poet Astrophil immerses himself in his models, "Oft turning others' leaves, to see if thence would flow / Some fresh and fruitfull showers upon my sunne-burn'd braine" (1.6–8). Yet his study falters because, "wanting Invention's stay," or the grounding of a proper subject, Astrophil loses himself among his sources (1.9). He wails that "others' feete still seem'd but strangers in my way," evoking the extra iambs in the long hexameter lines of this idiosyncratic sonnet (1.11). Astrophil retreats from the inspiration he might discover in the work of other poets and turns toward the experience of his own desire. The sonnet's expected volta is delayed until the final line, such that the poet is left to struggle until the last possible instant, when his muse finally appears and chides him to "looke in thy heart and write" (l.14).

The opening salvo in *Astrophil and Stella* marked a departure from the kinds of imitation that had proven so generative for the poets and publishers who, just before Sidney, had been experimenting with how to gather poems into larger compilations. Beyond a clever pun on the dual senses of "invention," as both discovery and imaginative creation, this sonnet speaks to an ambitious bid to take over a whole circuit of poetic transmission.[10] Sidney was attempting to bring under his control practices of poetic composition that were dynamically engaged with textual media. To be sure, the jarring arrival of insight at the end of the first sonnet does not replace imitation with an unmediated experience of emotion. "'Heart,'" as William A. Ringler observes, "refers to the mind in general, the seat of all faculties," not just love; it connotes an internalized store of wisdom.[11] But Sidney's sonnets did attempt to renovate the (sometimes tense) dynamic between a poet and his sources.[12] Literature was a mimetic art for Sidney, "a representing, counterfeiting or figuring forth," as he theorizes in *The Defence of Poesy* (ca. 1580, printed 1595). Instead of copying other writing, he advocated imitating abstract ideals: "the skill of the artificer standeth in that *idea* or fore-conceit of the work, and not in the work itself."[13] Sidney shifted imitation from copying other books to replicating the ideal of love itself. Sonnet 3 proposes that the poet's beloved ought to be the consistent origin for his invention: "in *Stella's* face I reed," Astrophil explains, "What Love and Beautie be, then all my deed / But Copying is" (3.12, 13–14).

In this claim for the value of immediate inspiration, Sidney was following the example of the master sonneteer Petrarch, who denounced imitation as compiling gone haywire. Petrarch insisted that poets who too closely follow other models are distorting their own voices. In one letter on poetic talent, he advocated writing "neither in the style of one or another writer, but in a style uniquely ours although gathered from a variety of sources."[14] The good poet is one "who does not, like the bees, collect a number of scattered things, but instead, after the example of certain not much larger worms from whose bodies silk is produced, prefers to produce his own thoughts and speech."[15] Petrarch here exchanged imitative compiling, or the collection of "scattered things," for a representation of the author's self. He thus revised Seneca's apian model of writing as a process of gathering nectar from the sweetest flowers. As Rosalie Colie observed, Petrarch "inveighed against the habit of florilegia, of anthologizing piecemeal, which robbed readers, he felt, of any sense of a work of literature as a made thing, as, literally, a poem."[16] The good poet instead consumes his very body as he spins writing out of the raw material he has ingested. He triumphs over his sources by making imitation invisible, immaterial, and secondary to his own thoughts and speech.

Sidney likewise replaced imitation with an idealized poetic selfhood. But where Petrarch's theories disavowed gathering as the foundation for eloquence, Sidney cast the writing of sonnets as a different kind of compiling. *Astrophil and Stella* reimagined the generic variety and social performance that was characteristic of multiauthor poetry compilations within the affective register of a single poetic speaker. Even as Astrophil praises himself for being "no pick-purse of another's wit," he was seduced by another and even sweeter source of eloquence: "what I speake doth flow / In verse," because "My lips are sweet, inspired with *Stella's* kisse" (74.8, 13–14). Inspiration— literally the "breathing in" of Stella's sweetness—comes directly from the beloved, not the imitation of other poets. When Astrophil returns to Stella, his sonnets replace metaphors of distributed floral gathering with the repeated accumulation of personal desire. He turned collaborative textual methods toward a singular and personal source of eloquence.

Sidney was scavenging the material practices of a long tradition of poetically engaged compiling in order to promote his own voice. Continuity of form and content was not the norm in English poetry compilations when Sidney was writing in the early 1580s. In both manuscripts and printed books from this moment, it was more common to find multiple, distinct kinds of poems—frequently from multiple authors. These juxtapositions required an explanation, and so the organizational features of printed compilations narrated both the origins of poems and how they were gathered into a given book. In *Astrophil and Stella*, by contrast, the variety of erotic experiences was attributed to a consistent occasion: the single poetic speaker who returned over and over again to his sweet beloved. This continuity made it possible to hide accounts of textual gathering behind a constant emotional conceit. With the iteration of a single form and expansive scenarios, Sidney occluded the secondary labor of compiling by allowing the sonnets to seem to link themselves together.

Sidney's poetics consolidated a whole network of textual activity within a fiction of individual authorship that only loosely harnessed the multiple influences on his writing. The burden of sonnets was to capture affective experiences on the verge of vanishing—the sudden arrival of Astrophil's muse or the eloquence that he finds in his beloved. But this project depended on drawing individual poems together in a textual form that was always just beyond the poet's control. The twisted and frequently interrupted chains of poems in *Astrophil and Stella* outline an erotic scenario that resists representation by dilating time, collapsing space, and dissolving the identities of both lovers. One sonnet opens with a doubled apostrophe of the instant in which the lovers' lips meet:

> O Kisse, which doest those ruddie gemmes impart,
> Or gemmes, or frutes of new-found *Paradise*,
> Breathing all blisse and sweetning to the heart,
> Teaching dumbe lips a nobler exercise.
>
> (81.1–4)

The kiss defies Astrophil's powers of description. All he is able to relate are the lingering effects of the encounter: the reddened cheeks—which might either be rubies or the fruits of an undiscovered paradise—as well as the lovers' joyous breath and the lessons their lips learn. Gathering together multiple descriptions, he attempts a second apostrophe:

> O kisse, which soules, even soules together ties
> By linkes of *Love*, and only Nature's art:
> How faine would I paint thee to all men's eyes,
> Or of thy gifts at least shade out some part.
>
> (81.5–8)

Failing once again, and this time with a paintbrush, the poet cannot muster even a partial outline of the aftereffects of the kiss. Astrophil gathers up—compiles even—his repeated but failed attempts to describe his inspiration. He is the better poet for turning the limits of individual poetic agency into the content of his sonnets.

When Sidney replaces the rote imitation of external sources with a repetition of the same scene, his protracted poetic failure exchanges one kind of copying for another. Even as the kiss vanishes without a trace, the iterative attempts to describe it allow Astrophil to reproduce the immaterial connections, the "links of *Love*," that join his soul to Stella's. He demands another kiss: "Stop you my mouth with still still kissing me" (81.14). The antanaclasis "still still" sets up at least three possible senses of time—"even now," "always," and "without change"—from which we must choose two senses to make the line parse. This compiling of multiple moments in time represents desire as a repetition that is specifically nonmimetic. Astrophil's links of love endure precisely because they replace imitation with iteration. In the final line of sonnet 81, the antanaclasis "still still" acts as a fulcrum that propels the scenario onward from one sonnet to the next, predicting a future continuation of kisses. The next poem "sweare[s] even by the same delight, / I will but kisse" (82.13–14). He ties the lovers' souls together by projecting this single instant forward as a duplicate of itself—as another kiss.

This repetition with a difference enacts, within the content of the erotic scenario, formal techniques that are characteristic of the abundant sonnets. Sidney flaunts his skill by accumulating scores of a single kind of poem, and this repetition in turn accommodates the experience of an erratic desire that extends forward, swerves abruptly, or reverses course altogether. The stalled time within each sonnet is set in motion both by the series of repeated kisses and by the iterative form of the quatorzains. Astrophil's pursuit of a constant delight in kissing actually begins two sonnets earlier as an expression of linguistic invention that was a kind of compiling but emphatically not an imitation: "Sweet kisse, thy sweets I faine would sweetly endite, / Which even of sweetnesse sweetest sweetner art" (79.1–2). This hyperbolic layering of six distinct senses of "sweet" launches a tiny story about how the poetic description of the kiss adds pleasure to pleasure itself. Rather than stealing nectar from other poets' flowers, Astrophil sources invention directly from language. This interplay between representation and action captures Sidney's interest in "bringing the meditative abilities of lyric into complex juxtaposition with the linear, event-based potentials of narrative," as Margaret Simon observes.[17] The clash between the distinct modes of lyric and narrative also reflects a specifically poetic attention to the intersection of writing and compiling because form, content, and organization all align to contribute to the same story. The endless kiss gathers sonnets into an iterative series that is perpetually on the verge of spilling over into an extended narrative sequence.

With a diffuse agency that draws on both poetic and textual arrangement, *Astrophil and Stella* subordinates the poet's voice to the love set loose across the work, accommodating a desire that is in excess of any single poem. Readings of Sidney's lyrics as a sequence have sought a single trajectory for Astrophil's lust. His desire is sparked in the early poems, partially (if incompletely) consummated in this cluster of kiss sonnets, yet ultimately thwarted by Stella's distance at the conclusion, "O Absent presence *Stella* is not here" (106.1). On this reading, the progressive arc of the sonnets is an object lesson in attaining a properly metaphysical, Neoplatonic union that can satisfy the soul of the desiring male poet whatever his real distance from the beloved's body.[18] But this teleological approach disregards Sidney's elastic erotic time, most especially in these poems that depict the kiss as an active agent of love, a "fastener of desire" that binds Astrophil and Stella by dissolving the boundaries between them (80.7). The motif of the kiss, Pablo Maurette has explained, "effaces dichotomies such as masculine and feminine, passive and active, giver and taker," producing a "liminal" erotics "that fluctuates invariably between the corporeal and the spiritual."[19] Far from a forceful seduction by the male poet, Astrophil and Stella are equally buffeted by desire in this cluster of kiss poems, "Teaching the meane, at once to take and give / The friendly fray, where blowes both wound and heale" (79.9–10). At least from the perspective of the male poet, their love is an optimistic yearning for a future connection, even as it constantly replicates the conditions of the poet's separation from his mistress. The song in which Stella responds to this scene, voicing her dissent, is not put into contact with these sonnets in the early compilations and would not be visible as a commentary on this lyric moment until the 1598 rearrangement in the folio.

This intermediate and oscillating (and osculating) erotics was intimately bound up with the arrangement of the compiled poems. While there is no extant autograph copy of *Astrophil and Stella*, we do have preprint manuscripts that treated the connections between Sidney's poems as self-evident. All four kiss poems appear on a single page of the Houghton Manuscript, now held at the British Library, where they were transcribed continuously and, at least originally, without intervening features like titles or numbered headings (see Figure 17).[20] Finding inspiration in the repetition of form and content—that is to say, finding consolation in genre—the affiliations between poems are vestiges of a poetics that developed out of the very practices of compiling that Astrophil claimed to reject.

Confronted with the problem of how to imitate ideas rather than their material instantiation in the world, Sidney's serial forms represented the active experience of desire. He captured the unmoored temporality of his inspiration in the aggregate network of bonds both between lovers and between poems. If Sidney's approach to the broader form of the gathered sonnets was partial, incomplete, or slightly beyond his control, the attenuated poetic

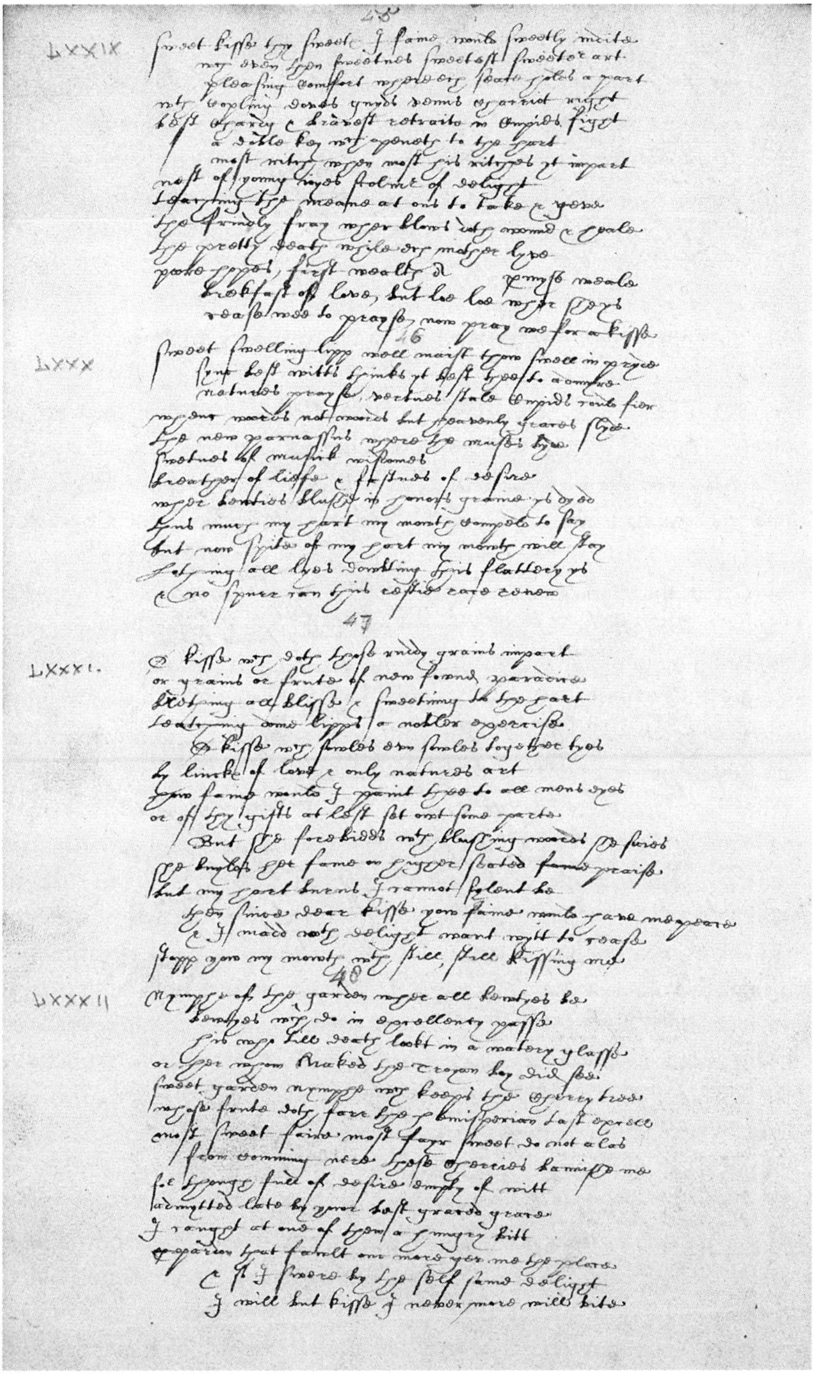

Figure 17. Sidney's kiss sonnets in the Houghton Manuscript, with two sets of numeration added by later readers, Add. MS 61822, fol. 96v. © The British Library Board.

agency that developed out of these methods of compiling was an echo of his fraught desire for an idealized beloved who was always just beyond the poet's reach. *Astrophil and Stella* improved on the arrangement of poetry compilations from the 1570s by devising an organization that was not external to the poems but rather grew out of Sidney's handling of poetic form and content.

Printing Genre: Mediating Compiled Emotions

The quarto of *Syr P. S. His Astrophel and Stella* was published three times, twice by Thomas Newman in 1591 and once by Matthew Lownes in 1597. Sidney had died the previous decade, in 1586. None of these posthumous editions were approved by his powerful family. In 1598, the sonnets were corrected against a manuscript provided by his sister, Mary Sidney Herbert, and included as the final component in the folio of *The Countesse of Pembrokes Arcadia.*[21] The revisions in the folio lashed the lyrics into a narrative sequence by splicing Sidney's sonnets together with his songs. The history of printing Sidney's lyrics—and hence the history of his significant influence on English poetry—has been understood as a natural accommodation of poetic authorship. In Gavin Alexander's reading, the generically diverse songs "contribute to the dramatization of Astrophil and Stella," by "observing the lovers as flesh and blood, not just as Petrarchan postures."[22] Yet before the folio, the quartos of *Astrophel and Stella* developed a representation of poetic emotions that was eloquent precisely because it was less constrained by textual design. Like the manuscripts containing Sidney's lyrics, Newman set the sonnets without titles or other organizational features, but in the second half of the book, which included both Sidney's songs and poems by other authors, he developed a more elaborate *mise-en-page*, adding multiple different numbering schemes. It was this division along the lines of lyric genre that actually made it possible to follow Sidney's expansive erotic scenarios across the limits of individual sonnets that required no secondary apparatus of material compiling.

The *Astrophel and Stella* quartos thus urge us to reconsider how Sidney came to occupy such a prominent position in English literary history. If we now take the lyric sequence as an expression of poetic authorship, we have forgotten how these traces were first produced by the affiliations that began to emerge within a profoundly unauthorial book. The features that we have come to identify as "literary," that is, as intrinsic to the language of the poem and the craft of the poet, were fashioned through the histories of production and circulation that made poetry available in the world. Scott A. Trudell has observed that Sidney's sonnets participated in "widespread communities of written and acoustic poesis, predicated on an unpredictable series of adaptations."[23] Newman was most invested in genre, and in treating poetic kind as a basis for organization, the quartos participated in Sidney's "proclivities toward media adaptation" by instantiating the connections between his poems.[24] Far from a model of authorship naturally consolidated by the technology of print, *Astrophel and Stella* expresses a more fitful media history of compiling as a transaction between poetic forms and textual formats.

In the first and third quartos of *Astrophel and Stella*, Sidney's writing was accompanied by dozens of poems from other writers.[25] The book opens with 107 of his sonnets, then gives ten of his songs, twenty-eight sonnets attributed to Samuel Daniel, five cantos by Thomas Campion, a poem signed "E. O." later included in Fulke Greville's *Caelica* (1633), and one anonymous poem later set to music in John Dowland's *The Second Booke of Songes or Ayres* (1600). Sidney was not named as the author of all this work. His songs were subscribed "Finis Syr P. S.," while the next section was headed "Poems and Sonnets of sundrie other Noblemen and Gentlemen."[26] Daniel's sonnets were subscribed with his name.[27] But the running title "Sir P. S. his Astrophel and Stella" also appeared on every opening, as though to signal the long shadow that Sidney cast over later poets. Newman in fact claimed that Sidney's legacy helped in perfecting the text of *Astrophel and Stella*, which "being spred abroad in written Coppies, it had gathered much corruption by ill Writers: I have used their helpe and advice in correcting & restoring it to his first dignitie."[28] The printing of Sidney's poetry is here depicted as an attempt to recover a more faithful copy text.

In this way, the simple arrangement of the sonnets without intervening titles or headings was a testament to how well the design of the quartos hid the labors of the publisher who was compiling for print. The desire for fidelity to Sidney in *Astrophel and Stella* led Newman to reject approaches to compiling poetry that had become conventional over the past several decades of English printing—even including his own. Just three years earlier, in June 1588, Newman and Thomas Gubbyn paid for a license to publish Abraham Fraunce's *The Arcadian Rhetorike*, a rhetorical treatise that drew examples from classical authors as well as from "Sir Philip Sydneis Arcadia, Songs and Sonnets."[29] In *The Arcadian Rhetorike*, Sidney's poetry was promoted through a model and a language of compiling that had become standard in England in the decades following Richard Tottel's phenomenally successful *Songes and Sonettes*.[30] Yet in the first 1591 *Syr P. S. Astrophel and Stella*, this description of the assorted "Songs and Sonets" was distributed across the book, which split the poems into generic sections. With a volume title that names only the fictional pseudonyms of the two lovers, Newman reimagined Sidney's compiled lyrics as a response to a single governing conceit, promoting the scenario that spans and unites the poems.

Newman retreated from the fictions of compiling that were so prominent in compilations published during the 1570s and 1580s, abandoning the elaborate narrative explanations of the origins and arrangement of poems. His layout of *Astrophel and Stella* owed more to manuscript than to printed poetry books, since it set pages asymmetrically and divided the quatorzains irregularly across openings and leaves (see Figure 18).[31] While all of Sidney's sonnets begin with drop capitals, they lack any verbal descriptions or symbolic markers to relate poems to one another. Newman and his compositors did attempt to alter the indentation of lines to account for the variety in Sidney's rhyme schemes, but this setting was at best sporadic, with multiple couplets that should have been set evenly but were not. The overall effect was of poems that were slightly at odds with the constraints of the printed page.

By turning genre into a principle of arrangement, the *Astrophel and Stella* quartos made the connections between sonnets a product of how readers moved through the book. Without organizational features, the links between poems lay dormant until they were activated by a process of interpretation. One pair of sonnets, both in alexandrines, retrospectively comes into focus as a very slight sequence with a necessary temporality (see the first two sonnets in Figure 18). The first opens with a simple statement of Stella's presence:

Shee comes, and straight therewith her shining twins do move
    Their raies to me: who in her tedious absence lay
Benighted in cold woe.[32]

The lengthy clause that spans the enjambed first and second lines replicates the conditions that motivate the sonnet. The beloved arrives and turns her eyes on the speaker, but that immediacy only recalls his memory of her absence, since Sidney reproduces this distance in a syntax that drives the lovers farther apart.

This play with distance also offers a way to temper Astrophil's continual yearning when the discussion of Stella's gaze reaches not just across the breaks

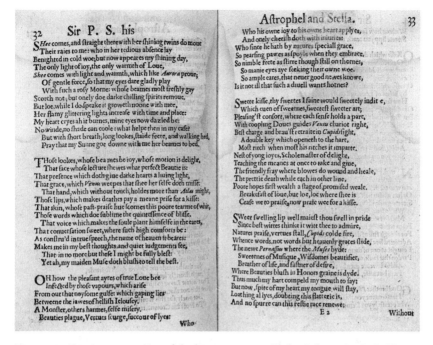

Figure 18. Continuous setting of the kiss sonnets, in Philip Sidney, *Sir P. S. His Astrophel and Stella* (London: [John Danter] for Thomas Newman, 1591), sigs. E1v–E2r, STC 22537. By permission of the Folger Shakespeare Library.

between lines but also across the gap between poems. This shifting coherence records a dynamic correspondence between poetic and textual order because the halting continuity becomes a formal expression of the lovers' interrupted connection. The following sonnet begins "Those lookes, whose beames be joy, whose motion is delight," returning to Stella's twinkling eyes (77.1). And the next nine lines all open with a deictic that refers back to her beauty: "That face," "That presence," "That grace," "That hand," "Those lips," "That skin," "Those words," "That voyce," and finally "That conversation sweet" (77.2–10). For the logic of these descriptions to succeed, these deictics need an earlier referent, an antecedent beauty already known to both the poet and the reader. The *Astrophel and Stella* quartos were a feedback loop through which Newman's iterative arrangement of poems begins to accumulate into a more expansive representation of erotic desire. They lent a format to the repetitive yearning of a poet who was continually thwarted in love and life. By linking the sonnets through their consistent and repetitive exploration of a single erotic occasion, Newman punctured the fictions of organization that had connected individual poems in earlier compilations.

Quite significantly, this performance of an unmediated compilation was limited to the sonnets. In the second half of the first and third quartos of *Astrophel and Stella*, Sidney's songs were preceded with a section title "Other Sonnets of variable verse" (see Figure 19), as though their diverse forms required a verbal explanation that the sonnets did not.[33] Each song was headed with an ordinal number, like "First Sonnet," and an arabic numeral was set in the first line of every stanza. These headings worked to cobble together a poetic series characterized by a variety of occasions, from meditations on the power of Orpheus to aggressive descriptions of the sleeping Stella to a pastoral that recasts the protagonists as rustic shepherds. Far from an expression of sequence or order, the abundant numeration was a sensitive response to the diverse forms of Sidney's songs, which ranged in length from eighteen to ninety lines and which experimented with an array of meters. With the addition of these organizational features that were absent in the first half of the book, the "Other Sonnets of variable verse" unfurled as a chain that was based on the essential differences between the poems. The series required an explanation of how and why the poems should or even could be grouped together.

The effect of these organizational features was to affiliate Sidney's longer songs with the work by other poets that appeared at the end of *Astrophel and Stella*. Daniel's sonnets were also headed with numbers and genre designations, like "Sonnet, 2."[34] The first and third quartos quite unconventionally set spaces between Daniel's cross-rhymed quatrains, perhaps to make them visually resemble Sidney's songs, which included spaces between the stanzas. Campion's songs bore ordinal numbers in their headings, though in Italian, like "Canto Secundo," and in one case, his stanzas were numbered.[35] Given these multiple resonances with the layout of Sidney's "Other Sonnets of variable verse," the primary division in the *Astrophel and Stella* quartos was not one of authorship but rather one of form. Instead of a contrast between the poems by Sidney and those by his imitators, the books performed a generic distinction between his sonnets and the rest of the more mixed compilation.

With this capacity to respond to genre, the design of the printed book transformed the history—and the historiography—of English poetics. *Astrophel and Stella* brokered a new relation between poetic form and lyric genre. This association was not inevitable.[36] When early moderns began to rediscover classical poetics, they found systems for categorizing poems according

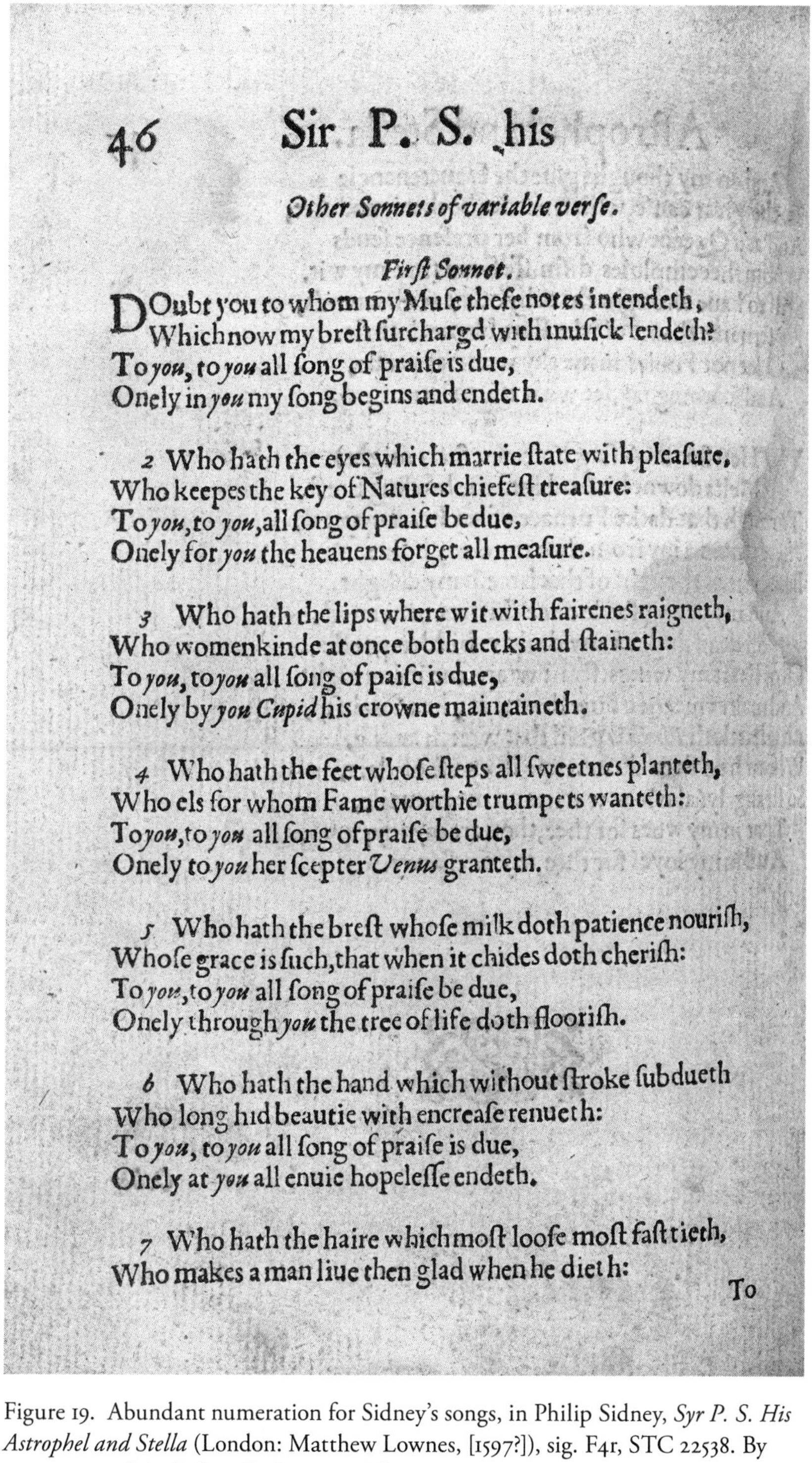

Sir P. S. his

Other Sonnets of variable verse.

First Sonnet.

DOubt you to whom my Muse these notes intendeth,
Which now my brest surchargd with musick lendeth?
To *you,* to *you* all song of praise is due,
Onely in *you* my song begins and endeth.

2 Who hath the eyes which marrie state with pleasure,
Who keepes the key of Natures chiefest treasure:
To *you,* to *you,* all song of praise be due,
Onely for *you* the heauens forget all measure.

3 Who hath the lips where wit with fairenes raigneth,
Who womenkinde at once both decks and staineth:
To *you,* to *you* all song of paise is due,
Onely by *you* Cupid his crowne maintaineth.

4 Who hath the feet whose steps all sweetnes planteth,
Who els for whom Fame worthie trumpets wanteth:
To *you,* to *you* all song of praise be due,
Onely to *you* her scepter *Venus* granteth.

5 Who hath the brest whose milk doth patience nourish,
Whose grace is such, that when it chides doth cherish:
To *you,* to *you* all song of praise be due,
Onely through *you* the tree of life doth floorish.

6 Who hath the hand which without stroke subdueth
Who long hid beautie with encrease renueth:
To *you,* to *you* all song of praise is due,
Onely at *you* all enuie hopelesse endeth.

7 Who hath the haire which most loose most fast tieth,
Who makes a man liue then glad when he dieth:

To

Figure 19. Abundant numeration for Sidney's songs, in Philip Sidney, *Syr P. S. His Astrophel and Stella* (London: Matthew Lownes, [1597?]), sig. F4r, STC 22538. By permission of the Folger Shakespeare Library.

to styles of mimesis as well as through common rhetorical figures and tropes. Sidney's own *Defence of Poesy* is a case in point, since he defined poetry through its capacity for representation. *Astrophel and Stella* helped to launch the centuries-long process of replacing these accounts with a modern focus on form and, specifically, with a focus on how form was an expression of the skill of the individual poet.

In William Scott's *The Model of Poesy* (1599), a recently rediscovered poetics treatise, classical genre taxonomies based on rhetoric were updated to accommodate the mimetic potential specific to lyric.[37] *The Model of Poesy* quite commonly defined the lyric as a musical form, "so called because properly they be appliable to music and song and might be married to some instrument."[38] But Scott also looked past the lyric's melodic origins to argue for both the common form and the common object of representation in these short "poesies wherein we imitate and discover our affections."[39] Imitation and discovery are paired here, not just as techniques of rhetorical invention, but also as faculties for capturing the emotions. Poets find ease in "representing and limning these affections" because lyrics reduce "the passions" that "be grievous and dreadful within us" into an "image and reflection" that tames the suffering of want.[40] *The Model of Poesy* is significant, even as an unpublished manuscript treatise, because it offers a contemporary perspective on the development of English poetics during the crucial decade of the 1590s. Scott in fact traced the English response to Petrarch, "the father or refiner of our vulgar kinds," through Sidney's pseudonym Astrophil, the "star-lover" of the celestial Stella, who further inspired the "English admirers of their sundry stars."[41] The lyric investment in representing affections was a product of the order and arrangement of small-format sonnet books like the first quartos of *Astrophel and Stella*.

But when Sidney's lyrics were republished within *The Countesse of Pembrokes Arcadia* in 1598, the revisions uncoupled the form and genre of compiled sonnets from the material format of the codex. The resetting of Sidney's lyrics took for granted an authorial sequence that was at first much more speculative. Mary Sidney Herbert elevated the poetic agency of her deceased brother, claiming that she was guided in her editorial work by a conjecture of "what was intended" and would proceed "no further then the Authors own writings," or what "knowne determinations could direct."[42] In the case of *Astrophel and Stella*, this recovery meant weaving Sidney's sonnets and songs together into a single sequence, restoring a narrative arrangement that Newman had apparently neglected in his division of the quarto into sections based on poetic genre. The folio added a heading above each poem: a simple arabic numeral for the sonnets and ordinal designations, like "Second song," for the longer verses that were mixed unpredictably into the regular quatorzains.[43] These textual features misapplied techniques of arrangement that had at first highlighted the serial organization of the diverse songs. In service of Mary Sidney Herbert's promise to restore "what was intended" by her brother, the numbered headings established a textual order that counted the forward progress of events by prioritizing content over lyric genre.

Through this imposition of a new fiction of authorial control, the revised *Astrophel and Stella* began to pry the representation of emotions apart from the design conventions of printed sonnets. More perniciously, the numbered headings heightened a basic violence against the female beloved. Compiling the divergent erotic episodes into a single sequence helped to consolidate an idealized and male textual agency by refocusing the fluid erotics within Sidney's sonnets. Stella comes in and out of focus in Sidney's lyrics. She is largely unheard in the sonnets but more audible in the formally diverse songs. When Sidney's songs were woven into the sonnets, they punctuated the regular series of quatorzains with their alternative forms and perspectives. The effect was to make Stella more visible—and more susceptible to Astrophil's vicious attacks. Following the 1598 rearrangement, the tiny sequence of kiss poems, which I considered above, now opens with a song in which Astrophil schemes to take advantage of the sleeping Stella:

Her tongue waking still refuseth,
Giving frankly niggard No:
Now will I attempt to know,
What No her tongue sleeping useth.
(ii.9–12)

The stunning violence of this scene consists of the poet's willful circumvention of the beloved's consent by too neatly equating the sleeping and the speaking tongue. Astrophil's desire for carnal knowledge triumphs over Stella's dissent with a homophonic repetition of "No," "know," "No." He "venture[s]" a "stealing kisse," then "flee[s]" hastily when "ah she is waking" (ii.23, 22, 27, 25). As is the case with Sidney's other songs, this depiction of the male poet's desire relates an unusual closeness to Stella's body and potential (if dormant) voice in the revised sequence of *Astrophel and Stella*. The scene of violence comes more clearly into sight when the conflation of the distinct kinds of poems mingles the divergent perspectives of the two lovers.

The essential misogyny of the male sonneteer is expressed not just through the content of his poems but also in the material form and format developed through the design of the printed book. Feminist readings have traditionally emphasized the inability of sonnets to represent the female beloved and her desire.[44] I would add that Stella's heightened presence in the revised *Astrophel and Stella* is a testament to how the organization of compiled sonnets mediates such essential qualities of poetic form. When the quartos at first divide this song from the sonnets, Stella is buffered from the poet's protracted meditation on the stolen kiss by the dozen pages that separate the more fluid erotics of the sonnets from the narrative of the songs. The nonsequential approach to textual arrangement distances the beloved's body and her voice from the scene of assault. In the 1598 arrangement, the assumption of a poetic sequence for more ambiguously arranged poems has the effect of marginalizing other textual and erotic agents. The consolidation of authorial emotions comes at the cost of the range of potential readings—and perspectives—within an arrangement that links poems by their own qualities rather than a seeming truth established by the poet.

Serial Sonnets: Counting and the Agency of Compiling

The representation of emotions that has been understood as fundamental to compiled sonnets looks different when we approach authorship as a textual effect produced by how these poems were materially organized. The publication of *Astrophel and Stella* left a complex, even contradictory legacy to the poets who were chasing Sidney's success: how might they join a fashion for English sonnet books that was driven by print, while simultaneously claiming that their work was unsullied by textual imitation? The second half of this chapter considers how sonneteers began to appropriate and transform the poetics of compiling that had previously been the purview of nonauthorial textual agents. Because this transformation was accomplished by virtue of imitating Sidney, it required a paradoxical disavowal of the very material practices that enabled their expansive poetic craft. The solution was to present sonnets as apparently uncompiled by introducing them only with numbered headings. This organization has traditionally been read as sequential, but I want to suggest that before the 1598 revisions to *Astrophel and Stella* there was little expectation of any overarching order for printed sonnets. Instead, the sonnet books published between the two formats of the Sidney editions cast the broader compilation as a modular accumulation of repeated forms. Because each book was a series, not a sequence, their design left the bonds between sonnets open, malleable, and unfixed by any narrative chronology of composing or compiling.

While sonnets had not been printed in large gatherings before *Astrophel and Stella*, nineteen books in which quatorzains outnumbered other types of poem were published by 1598, often with countergenres of songs and complaints mixed in (see Table 1).[45] Compilations from the first two years of this trend were particularly successful. *Astrophel and Stella* (1591), Samuel Daniel's *Delia* (1592), Henry Constable's *Diana* (1592), and Henry Lok's *Sundry Christian Passions* (1593) all went through multiple editions.[46] Sonnets were published in small formats, at first mostly in quarto, but more often in octavo between 1595 and 1598. The features that organized sonnets were visual and symbolic—numbered headings instead of the discursive fictions in earlier compilations. Of the nineteen first-edition sonnet books from the 1590s, eighteen had a layout that was symmetrical across the page opening, with either one or two complete lyrics on each. The regular, diminutive form of the sonnets left ample room around the poem texts, and in seventeen of the first editions, that white space was filled with decorative headpieces and tailpieces, creating ornamental borders that ran along the top or the bottom, or even in between lyrics.

Like Newman's *Syr P. S. His Astrophel and Stella*, later volume titles emphasized the singular focus of the scores of sonnets within each book. More than half of the sonnet books announced the fictional identities of lovers or mistresses: Sidney's *Astrophel and Stella* (1591), Daniel's *Delia*, Constable's *Diana*, Thomas Lodge's *Phillis* (1593), Giles Fletcher's *Licia* (1593), the anonymous *Zepheria* (1594), William Percy's *Coelia* (1594), Drayton's *Ideas Mirrour* (1594), Richard Barnfield's *Cynthia* (1595), E. C.'s *Emaricdulfe* (1595), Bartholomew Griffin's *Fidessa* (1596), Richard Linche's *Diella* (1596), William Smith's *Chloris* (1596), and Robert Tofte's *Laura* (1597). Five other compilations were titled with descriptions of the poetic contents that also downplayed the process of compiling by naming the consistent forms or conceits of the poems: T. W.'s *Tears of Fancie* (1593), Henry Lok's *Sundry Christian Passions Contained in two hundred Sonnets* (1593), Barnabe Barnes's *A Divine Centurie of Spiritual Sonnets* (1595), Edmund Spenser's *Amoretti and Epithalamion* (1595), and Thomas Rogers's *Celestiall Elegies* (1598). These titles cast the

Table 1. First Edition Sonnet Books by Year

Author	Title	Year	Format	Layout	STC #
Philip Sidney	*Syr P. S. His Astrophel and Stella*	1591	quarto	asymmetrical	22536
Samuel Daniel	*Delia: Contayning certayne Sonnets*	1592	quarto	symmetrical	6243.2
Henry Constable	*Diana: The praises of his Mistres, in certaine sweete Sonnets*	1592	quarto	symmetrical	5637
T. W.	*The Tears of Fancie, or Love Disdained*	1593	quarto	symmetrical	25122
Henry Lok	*Sundry Christian Passions Contained in two hundred Sonnets*	1593	16mo	symmetrical	16697
Thomas Lodge	*Phillis: Honoured with Pastoral Sonnets, Elegies, and amorous delights*	1593	quarto	symmetrical	16662
Giles Fletcher	*Licia, or Poemes of Love*	1593	quarto	symmetrical	11055
William Percy	*Sonnets to the Fairest Coelia*	1594	quarto	symmetrical	19618
Anonymous	*Zepheria*	1594	quarto	symmetrical	26124
Michael Drayton	*Ideas Mirrour: Amours in Quatorzains*	1594	quarto	symmetrical	7203
Richard Barnfield	*Cynthia: With Certaine Sonnets*	1595	quarto	symmetrical	1484
Barnabe Barnes	*A Divine Centurie of Spirituall Sonnets*	1595	quarto	symmetrical	1467
E. C.	*Emaricdulfe: Sonnets Written by E. C. Esquier*	1595	octavo	symmetrical	4268
Edmund Spenser	*Amoretti and Epithalamion*	1595	octavo	symmetrical	23076
B[artholomew] Griffin	*Fidessa, more chaste then kinde*	1596	octavo	symmetrical	12367
Richard Linche	*Diella, Certaine Sonnets*	1596	octavo	symmetrical	17091

William Smith	Chloris, or The Complaint of the passionate despised Shepheard	1596	quarto	symmetrical	22872
R[obert] T[ofte]	Laura: The Toyes of a Traveller; or, The Feast of Fancie	1597	ocatvo	symmetrical	24097
Thomas Rogers	Celestiall Elegies of the Goddesses and the Muses	1598	octavo	symmetrical	21225
John Davies	Wittes Pilgrimage (by Poeticall Essaies)	1605	quarto	symmetrical	6344
Alexander Craig	The Amorose Songes, Sonets, and Elegies	1606	octavo	symmetrical	5956
William Shakespeare	Shake-speares Sonnets	1609	quarto	asymmetrical	22353

gathered sonnets as new writing that had no previous life in manuscript or print.[47]

In every sonnet book following *Delia*, the arrangement of the compilation was explained only through nonverbal symbols that held no clues about how poems found their way into print. Lyrics were titled with numbered headings, typically a roman numeral and a designation of genre, like "Sonnet III" in Thomas Lodge's *Phillis* (1593). There was a slight variety in a few cases, like the Italianate "Sonnetto terzo" in Henry Constable's *Diana* (1592), or simply "III" in Robert Tofte's *Laura* (1597). Earlier compilations had incorporated the perspective of a compiler into the material organization of the book. For instance, Tottel's *Songes and Sonettes* introduced headings that gave a synopsis of the events within poems, like "How the lover perisheth in his delight, as the flie in the fire."[48] But sonnet numbers hid that process when they introduced a new kind of abstraction. The very existence of the process of compiling was obscured by offering a metareading of genre, and this design would ultimately allow sonnet books to be read as authorial because they disguised the labor of production.

Despite this prominent history of mediation, the very naturalness of the terms through which we conceptualize gathered sonnets has foreclosed an attention to the practices that allowed these books to generate effects of an authorial order. While it is a critical commonplace that the term "sonnet sequence" originated in the nineteenth century, a sense of a sequential and temporal order has remained inescapable for readings that identify the author with compiled sonnets.[49] C. S. Lewis declared that "the first thing to grasp about the sonnet sequence is that it is not a way of telling a story," but despite this dissatisfaction with a narrative approach, he still read gathered sonnets as a poet's "prolonged lyrical meditation," an extended encounter with his own mind.[50] Perhaps most adamant about the "insidious fallacy" of reading sonnets sequentially, Thomas Roche insists that the language implies "images of progression, which automatically transfers the term to the realm of psychology."[51] But Roche also falls back on a temporal model in two ways, both identifying a numerological significance to the placement of individual poems and even maintaining that the "phrase *sonnet sequence* is so deeply embedded in our critical vocabulary that it would be fruitless to want to do it in."[52]

We need a new language that can describe how the emerging conventions for sonnet books transformed poetic authorship without anticipating modern ideals of psychology and sequence. Against totalizing accounts of order, histories of printing sonnets have recognized the recombinant potentials of the arrangement of these innovative books, even as they maintain an authorial yearning for control over the order of poems. Marcy North observes how the "exceptional standardization of the sonnet vogue," and in particular the symmetrical setting of pages, allowed poets to rearrange their work in successive editions.[53] Heather Dubrow has likewise identified, in the modular structuring of gathered poems, a much looser approach to the books she calls "sonnet cycles," because the degree of "narrativity varies so much from one collection to another and often within a given collection."[54] Dubrow is right to resist modern presumptions of a totalizing narrative, but my survey of the habits of numbering proposes that we need an even sharper distinction between the order of events within sonnets and their placement within the printed compilation. Considered in the context of a slightly longer history of assigning titles to printed poetry, sonnet numbers measure the quantity of poems within a single volume. They chart the accumulation of a series of discrete poems and reflect the sense that denominating genre might be a guide for reading.

To that extent, printed sonnet books could not have been further away from the contemporary understanding of the poetic sequence. Gascoigne twice referred to "Sonets in sequence" in his 1573 *A Hundreth sundrie Flowres*, and he knit lyrics into slight chains with additive titles like "An other Sonet written by the same Gentlewoman upon the same occasion."[55] Such expansive occasions disappeared in the sonnets printed in collections during the 1590s. The innovation of numbered headings was to make the arrangement of poems a condition of their temporary placement within a given book. "Numerical designations," Wendy Wall explains, "called attention to the reading experience rather than the social world in which the poem could function."[56] This reading experience changed when sonnets were reordered and assigned new numbers in subsequent editions. For instance, the poem headed "Sonnetto terzo" in the 1592 edition of Constable's *Diana* became "Sonnet II" in the 1594 and 1595 revisions made by the publisher Richard Smith.[57] As expressions of the shifting organization determined by a compiler, these numbered headings show how the order of the sonnets was contingent on the arrangement of the printed book, neither the chronology of composition nor lyric occasion.

The paradox is that even if the headings in sonnet books had little to do with an author's organization of his own work, they made it possible to forget that compilers like Smith had intervened in the order of *Diana*. The abstract numbers seemed definitive, absolute, and unsullied by the process of compilation. We can get a sense of how these abstract and symbolic headings flattened out the occasions of composition by comparing printed sonnets to the few examples of mixed genre books with numbered headings. Prior to the rush of sonnets in the 1590s, numerals were not applied to formally repetitive poems but rather to a variety of styles, topics, or authors. Like the mixed portion of the *Astrophel and Stella* quarto they worked to draw dissimilar—and perhaps initially unrelated—texts into a legible compilation. In *The Paradyse of daynty devises* (1576–1606), each of the first sixty-odd poems is headed with both a title and a number. Thus, a warning about the treacherous duplicity of false friends began "21. Trye before you trust," while the very next poem was an erotic lament entitled "22. A Lady forsaken, complayneth."[58] Weaving together poems that were unrelated by form or scenario, the numbers created a series characterized by diversity, not by sameness. The headings reached beyond the basic distinctions between individual poems, teaching readers to perceive the broader coordinates of the compiled book, and this lesson seems to have been a success. In a 1578 copy of *The Paradyse of daynty devices* now held at the Bodleian, a contemporary hand has worked to complete the count, supplying numbers for the poems printed without them in the final pages (see Figure 20).[59]

In sixteenth-century poetry books, numbered headings were understood as a sign of a basic discontinuity that stationers resolved through the extra cost and labor of adding organizational features. They were also used to connect formally diverse poems from the same poet, signaling individual skill by demonstrating the variety of modes in which an author could work. In Thomas Watson's *The Hekatompathia, or Passionate Centurie of Love* (1582), every poem is preceded by a roman numeral and then an explanation of how to read the lyric that follows. The heading for "XXII" describes how "The substance of this passion is taken out of *Seraphine* sonetto 127," but that "the Author hath in this translation inverted the order of some verses of *Seraphine* and added the two last of himselfe to make the rest to seeme the more patheticall."[60] This poem is undoubtedly singular, the product of Watson's reworking of his source, which is different in almost every case. But the roman numeral above the narrative title situated this individual translation as one component within a broader series of poems, folding Watson's *inter*textual reading and writing into an *intra*textual organization. In the same fashion, Thomas Lodge's *Scillaes Metamorphosis: Enterlaced with the unfortunate love* *of Glaucus* (1589) concludes with a short run of "Sundrie sweete Sonnets written by the same Gent," twelve poems drawn together only with unevenly sized and spaced arabic numerals.[61] These numbers were placed above individual poems early in the section, but they migrate to the margins next to the later items, probably to save space (see Figure 21). Ranging in length from six to forty-eight lines and with correspondingly varied meters and rhymes, the sundry sonnets do not themselves imply a continuous reading but instead lurch fitfully from scenario to scenario in the oddly sized gaps between the poems. The only unity to these diverse poems is provided by the irregularly placed numbers—which we might hesitate to even call "headings"—that draw them into a series.

After these early forays into organizing diverse poems, compilations used numbers to call out lyrics of the same genre, counting kinds of poems. Far from capturing the emotional development of a single author, these headings were markers only of the order of the book. They expressed the process of compiling poems for print. Barnabe Barnes's *Parthenophil and Parthenophe* (1593) appeared early in the fashion for sonnet books, just two years after *Astrophel and Stella* and one year after Daniel's *Delia*. When compared to *The Paradyse of daynty devises* or *The Hekatompathia*, the headings in Barnes's compilation demonstrate how quickly sonnets changed conventions for drawing poems together within the material apparatus of the printed book. *Parthenophil and Parthenophe* was divided roughly in half. The first section consisted primarily of sonnets with madrigals spliced in as a countergenre, while the second half, under a new running title, contained mostly elegies and a few infrequent odes. Regardless of this organizational split down the middle, all the poems are headed with numerals that, stunningly, trace each genre across the *entire* book. They gave the order of distinct lyric kinds even when the poems were not continuous. For instance, "Madrigall 2" and "Madrigall 3" appear on a single opening, separated by "Sonnet XII" and "Sonnet XIII," and the verso of the same page gives "Madrigall 4" next.[62] But "Madrigall 5" does not appear until after "Sonnet XLIII," following fifty intervening poems spread across seventeen pages.[63] In the same way, "Sonnet CIIII" at first seems to be the final quatorzain in *Parthenophil and Parthenophe*, since it concludes the first section devoted to sonnets. But the very end of the book holds a surprise, slipping "Sonnet CV" in after nearly seventy pages filled with sestinas and odes.[64] This late addition to the tally of sonnets shows how, far from capturing a poetic sequence dictated by Barnes as an author, numbered headings were a secondary attempt to organize an abundance of

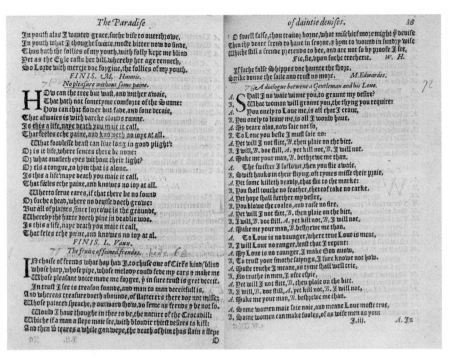

Figure 20. Poem numbers supplied by a contemporary reader in a copy of *The Paradyse of daynty devises* (London: Henry Disle, 1578), sigs. I2v–I3r, Wood 482 (6). By permission of the Bodleian Libraries, The University of Oxford.

poetic forms. Headings were inherently a product of compiling, even as they work to disguise that agency. The patchy numbering scheme in *Parthenophil and Parthenope* reflects an attention to the quantity and genres of gathered poems—and to how this series of accumulated forms constellates unevenly within the compiled book.

This microhistory of poetic numbering draws out modes of gathering and reading poetry that have been lost as a result of modern presumptions about the authorial sequencing of sonnets. The poetics of compiling in earlier printed books never really disappeared, of course. The appearance of numbers above formally identical lyrics rather helped devise a textual arrangement that merely appeared free from the imitation of extant sources. In *Ideas Mirrour: Amours In Quatorzains* (1594), Michael Drayton calls his work "mine owne" not "filch[ed] from *Portes* nor *Petrarchs* pen," even as he splices Sidney's prohibition of imitation into the couplet of his dedicatory sonnet: "Divine Syr *Phillip*, I avouch thy writ, / I am no Pickpurse of anothers wit."[65] Instead of stealing from other poets, Drayton promises that the pages of the book will offer a direct expression of his emotional state:

> Reade heere (sweet Mayd) the story of my wo,
>   The drery abstracts of my endles cares:
>   With my lives sorow enterlyned so,
>   Smok'd with my sighes, and blotted with my tears.[66]

Loading his lines with cares, sorrows, sighs, and tears—expressions that exceed verbal representation—Drayton's sonnets are visibly stained with his suffering. This physical intimacy between the poet and the reader took the form of an apparently artless or unmediated arrangement of sonnets.

If numbered headings were signs of an amorphous tally of love, not vestiges of the chronology of composition, they did begin to suggest how claims for authorship began to intrude upon the unknowable gap between writing and gathering poetry. In *Sonnets to the Fairest Coelia* (1594), William Percy describes "my Sonnets, as thinges privie to my selfe" and explains that they "were secretlie committed to the Presse, and almost finished, before it came to my knowledge."[67] Despite this fugitive publication, Percy did not attempt to revise or restrict his sonnets, adding only a disclaimer of the trivial subject matter of the work: "I did deeme it most convenient to praepose mine Epistle, onely to beseech you to account of them as of toyes and amorous devises."[68] Like Drayton's smudged and blotchy abstract of cares, Percy's "privie" sonnets are implicitly personal because the work claims to have hardly been touched by compilers. Little seemed to stand between the poet's pen and the pages of the printed book.

It is not that sonneteers were unconcerned with the organization of their work, but rather that they were pursuing a modular and shifting structure for their poems instead of a totalizing sequence.[69] Poets exchanged the imitation of extant sources for a visceral account of their own experiences. Daniel opens *Delia* with an announcement that the book is a tally of his suffering, a raw accumulation of emotions:

> Heere I unclaspe the booke of my charg'd soule,
> Where I have cast th'accounts of all my care:
> Heere have I summ'd my sighes, heere I enroule
> Howe they were spent for thee.[70]

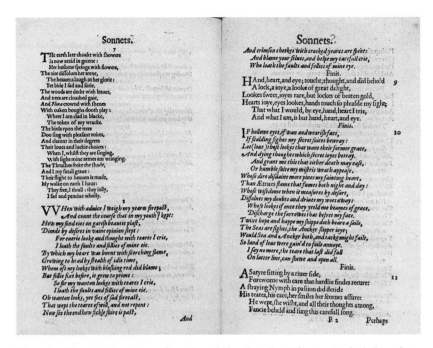

Figure 21. Erratic placement of numbered "headings" in Thomas Lodge's "Sundrie sweete Sonnets written by the same Gent," *Scillaes Metamorphosis: Enterlaced with the unfortunate love of Glaucus* (London: Richard Jones, 1589), sigs. F1v–F2r, RB 31529. By permission of the Huntington Library, San Marino, California.

Quantifying his expenditures in love, Daniel's imagery of accounting uses the seemingly objective, incorruptible practice of bookkeeping to cast *Delia* as an accurate record of his desire.[71] The mathematical fixation with quantity requires the impression of uncountable disorder to capture the vehemence of passion. This intimate registry was added to the first complete edition of *Delia* published in 1592, where it was probably meant to remedy the public exposure that Daniel suffered when some of his sonnets were included in the *Astrophel and Stella* quarto. He writes of Thomas Newman's 1591 edition: "I was betraide by the indiscretion of a greedie Printer, and had some of my secrets bewraide to the world, uncorrected."[72] With the new claim to have summed his own sighs, Daniel performatively evaded the interference of any other figures involved in publishing *Delia*. Taking control of his (now apparently corrected) secrets, Daniel mixed dozens of new sonnets into the set published with the Sidney volume. He continued to expand and shuffle the order of *Delia* over the years, adding four more sonnets in the second edition from 1592 and yet another in the third edition from 1594. This growing count of sonnets, an ever-larger compilation of sighs, was made possible by the additive logic of the numbered headings, which could expand endlessly to accommodate the addition of new poems.

By linking poems into a repetitive series, not a totalizing sequence, sonnet books contributed to the representation of emotions explored earlier in this chapter, though in a fashion that expresses poets' sense of an increasing distance from how their work was arranged for print. At times, a poet's hand actually became legible because sonnets were organized badly. Robert Tofte's *Laura* (1597) includes a postscript from a "Frend" who bemoans his inability to correct the damage wrought in the poet's absence: "Without the Authors knowledge, as is before said by the Printer, this Poeme is made thus publiquely knowen." The "Gentleman himselfe . . . earnestly intreated me to prevent" this publication. "But I came at the last sheetes printing, and finde more than thirtie Sonnets not his, intermixt with his."[73] The vast quantity of "Sonnets not his" suggests that something has gone drastically wrong, since *Laura* only contains forty poems, meaning that perhaps just ten are actually Tofte's. Yet the friend claims that the collection's "intermixt" poems promoted a new attention to authorship: "helpt it cannot be but by the wel judging Reader, who will with lesse paine distinguish betweene them, than I on this sodaine possibly can."[74] Given enough time, the mixture of writing will teach the discerning reader to recognize which poems can safely be ascribed to Tofte.

Such gaffes in material organization illuminate how printed sonnet books were active and evolving responses to the formally identical quatorzains. The complex process of making poems into a book contributed to a dynamic version of poetic authorship that was driven both by a Petrarchan desire to transcend mediation and by the real contingencies involved in printing compiled sonnets. In T. W.'s *The Tears* of *Fancie* (1593), both roman and arabic numerals were used as headings, usually for sonnets set on different formes. Both systems of numeration did appear on the same page once, in the case of the comically bungled roman numeral "Sonnet XXX.XIX," which was immediately followed by "Sonnet 40" (see Figure 22).[75] If these organizational features seem to have challenged the numeracy of the compositor, they also show how the design of compiled sonnets was at first an expediency of printing the short poems: it was better to include such messy numbering than to leave a sonnet without a heading.

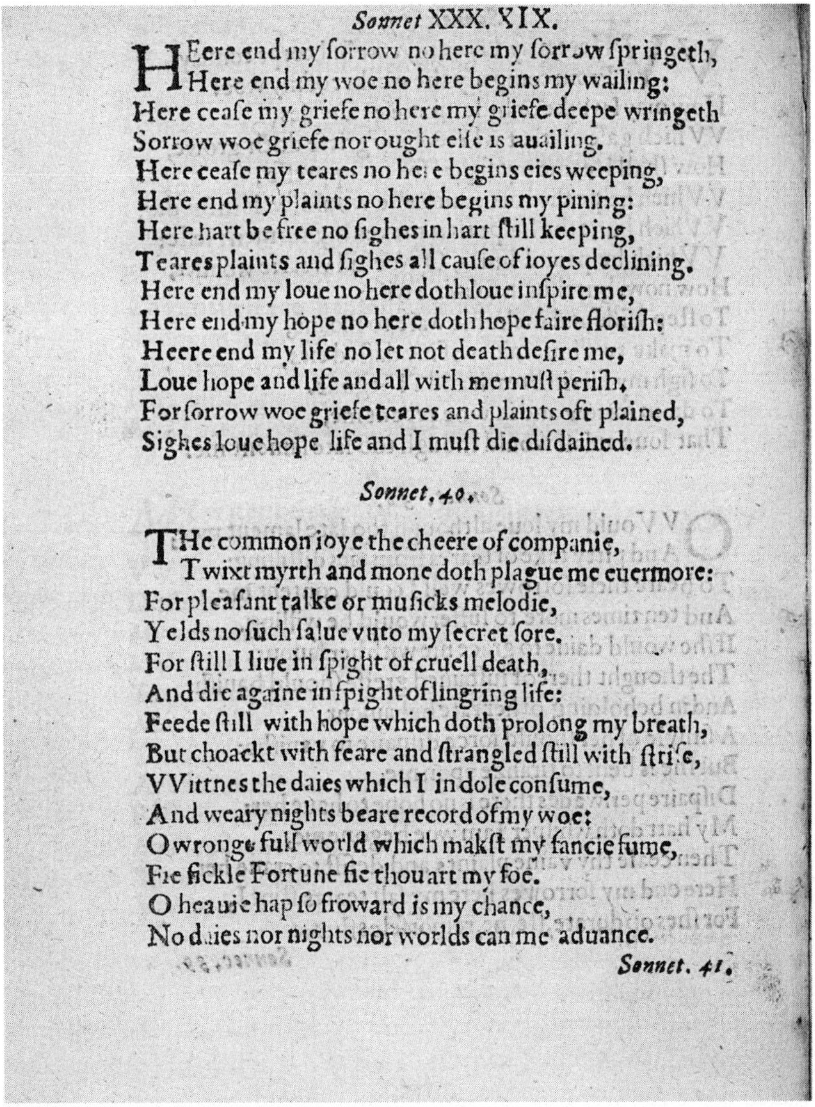

Sonnet XXX. ℣IX.

HEere end my sorrow no here my sorrow springeth,
Here end my woe no here begins my wailing:
Here cease my griefe no here my griefe deepe wringeth
Sorrow woe griefe nor ought else is auailing.
Here cease my teares no here begins eies weeping,
Here end my plaints no here begins my pining:
Here hart be free no sighes in hart still keeping,
Teares plaints and sighes all cause of ioyes declining.
Here end my loue no here doth loue inspire me,
Here end my hope no here doth hope faire florish:
Heere end my life no let not death desire me,
Loue hope and life and all with me must perish.
For sorrow woe griefe teares and plaints oft plained,
Sighes loue hope life and I must die disdained.

Sonnet. 40.

THe common ioye the cheere of companie,
Twixt myrth and mone doth plague me euermore:
For pleasant talke or musicks melodie,
Yelds no such salue vnto my secret sore.
For still I liue in spight of cruell death,
And die againe in spight of lingring life:
Feede still with hope which doth prolong my breath,
But choackt with feare and strangled still with strife,
VVittnes the daies which I in dole consume,
And weary nights beare record of my woe:
O wrongfull world which makst my fancie fume,
Fie fickle Fortune fie thou art my foe.
O heauie hap so froward is my chance,
No daies nor nights nor worlds can me aduance.

Sonnet. 41.

Figure 22. Mixed roman and arabic headings in T. W., *The Tears of Fancie, or Love Disdained* (London: William Barley, 1593), sig. C4v, RB 32085. By permission of the Huntington Library, San Marino, California.

For minor collections that were chasing the success of *Astrophel and Stella* and *Delia*, compilers used the conventions of *mise-en-page* to nudge volumes that mixed in other kinds of poems closer to the genre expectations for the printed books. Lodge's *Phillis*, Drayton's *Ideas Mirrour*, Smith's *Chloris*, Linche's *Diella*, and the anonymous *Zepheria* all included a few poems that were longer or shorter than fourteen lines. Usually these variations were slight and could be shoehorned into the otherwise regular pages by shifting or removing an ornamental border. But one poem in *Diella* posed a more substantial challenge—and solicited a more creative solution. Linche's "Sonnet XIII" is a tearful acknowledgment of the futility of the poet's extravagant suffering, which still "will not remove / flynt-harted rigour from your rocky breast."[76] Yet while Linche deployed traditional Petrarchan imagery, this poem did not match the rest of the sonnets in *Diella* because it is far longer, spanning twenty-six lines of cross-rhymed quatrains and a final couplet. Unable to fit it on a single octavo page, the compositors in printer James Roberts's shop split the poem in two, with the first fourteen lines given on one page and the remaining twelve on the overleaf, each with regular borders running along the top and the bottom. The advantage of this approach was that it preserved *Diella*'s uniform *mise-en-page*, allowing for two pages with almost the correct number of lines. But there was a problem: was the border a marker of division interrupting the single poem? And did the second half need a heading? The solution was slightly counterintuitive. Instead of leaving a page without a title, the heading "Sonnet XIII" was repeated, appearing above both halves of the divided poem.[77] If the desire for a regular page layout succeeded in *Diella*, the repetition of the numbered heading introduced a stutter in the arrangement of the book by allowing for what looked like two identically titled sonnets.

In all these cases, sonnet books were simultaneously sensitive readings of poetic form and slightly heavy-handed influences on authorial craft. Their formulaic page layout has disguised how they manufactured coherence—as well as all the gaps and fissures in those presumptions of order—by hiding the influence that professional compilers wielded over textual arrangement and even over poems themselves. The fine line between a sensitive and a rather foolhardy setting of copy in *Diella* shows how agents of the book trade read individual lyrics carefully enough to recognize deviations in form but also used organizational features to remake poems. When we recognize the basic contingency of this approach to arranging compiled poetry, it is stranger still to think that sonnet books would become the origin for presumptions of an authorial sequence. The belief that narrative continuity is desirable, or even possible, follows from placing too much faith in the textual features that linked diverse poems but that ultimately did little to specify the nature of those connections, leaving them open to the desires of readers.

Preposterous Placing

The sonnet books that proliferated during the 1590s opened the arrangement of compiled poetry to interpretation, cultivating a dynamic tension between a meaningful investment in textual design and a practical response to the demands of print. Literary history has simplistically taken this tension as a spectrum of order and disorder, signs of the varying degrees of authorial control. But early modern poets and compilers valued this dynamic as intrinsic to the meaning of gathered sonnets and exploited it to heighten the expression of erotic desire and religious affect. The impact of this modular, shifting organization on the representation of emotions is particularly evident in two sonnet books that express the outsize influence of their stationers: Henry Constable's *Diana*, published three times by Richard Smith in 1592, 1594, and 1595, and Henry Lok's *Sundry Christian Passions*, which Richard Field printed twice in 1593 and 1597. Both intervened in the order and material setting of the compiled sonnets, albeit in ways that variously respected poets' agency. Field met Lok's demands for specific textual features, while Smith took advantage of Constable's exile to impose the abstract conventions of the printed sonnet book on poems that were arranged differently in manuscript.[78] Taken together, *Diana* and *Sundry Christian Passions* show the significance that conventions of material design invested in a series of repeated quatorzains. Their modular arrangement, which was patently an artifice of print, could claim to be the more expressive because it denied the interventions of compilers.

Diana included all the features of a conventional sonnet book, but it was not in the least authorial. Constable had been stranded in France since 1591, so the path was clear for the publisher Richard Smith and the printer John Charlewood to reframe the poet's work.[79] First published as a compilation of twenty quatorzains, *Diana* retrospectively introduced the stock imagery of a Petrarchan lover lamenting his absent mistress. In multiple manuscript copies of Constable's erotic sonnets, the beloved is not identified, and in the poems themselves she is simply called "My Ladie."[80] The only place we learn her name is in the heading of an introductory sonnet, "To his absent Diana," a poem that was introduced—and probably written—after Constable's departure.[81] Given that "Diana" appears only in a textual frame, it is possible that Smith and Charlewood slipped in this reference in an attempt to meet the current fashion for printed sonnets that were unified around the identity of a consistent beloved.

In ascribing all of the sonnets to a single erotic scenario, *Diana* scoured away every trace of the world in which Constable's work was written and circulated. Unlike the printed sonnets, the manuscript copies incorporated social contexts and the occasions of composition into the features that organized the poems. Fifteen of Constable's sonnets appear in a continuous run in a composite volume now held at Marsh's Library, where they are given titles like "To hir maiesty for a p[re]face to his booke."[82] In the Arundel Harington manuscript, twenty quatorzains are arranged under the heading "Mr Henry Conestables sonets to the Lady Ritche. 1589."[83] Most impressive is the Todd manuscript, now held in the Dyce collection at the Victoria and Albert Museum, which contains sixty-three of Constable's sonnets, along with extensive framing devices, all in a single italic hand.[84] A note entitled "The order of the booke" explains: "The sonets following are divided into 3 parts, each parte contayning 3 severall arguments, and every argument 7 sonets."[85] These scores of sonnets were further divided by topic. "The first parte is of variable affections of love" and was wholly devoted to the poet's mistress, while "The second is the prayse of perticulars" and comprises sonnets to notable figures including "the Q: of England and K: of Scotts" and "Sir Philip Sydneyes soule."[86]

These elaborate headings sorted Constable's sonnets according to multiple intersecting logics. The final section was defined not just by the addressees but also by the mode of the sonnets, remarking on the tragedy that draws the compilation to a close: "The thyrd parte is tragicall conteyning only lamentations wherein the first 7 be complaints onlye of misfortunes in love, the second 7 funerall sonets of the death of perticulars, the last 7 of the end and death of his love."[87] The arrangement of this manuscript was certainly invested in authorship, since the placement of the individual sonnets accounted for the poet's relation to his audience. But that complex and networked order was a reflection of the social world in which Constable wrote, not an abstract, forward progress of lyric events.

Smith cut all these narrative occasions when he published Constable's work as *Diana*. Instead, the symbolic conventions of sonnet books produced

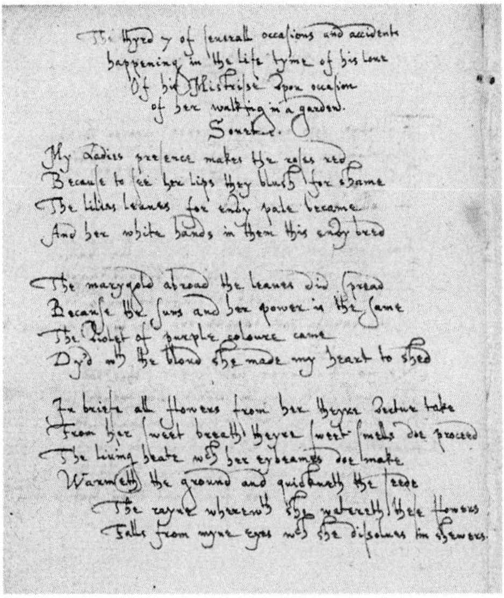

The thyrd 7 of severall occasions and accidents
happening in the life tyme of his love
Of his Mistrisse upon occasion
of her walking in a garden.
Sonet. 1

My Ladies presence makes the roses red
Because to see her lips they blush for shame
The lilies leaves for envy pale became
And her white hands in them this envy bred

The marigold abroad the leaves did spread
Because the suns and her power is the same
The violet of purple colour came
Dyd with the blood she made my heart to shed

In briefe all flowers from her theyre vertue take
From her sweet breath theyre sweet smells doe proceed
The living heate wch her eyebeames doe make
Warmeth the ground and quickneth the seede
The rayne wherewth she watereth these flowers
Falls from myne eyes wch she dissolves in showers.

Figure 23. Frame of "occasions and accidents" for Henry Constable's sonnet in the Todd manuscript, fol. 19v. Dyce 25.F.39. © Victoria and Albert Museum, London.

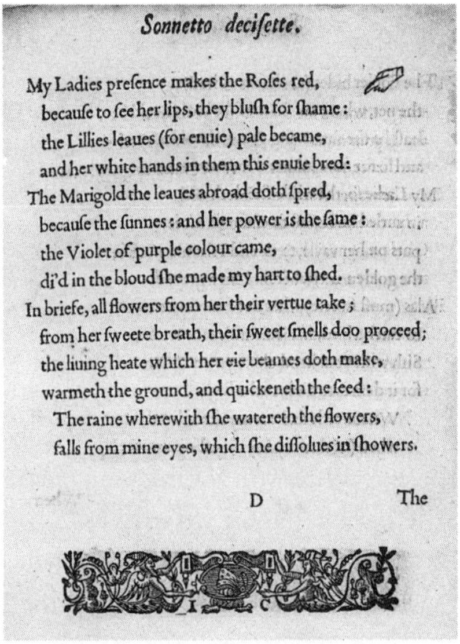

Sonnetto deciſette.

My Ladies preſence makes the Roſes red,
becauſe to ſee her lips, they bluſh for ſhame:
the Lillies leaues (for enuie) pale became,
and her white hands in them this enuie bred:
The Marigold the leaues abroad doth ſpred,
becauſe the ſunnes: and her power is the ſame:
the Violet of purple colour came,
di'd in the bloud ſhe made my hart to ſhed.
In briefe, all flowers from her their vertue take;
from her ſweete breath, their ſweet ſmells doo proceed;
the liuing heate which her eie beames doth make,
warmeth the ground, and quickeneth the ſeed:
The raine wherewith ſhe watereth the flowers,
falls from mine eyes, which ſhe diſſolues in ſhowers.

D The

Figure 24. "Sonnetto decisette" in Henry Constable, *Diana* (London: Richard Smith, 1592), sig. D1r, RB 58467. By permission of the Huntington Library, San Marino, California.

a compilation that aspired to be free from the contingencies of gathering and arranging poems—and from the contingencies of love. The printed *Diana* was a single series of numbered sonnets, thereby creating the conditions for the expansive linking of intimate emotions. Most pointedly, the lengthy headings were exchanged for sonnet numbers in Italian. In the Todd manuscript, a poem was called "The thyrd 7 of severall occasions and accidents happening in the life tyme of his love. Of his Mistrisse upon occasion of her walking in a garden. Sonet 1" (see Figure 23).[88] In the printed *Diana* this heading was radically simplified to "Sonnetto decisette" (see Figure 24).[89] Liberated from the "occasions and accidents" that inspired the sonnets, *Diana* developed an expanded scenario that was unique to this compiled book. This sonnet preserves the influence that the beloved has over her surroundings: "My Ladies presence makes the Roses red, / because to see her lips, they blush for shame."[90] Yet without the lengthy heading, the beloved's presence is no longer an artifact of the time in the garden but is instead contextualized by the other sonnets printed in *Diana*. The statement of the mistress's presence reads as the poet's imaginative description of an erotic desire that is private and particular to his own experience. When this instant is set within the rest of the compiled sonnets, becoming "Sonnetto decisette," the attenuated context exposes the links between poems to a scrutiny that was once explained through the occasions of composing and compiling. The arrangement of sonnets was cast as an expression of Constable's desire, even though that design and organization was determined by a secondary compiler.

Poets and stationers alike took advantage of this new orientation to the poetic context created by printed sonnet books. The potential impact of the order—as well as the palpable disorder—of poems that were gathered and arranged for print was appealing to poets working in Sidney's wake because sonneteers could claim their poetry was free from rote material compiling even when they willingly sought publication. Henry Lok worked closely with Richard Field on two editions of his sonnets, published first as *Sundry Christian Passions Contained in Two Hundred Sonnets* in 1593 and then "annexed" at the end of his 1597 translation of *Ecclesiastes, Otherwise Called the Preacher* as "other affectionate Sonets of a feeling conscience of the same Authors."[91] In both, Lok's sundry, affectionate, and feeling poems were divided into two sections that mapped the poet's progress toward spiritual redemption, from "The First Part of Christian Passions, containing a hundreth Sonets of *meditation, humiliation, and prayer*" to "The Second part of Christian passions, Containing a hundred Sonets of comfort, joy, and thankesgiving."[92] The book's binary split at the instant of salvation produced an organization that was superficially temporal but not in the least sequential. Each section was a testament to an ongoing, repetitive affective experience. With a muse trapped by the poet's desire to express his devotion, the sonnets simply repeated Lok's sentiments, often to pedestrian effect. The first section demonstrates the constant, irresolvable yearning of the penitent sinner: "How should my soule Lord clad in earthly mold," the poet worries, "Unto one thought of hope or helpe incline."[93] This pensive fear vanishes in the set of sonnets following his salvation, when his spiritual struggle is replaced with a basic inability to capture his transcendence: "The more I seeke to dedicate my power," the "more my dutie groweth everie hower" until "I cannot write, such maze my muse is in."[94] Without the ability to coalesce into longer chains of sonnets, as we saw in the case of Sidney's iterative clusters of kiss poems, Lok's writing was a static repetition of form and content.

This maze of repetitive sonnets offered an exceptionally vivid representation of the human experience of divine providence. Lok opened *Sundry Christian*

Passions with an address "To the Christian Reader" in which he defended using poetry to express his religious devotion: as "for my deducing these passions into Sonnets, it answereth (as I suppose) best for the shortnesse, to the nature of passions, and common humor of men."[95] Beyond the common and short form of these passions, Lok describes the value of "the confused placing of them without speciall titles," that is, without any narrative or occasional headings.[96] *Sundry Christian Passions* instead provided numbered headings in distinct runs for each half of the book. Lok claimed, once again, that this arrangement was a kind of verisimilitude: "as for the cause of my so preposterous placing of them and devision onely into two sorts, I confesse indeed I am perswaded their disorder doth best fit the nature of mankind, who commonly is delighted with contraries and exercised with extreames."[97] The apparent disorder of the several hundred sonnets, divided into two unwieldy extremes of religious experience, captured the tumult of an emotional life that was beyond the poet's control. "Preposterous," in early modern England, was a term for "the disruption of orders based in linearity, sequence, and place," from the "reversal" of status and hierarchy to the "transgressions of the linear ordering" of narrative and rhetorical structures.[98] With the topsy-turvy, upside-down, and transgressive arrangement of his *Sundry Christian Passions*, Lok achieved a compiled form that would allow his affections to be both "plac[ed]" and yet still palpably "disorder[ed]." The imitation of affections in this book expresses the limits of human agency—or even more basically, of a human understanding of the forces governing the world—in the face of divine providence.

This savvy handling of the affordances of the printed sonnet book was responding to and adjusting the dominant model of religious poetry in sixteenth-century England: the psalm translations that had circulated for decades in both manuscript and print. Contemporary poetic theorists including Sidney and Scott had identified psalms as a powerful model of lyric craft. Lok was drawing in particular on the example set by his mother, Anne Vaughan Lock, who published a translation of Psalm 51 entitled *A Meditation of a Penitent Sinner* in 1560. Anne Lock's paraphrase is a series of twenty-one sonnets, each of which is an expansive dilation of a single verse. Henry Lok leaned heavily on *A Meditation of a Penitent Sinner*, learning "both structure and strategy" from his mother.[99] His binary split between the sonnets of penitence and redemption in *Sundry Christian Passions* instantiates the process of redemption narrated in Psalm 51.

But in taking this spiritual development as the inspiration for the material arrangement of his compilation, Henry Lok also reframed his mother's poetic and devotional example through the new bibliographic paradigm offered by the sonnet book. The design conventions of printed sonnets changed the traditional expression of religious devotion in English translations of psalms by poets such as Thomas Wyatt, Philip Sidney, and Mary Sidney Herbert, as well as the liturgical psalter, *The Whole Book of Psalms* (1562).[100] Psalters had a set sequence. Though the verses were divided slightly differently in the Catholic and Protestant traditions, the order and quantity of the 150 psalms was constant and not impacted by the design or production of any particular book. Unlike sonnets, individual psalms could be identified by number. *The Booke of the Common Praier* (1549), for instance, included a calendar dictating "the ordre how the Psalter is appoynted to bee redde" through in its entirety every month: "in this table . . . the nombre is expressed after the greate Englishe Bible."[101] When Anne Lock announced that she was translating Psalm 51, her readers would have known that her string of sonnets was a version of the *Miserere*.[102] Psalm numbers thus functioned as titles, not relational markers of position, and Henry Lok broke with this tradition in *Sundry Christian Passions* when he refashioned the affective experience of redemption according to the conventions of printed sonnet books. Although he was exploring the same religious experience as his mother, the sets of numbered headings in each half of his book exchanged the expectations of a set poetic order for a preposterous (and redoubled) maze of repetitive sonnets that was particular to the compilation.

Henry Lok's investment in the disorderly poetics of the printed sonnet book found a ready partner in Richard Field. The printer was known for the quality and detail of his work, as well as his willingness to meet the demands of authors who were invested in typography.[103] By 1593, Field had printed elaborate books such as George Puttenham's *The Art of English Poesy* (1589) and John Harington's translation of *Orlando Furioso* (1591), an edition for which Harington gave explicit instructions about the marginal citations, print ornaments, and division of copy.[104] Lok was similarly involved in printing his own work. In the 1597 *Ecclesiastes, Otherwise Called the Preacher*, the book that contained his expanded sonnet collection, Lok described his approach to translation: "I have caused the same to be quoted in the margent, reducing for memorie sake into two abstract lines of verse set in the top of everie leafe: the substance of every pages content, which afterward as thou seest, is paraphrastically dilated page by page."[105] Lok was aligning units of the printed text with units of rhetorical expression. To write and then dictate the placement of these two kinds of marginal glosses, the poet must have worked closely with the printer. One of the additions to the compilation in 1597 was a clutch of sixty new sonnets seeking the favor of named patrons, which appeared under the heading "Sonnets of the Author to divers, collected by the Printer."[106] Somewhat unusually, Field here announced his role in bringing these dedicatory verses to print. Perhaps he included this note of his own compiling because he had assisted Lok in the massive expansion of the collection, which almost doubled in size, growing by 184 sonnets between the two editions.

Beyond adding to the quantity of sonnets, this collaboration was essential to the poetics of disorder through which Lok developed his account of the Christian passions within a modular textual arrangement that could be read in any order. The most stunning example of this collaboration was an elaborate grid entitled "A Square in verse of a hundred monasillables only," which was faced by a set of instructions for reading in at least eight different geometric configurations and followed by a verse ("The Square plainely set downe") of all the words (see Figure 25).[107] This is poetry fashioned through the recombinant affordances of typography. Ten lines of ten words are divided into a hundred squares that are syntactically and semantically interchangeable, such that every potentially divergent reading arrives at a universal truth of the queen's glory: "Describing the cause of Englands happinesse."[108] Equally, Lok's engagement with Field's book design produced a textual structure in which the disorder of poems helped to capture a universal religious truth. He casts his tangled sonnets as an expression of divine guidance: "as they were by God ministred to my minde, to set downe by sundry accidents in my private estate and feeling; so I suppose my providence could not by a formall placing of them so soone hit the affections of everie Reader as Gods direction (by that which men call chaunce)."[109] Defending the sundry and accidental arrangement of his sonnets, which from a human perspective looks like the haphazard result of chance, Lok shows they should actually be understood as the poet's responsiveness to God's own direction.

With this defense of the apparent disarray of his work, Lok joined the ranks of sonneteers like Sidney who denounced the piecemeal imitation of sources and of those like Daniel who claimed that the seeming artlessness of their collections offered an emotional intimacy. *Sundry Christian Passions* allows readers to encounter divine providence when they move through the modular arrangement of the sonnet book. The paradox is that Lok accomplished this intimate religious expression by embracing the typographic conventions and features that other sonneteers rejected as mere imitation.

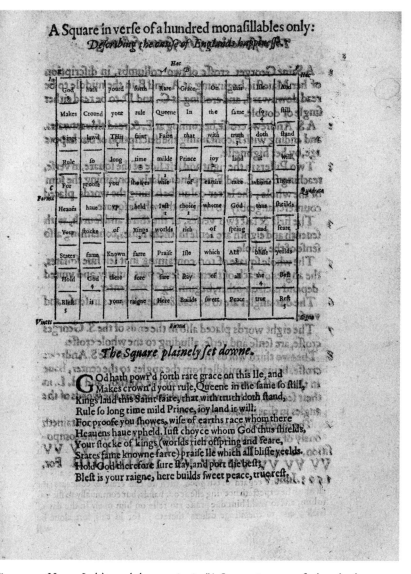

Figure 25. Henry Lok's modular poetics in "A Square in verse of a hundred monosillables." From *Ecclesiastes, Otherwise Called the Preacher* (London: Richard Field, 1597), sig. I7r, STC 16696. By permission of the Folger Shakespeare Library.

Reveling in "the confused placing" of sonnets "without speciall titles," he transformed the poetics of compiling that had structured earlier poetry books. In this way, Lok could embrace the affordances of the sonnet book while still claiming to be copying his own divine inspiration, in fact, making the design of the compilation integral to that experience of providence.

Shakespeare's Sequence

The modular poetics of arrangement that Lok found so productive would not fare well in future estimations of his work, nor indeed in the future of printed sonnets more generally. Less than a decade after the second edition of *Sundry Christian Passions*, the university play *The Returne from Pernassus* (1606) burlesqued Lok's interest in printing his poetry, condemning him to "sleepe . . . among the shavings of the presse, and let your bookes lie in some old nookes among old bootes and shooes."[110] The play's censure of other sonneteers was almost as harsh. Constable was mocked as a poet who "doth take the wondring eare, / And layes it up in willing prisonment," while "Sweete hony dropping Daniell" was warned to "let him more sparingly make use, / Of others wit."[111] Sonnets and the books in which they were published were well past their heyday by the time this play was printed.[112] Once poets returned to a greater variety of lyric forms, it was impossible to maintain the design conventions that had allowed for the regular, symmetrical pages.

But if sonnet books only dominated the market for English poetry for a few years, they did go on to transform subsequent printed compilations by retrospectively allowing textual organization to be theorized as an expression of authorship. Philip Sidney's legacy was once again responsible for this pronounced shift in printing poetry. The revisions to *Astrophel and Stella* in the 1598 *The Countesse of Pembrokes Arcadia* brought an end to the fashion for small books devoted completely to sonnets. The 1598 folio used the print conventions of the sonnet books published in the years after the *Astrophel and Stella* quartos to retrospectively impose a rigid and totalizing order on a compilation that was at first less constrained. By taking for granted an authorial design that was at first much more speculative, Mary Sidney Herbert's corrections broke the link between poetic form and the material format of the compilation.

While the 1598 *Astrophel and Stella* adopted the numbered headings that had become conventional in sonnet books, it abandoned other features, particularly the ornamental borders and symmetrical *mise-en-page*, because the larger folio format and the interspersed songs made it impossible to set pages regularly. Most significantly, Sidney's lyric poetry no longer filled the entirety of the codex. His sonnets were relegated to the end of *The Countesse of Pembrokes Arcadia*, which did not even advertise *Astrophel and Stella* on the title page, promising only that the romance would be followed by "sundry new additions of the same Author."[113] Valued as one component within Sidney's whole body of work, *Astrophel and Stella* was no longer legible as a book filled with and defined by the regular form of the sonnet.

This change of status for Sidney's lyrics again transformed the market for printed poetry. After *Astrophel and Stella* was included in the 1598 edition of Sidney's work, there were no published poetry compilations that met all the conventions of the sonnet book. There have been many plausible suggestions for the cause of the sudden passing of the fashion for sonnets, from the literary historical explanation that the "form exhausted itself" to the sociological argument that the genre was tied to the power structures of Elizabeth's court.[114] But these accounts have focused more on the poems than on how the trend for sonnets was driven by innovations in printing collected poetry. In light of the history of textual design told in this chapter, I want to suggest one more possibility. Sonnet books created the conditions for their own demise by developing a poetically sensitive page layout that would eventually become the foundation for a new model of authorship. By disguising the poetics of compiling, and by setting poems without narrative or occasional titles, they supplanted the efforts of professional compilers like Thomas Newman, Richard Smith, and Richard Field. The mimesis of emotions, which had first depended on how sonnets could be brought into material contact with one another, evolved into a sense that a poet could order his own work. In turn, the nexus of design conventions in the sonnet book became obsolete once the repetitive series of quatorzains began to be legible in the corrected *Astrophel and Stella* as a sequence based on narrative content.

After 1598, it was harder to confuse the sonnet sequence with a series of repeated forms because gathered poems took on a different relationship to the printed book. In most cases, sonnets appeared only as subsections within larger poetry collections, like Francis Davison's *A Poetical Rapsody* (1602–1621), which included multiple runs of sonnets with both numbered headings and occasional titles, like "Sonet. I. Dedication of these Rimes, to his first love."[115] Michael Drayton similarly incorporated *Ideas Mirrour*, his sonnet book from 1594, into larger collections of poetry, first his *Englands Heroicall Epistles* (1599, 1600, 1602), then his even more comprehensive *Poems* (1605, 1608, 1610, 1613, 1616, 1619, and 1630).

The formal and ideological operations of the "sonnet book" had become so successful that they no longer needed the material support of the printed form of the small codex. The two volumes of Shakespeare's poems published during his life are a case in point. In 1599, the publisher William Jaggard included Shakespeare's name on the title page of *The Passionate Pilgrim*. Consisting of twenty poems, of which only five are now thought to be written by Shakespeare, Jaggard's compilation met many of the print conventions of the sonnet book. Poems were evenly spaced, one to a page, and each was framed with ornamental borders. But although Jaggard emphasized similarities with the sonnet book, even opening *The Passionate Pilgrim* with six quatorzains, he did not include any numbered headings.[116] The effect of this partial affinity was to cast the order of the compiled poems as jumbled and undetermined by contents because there were no guides for moving through them. Thomas Thorpe took precisely the opposite approach when he published *Shake-speares Sonnets* in 1609. As a quarto with 154 numbered quatorzains and the narrative "A Lover's Complaint," *Shake-speares Sonnets* also met many of the conventions for the sonnet book.[117] But the design of this collection privileged a sequential poetic order. *Shake-speares Sonnets* set pages asymmetrically, with poems divided unevenly across openings, and removed all mention of genre from the headings. Dropping every pretense of counting lyric kinds, each sonnet was introduced only with a numeral. This was precisely the setting innovated in the 1598 revised *Astrophel and Stella*, which only included references to genre for the intrusive songs. In a further imitation of Sidney's authorial corpus, *Shake-speares Sonnets* announced the name of the poet in the volume title, puncturing the erotic fictions that had marketed the sonnet books printed during the 1590s.

In reading *Shake-speares Sonnets* as an attempt to heighten a sequential arrangement popularized by Sidney, I am not arguing that Shakespeare himself was involved in publishing his work. On the contrary, the two arrangements of Shakespeare's printed poetry shed light on how publishers took distinct approaches to updating the conventions of the sonnet book when the revisions to *Astrophel and Stella* had introduced new presumptions of authorship. If we have not typically identified a connection between Shakespeare's two compilations—each published after the fashion for sonnet books had passed—it is because his poetry has too easily been subsumed into a history of authorship that has disregarded the active poetics of compiling for print. Where Thorpe deployed features that (perhaps erroneously) implied the poet's investment in ordering and arranging *Shake-speares Sonnets*, Jaggard used a setting that cast the gathered work as a series of poems without necessary connections between them. We have since come to read *The Passionate Pilgrim* as miscellaneous because its motley arrangement seemed to damage claims for Shakespeare's control of his work.

The more nuanced account of poetic selfhood in this chapter depicts a prominent shift in the history of the poetry miscellany in early modern England. Sonnet books changed the nature of the relationship between imaginative writing and the media in which it circulated. By rejecting the speculative fictions of compiling that had organized previous compilations, the restrained, abstract, and nonverbal layout of sonnet books began to disguise the basic contingency of early modern printing practices. Sonnet books made prior modes of compiling appear disorderly and poetically insensitive because, in implicitly positing the textual control of a single author, they consolidated an agency that was at first distributed among multiple, unknown participants in the book trade. The brief moment in the 1590s in which sonnets dominated the market for published poetry made compilations like Tottel's *Songes and Sonettes* feel palpably miscellaneous by beginning to occlude the poetic sensibilities that were distinct to professional stationers. Looking forward into the seventeenth century, this new distinction between material and poetic practices would finally make it possible to identify the much more ephemeral links of authorial style within books that were called, simply, *Poems*.

CHAPTER 5

Books Called *Poems*

Authorship and the Miscellany

After the fashion for sonnet books waned with the 1590s, poetry compilations from the early seventeenth century returned to a greater variety of lyric forms and genres. Publishers mingled diverse odes, elegies, madrigals, pastorals, and many kinds of songs in their printed books. At the same time, the media landscape for imaginative writing was changing profoundly in early modern England. The circulation of poetry moved away from print during the 1620s and 1630s, with manuscript transmission becoming so common and so widespread as to constitute a system of publication.[1] This chapter considers how a burgeoning scribal culture transformed the poetics of compiling that, so far in this study, has been more affiliated with printed books. I argue that the rush of poetry manuscripts helped to consolidate a sense of the miscellany as a textual genre characterized by its diverse contents. This shift was not just a matter of the distinct affordances of the different media, since many manuscripts were copied from printed books and even adopted features, like poem titles, that originated with publishing stationers. Manuscript transmission rather contributed to the development of the miscellany as a conceptual category. More than just a material practice, textual arrangement came into focus as the result of prior decisions about how to read and understand diverse poems together.

The firsthand experience of gathering and arranging poetry taught manuscript compilers to think through the significance of textual context. By encountering large, varied compilations, readers developed a newly sophisticated approach to juxtapositions of poetic form, content, mode, authorship, and even audience.[2] A broad network of compilers explored the fissures and gaps—as well as the continuities and links—between poems they had not written themselves. This reading of context made it possible to define the miscellany as a book characterized by an apparent mixture of contents. Diverse collections had always existed in practice, but the term "miscellany"— from the Latin *miscere*, "to mix"—was just beginning to enter the English language at this moment. As Joshua Eckhardt and Daniel Starza Smith explain, while phrases like "miscellanea" and "miscellany poems" had been common earlier, it was not until the seventeenth century that the "English noun 'miscellany' gradually came to refer not only to the miscellaneous parts or contents of a volume but also to the volume itself."[3] The incremental development of a lexicon that could explain poetic variety was the result of several decades of experimenting with textual arrangement for print. English needed a new, more concrete name for miscellaneous collections because the culture was grappling with an evolving sense of how composing poems was distinct from compiling them.

The second argument of this chapter is that a new model for the authorial poetry book was consolidated in the same moment as the miscellany, such that each type of compilation came into sight as an opposing end of a broad spectrum of textual order and disorder. In both practice and theory, poetic authorship and miscellaneity were constituted mutually by the habits, actions, and desires of compilers, not the poets who wrote the poems. These compilations introduced new ways of understanding a textual corpus, of thinking across the connections between gathered writing, and of reading at scale. My primary case is the proliferation of John Donne's poetry in both manuscript and print. By any account, Donne had an extraordinary influence on seventeenth-century poetry, with thousands of extant scribal copies of his poems and a posthumous printed collection that was republished for nearly four decades. Donne's legacy inspired new approaches to compiling, I suggest, because his refusal to print his secular poetry left a vacuum that readers were all too eager to fill with their own sense of how to organize his extremely diverse work.[4] By gathering scores of poems that were first written to be read singly or in small clusters, compilers fashioned a poetic authority characterized by variety, not the generic sameness of sonnet books. At the same time, they expressed an authorial style that denied the classicizing model of deliberate, laureate authorship in the publications of slightly earlier English poets, including Edmund Spenser and Ben Jonson.[5] The broad scene of compiling in mid-seventeenth-century England was an opportunity to experiment with how a dispersed textual agency might come to represent Donne's body of work—and even his physical body—precisely because the poet was absent from the process of making his books.

In the pages that follow, I consider Donne's posthumous compilations as the development of a new paradigm for how printed books could use material organization and design features to articulate the fleeting authorial connections between poems. Two years after Donne's 1631 death, John Marriot published *Poems, By J. D.* (1633), a volume title that was stunningly simple yet almost unprecedented in English print history. Recovering the origins of this innovative title, I show how Marriot promoted Donne's spectral influence on the posthumous book by advocating for a sensitive reading of his diverse poetry.[6] The breadth of the title *Poems, By J. D.* was an attempt to devise a compiled form that could encompass the variety of genres in which Donne worked. To that extent, Donne was an absent presence in his own book, conjured into being as an author because he was deceased. This model of a compilation that was at once physical and conceptual, visceral and idealized was provocatively in dialogue with much of Donne's poetry, which consistently returned to questions of the problematic relation between the body and the soul. These thorny questions found expression in an equally fraught poetic style, which Donne expressed in idiosyncratic approaches to imagery, lineation, and voice. Picking up on Donne's characteristic complexities, *Poems, By J. D.* entangled the formal qualities of his writing with material formatting and design. In the second edition from 1635, the organization of the book was revised to hypothesize a poetic biography that attempted to explain the variety of his corpus as a development from erotic to divine verses.

The multiple printings of Donne's work produced an authorial identity that was so influential that it would actively sway the publication of later poetry compilations. *Poems, By J. D.* even reshaped and redefined Shakespeare's poetic authorship in the moment when that writer was becoming known for his collected drama. Although *Shake-speares Sonnets* (1609) was published decades earlier, this chapter concludes by exploring how *Poems, By J. D.* was the most prominent model for a belated "edition" entitled *Poems: Written by Wil. Shake-speare, Gent.* (1640). Published by the young stationer John Benson, this compilation of Shakespeare's lyric poetry adopted both Donne's bibliographic example and the poetic texture of his idiosyncratic verses, conflating Shakespeare's regular fourteen-line sonnets and repackaging them as stanzas within "poems" of various lengths. *Poems: Written by Wil. Shake-speare, Gent.* was a timely reading of Shakespeare's outmoded sonnets, updating his work for a new moment in literary history. In this anachronistic refashioning of Shakespeare after Donne, Benson's new forms and format register the outsized influence of habits of compiling on the elements of poetic style that seem to precede the printed book.

Matter and Form: Donne's Mixtures

John Donne's writing was characterized by an impressive variety of genres, styles, and modes. In addition to the prose sermons, polemical pamphlets, and devotional meditations that he willingly sent to press, Donne wrote verse letters, satires, epigrams, funeral elegies, erotic elegies, love lyrics, and devotional poems. While some of this poetry made it to print during his lifetime, most was limited to manuscripts that he sent to close friends, but which were copied over and over again, gradually reaching a wide circle of readers. The quantity and complexity of Donne's compiled poems solicited a particular approach to reading. His highly personal style, along with the numerous genres in which he worked, encouraged a habit of contextual interpretation that moved fluidly across different scales of meaning. In puzzling through the images layered within his conceits, readers gained practice in considering the relations between individual poems and larger compilations. This sensitivity to context allowed the judgments of (usually unknown) manuscript compilers to inform critical categories for making sense of Donne's body of work.

Donne understood his diverse poems, first, as individual compositions, not as components of a single corpus. He apparently did not keep copies. In 1614, as he was about to take orders in the Church of England, Donne was contemplating the "necessity of printing my poems" as "a valediction to the world," and he wrote to his close friend Henry Goodere, asking "to borrow that old book of you" because it would "cost me more diligence, to seek them, then it did to make" the poems in the first place.[7] "Valediction" is a Latinate expression meaning a speech or words uttered at leave-taking; it was a recent coinage most closely associated with Donne, perhaps even his own neologism.[8] In this moment of leaving behind the world, Donne recognized that his status as a poet was embodied in a compilation—namely, "that old book"—produced by someone who had exercised more care for his corpus than the poet had himself. Perhaps the effort of recovering these far-flung verses was too great, or perhaps Donne reconsidered the liabilities of sending his private writing to press, because we have no further mention of the project.

His poetry was not published until two years after his 1631 death, when the posthumous compilation could offer an illusion of completeness because Donne was himself absent.

If the majority of Donne's poems never saw print during his lifetime, restricting them to manuscript seems only to have fueled readers' desire for his work. Just one of his poems has survived in an authorial copy: a verse letter Donne sent to Lady Carey in 1612. But at current count, we have over 4,000 manuscript copies of individual poems in at least 239 different manuscripts.[9] The extant copies, which are certainly a fraction of the manuscripts originally in circulation, testify to the range of textual forms assumed by Donne's poetry. His work appeared in large and small collections put together by many different kinds of compilers. An early gathering of satires, elegies, and verse letters was owned by his close friend Roland Woodward.[10] Many composite volumes grew across time, like a manuscript maintained for generations by the Skipwith family.[11] Some compilations were produced collaboratively by mixing Donne's poems with work by his contemporaries.

The many forms and formats of Donne's compiled poetry reflect both how he shared his own writing and how his verses circulated for decades in manuscript before and after they were printed. Donne likely distributed some of his earliest poems in a small booklet. Later transcriptions frequently group his five satires together and in a consistent order, along with "The Storm" and "The Calm," two verse letters on his expedition to the Azores in 1597. Yet if Donne set the sequence of the satires, his love lyrics and elegies probably only began to come together in larger collections around 1620, thirty years after he started writing.[12] The order of these occasional poems is far less consistent in extant manuscripts, suggesting that they first circulated in separate sheets, booklets, and fascicles. Compilations of Donne's poetry were accretive and tended to grow across time as readers sought to make their books "as complete as possible."[13] After the publication of *Poems, By J. D.*, manuscripts continued to be copied and recopied, with scribes at times taking the printed books as sources.

Through this broad dissemination of his work, Donne's strikingly idiosyncratic, even personal poetics allowed the figure of the individual author to come into focus as a potential influence on the organization of the gathered poetry. To be clear, by "authorship," I do not mean proximity to the poet's hand, nor am I referring to accurate or faithful copies. A "Donne" poem does not need to be written by Donne—or "J. D.," "Jack Donne," "Doctor Donne," or any other name that proliferated around the popular poet and prominent clergyman. Rather, we need to trace how these diverse poems were physically and imaginatively affiliated with Donne's reputation, which had taken on an outsized celebrity by the time he died as the popular dean of St. Paul's. Donne's status as a poet was conferred by the manuscript transmission that, from the perspective of modern textual criticism, introduced multiple kinds of corruption: inadvertent scribal errors, deliberately rewritten lines, even a basic confusion over which poems were his.[14] Instead of disavowing the ways in which manuscript transmission warped or distorted this corpus, Marcy North has argued that these profoundly unreliable attributions "represen[t] the community's formulation of the author."[15] Donne's prominence was elaborated through the social processes that lent value to his poems while they circulated among a vast network of contemporary writing, which included his own work, certainly, but also that of other known and unknown poets. To that extent, the use of the phrases "falsely attributed" or "misattributed" are at best misleading—at worst, they are wholly without meaning—because the act of attribution was itself a measure of what contemporary readers *thought* was Donne's, even if they were later proven wrong.

With Donne's poems being recopied for decades, scribes had ample opportunity to experiment with how his writing should be related to the work of other poets as a matter of both physical organization and literary form. One manuscript collection, now held at the Folger Shakespeare Library, shows how organizational features like headings, attributions, and designations of genre expressed personal readings.[16] Such features, as Lara M. Crowley observes, "deserve attention, in part because they indicate frequently how readers interpreted works."[17] Pages in the first part of this quarto blank book were organized with running headers that named distinct kinds of poems, like "Laudatory Epitaphs," "Satyres," and "Love Sonnets." These headings engage with the genres named in these phrases, even as they work to redefine them. To take just one example, the two poems that begin "Hee is starke madd who ever Saies" and "I am two Fooles, I know," which were more typically read as love poems, appeared among the "Satyres." The compiler was perhaps struck by their conflicted and ironizing tone. He observed their shared contrarian stance in the two headings, which appeared in a single opening: "Dr. Donne. Against Love" and "A Lover against himselfe. Dr. Donne."[18] With the introduction of these multiple organizational features, which both divided and united poems, the compiler materialized both continuities and rifts within the field of contemporary poetry. He was seeking a way to represent more attenuated connections between the diverse, mixed texts in his manuscript.

The headings were also the expression of contextual links between several poems attributed to Donne. The "Love Sonnets" section, for instance, contains the poem beginning "Busy old fool, unruly sun," which is given the title "Mr. Dunne. To the Sunne that rise too early to call Him and his love from bedd."[19] On the very next page, the erotic topics continue with another poem headed "Mr. Dunne. To his Scornefull Mistresse," which begins, "Cruell, since that thou dost not feare the curse," a verse that editors no longer believe to be Donne's.[20] The fluidity of these genre designations and attributions shed light on how Donne's poetry fit into the cacophonous environment of contemporary manuscripts. These evolving texts are a window onto a literary history in the process of being written and theorized, not from the centralized agency of the author, but from the margins—that is, from the points of material contact between poems within a shifting body of work that have necessarily been excluded from a modern editorial focus on the identity of the individual poet.

But this scribe's yearning for an organizational clarity also introduced its own challenge: what to do with poems that did not quite fit into the precise genre categories that he had devised? He was left with several pieces that he apparently did not want to place in the manuscript's existing sections, even though ample blank pages remained. The solution was to affiliate all the verses that defied categorization in a slight section at the end of the manuscript called "Miscellanea." This heading was a catchall for poems rejected from the other categories, naming the motley remnants of an impossible cataloging scheme—as indeed all catalogs are. Donne was the first poet to appear in this slight clutch of four verses, which opens with his poem "Like one who in her third widdow[hoo]d doth profess," appearing under the title, "Dr. Donne. A Retyring of himselfe into himselfe; Or, An Eternall Farewell to Love & Poetry" (see Figure 26). This poem, more often identified as a letter to Roland Woodward, describes the newfound chastity of a muse "tir'd to retirednes," prompting a time of solitary reflection: "Seeke wee then o[u]r selves in o[u]r selves."[21] It is followed on the next page by "Dr. Donne. Making of Men," an erotic elegy that starts "Till I have peace with thee, warre other man" and then goes on to depict a lover willing to "warre, in these armes," to "parly, batter, bleed, and dy" with his mistress.[22] When these diverse poems appear together under the heading "Miscellanea," Donne's work is linked through the very

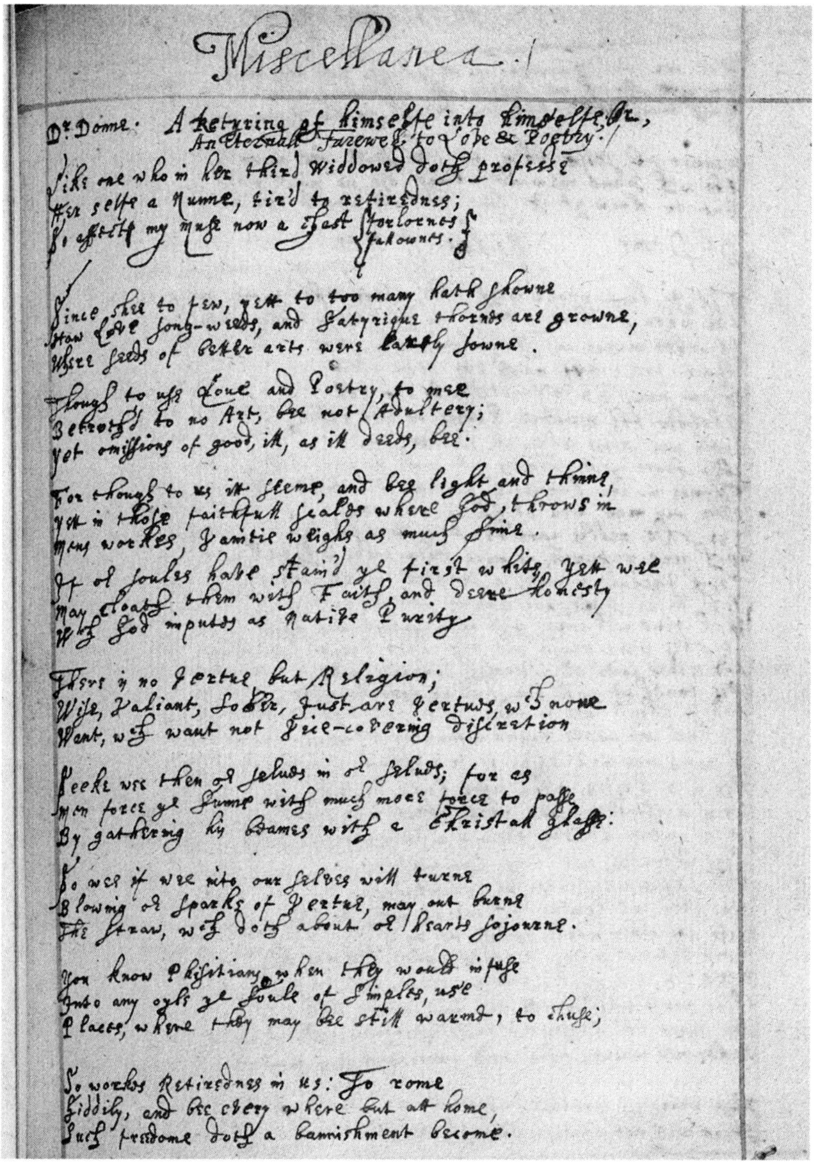

Miscellanea. 1

Dr Donne: A Retyring of himselfe into himselfe &c,

An Eternall fareweel: to Ode & Poetry:

Like one who'in her third widdowhood doth professe
Her selfe a Nunne, tir'd to retiredness;
So affects my muse now a chast forlornes / fallownes.

Since, shee to few, yett to too many hath showne
How Love song-weeds, and Satyrique thornes are growne,
Where seeds of better arts, were lately sowne.

Though to use Loue and Poetry, to mee
Betroth'd to no Art, bee not Adultery;
Yet omissions of good, itt, as itt deeds, bee.

For though to us itt seeme, and bee light and thinne,
Yet in those faithfull scales where God, throws in
Mens workes, Vanitie weighs as much sinne.

If of soules have stain'd ye first white, yet wee
May cloath them with Faith, and deere honesty
Which God imputes as natiue Purity.

There is no Vertue but Religion;
Wise, Valiant, Sober, Iust, are Vertus, wch none
Want, wch want not Vice-couering discretion

Seeke wee then of selues in of selues; for as
men force ye Sunne with much moer force to passe,
By gathering his beames with a Christall glasse:

So wee if wee into our selues will turne
Blowing of Sparks of Vertue, may out burne
The straw, wch doth about of hearts sojourne.

You know Phisitians, when they would infuse
Into any oyle ye soule of Simples, use
Places, where they may lie still warmd, to chuse;

So workes Retiredness in us. To rome
Giddily, and bee every where but att home,
Such freedome doth a banishment become.

Figure 26. Opening of the "Miscellanea" section in the Smith family manuscript, fol. 76r, V.a.103. By permission of the Folger Shakespeare Library.

variety that excluded it from the elaborate set of genre categories the compiler had devised.

The designation of "Miscellanea" helps us see how an unruly mixture of genres, occasions, and scenarios was neither natural nor innate. This material and generic juxtaposition was rather produced through the scribe's attempt to explain the placement of poems for which he could not find any apparent relation. While seeming to express an arbitrary organization, it actually grew out of a desire for a materially sensitive expression of poetic form and content. Far from the limit case of a whimsical cataloger, this slim miscellany section was the necessary result of an attempt to divide or organize poetic genres with any illusion of completeness.

This mutual constitution of order and disorder, of mixture and unity, has been occluded by literary histories that reach proleptically toward the agency of individual poets, forgetting the influence of amateur and professional compilers. From the first histories of English poetry, the early modern awareness of Donne's mixed body of work was replaced with an attention to the mixtures of imagery *within* his poems. In 1779, Samuel Johnson identified Donne as the progenitor of a whole "race" of "metaphysical poets," who reveled in "a combination of dissimilar images, or discovery of occult resemblances in things apparently unlike."[23] The fraught, overblown conceit was the characteristic feature of this supernatural poetics in which "the most heterogeneous ideas are yoked by violence together."[24] Donne's poetic mixtures were reduced to violent, chaotic metaphors, particularly in terms of his contradictory handling of the physical body and transcendent soul. In the most influential account of Donne's "metaphysical" poetics, T. S. Eliot described how he "elevates sense for a moment to regions ordinarily attainable only by abstract thought, or on the other hand clothes the abstract, for a moment, with all the painful delight of flesh."[25] In "A Valediction Forbidding Mourning," for example, Donne exposes his lovers' souls to earthly indignities:

> Our two souls, therefore, which are one,
> Though I must go, endure not yet
> A breach but an expansion,
> Like gold to aery thinness beat.[26]

For Eliot, this comparison overturns the proper workings of metaphor. As he puts it, "The figure does not make intelligible an idea, for there is properly no idea until you have a figure." "If gold can be beaten out thin," he asks, "why should not a soul?"[27] The metaphor, in Eliot's estimation, overcomes Donne's description, siphoning attention from the relationship between the two lovers that the conceit ought to express. When the poem spins off into multiple different and even competing conceits, this fluid form actually distracts from the scenario of the lovers' impending separation.

Following accounts like Johnson's and Eliot's, literary history has treated Donne's mixed descriptions as a personal habit of mind, focusing narrowly on single poems as the horizon of interpretation. Studies of poetic form have filtered out how the distributed, collaborative, and contextual poetics of the compilations first elaborated categories for understanding his poetry. Yet Donne himself advocated a much more capacious mode of reading in which forms and scales overlapped, each nudging the other into a creative reading of context. Like the manuscript compiler who quite pragmatically invented a "Miscellanea" section, he was sensitive to multiple kinds of material and semantic connections. In "Obsequyes upon the Lord Harrington the last that dyed," Donne describes "a perfect Reader" who:

> doth not dwell
> On every sillable, nor stay to spell
> Yet without doubt hee doth distinctly see
> And lay together every A and B.[28]

This nimble reader moves surely from point to point. Without pausing to spell, he follows precisely the meaning of what he's reading, grasping the sense and the syllables together. At the same time, he does *see* the individual letters because he recognizes their distinction from each other without agonizing over the process that produces meaning. Reading is here a kind of perception; it happens in an instant when the eye connects letters and the mind simultaneously gleans the meaning carried by those building blocks of signification. Where Eliot and Johnson fret over the violent combination of unlike things, Donne praises a reader who is open to the interpretive potentials of context, swayed by the significance that exceeds the boundaries of discrete semantic units, such that "All the world growes transparent, and I see / Through all."[29]

Donne further developed this model of contextual interpretation in *Devotions Upon Emergent Occasions* (1624), a spiritual meditation on his own mortality prompted by a near fatal bout with an epidemic of fever sweeping London. A passage on the incessant tolling of the death knell hyperbolically extends reading from the level of the letter to the cosmos. Donne figures human life as textual transmission, whereby "all mankind is of one author, and is one volume" and "when one man dies, one chapter is not torn out of the book, but translated into a better language."[30] Divine power is compared to an author with an expansive purview over a whole circuit of book production, use, and storage: "God's hand is in every translation and his hand shall bind up all our scattered leaves again." He will compile a heavenly "library where every book shall lie open to one another."[31] This conceit represents divine power over human progress from creation to salvation as control over multiple moments in the life cycle of a book. Like the "perfect Reader" who identifies the links between letters, God is a compiler or binder who makes it possible to identify the unexpected continuities between the impossibly diverse texts gathered into a single (if limitless) collection.

With this mode of reading that can span the distance from syllables to souls, Donne modeled a habit of mind that was attuned to the collision of distinct kinds of writing within textual collections. Both his poems and the manuscripts in which they circulated demanded an attention to the surprising continuities between unlike things. If mixtures of poets and styles were newly perceptible in the seventeenth century, it was because readers were learning how to understand the poetic significance of juxtapositions that, in earlier printed collections like Gascoigne's *A Hundreth sundrie Flowres* (1573), were understood as traces of the process of compiling. "Miscellany" emerged in this moment as the name for a set of textual attributes that were not apparent until compilers were able to perceive a shifting network of relations and to imagine alternative ways to structure gathered writing. The corollary of that sense of miscellaneity was the desire for a book in which context was harmonious and no longer at odds with the meaning of individual poems.

Donne's Relations

Like Donne's mixed imagery, which drew together unwieldy juxtapositions of things and thoughts, compilations of his scattered verses gestured to a network of ephemeral links in excess of material arrangement. Seventeenth-century approaches to compiling Donne's poetry shed light on the uneven, fitful process through which the arrangement of gathered writing came to be interpreted as authorial, even when a poet had never collected his own work. Confronted with verses from many different moments and on an array of

topics, manuscript compilers articulated new and sometimes arbitrary continuities between poems, using organizational features to stitch discordant
writing into larger volumes. Along the way, the poetry compilation came
into focus as an idealized corpus that was measured against the physical disorder of the text. The value judgments of mixture and disorder actually constituted the conditions of possibility for a coherent form of poetic authorship
that, in its moment of origin, was distinct from how we now understand that
category.

The evolving organization of Donne's poetry holds the history of a *metaphysical* compilation. That is to say, Donne's compilations reflect the process
through which a body of work that was at first experienced materially, in the
connections between poems within particular manuscripts, came to encourage broader, more allusive relations by figuratively loosening the constraints
of arrangement. Beyond attending to the significance of physical context,
compilers gestured to and anticipated an ideal collection that was yet to be
materialized. Practices of active reading like cross-referencing and indexing
imaginatively contorted, twisted, bent, and stretched the material arrangement of poems in order to draw out thematic or stylistic connections between
work that was not at first proximate. Donne's readers turned compilations of
his work into a self-referential circuit, a network of shifting and flexible connections that ultimately forged an idealized bond between the poet's body
and his book. By entangling Donne's metaphors with the arrangement of his
poems, compilers yoked his dissonant images together into an expanded context.[32] While literary histories, like Samuel Johnson's genealogy of a "metaphysical race," have understood this bond as the emergence of a modern
author function, the broadly intertextual reading of his contemporaries
demonstrates that there were multiple other ways of understanding the connection between poems and books. The shifting approaches to compiling
Donne's work instead show how the material arrangement of poems—and
particularly the uneasy mixtures of forms and agencies that those arrangements
contain—helped to fashion the public reputation of this poet.

Manuscript compilers were alert to the echoes between the formal composition of Donne's wild images and the idiosyncratic arrangement of his
gathered texts. The Huntington Library holds a carefully copied manuscript, once owned by Frances Egerton, Countess of Bridgewater, that contains 123 poems by Donne and a smattering of work by other poets.[33] While
the majority of this compilation is in one hand, a second contemporary
scribe has supplemented and corrected the initial transcription in places.

Besides filling in ten blank leaves with additional work, this later hand tried to adjust the connections between poems. One page containing two short love lyrics was initially headed "Doctor Dunnes Sonnets," but this marker of authorship and genre has been roughly obliterated (see Figure 27). Yet the title of the second poem, "Another Sonnett," was left alone, even though that designation of a companion makes little sense by itself. The obliteration was probably meant to correct the attribution, since the first poem, which begins "Love bredd of glannces, twixt amorous eyes," is not consistently taken as Donne's, while the second, which begins "When by thy scorne (o murdress) I am deade," is canonical.[34] But if this intervention was an attempt to correct authorship, it also adjusted the network of conceptual links within this compilation, a manuscript attributed at the opening to "Dr. Donne."[35] By obscuring the "Doctor Dunnes Sonnets" heading, the correcting hand broke the potential link between these love poems. The obliteration transformed what had first been a single-author cluster into a miscellaneous mixture, leaving the basis for comparison as merely the material organization of this manuscript.

If this correction dissolved the organization of the page, such secondary pressure on the material links between poems ultimately had the effect of distinguishing an idealized, immaterial collection of Donne's work from the physical arrangement of any particular manuscript or printed book. The scribe who attempted to unravel the attributions was pursuing a network of contextual links that he saw fanning out across the manuscript—and even across multiple other sources that ought to be included in this large compilation of Donne's work. Under the heading "Another Sonnett," he slipped in the note "see ye beginning of this after ye obsequies," along with a clover symbol that lured the reader forward several dozen leaves to the slight run of poems that he had added to the primary transcription.[36] There, following a matching clover, the correcting scribe included a heading that cross-referenced the earlier poem: "This hath relation to [when by thy scorne O Murdresse &c" (see Figure 28).[37] This "relation" reflects an attention to the continuity of a scenario that spans noncontiguous poems, affiliating texts that are materially divided by the layout of the manuscript. The annotator may well have recognized that he was evoking a secondary connection. He marked the new poem as an addition, including "Sup" for "sup[plement]" in the heading. These annotations chart a reading practice that could leap across pages, collapsing the gap between poems that were distant and, originally, not even in the same compilation.

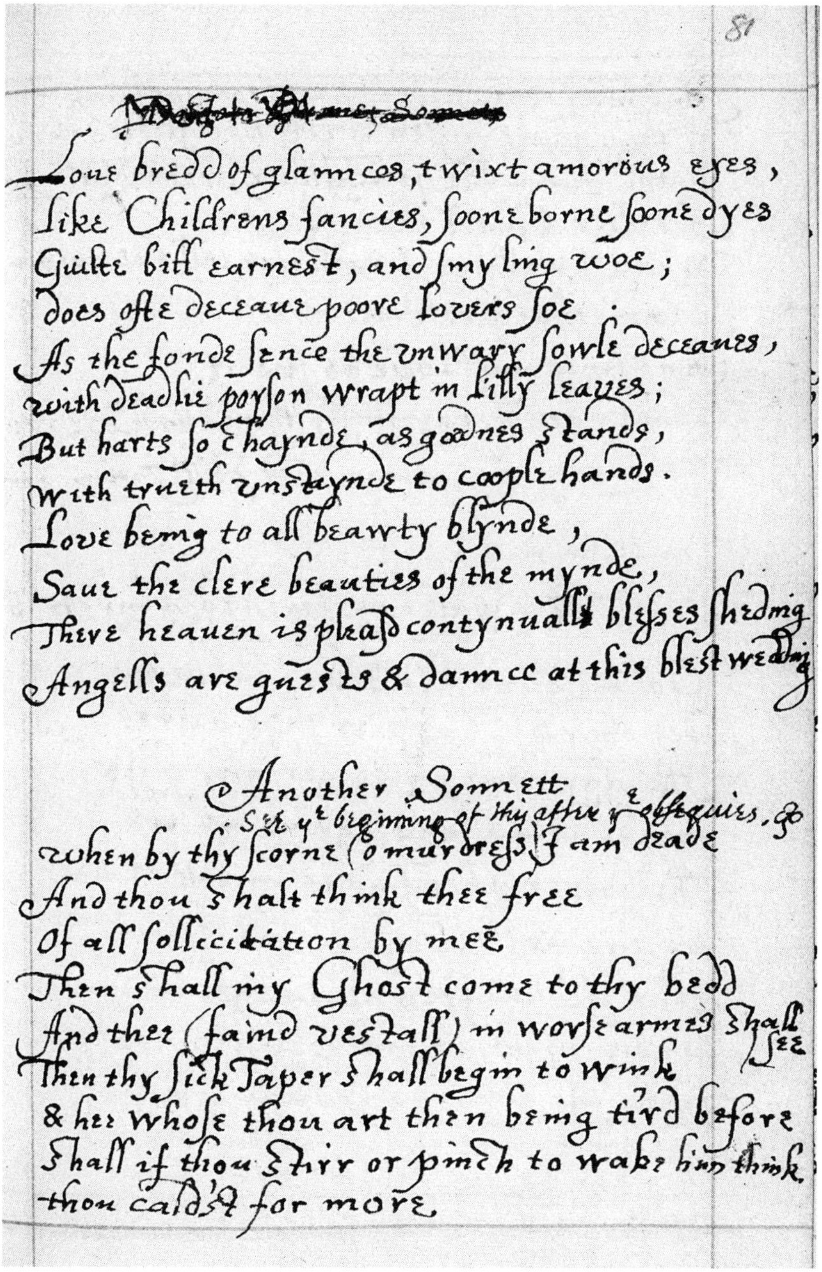

~~Mr John Dunne Sonnets~~

Loue bredd of glannces, twixt amorous eyes,
Like Childrens fancies, soone borne soone dyes
Guilte bill earnest, and smylnig woe;
does ofte deceaue poore lovers Joe.
As the fonde sence the vnwary sowle deceaues,
with deadlie poyson wrapt in lilly leaues;
But harts so chaynde, as goodnes stands,
With trueth vnstaynde to cople hands.
Love beinig to all beawty blynde,
Saue the clere beauties of the mynde,
Theyre heauen is pleasd contynuall blesses shedmig
Angells are guestes & daunce at this blest wedding

Another Sonnett
See ye beginning of this after ye effequirs. go
when by thy scorne (o murdresse) I am deade
And thou shalt thmk thee free
Of all sollicitation by mee.
Then shall my Ghost come to thy bedd
And thee (faind vestall) in worse armes shall see
Then thy sick Taper shall begin to wink
& hee whose thou art then beinig tir'd before
Shall if thou stirr or pinch to wake him thmk,
thou cald'st for more.

Figure 27. Revisions to poem headings in the Bridgewater manuscript, fol. 81r, EL 6893. By permission of the Huntington Library, San Marino, California.

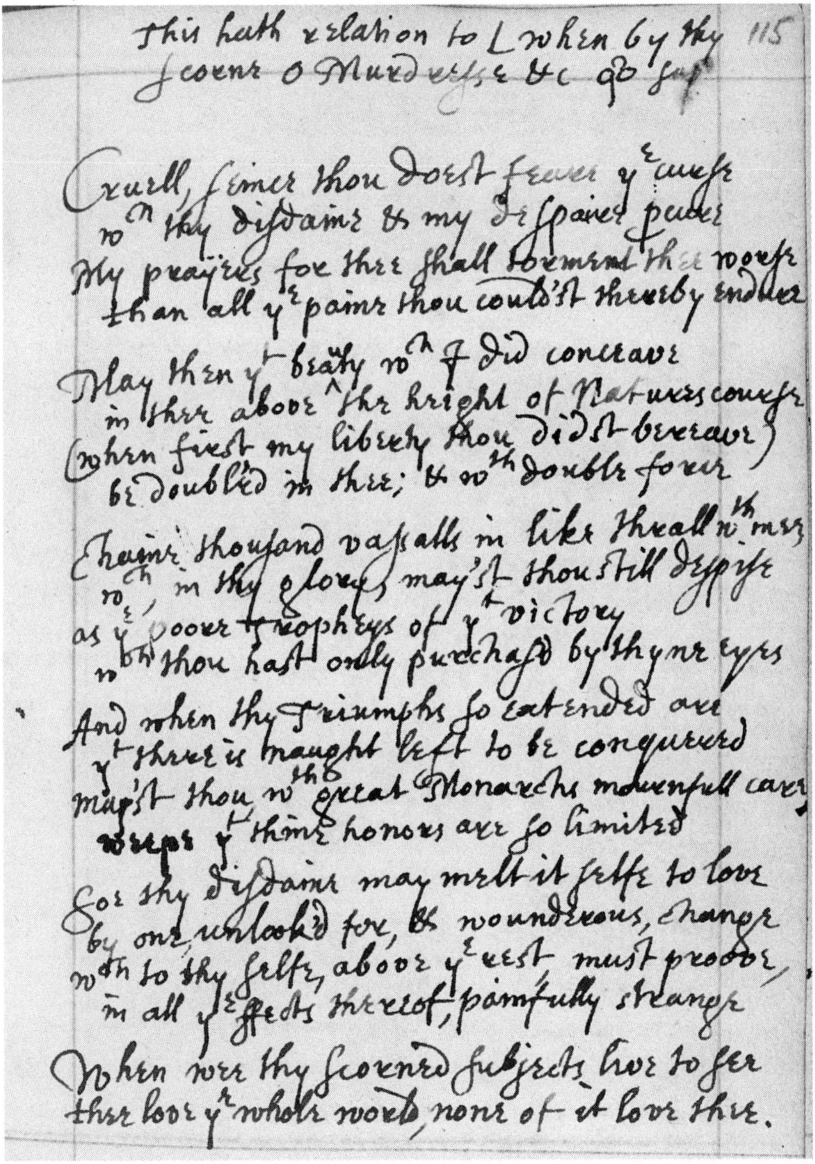

This hath relation to L when by thy 115
scorne O Murdresse &c qd sup

Cruell, since thou doest feare ye curse
wch thy disdaine & my dispaire procure
My prayers for thee shall torment thee worse
than all ye paine thou could'st thereby endure

May then yt beauty wch I did conceave
in thee above the height of Natures course
(when first my liberty thou didst bereave)
be doubled in thee; & wth double force

Chaine thousand vassalls in like thrall wth mee
wch in thy glory, may'st thou still despise
as ye poore trophyes of yt victory
wch thou hast only purchas'd by thyne eyes

And when thy Triumphs so extended are
yt there is naught left to be conquered
may'st thou wth great Monarchs mournfull care
weepe yt thine honors are so limited

For thy disdaine may melt it selfe to love
by one, unlook'd for, & wounderous, change
wch to thy selfe, above ye rest must proove,
in all ye effects thereof, painfully strange

When ere thy scorned subjects live to see
thee love ye whole world, none of it love thee.

Figure 28. "Supplement" that articulates a relation to an earlier poem in the Bridgewater manuscript, fol. 115r, EL 6893. By permission of the Huntington Library, San Marino, California.

Reaching beyond the continuities forged by material arrangement, this mode of reading was imaginatively tracing the thematic links between multiple poems in which speakers condemn their cruel mistresses to a loveless future. In the first example, which the primary scribe had called originally called "Another Sonnett," Donne's speaker visualizes a time when his lover will find herself "neglected" and "bath'd in a colde quicksilver sweat shalt lye / A verier Ghost then I."[38] In the second, which editors no longer attribute to Donne, the speaker predicts that, although she will "love ye whole world, none of it love thee."[39] The correcting scribe was thus working to bend the order of the book, figuratively beginning to produce a corpus defined by complex networks of materials and styles. He found a way for the physical book to encompass, foster, and preserve an intertextual reading process that was integral to defining Donne's body of work.

Beyond an attention to thematic continuity, the somewhat imprecise language of "relation" in the supplementary heading is a provocative expression of how manuscript compilers could accommodate overlapping—and, at times, conflicting—approaches to organizing poems. Flipping between two different places in a manuscript that was compiled in (at least) two different moments, the correcting hand used the material form of the codex to foster a radiating network of connections among the poems. Like Donne's formally mixed images, these "relations" uneasily mingle physical and conceptual continuities, at times joining poems into slight sequences based on proximity, and at others demanding that readers look past the arrangement of the manuscript book. With these mutable bonds, the fits and starts of an unfolding process of compiling became central to an emerging sense of both Donne's body of work and a new kind of authorial poetry book that could express multiple different kinds of relations between discrete pieces of imaginative writing.

The Metaphysical Codex

The conceptual category of the miscellany was a response to attempts to explain the juxtapositions between gathered poems that were not initially related by form, content, or occasion. As the name given to mixed poetry books, the designation of "miscellany" was neither natural nor timeless; it rather developed out of new discourses of poetic authority and the burgeoning manuscript culture of seventeenth-century England. So, how did this new ability to conceptualize mixed compilations impact books devoted to the work of individual poets? Far from a sensitive response to Donne's mixed conceits, collections of his work have been understood as a testament to the increasing distance between the moment in which he composed his poems and their long reception in the seventeenth century and beyond. As Arthur F. Marotti puts it, in the published *Poems, By J. D.*, Donne's writing was uprooted from its origins in "a series of social relationships spread over a number of years," such that the "rich interplay of text and context has been falsified" as a "poetical corpus."[40] This opposition of a social context with an expansive temporality and the false present of the poetic collection is slightly too easy for the uneven mixtures of Donne's work. If the process of gathering Donne's poetry in manuscript and print attenuated the circumstances of composition and transmission, these compilations also hold a history of how his contemporaries treated aspects of poetic form as a rationale for relating individual verses. The social context that remains is of a broad community of early readers. Where scribes had first experimented with the connections between proximate poems, print publishers extended those local links, articulating authorship through an immaterial network of relations that allowed for mixing poetry characterized by diverse occasions, styles, and genres. Authorial presence was a textual effect produced by bringing the writer's poems into contact with other one another, allowing the harsh language from a misogynist love elegy to collide with the request for divine transcendence in a holy sonnet or the plea for patronage in a verse letter. As a result, the arrangement of the printed compilation was shot through with the powerful mixtures of forms within Donne's poems.

In 1633, Miles Flesher printed *Poems, By J. D. with Elegies on the Authors Death* for the publisher John Marriot. This quarto contained Donne's abundant religious, erotic, and satiric poems, but Marriot and Flesher did little to lend an apparent order to the mixture of diverse genres and styles. The book opens with "Metempsychosis," a lengthy narrative that tells the "progresse of a deathlesse soule" passing through multiple transfigured states.[41] This mock epic is followed by nineteen "Holy Sonnets," fourteen brief "Epigrams," and eight Ovidian erotic elegies, before turning with little fanfare to occasional verses for named and unnamed patrons, additional elegies, religious verses, love lyrics, and finally, satires.[42] The uneven distribution of genres suggests that Marriot was working from multiple sources. Rather than consolidating, say, all of the elegies into a single section, he pursued a "strategic miscellaneity" as a way to market Donne's work to a wider reading public that was clamoring to gain access to the manuscript compilations.[43]

Poetic mixture and miscellaneity paradoxically came to sustain Donne's authorship because a shared origin in the hand of a single poet was posited as the grounds for reading his diverse poems together. If the internal, intratextual relations within the collected *Poems, By J. D.* were fraught and tangled, the effect of this inconsistent arrangement was to demonstrate the impressive range of the poet's work. A reader might quickly glean the connection between the love poems "The Indifferent" and "Loves Usury," which were set continuously and on facing pages, but in other instances the relations between poems were more tenuous.[44] "Obsequies to the Lord Harringtons brother / To the Countesse of Bedford," a poem addressed to the "Faire soule" of the named departed, is followed without any explanation by the erotic "Elegie" to an anonymous mistress, beginning "As the sweet sweat of Roses in a Still."[45] To further confuse matters, some poems were left entirely without headings, like the love lyric that begins "Some man unworthy to be possessor," and which would be entitled "Confined love" in later editions.[46] In this mixed compilation, the agency of the author was constructed though a dynamic feedback loop with the disorderly arrangement of the printed book, becoming legible as a rationale for the fits and starts between the often poorly organized poems.

This version of mixed authorship was a way to promote the value of the printed compilation, which might otherwise seem superfluous in a textual culture already inundated with manuscript poetry. *Poems, By J. D.* drew Donne's work into a self-referential circuit, casting the poet's own words— and even his projected image—as a standard for interpretation. A prefatory letter from the "Printer to the Understanders" chastises any reader "who so takes not as he findes it, in what manner soever," and objects to the imperfect and fragmentary nature of this poetic corpus.[47] Marriot is suggesting, first, the extent of Donne's skill, claiming that "a scattered limbe of this Author, hath more amiablenesse in it, in the eye of a discerner, then a whole body of some other."[48] The publisher is saying quite conventionally that the tip of Donne's little finger—or a single line lifted from one of his poems—holds more greatness than the complete body of another poet's work. But this appeal to the discerning eye of the "understander" was also making a more nuanced argument for the consistent quality of all the pieces of the corpus scattered across *Poems, By J. D.* Marriot quotes Donne's own work as evidence of the continuities that span the gathered poetry:

Or, (to expresse him best by himselfe)
  —A hand, or eye,
  By Hilyard drawne, is worth a history
  By a worse Painter made.[49]

A printed marginal note, "In the Storme," gives the source of these three lines as Donne's verse letter to his friend Christopher Brooke. That poem attempts to recreate the speaker's experience for a reader who is physically absent but emotionally so close as to be nearly a second self:

Thou which art I—'tis nothing to be so:
Thou which art still thyself, by these shalt know
Part of our passage.[50]

In citing these lines from a poem that attempts to close the distance between the speaker and his friend, Marriot also closed the distance between readers and the poet. The compiling publisher made Donne's own bid for textual intimacy into a tool for understanding his work as a compiled whole.

The compiling publisher was modeling a careful engagement with Donne's work and, as a result, allowing the book to represent the poet himself. The reference to Nicholas Hilliard is particularly stunning because, in picking up on Donne's allusion to a visual artist known for his portraits, Marriot entered into an extended game of *ut pictura poesis* in which the verbal description of the poetic author was crafted through Donne's own act of intermedia translation. *Poems, By J. D.* would not include an image of Donne until the addition of William Marshall's engraving of his portrait as a youthful lover in the 1635 second edition. Before acquiring this visual emblem of the author, Marriot found another way to gesture to his image, using the powerful illogic of the poet's own mixed figures to ensnare his image within the material design of the printed compilation.

With this set of implicit relations, *Poems, By J. D.* took the arbitrary arrangement of the compiled texts as an opportunity to articulate the stylistic, thematic, and formal connections within Donne's work. This process of thinking across the form and format of the printed book drew on a mode of reading practiced in contemporary encounters with scripture. The Christian codex was "above all *indexical,* a technology that uses bookmarks like prosthetic fingers to take the reader easily from place to place" within the Bible, the psalter, or the prayer book.[51] The individual experience of reading was a dynamic encounter between the compiled texts and the physical affordances of the sacred book. Concordances, indexes, digests, and other tools for navigating scripture supported an active reading practice by helping to make visible for novices the latent textual connections that were already apparent for skilled readers. William Strode, one of Donne's contemporaries, observed the basic humanness of the string bookmark in a poem called "A Register for the Bible":

I am the faithfull deputie
Unto yo[u]r fading memory,
Yo[u]r Index long in search doeth hold,
Your folded wrinckles make bookes olde;
But I the scripture open playne,
And what you heard soone teach againe.[52]

The register string was a bookmark attached to the spine or endband of a codex. Here, Strode was personifying a tool for discontinuous reading that, unlike the tedious index or unsightly dog-eared pages, lends life to the lessons of the Bible because it is movable and leaves no trace of previous readings.[53] The impermanence of the register string helps readers cross-reference multiple different points within the same book while they reconstruct the shifting, immaterial relations between texts.

Just as Strode's speaking bookmark sustains the lessons of scripture, the unruly mixture of genres, styles, and forms within *Poems, By J. D.* solicited a mobile, discontinuous reading practice. Donne's corpus became legible through readers' engagement with a book in which the organizational premise of authorship allowed them to identify relations between poems that were not materially proximate. It was this active reading across the codex that produced a sense of Donne as a poet with a mixed and proleptically metaphysical body of work. In one copy of the 1633 *Poems, By J. D.* now at the Folger, a contemporary reader has added his own index of the topics that spanned the compilation, including headings such as "Delight," "Graves," "Obedience," and "Sinn," along with page numbers for the multiple passages where these phrases appear (see Figure 29).[54] While this indexer focused more on the religious than the erotic poems, his headings did occasionally mingle those topics. The entries "Beauty 38 · 52 · 181·" correspond to the holy sonnet that begins "What if this present were the worlds last night," the love elegy that opens "Here take my Picture, though I bid farewell," and the stanza of "The Litanie" that begins "Through thy submitting all, to blowes."[55] Cross-referencing just a common

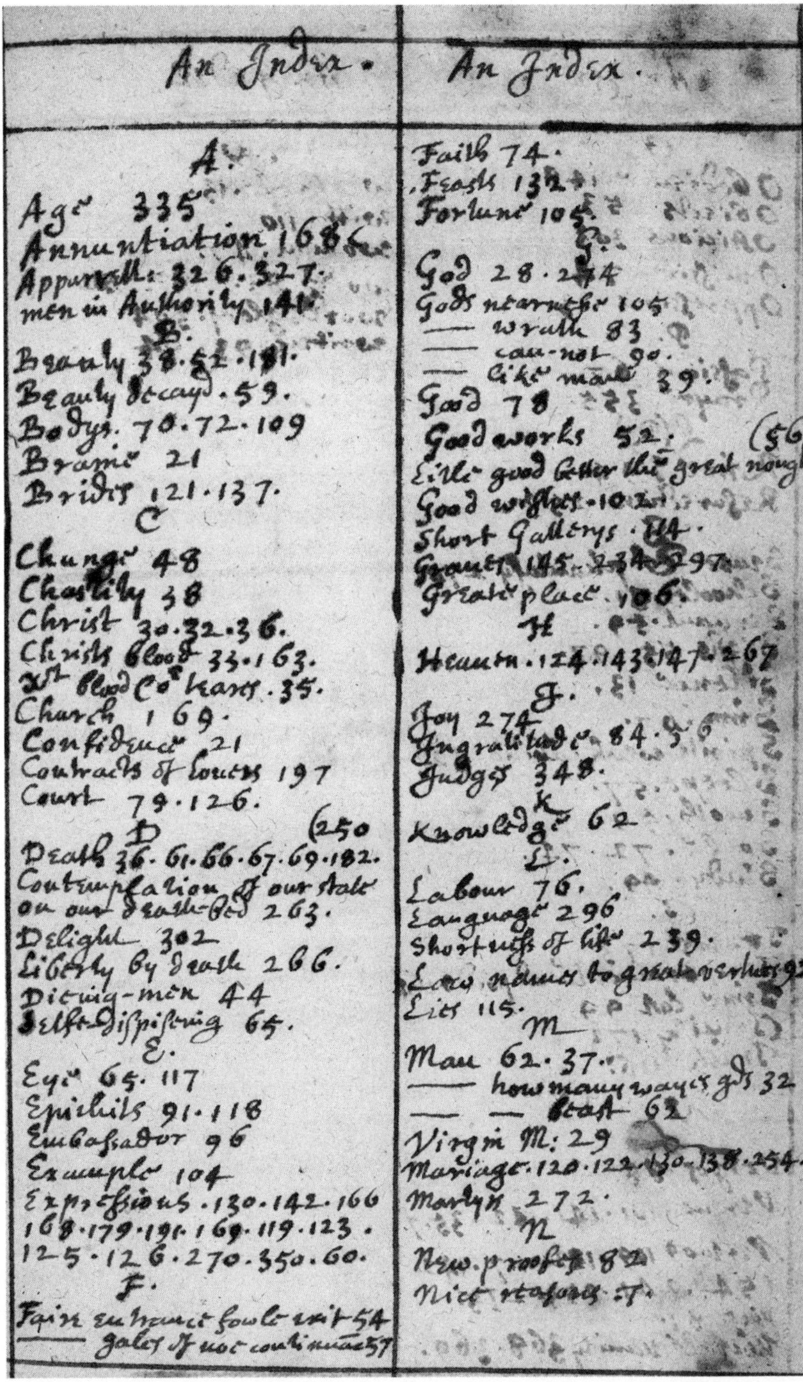

An Index. An Index.

A.

Age 335
Annuntiation 168.
Apparells 326. 327.
men in Authority 141

B.

Beauty 38. 51. 181.
Beauty decayd. 59.
Bodys. 70. 72. 109
Brayne 21
Brides 121. 137.

C

Change 48
Chastity 38
Christ 30. 32. 36.
Christs blood 33. 163.
Xt blood Co heares. 35.
Church 169.
Confidence 21
Contracts of louers 197
Court 79. 126.

D (250

Death 36. 61. 66. 67. 69. 182.
Contemplation of our state
on our death-bed 263.
Delight 302
Liberty by death 266.
Dieing-men 44
Selfe dispiseing 65.

E.

Eye 65. 117
Epistles 91. 118
Embassador 96
Example 104
Expressions .130. 142. 166
168. 179. 191. 169. 119. 123.
125. 126. 270. 350. 60.

F.

Faire entrance foule exit 54
— gates if not continued 57

Faith 74.
Feasts 132.
Fortune 106

God 28. 274
Gods nearness 105
— wrath 83
— can not go.
— like man 39.
Good 78
Good works 52. (56
Litle good better thē great nough[t]
Good wishes 10
Short Gallerys 114.
Grave 115. 234. 297.
Greate place 106.

H

Heauen 124. 143. 147. 267

J.

Joy 274
Ingratitude 84. 36
Judges 348.

K

Knowledge 62

L.

Labour 76.
Language 296
Shortness of life 239.
Easy names to great vertues 92
Lies 115.

M

Man 62. 37.
— how many wayes g[o]ds 32
— beast 62
Virgin M: 29
Mariage. 120. 122. 130. 138. 254.
Martyr 272.

N

New proofe 82
Nice reasons 57.

Figure 29. Handwritten index for John Donne, *Poems, By J. D.* (London: John Marriot, 1633), unsigned, STC 7045, copy 2. By permission of the Folger Shakespeare Library.

word, "Beauty" traces a reading practice that collapsed the material and generic gaps between poems on diverse topics that were spread across nearly 150 pages.

As a relic of a personal engagement with *Poems, By J. D.*, the index treats the material book as both an obstacle and an opportunity for articulating unforeseen poetic connections. It is a material archive of a reading practice that has more often been lost to history. The indexer did not approach Donne's corpus as a set of deracinated poetic fragments, that is, as a jumble of portable quotations that were distinct from the book that held them together. He rather used the affordances of the printed codex to draw out the relations between Donne's diverse poems. The heading "Contemplation of our state on our death-bed 263," appearing under "D," is lifted from a gloss in the margin: "Of the Progress of the Soule / The Second Anniversarie," which Marriot himself had copied from the first edition of that poem in 1612.[56] With this attention to textual formatting, the index archives a spiraling chain of readings. It is a testament to the poetic hermeneutics that was at once enabled by the arrangement particular to this book and an attempt to imagine a collection that could exceed the physical limitations of any single codex.

This shifting relation between the immaterial text and the physical book was at least in part a response to the form and content of Donne's poetry. When Donne's mixed, metaphysical conceits inspired readers to seek out the connections within *Poems, By J. D.*, those immaterial bonds reflected an author who was simultaneously absent and present, a living voice and a ghostly echo, a physical body and an immaterial soul. In the Folger's indexed copy, the annotator placed lines from Donne's letter to the Countess of Bedford in celebration of the New Year under the heading "Verses":

Verse embalmes vertue; and Tombs, or Thrones of rimes
    Preserve fraile transitory fame, as much
    As spice doth bodies from corrupt aires touch.[57]

The poetic line is a technology that seals frail reputation off from the corruption of the world, enshrining virtue in rhymes. Donne goes on to lament the failure of his "short liv'd" verses, because the Lady Bedford is herself so worthy of praise:

    the tincture of your name
Creates in them, but dissipates as fast,
New spirit.[58]

His patroness's example at once necessitates and obviates the fleeting lines that Donne can offer her. This modesty is false, of course, but when Donne wrote this letter there was at least a material truth to his claim for the power of his impermanent, self-consuming lines. In the published compilation, by contrast, those vanishing verses were imperfectly gathered together, reconstituted within and through a dynamic exchange between the immaterial poetic collection and the printed book that Donne himself never thought would come to fruition. *Poems, By J. D.* used the compiled verses to preserve the transitory fame of the poet himself.

A Book of Poems

The print history of Donne's poetry shows how an increasing attention to textual organization transformed the poetics of compiling that *Making the Miscellany* has been tracing across the sixteenth and seventeenth centuries. John Marriot substantially changed the organization of *Poems, By J. D.* when he published a second edition in 1635. He first sorted the work into sections according to genre and then used this arrangement to divide the erotic from the religious poems. The effect of these revisions was to distinguish Donne's efforts as a writer from the labors of the press agents who gathered, organized, printed, and sold his work.[59] In untangling Donne's mixtures, Marriot cast the order of the book as a response to qualities of the writing that were distinct from the circumstances of textual transmission. Abstraction and immateriality were the conditions that enabled poetic authorship, particularly in the posthumous printed books over which Donne himself had no control.[60] This distinction turned a sense of how the printed book might accommodate aspects of poetic form and content into a claim for an ability to represent the life of the author.

Marriot adjusted the structure of the compiled book, connecting and dividing poems by form, speaker, subject, and theme. The revised *Poems, By J. D.* followed the genre categories first elaborated in the O'Flahertie manuscript, a compilation of 169 of Donne's poems and prose works that was copied in October 1632, likely for publication. Marriot received O'Flahertie in the midst of printing the first edition, allowing him to introduce only word-level changes.[61] In 1635, when he did adopt the manuscript's organization by poetic genre, Marriot's innovation was to use the organization of his book to express the hierarchy of the multiple kinds of poems. The organization of the O'Flahertie manuscript oscillated between sections of religious and secular poetry. But the revised *Poems, By J. D.* disentangled those categories, running from the "Songs and Sonets" to the "Epigrams"; "Elegies"; "Epithalamions, or, Marriage Songs"; "Satyres"; "Letters to Severall Personages of Honor"; "Funerall Elegies"; more "Letters," this time in prose; "The Progresse of the Soule"; and finally the "Divine Poems." Following this progress from erotic to spiritual topics, the book closed with a section of "Elegies upon the Author" in which other poets praised the memory of the recently deceased Donne.

The new organization of the 1635 *Poems, By J. D.* outlines a poetic and personal transformation that still informs how we approach Donne today. The movement from erotic to religious poetry within the order of the book, which was maintained in all subsequent seventeenth-century editions, has been taken as an expression of how the rakish young lover turned away from his indiscretions and became the mature dean of St. Paul's.[62] But if Marriot disentangled Donne's mixed writing, the revised *Poems, By J. D.* did not replicate the life of the poet in any simple way. As in so many early modern compilations, the organizational features and structures that now seem authorial were not initially signs of "a story centered" on a "man or writer himself" but rather of his multiple "authorial personae created, bought, and sold by the early modern book trade."[63] Erin A. McCarthy has rightly challenged the sense that the 1635 *Poems, By J. D.* was inspired by biography, showing instead that "details of this narrative" of personal development "remained unsettled" before Izaak Walton's account of Donne's life in 1640, and, in fact, that "the printed book *created*" the now familiar story of redemption.[64] If the 1635 edition settled on authorship as the rationale for the collection, that apparently simple motive had to be distilled out of the much more complex network of agencies that went into printing English poetry.

Marriot found, in the seeming objectivity of genre, a way to supersede the contingent, ad hoc acts of compiling that had contributed to the interpretation of Donne's work in earlier compilations. The abstraction introduced by the genre categories in the 1635 *Poems, By J. D.* is particularly apparent in "Songs and Sonets," the opening section of fifty-six erotic lyrics, many written in idiosyncratic stanzaic forms that are uttered by multiple distinct poetic speakers addressing different lovers. Like the "Miscellanea" designation in the Smith family manuscript considered above, "Songs and Sonets" names the poems that do not fit into the more traditional categories of elegies, satires, and epigrams. This opening section juxtaposes wildly divergent accounts of erotic desire. "Aire and Angels," for instance, is a meditation on a beloved so ethereal as to be deemed a "lovely glorious nothing," but this Neoplatonic poem is immediately followed by "Breake of Day," a bawdy aubade in which the speaker lingers in the beloved's bed: "Why should we rise, because 'tis light? / Did we lie downe, because 'twas night?"[65] With so many conflicting accounts of love and desire, the arrangement of this section works against the consolidation of any narrative sequence or occasional connection between the discrete compositions.

If "Songs and Sonets" mixed poems without regard for continuity of speaker or scenario, the section also worked to divide the erotic verses from the rest of Donne's capacious and varied body of work. The opening section of *Poems, By J. D.* instantiates a new genre category for poems that were composed and read singly, creating a compilation that Donne himself probably never imagined. It is a "miscellanea" section that is given priority—at least in the book, if not in the narrative of a poetic biography that the book presents— for the public persona of a poet who was read as the creator of a mixed and miscellaneous body of work.

In reorganizing *Poems, By J. D.* between the first and second editions, Marriot was following print trends that were first concerned with making compiled poetry legible for future readers. After the 1590s fashion for sonnet books, multiauthor compilations like *Englands Helicon* (1600) and Francis Davison's *A Poetical Rapsody* (1602) were increasingly invested in how material organization might accommodate poetic genre. In 1621, the retitled *Davisons Poems, or A Poeticall Rapsodie* promised on the title page that the book had been "put into a forme more pleasing to the Reader."[66] Where the first three editions of *Poetical Rapsody* were advertised simply as "Containing Diverse Sonnets, Odes, Elegies, Madrigalls, and other Poesies," the revised fourth edition was "Devided into sixe Bookes," with

> The first, contayning Poems and Devises.
> The second, Sonets and Canzonets.
> The third, Pastoralls and Elegies.
> The fourth, Madrigalls and Odes.
> The fift, Epigrams and Epitaphs.
> The sixt, Epistles and Epithalamions.[67]

In the same fashion as the 1635 *Poems by J. D.*, these internal divisions articulated the distinct subsections by lyric genre. The designations from the title page were echoed in the introductory headings, divisional running titles, and explicits marking the end of each internal "book." Far from an overarching order for the entire collection, multiple and coordinating organizational features sponsored local and contextual readings of poems that were related by a common form or mode.

Like *Davisons Poems, or A Poeticall Rapsodie*, Marriot's new organization was not primarily motivated by the chronology of authorship, but he was invested in how a poet's name might promote and sell his book. The volume title *Poems*, which now seems naturally descriptive, was not common when Marriot applied it to Donne's work in the early 1630s. In previous compilations, "poems" had appeared as a title-page description of the multiple components within a volume, particularly for items with a recent history of publication. Robert Southwell's *Moeoniae; or, Certaine excellent Poems and spirituall Hymns* (1595) carried the subtitle *Omitted in the last Impression of Peters Complaint.*[68] Samuel Daniel's *Certaine Small Poems Lately Printed: With the Tragedie of Philotas* (1605) joined his new tragedy to earlier plays, complaints, and narrative verse letters.[69] Daniel's simple title proposed that his reputation was a sufficient lure for potential buyers. Without any mention of the diverse contents of the compilation—most of which was not actually "small poems"—the title page allowed his name to take the place of a description of the work or how it was compiled.

When "Poems" did stand alone as a volume title, it likewise served to elevate the status of the poet by minimizing the interventions made by other agents of the book trade. Michael Drayton's *Poems* (1605) was an omnibus gathering of his earlier books of pastorals, sonnets, histories, and verse letters. The simple title belonged almost exclusively to Drayton. The one other compilation that adopted the designation of "Poems" before the 1630s was William Drummond's, published in Edinburgh in 1614, but Drummond had likely gleaned the title from Drayton, since the two poets had corresponded extensively.[70] Drayton's *Poems* was republished throughout the last twenty-five years of his life, and there were even more editions posthumously.[71] Although the book's contents, order, and even format size changed when it was reprinted, the title minimized those acts of compiling. Where earlier books had described the work of gathering and organizing the diverse poetry, Drayton's *Poems* was sold as "Newly Corrected by the Author," as though the compilation had been produced by the poet himself.[72]

By moving away from the poetics of compiling that had been so important in sixteenth-century printed collections, books called "Poems" contributed to a new sense of how a body of work could express qualities particular to a given author. John Marriot played a crucial role in this development. After Drayton, the next volume to use the title was Marriot's 1630 publication of Frances Quarles's *Divine Poems*, another omnibus compilation of multiple earlier works, including *The Histories of Jonah, Ester, Job* and *Sion's Sonets* and *Elegies*, as well as *An elegie on Dr. Ailmer, not formerly printed*. In 1633, Marriot used the title for Robert Gomersall's compilation, which included a brief run of nine occasional verses; a play, *The Tragedie of Lodovick Sforza*; and a long narrative poem, *The Levites Revenge*. Marriot had published both the play and the narrative poem separately in 1628, but he added a new preface to Gomersall's *Poems* in 1633: "The Booke-seller to the Reader," which explained his financial interest in this reprint. "To praise the worke, were to set my selfe to sale," Marriot wrote, "since the greater its worth is, the more my benefit, & not the Authors." The poet "may have an Ayery, but I a reall profit."[73] The profiteering publisher nonetheless let his language of gain slip from financial to poetic terms: "if ever it were worthy the reading, now the worth of it is multiplied, the whole being perused by the Author, and some, not deformed pieces added, which as they mend the bulke, so they take nothing from the Dignity of the Poem."[74] In lauding the quantity and the quality of the newly expanded compilation, this preface worked to distinguish between the labors of poets and stationers. Crucially, Marriot was not claiming to protect Gomersall from the stigma of print, since the poet had agreed to publication multiple times over. His gambit was instead to divert attention from the shape of this particular compilation to the writer who stood behind it. Marriot concluded by stepping back from his praise for the quality of the poems, admitting that "I beginne to talke rather like a Maker, then a seller of Bookes."[75]

With these projections of authorship, books titled *Poems* were downplaying the process of compiling, minimizing the expressions of material disorder that would have been newly visible to readers who, as a result of the seventeenth-century flourishing of manuscript culture, were learning to gauge the significance of poetic context, juxtaposition, and arrangement. In the case of *Poems, By J. D.*, Marriot recognized the need to explain his novel design of the book. His prefatory letter in the second edition described the elegies written by "some, who had studied and did admire him, to offer to the memory of the Author," and then goes on to defend his unusual placement of these poems of praise: "had I placed them in the beginning, they might have serv'd for so many Encomiums of the Author (as is usuall in other workes, where perhaps there is need of it, to prepare men to digest such stuffe as follows after)."[76] The language of digestion here is a vestigial trace of Senecan floral gathering, an echo of an outmoded practice of textual compiling that Marriot deemed an unnecessary introduction for Donne's poetry. Instead, he wrote, "you shall here finde" the elegies "in the end, for whosoever reads the rest so farre, shall perceive that there is no occasion to use them to that purpose."[77] With this relocation of the usual front matter, utility trumped tradition. Marriot was changing how the layout of his book joined individual poems. *Poems, By J. D.* omitted descriptions of the previous textual life of Donne's work, from the extensive manuscript copies of his secular and religious poetry to the publication of his *Anniversaries* (1611, 1612) commemorating the death of Elizabeth Drury. By erasing this history, Marriot cast the arrangement of the posthumous compilation of Donne's poetry as an extension of the natural and timeless qualities of the poems, which he was a good enough reader to recognize and posit as a model for the material organization of the distinct genres.

The revised *Poems, By J. D.* thus disrupted and obscured the intricate tangle of relations that, in earlier compilations, had been an expression of the indistinct boundary between writing and organizing poetry. These attenuated connections were particularly evident in the final section of "Divine Poems," which drew together Donne's shorter pieces on explicitly religious topics.[78] Like the opening "Songs and Sonets," the concluding section invented a genre category for work that was not necessarily meant to be read together. The form and tone of Donne's religious poetry varies widely, from the fraught turmoil of a nameless, self-doubting speaker in the "Holy Sonnets" to "A Hymne to Christ, at the Authors last going into Germany," which drew on Donne's own travels in 1619. Nor was the variety of these "Divine Poems" given any coherent sequence. "Resurrection, Imperfect," "The Annunciation and Passion," and "Goodfriday, 1613. riding Westward"—three poems celebrating events in the life of Christ—resist the obvious opportunity to follow the chronology of the liturgical year.[79] The poems appeared in this order and with other work mixed in. In the same fashion as the opening erotic lyrics, the concluding "Divine Poems" made organization a matter of shared topic and origin in Donne's hand. The section proposed that the connections between the various pieces were beyond the manipulations of secondary compilers. In the 1635 *Poems, By J. D.*, authorship stepped in to span the gaps between poems that, in much earlier printed compilations, had been filled with elaborate headings and organizational features narrating the contents of the poems.

By situating Marriot's publication of Donne's work within a quite precise moment for the English poetry collection—the instant in which it became possible to call a book *Poems*—I mean to refine the literary history that has treated Donne's work as the inevitable result of experiments that began in Richard Tottel's print shop.[80] Commenting on the use of "Songs and Sonets" as a genre designation for the section of erotic poetry, John T. Shawcross observed "a conscious effort to recall Tottel's Miscellany," even going so far as to propose that "perhaps the 1635 editor was suggesting that Donne's poems were the source of another poetic outpouring."[81] But this teleology of the title *Songes and Sonettes* leaps precipitously across seven decades of innovations in book production and use. Shawcross's literary history compressed the slow development of the discursive categories for naming mixed books, which always trailed the material practices of making them. The miscellany was a textual genre that had to be invented. This conceptual category for poetic mixtures was not a natural or innate way of thinking about compilations, and it could only be retroactively applied to multiauthor books from the sixteenth century *after* the advent of poetry books invested in the persona of the author.

By anachronistically using the miscellany to collapse the distance between Tottel's book and Marriot's, standard literary histories forget the more diffuse legacy of *Songes and Sonettes* within sixteenth- and seventeenth-century poetry compilations. They overlook the regularization of poem titles, the experiments in laying out pages, and the ideals of connecting or dividing poems according to author, topic, or style. It was precisely this gradual evolution of a comprehensive approach to arranging poetry that disguised the approaches to compiling that had been so important for earlier multiauthor collections from publishers including Tottel and Richard Jones. By working to consolidate the independent agency of poets, books called *Poems* cast overt performances of gathering and organization as heavy-handed interventions wrought by agents of the book trade.

Turning *Sonnets* into *Poems*

The bond between poets and their books in *Poems, By J. D.* was taken up as the model for a new kind of English poetry compilation. After the publication of Donne's poetry in three editions in the 1630s, there was a sudden rush of books called *Poems*. At least ten different compilations used the title between 1638 and 1650, first for the work of deceased poets and then more frequently for living ones.[82] These books drew on Marriot's investment in a metaphysical commemoration, taking up the preoccupation with the material and spiritual dimensions of the afterlife in the publication of Donne's work. Thomas Randolph's *Poems with the Muses Looking-Glasse* (1638) contained a letter by Ralph Brideoake "Upon Mr. Randolph's Poems, collected and published after his Death" that described how the poet's "diffusive soule, and fluent parts" had left "Flouds of Wit" for his "dull" earthbound readers: a "bloud of verse" "pump't from our dry Braines, / Sprung like a rushing Torrent from thy Veines."[83] Thomas Beedome's *Poems Divine and Humane* (1641) opens with an astonishing twenty-four pages of elegies lamenting his premature death, including Henry Glapthorne's account of how "Bookes are the pictures of mens lives delineated" and preserve "the living Idea of him that writ it, who though now dead, has a living Monument to his worth."[84] Beedome even celebrated Donne's example, praising "the memory of his honoured friend, Master John Donne, an Eversary" and calling on his "blest dust, and better soule" to "Burst ope thy Cell" and "rise that we / May doe some homage to thy excellency."[85] Donne's legacy was to live on not only in his own work, but also in the outpouring of publications that fashioned themselves after the bibliographic form of his compilation.

One of these living monuments to a recently deceased poet was a book called *Poems: Written by Wil. Shake-speare, Gent.* Published by the young stationer John Benson in 1640, Shakespeare's *Poems* was a small compilation of poetry by an author who, from the mid-seventeenth century on, was better known for his large books of plays.[86] Like other omnibus compilations, Benson gathered and republished work that had already been attributed to Shakespeare in print: the 1612 edition of William Jaggard's *The Passionate Pilgrime* and especially *Shake-speares Sonnets*, a volume of 154 sonnets and "A Lover's Complaint" published by Thomas Thorpe in 1609. Benson drew on the commemorative tradition established in *Poems, By J. D.* For instance, he included a dedicatory verse by Leonard Digges, "Upon Master William Shakespeare, the Deceased Author, and his Poems," that aimed to lend new life to this deceased poet by evoking "the glad remembrance" of "never dying Shakespeare."[87] By transforming Thorpe's quarto of *Shake-speares Sonnets* into a slight octavo called *Poems*, Benson was creating a new market for poetry that had been conspicuously out of date from the moment of its first publication in 1609, more than a decade after the Elizabethan fashion for printed sonnet books.

In republishing Shakespeare's lyrics, Benson went further than most collected *Poems* by fundamentally altering not only the bibliographic format but
also the poetic texture of his sources. Where the pages of the 1609 *Sonnets*
were punctuated by the iteration of fourteen-line quatorzains, those of the
1640 *Poems* were broken up by lyrics of various lengths. Benson conflated
many of the sonnets into larger poetic units, removing the spaces and numbered headings that first separated them in Thorpe's quarto. Some sonnets
remained single, but most became stanzas within longer poems, each containing between two and five "sonnet stanzas." In place of numbers, Benson
assigned each of these "new" poems a title, usually an abstraction of the sonnet group's content. Thus, "In prayse of his Love" identified Sonnets 82 to 85;
"Selfe flattery of her beautie," Sonnets 113 to 115; "Tryall of loves constancy,"
Sonnets 117 to 119; and "Retaliation," Sonnets 78 and 79.[88] Shakespeare's quatorzains did remain visible in 1640, both in the sonnets printed individually
and in new stanzas that preserve the indented couplets from the 1609 collection, but Benson never called any of these lyrics "sonnets." He instead referred to them as "some excellent and sweetely composed Poems, of Master
William Shakespeare."[89]

Regardless of these pervasive emendations to the material and poetic
forms of the 1609 *Shake-speares Sonnets*, I think we should take Benson at his
word, accepting both his designation of these conflations as "poems" and his
title that casts the compilation as a book called *Poems*. The 1640 edition reveals a surprising sensitivity to the organization of the 1609 *Sonnets*: inside of
his new poems, Benson never once disrupted the local order of his source.[90]
Even as Shakespeare's quatorzains were joined together to fashion longer poems, the new units of poetry always placed sonnets that appeared earlier in
the quarto before later ones and, within a given cluster, they only rarely omitted internally sequential sonnets.

The first explanation for why the 1640 conflations reproduced the local
order of the 1609 compilation is that Benson took Thorpe's quarto as a guide
to the poetics of the gathered sonnets, finding meaning in the organization
of his source text. But *Poems* does not demonstrate a totalizing concern with
the sequence of the 1609 *Sonnets*. Like the compilers of Donne's scattered
corpus, Benson used the material form of the codex to change how poems
might be read together. To take one example, in the opening pages of *Poems*,
we can see him move forward through the quarto *within* each of his poems
but turn backward when he starts a new unit. So, the book opens with a conflation of Sonnets 67 to 69 as "The glory of beautie," after which Benson

jumps back to make a poem by combining Sonnets 60 and 63 to 66 as "Injurious Time."[91] Having worked his way through the 60s, Benson again turned back in the sequence of the quarto, printing Sonnets 53 and 54 together as "True Admiration."[92] The effect was to maintain local connections between proximate sonnets without replicating the 1609 edition in any simple way.

Benson's "poems" are a valuable record of how seventeenth-century readers understood the significance of the order and arrangement of a compiled book. By treating his conflated sonnets as any other unit of verse—that is, by attending to the formal composition of poetic structures that were explicitly not authorial—we can begin to recover how this publisher responded to the intellectual work prompted by the quarto's organization. Not all of his conflations function perfectly. Although "A disconsolation" joins Sonnets 27 to 29, the final sonnet stanza does not seem to follow: Sonnets 27 and 28 are an expanded treatment of the sleeplessness brought on by the poet's longing for the beloved, while Sonnet 29 introduces a new meditation on disgrace and solitude.[93] It is precisely in the new poem's attempt to contain such semantic difficulty within a tighter poetic unit that we see how Benson's organization hypothesized and then preserved the effort of interpretation required to get from Sonnet 27 to 29. As conflations like "A disconsolation" retransmitted the shifting connections between sonnets in 1609, the inferential work solicited by this intratextual poetics became the foundation for new poems in the 1640 publication.

Recent scholarship has done much to nuance our understanding of the agency that Benson exercised over Shakespeare's lyrics, in contrast to earlier views that the 1640 *Poems* had badly distorted the *Sonnets*. In the 1944 New Variorum edition of the *Sonnets*, Hyder Rollins concluded that *Poems: Written by Wil. Shake-speare, Gent* was a testament to "Benson's chicanery." In "jumbl[ing] together in a new, unauthorized, and deceptive order all but eight of the sonnets" and "various poems by miscellaneous authors," the 1640 *Poems* has long seemed "a deliberate, and evidently a successful, attempt to deceive readers and to hide the theft" of Shakespeare's lyrics.[94] Against this traditional concern with fraud, Arthur F. Marotti locates the *Poems* in a broader culture of "textual instability," proposing that Benson "creatively exercised his prerogatives as an editor" within the commercial world of "a developing literary institution."[95] Margreta de Grazia further recuperates Benson as an invested reader of Shakespeare's poetry, observing that we can discern in his conflated poems "some principle of coherence that is often highlighted by the title."[96] The softening of Benson's reputation as a rogue publisher has helped us begin to read the 1640 *Poems* as an early canonization

of poetic authorship that "gathered the far-flung pieces of Shakespeare's poetic corpus and gave them a second life."[97] Such defenses of Benson recognize
that his *Poems* refashioned Shakespeare's lyrics according to seventeenth-
century poetic models, particularly Ben Jonson's influential Cavalier mode.[98]

Although accounts of Benson's integrity have allowed us to reconsider
the 1640 *Poems* as an important moment in the long reception of Shakespeare's writing, it is striking that scholars continue to direct their attention
more to how Benson jumbled, fragmented, and distorted Thorpe's quarto
than to how he locally preserved that volume within his reimagined poetry
book. I am sympathetic to readings of the intertextuality of Benson's edition,
but in focusing on miscellaneous mixtures, we have overlooked the explicitly
poetic significance that Benson identified in the organization of the 1609
Sonnets and then carried forward into the 1640 *Poems*. Unlike the manuscript
index in the Folger's copy of the 1633 *Poems, By J. D.*, for instance, Benson's
attention to the organization of the quarto largely prevented him from combining sonnets from opposite ends of the collection, and he never disrupted
the order of constituent sonnets within his new poems, as a reading most
concerned with the aesthetic potential of fragments might. Perhaps like other
readers of *Shake-speares Sonnets*, Benson was always reading whole sonnets
and even clusters of sonnets drawn together by that book's material design.
When features that might seem merely organizational were actively transmit-
ted along with the "poems," Benson was grappling with the 1609 *Sonnets* as a
book, a material form in which textual order contributed to the aesthetics of
Shakespeare's poetry.

Benson's response to the compiled poetics of the *Sonnets* is evidenced
particularly well by "Magazine of beautie," a new poem that traces a dynamic
account of the beloved's profligate self-use. In this conflation of Sonnets 4 to
6, all three "sonnet stanzas" argue that the beloved should recognize the
value of his beauty and consequently that he should preserve it.[99] The new
poem opens by questioning the beloved's hoarding of himself:

> Unthriftie lovelinesse why dost thou spend,
> Upon thy selfe thy beauties legacy?
> . . . .
> Then beautious niggard why doost thou abuse,
> The bountious largesse given thee to give?
> Profitles Usurer, why dost thou use
> So great a summe of summes yet can'st not live?[100]

"Unthriftie loveliness," "beautious niggard," "Profitles Usurer": this series of paradoxical descriptions multiplies the qualities attributed to the beloved, reflecting the poet's inability to isolate a singular representation. Later in the same sonnet stanza, the speaker animates these multiple images, accusing the beloved of self-abuse in a scene of solipsistic commerce: "For having traffike with thy selfe alone, / Thou of thy selfe thy sweet selfe dost deceive."[101]

By incorporating this new "Magazine" into his book of *Poems*, Benson filtered Shakespeare through the predominant model for seventeenth-century poetry collections. Along the way, he subordinated his own interventions as a compiling publisher to a newly conventional performance of authorship. The new poems grew out of the presumption that the speaker and his beloved were locked in an erotic scenario that spans the gaps between sonnets. Given this continuity, it is especially noteworthy that the rapidly proliferating images of the beloved in the first sonnet stanza of "Magazine of beautie" are so often addressed with rhetorical questions because the remainder of the poem disrupts this strategy. Where the first sonnet stanza revolves around anxious queries, the second and third offer answers, even as the beloved comes into focus as a single "substance."[102] Sonnet 5 proposes that "summers distillation," a "liquid prisoner pent in walls of glasse," might preserve "beauties effect" even after death, when "beautie were bereft." And this alchemy continues in the final sonnet stanza, which entreats the beloved to "Make sweet some viall; treasure thou some place."[103] Across the new poem, the beloved, who has been destabilized into multiple paradoxical selves in stanza 1 (Sonnet 4), is transfigured into a more durable object of value, preserving "beauties treasure ere it be selfe kil'd."[104] Organized around metaphors that quantify the worth of a singular (and single) beloved, "Magazine of beautie" gathers and increases this valuation, producing a formal expression of the meaning that Benson found, not in any one poem, but in the local order of his source.

By removing the spaces between the three sonnets, subordinating them as stanzas under the rubric of the "magazine," Benson created a single poem that accretes the "bountious largesse" alluded to in the first sonnet stanza. This consolidation is supported by his title, a strategic amplification of the thematics of Sonnets 4 to 6.[105] A word new to English in the sixteenth century, "magazine" refers to a location that contains and protects wealth, a "storehouse."[106] Benson's conflation operates as a storehouse for the beloved, with the new poem protecting his beauty as a function of its longer form. A number of passages in "Magazine" play with the relation between "use" and "usury," each time dismissing claims about the potential misuse of value. Increase is permitted because it ensures the beloved's future presence: "Ten times thy selfe were happier then thou art, / If ten of thine ten times refigur'd thee."[107] We can see how the shared endeavor of Sonnets 4 to 6 might have inspired Benson to call this poem a "magazine." Like these generations spawned by the poet's imagination, "Magazine of beautie" multiplies the images of the beloved containable in a single poem, drawing together in one magazine what was at first spread across multiple sonnets.

Through this gathering that attends to the presumed agency of the author, not the secondary compiler, "Magazine" reveals how closely Benson followed the local order of the quarto, even when that principle of organization risked destabilizing the new unit of verse. It is a critical commonplace that Sonnets 5 and 6 are companions. In an evaluation that almost validates the agency that Benson exercised in his conflations, Stephen Booth finds that Sonnets 5 and 6 are "logically linked," in fact, related so "tightly . . . as practically to make [Sonnet 6] the second half of a 28-line unit."[108] Both sonnets explore how distillation might preserve the beloved. Sonnet 5's couplet announces that "flowers distil'd though they with winter meete . . . / . . . their substance still lives sweet."[109] Sonnet 6 begins with a rhetorical and temporal hinge: "*Then* let not winters wragged hand deface, / In thee thy summer ere thou be distil'd."[110] The third sonnet stanza of "Magazine" thus applies the abstractions of the second to the specific issue of the beloved's perpetuity.

But "Magazine of beautie" also includes Sonnet 4, a poem that attacks the beloved's self-hoarding with a different poetic logic: by multiplying rather than distilling him. Initially, this semantic gap makes the new poem slightly unsteady, as the reader struggles to discern the connection between the first and second sonnet stanzas. This "Magazine" generates a kind of retrospective coherence, asking the reader to recall the opening gambit when the language of usury and legacy reappear at the end. In the final sonnet stanza, we hear "That use is not forbidden usury, / Which happies those that pay the willing lone." The final couplet concludes with a gesture to posterity: "Be not selfewil[le]d for thou art much too faire, / To be deaths conquest and make wormes thine heire."[111] Taken together, these lines refer back to the couplet concluding the first sonnet stanza (Sonnet 4): "Thy unus'd beautie must be tomb'd with thee, / Which used lives th'executor to be."[112] With this return to "use" as a way to escape the ravages of death, "Magazine of beautie" shows how the quarto's local clustering of Sonnets 4 to 6 might have led readers like Benson to identify a relation between textual order and poetic meaning.

Even as this new poem initially seems somewhat disjointed, it contains a record of Benson's active reading across textual gaps, taking the mobile resonances between sonnets as integral to the poetics of Shakespeare's compiled verses.

By reading Benson's conflations as "poems," we can see how the compiling publisher was surprisingly responsive to the organization of the 1609 quarto, preserving a hidden but active relation between poetic effects and textual order. He presumed a local sequence for sonnets that, in their first printing, were much less securely tethered together. "Magazine of beautie" also suggests that this very sensitivity with the structure of *Shake-speares Sonnets* distorted the form that new poems took in the 1640 edition. Benson drew the sonnets together in a way that was at once an alert reading of their arrangement in the quarto and an intensification of those intratextual poetics so literal as to diminish the semantic gap between Sonnets 4 and 5. *Poems: Written by Wil. Shake-speare, Gent.* is a testament to how the larger form of the printed book could place pressure on individual poems, since as subsequenced sonnets grew into longer and irregular verses, poetic and erotic structures were themselves produced by the process of textual transmission.

Shakespeare After Donne

Shakespeare's 1640 *Poems* is a testament to the imprecise line between poetic reading and the material practices of making books, even in the moment when multiple and distinct textual agencies began to be consolidated around the figure of the individual author. I want to offer Benson's literal reading of the arrangement of the 1609 *Shake-speares Sonnets* as evidence for how commercial publication helped consolidate literary status and value. By transforming the outmoded *Sonnets* into a book titled *Poems*, Benson was updating Shakespeare's verses for a new moment in literary history, and he was doing so through Marriot's model of posthumous commemoration in *Poems, By J. D.* This refashioning was at once textual and poetic. In his letter "To the Reader," the publisher claimed an evident simplicity to Shakespeare's poems: "in your perusall you shall finde them Seren, cleere and eligantly plaine, such gentle straines as shall recreate and not perplexe your braine, no intricate or cloudy stuff to puzzell intellect, but perfect eloquence."[113] As in "Magazine of beautie," this picture of eloquence could not be further from the experience of reading the 1609 *Sonnets*, where the erotic scenario overflowed individual poems and worked against the regularity of the sonnet form. Where the earlier sonnet book demanded effort from readers who sought out the connections between any particular cluster of verses, in "Magazine of beautie" and other new poems, Benson tamed Shakespeare's semantic difficulty by combining sonnets into more predictable lyric units.

This chapter concludes by showing how this smoothing or calibrating of poetic and textual craft was sustained by the larger form of *Poems: Written by Wil. Shake-speare, Gent.* Broadening my claim that Benson preserved aspects of the quarto within his new edition, I show that he also read the outmoded sonnet book through the more contemporary example of *Poems, By J. D.* Although Donne's knotty, mixed poetics are distinct from Benson's interest in Shakespeare's serenity, I argue that in drawing sonnets together into longer poems, the stationer was using the paradigm of commercial authorship created for Donne by Marriot to unite a diverse variety of poetic genres and forms within a single book. Benson's imitation of *Poems by J. D.* is a testament to that volume's influential bibliographic legacy, which not only informed how Shakespeare's poetry was organized for print but also how poetic style was interpreted at multiple moments in the seventeenth century. Poetry exceeds the material form of the book, even as literary form preserves the complex interactions of the people and things that produced it.

There are, of course, reasons to question Donne's influence on Benson's book, particularly as a model of eloquence and poetic serenity.[114] David Baker has proposed that Ben Jonson's restrained and classicizing Cavalier mode offers a better model than Donne for the 1640 *Poems: Written by Wil. Shake-speare, Gent.*[115] There is much to recommend Baker's view. Jonson played a profound role in the mid-seventeenth-century publication of poetry and, specifically, in Benson's career. In the same year as Shakespeare's *Poems*, Benson published *Ben Jonson's Execration against Vulcan* and *Q. Horatius Flaccus: His Art of Poetry, Englished by Ben Jonson.*[116] Further, the Cavalier mode was often self-consciously composite, like Benson's claims for presenting a Shakespeare cast in the image of Jonson's restraint. Thomas Carew, for instance, wrote in praise of Donne's rough lines, but in an explicitly Horatian mode, thus showing his debt to Jonson.[117]

Inside this tangled network of influences on Shakespeare's 1640 *Poems*, Benson was taking seriously the mixture of agencies responsible for writing poems and organizing printed books. Although the stationer expressed a desire for a stylistic synthesis of Jonson and Shakespeare, his ambition was manifested through a textual synthesis of Shakespeare and Donne that ended up producing its own stylistic effects.[118] If Benson's stated preference for plain verse evokes a Jonsonian model for Shakespeare's individual poems, nevertheless Jonson's model is less prominent if we think about the features that made the 1640 *Poems* legible as a compilation. Recall that Jonson's ambitious *Workes* (1616) was revolutionary not for containing his poetry, but for presuming to include his drama. Plays are missing in *Poems: Written by Wil. Shake-speare, Gent.*, where the only sense we get of Shakespeare as a dramatist is in Leonard Digges's prefatory poem, which explicitly contrasts Shakespeare to Jonson.[119] It opens, "Poets are borne not made," countering Jonson's famous "a good *Poet's* made, as well as borne," and then goes on to attack "needy Poetasters" and "tedious *Catilines*," ultimately calling *Sejanus* "irksome."[120] Of course, Benson could not have included the plays because those rights were tied up in two recent editions of the folio *Mr. William Shakespeares Comedies, Histories & Tragedies* (1623, 1632). Equally, *Venus and Adonis* (1593) and *Rape of Lucrece* (1594) were still being actively reprinted. Left with the possibility of publishing only Shakespeare's nonnarrative poetry, Benson needed a model for this kind of book and neither Jonson's multigeneric folio nor Shakespeare's dramatic folio could adequately fill this role.

In identifying Shakespeare as the author of a posthumous *poetry* collection, Benson was fitting him into the textual paradigm that was consolidated not around Jonson but around Donne. *Poems, By J. D.* was printed three times in the decade before *Poems: Written by Wil. Shake-speare, Gent.*, and it would have been difficult to hear Benson's title without connecting it to Donne. Benson also followed the broader order of *Poems, By J. D.*, giving work by other poets, some of them mourning Shakespeare's death, at the end of *Poems: Written by Wil. Shake-speare, Gent.* Three elegies—one by Milton from the Second Folio of Shakespeare's plays, one by an unknown author, one by "W. B." (William Basse)—were spliced in between the verses attributed to Shakespeare and a concluding section titled "Addition of some Excellent Poems . . . By other Gentlemen," contemporary poets including Jonson, Carew, Francis Beaumont, Robert Herrick, and William Strode.[121]

More than just adopting the conceptual framework for a book called *Poems*, Benson lifted multiple organizational features from Marriot's compilation. Like *Poems, By J. D.*, Shakespeare's *Poems* opens with a portrait of the youthful author by William Marshall. Both poets are depicted with an arm cocked across their torsos and clutching an iconic implement of their trade, a sword in Donne's case and a laurel in Shakespeare's.[122] In the same way, the *mise-en-page* of Donne's *Poems, By J. D.* offers an alternative source for an aspect of Shakespeare's *Poems* that seems explicitly "Cavalier." Throughout the 1640 volume, every page was headed with a running title that inserts a diaeresis over the vowels in *Poëms*. Although this heading appears neither in Jonson's folio, nor in his two shorter volumes that Benson published in 1640, "Poëms" runs on every page of Donne's 1633 collection and on every verso page of the subsequent editions.[123] One of the most apparently classicizing details of Benson's book thus looks more like an instance of textual impersonation—and of impersonating Donne rather than Jonson.

While the influence of *Poems, By J. D.* on Shakespeare's *Poems* is most visible as a confluence of organizational features, his bibliographic example had an effect on the new units of poetry that unevenly conflated the earlier sonnets. This is, of course, not to say that Benson necessarily set out to imitate Donne's style; but in the process of framing his compilation of Shakespeare's poetry in the bibliographic model of *Poems, By J. D.*, Benson discovered how to make longer, more semantically contained lyrics. A complex poetics followed as a result of joining together groups of Shakespeare's already difficult sonnets.

If Benson approached both Shakespeare's sonnets and Donne's example of authorship through the organization of their respective collections, preserving the local order of the 1609 quarto within the reimagined *Poems*, his conflations were also attuned to the internal structures of Donne's verses. My case is the poem that Benson called "A Valediction" (see Figures 30 and 31). As with the volume title *Poems*, the evident anachronism of "A Valediction" sheds light on how Benson updated Shakespeare's poetry thirty years after its initial publication.[124] The distinctly mixed, metaphysical handling of erotic time in Donne's valedictions inspired Benson to deviate from his habitual treatment of the quarto's local clusters of sonnets: this new poem contains Sonnets 71, 72, and 74, but not a trace of Sonnet 73. Through this omission, the conflated "Valediction" registers the afterlife of the Elizabethan sonnet book within the greater formal variety of mid-seventeenth-century poetry books.[125] Breaking down the iterative repetition of form and content in the 1609 *Sonnets*, the 1640 *Poems* instead unfolds as a compilation of discrete instants, a continuous lyric present that never fully reconciles the multiple temporalities Shakespeare explores in the sonnets.

As a linguistic and poetic invention that postdated the 1609 *Shake-speares Sonnets*, the valediction is a hallmark of Donne's mixed poetics. The term appeared consistently in manuscript and print as the title for his poems that meditate on how, in the instant of taking leave, the poet allows his future

Poëmes.

Doſt thou deſire my ſlumbers ſhould be broken?
While ſhadowes like to thee doe mocke my ſight?
Is it thy ſpirit that thou ſend'ſt from thee
So farre from home into my deeds to pry,
To finde out ſhames and idle houres in me,
The ſcope and tenure of thy Iealouſie?
O no, thy love though much, is not ſo great,
It is my love that keepes mine eye awake,
Mine owne true love that doth my reſt defeat,
To play the watch-man ever for thy ſake.
　For thee watch I, whilſt thou doſt wake elſe-where,
　From me farre of, with others all too neare.

A Valediction.

NO longer mourne for me when I am dead,
Then you ſhall heare the ſurly ſullen bell
Give warning to the world that I am fled
From this vile world with vildeſt wormes to dwell:
Nay if you read this line, remember not,
The hand that writ it, for I love you ſo,
That I in your ſweet thoughts would be forgot,
If thinking on me then ſhould make you woe,
O if (I ſay) you looke upon this verſe,
When I (perhaps) compounded am with clay,
Doe not ſo much as my poore name rehearſe;
But let your love even with my life decay.
　Leaſt the wiſe world ſhould looke into your mone,
　And mocke you with me after I am gone.

D 2

Poëms.

O Leaſt the world ſhould taske you to recite,
What merit liv'd in me that you ſhould loue
After my death (deare love) forget me quite,
For you in me can nothing worthy prove,
Vnleſſe you would deviſe ſome vertuous lye,
To doe more for me then mine owne deſert,
And hange more prayſe upon deceaſed I,
Then nigard truth would willingly impart:
O leaſt your true love may ſeeme falſe in this,
That you for love ſpeake well of me untrue,
My name be buried where my body is,
And live no more to ſhame nor me, nor you.
　For I am ſhamd by that which I bring forth,
　And ſo ſhould you, to love things nothing worth.
But be contented when that fell areſt,
Without all bayle ſhall carry me away,
My life hath in this line ſome intereſt,
Which for memoriall ſtill with thee ſhall ſtay.
When thou revieweſt this, thou doſt review,
The very part was conſecrate to thee,
The earth can have but earth, which is his due,
My ſpirit is thine the better part of me,
So then thou haſt but loſt the dregs of life,
The prey of wormes, my body being dead,
The coward conqueſt of a wretches knife,
To baſe of thee to be remembred.
　The worth of that, is that which it containes,
　And that is this, and this with thee remaines.

Figure 30. Sonnet 71 as the first stanza of "A Valediction" in William Shakespeare, *Poems: Written by Wil. Shake-speare, Gent.* (London: John Benson, 1640), sig. D2r, STC 22344 copy 6. By permission of the Folger Shakespeare Library.

Figure 31. Sonnets 72 and 74 as the second and third stanzas of "A Valediction" in William Shakespeare, *Poems: Written by Wil. Shake-speare, Gent.* (London: John Benson, 1640), sig. D2v, STC 22344 copy 6. By permission of the Folger Shakespeare Library.

absence to color his present relation to the beloved. This consistent repetition by seventeenth-century compilers worked to consolidate the valediction as a poetic genre. Donne's "A Valediction: Of Weeping" begins by begging "Let me pour forth / My tears before thy face whilst I stay here."[126] With this plea for the beloved to witness the sadness that will fill his time away, the poet collapses present and future, demanding that the current conversation be seen only in light of the coming separation. The rest of the poem spins a fantasy in which the tears are globes that might drown both lovers if the poet's watery orbs happen to collide with those of the beloved. It concludes with a claim for how such protracted emotional displays threaten the lovers' current union: "Since thou and I sigh one another's breath, / Whoe'er sighs most is cruellest, and hastes the other's death."[127] The valedictory speech unites the lovers' experience of absence and presence in a single unit of verse, concluding with the ultimate separation, a final image of death.

In "A Valediction: Forbidding Mourning," Donne's metaphysical collapse of time—which pulls together presence and absence, life and death—produces a strange causality in which a poetic imagination of the future causes effects in the present. Benson's "A Valediction" troubles temporal boundaries in precisely the same way. In the conflated poem, the speaker repeatedly attempts to communicate from beyond the grave by producing constructions filled with hypotheticals: statements about the future that nonetheless operate in the present. The first sonnet stanza, the quarto's Sonnet 71, announces that if the beloved is reading this verse, the poet must already be dead and, paradoxically, should be forgotten:

> if you read this line, remember not,
> The hand that writ it, for I love you so,
> That I in your sweet thoughts would be forgot.[128]

In Sonnet 72, the conditional "ifs" become more emphatic warnings—"Least," Unlesse," "so should you"—of how the beloved should fear the poet's posterity, so that he is not "shamd by that which I bring forth."[129] The poet in fact demands "After my death (deare love) forget me quite," so that the beloved will not be forced to recount his memory to others: "Least the world should taske you to recite."[130] While Sonnet 74 removes the conditionals that qualify the earlier sonnet stanzas, it is still located at the very limits of future life: "But be contented when that fell arest, / Without all bayle shall carry me away."[131] Like Donne's complex metaphysical conceit, the mixed time of this conflation unites the lovers' experience of absence and presence in the transitional instant of the valediction. The poem speaks from a future that is located beyond the current moment, imagining itself as an artifact of the poet's posthumous presence: "The worth of that, is that which it containes, / And that is this, and this with thee remaines."[132]

Like "Magazine of beautie," "A Valediction" condenses meanings that originally unfolded across a cluster of sonnets, contracting the extended temporality of love (and of its leavings) into a single instant of departure.

Although this poem follows the local order of the quarto, giving Sonnet 71 and then Sonnets 72 and 74, Donne's neologism and, most important, the poetic model of desire implied by that word in the governing title led Benson to omit one of the sonnets in the sequence. I take it that this omission was required by the characteristic temporality of the valediction. Contrary to the provisional futurity of the other three sonnet stanzas, which contract the temporal gap between present and future, Sonnet 73 more simply sketches a scenario in which the poet embodies an extended present. His aging body is described with metaphors that pause multiple instances of waning—of a year, a day, a fire:

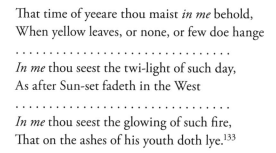

> That time of yeeare thou maist *in me* behold,
> When yellow leaves, or none, or few doe hange
> . . . .
> *In me* thou seest the twi-light of such day,
> As after Sun-set fadeth in the West
> . . . .
> *In me* thou seest the glowing of such fire,
> That on the ashes of his youth doth lye.[133]

With "in me" appearing in each quatrain, the triply repeated call to recognize that the poet's body illustrates the instant in which age eclipses youth is uttered in a resolute present tense, one determined to freeze these transitions. Where the three sonnets in "A Valediction" imagine a moment after the poet's death—"When I (perhaps) compounded am with clay"—his aging body is necessarily present in Sonnet 73, standing as an emblem for the various images of waning.[134] Each quatrain contains a tiny, constrained exploration of encroaching death, with naked boughs replacing leaves, "blacke night" entombing day, and the fire's ashes suffocating any remaining flames. Most bravely—and perhaps most blindly—the final couplet of Sonnet 73 asserts that "this thou percev'st," the frozen progression of time, is actually what makes the poet desirable: it "makes thy love more strong, / To love that well, which thou must leave ere long."[135]

That Benson's "Valediction" omits all of this brave posturing from Sonnet 73 suggests how he correlated poetic and material structures, intertwining features that were at once Shakespeare's and Thorpe's, Donne's and Marriot's. To that extent, it is difficult to discern where a practice of compiling ends and literary reading begins. Learning from Donne how lyric length might reflect the erotic scenario, Benson created units of poetry that could contain the desire that had originally unfolded across multiple sonnets in the quarto. In this case, Sonnet 73 would have inserted the poet's waning body into a posthumous speech, thereby interrupting the consistent time that Benson's conflation required. The solution was clear. Benson leapt across to Sonnet 74, allowing his imaginative discovery of a poetic form distinctly associated with Donne, but which was only a primordial cluster in the 1609 publication, to draw him across an intervening verse just as he more often read across the gaps between sonnets. By removing Sonnet 73 from "A Vale-diction," Benson stabilized the speaker's voice, providing a uniform perspective that operated only from beyond the grave rather than oscillating between the hypothetical future and an expanded present. Benson's arrangement of the 1640 *Poems* enacted the experience on which this cluster of poems medi-tates: life after the poet has died. He cut the poet's voice from the present moment and, as promised in the first sonnet stanza, allows us to hear him speak only as an absent presence.

Reading the conflated "Valediction," we attribute the lines to the poetic speaker, the posthumous voice begging the beloved to forget him: "if you read this line, remember not, / The hand that writ it." But taking this poem seriously also requires us to forget the operations of another hand, that of the professional compiler who arranged this printed book. The power of "A Vale-diction" derives from the scenario that Benson imaginatively discovered in the 1609 *Sonnets* and amplified within his own textual fiction of a new kind of poetry collection. I have singled "A Valediction" out as a product of both Benson's attention to the 1609 text and his slightly presentist reading of Don-ne's paradigm because it resists modern critical tendencies to overlook the complex, tangled agencies that come to rest within poetic structures. The stunning anachronism of this poem made it possible for Shakespeare to pen (or, more precisely, to have penned) a valediction. This strange hybrid poem uncovers a literary history driven by books themselves.

More than just fostering a mixed and metaphysical time within "Shake-speare's" lyrics, Benson's 1640 *Poems* unsettled neat chronologies of poetic influence. If "A Valediction" manufactures a false fidelity to the poet's hand, it also attempts to cast Shakespeare as an author who could withstand the passing of time and literary fashions. In Digges's prefatory verse, "The De-ceased Author, and his Poems," Zachary Lesser and Peter Stallybrass have read a new disdain for habits of textual compiling. Digges praised Shake-speare for a natural, unlearned "wit" that was distinct "from the commonplace tradition" and from "any relation at all to knowledge acquired through reading." Unlike Jonson's belabored classicisms, *Poems: Written by Wil. Shake-speare, Gent.* made it possible for "an emergent vernacular literature to reproduce [a] timeless and impersonal authority" without relying on the "crutch" of commonplacing.[136] In fashioning Shakespeare around Donne's paradigm of absent authorship, Benson reinforced the agency of the deceased poet but also articulated this public identity through the shifting relations between gathered poems, lending value to the poetic connections over which neither Shakespeare nor Donne had any control.

This chapter has accounted for the development of the poetry miscellany by drawing on innovative authorial compilations—books with the title *Poems*—using a new understanding of the connections between poems to illuminate the history of a textual genre defined by an irreducible and irresolvable variety. The consolidation of compiled forms that simultaneously embraced and spurned authorship speaks, ultimately, to the decline of a poetics of compiling across the seventeenth century. The material arrangement of poetry books came to be taken quite naturally as an expression of their contents, not of how they were made. Yet if the interventions of secondary compilers were lost from sight, those practices nonetheless remained present within the literary histories of authorship that came to stand in their place. These books condense a loose and protracted network of circulation into the most personal expressions of poetic affect.

Taken together, the trajectory from Donne's uncollected lyrics to the multiple posthumous editions of *Poems, By J. D.* and the derivative *Poems: Written by Wil. Shake-speare, Gent.* suggests that, even in the moment in which England begins to consolidate a vernacular poetic authorship, the formal features that seem to point directly to the poet's own hand are expressions of how his work was read and understood at multiple moments in time. Like the mixed temporality of Donne's valedictions, which allow the future to act within the lyric present, this is a literary history that was unfolding in an extended moment. Authorship was constituted through the influence that compilations could exercise retrospectively on poetic form, even decades—or centuries—after the instant of composition.

Coda

Shakespeare's Miscellanies: The Poetic
History of the Book

Making the Miscellany has argued that the material design of early modern printed books was an active response to poetic form. Throughout this book, I have traced the textual formations that were obscured by the seventeenth-century invention of the miscellany as a conceptual category that made mixed compilations seem natural and timeless. The project of making poetic diversity visible, in other words, rendered multiple practices of compiling invisible. The organizational features and arrangements that *Making the Miscellany* has discussed were the result of consistent experiments in turning discrete poems into legible books: from Richard Tottel's innovative poem titles to John Benson's imaginative rereading of Shakespeare's sonnets as a valediction. If I have ended with an articulation of authorship, reinscribing a teleology that has often been assumed of early modern print, I hope to have shown the consolidation of this agency to be more complex, fitful, and unpredictable than it has often seemed. The long process of aligning authors with the material form of their gathered poetry—or excluding them from it, in the case of the miscellany—reflects the poetic reading of multiple generations of compilers.

In recognizing that perspectives on textual organization have a morphology—that is to say, the miscellany as a genre is bound by time and has changed across time—we can begin to account for a much fuller range of approaches to compiled poems. The conceptual category of the miscellany holds a history of how we came to read the past through modern eyes, collapsing the real distance between our own moment and when these books were first made and used. What emerges is a new method for a formal history of the book that is distinct to the development of early modern poetry. While genre-specific studies of playbooks have been foundational for book history, that approach has not been as fully applied to other kinds of writing.[1] In the case of poetry books, this blindness to the intersection of material and poetic craft has elided the forms produced within and by printed books, from the powerful figures in floral volume titles to the numbered headings that string sonnets into iterative series. The poetics of compiling thus offers a corollary literary history of multiple aesthetic, conceptual, and material forms in the sixteenth and seventeenth centuries. Indeed, the poetry compilation expands our sense of what even counts as *literary*, showing the unexpected agency of form on the material text.

By way of conclusion, I turn briefly to the legacy of John Benson's *Poems: Written by Wil. Shake-speare, Gent.* (1640) because eighteenth-century responses to that book show very clearly how the status of compiled poetry changed following the invention of the miscellany. After Shakespeare's poetic authorship was remade in 1640, his lyrics remained entangled with Donne's complex, mixed forms for more than a century. This was the moment when the public awareness of Shakespeare's drama supplanted his reputation as a poet, and his lyrics were not reprinted for more than six decades.[2] But new approaches to publishing the plays did eventually create opportunities for editions of Shakespeare's poems. In 1709, Nicholas Rowe edited a six-volume set of *The Works of Mr. William Shakespear*, which contained all the plays as well as "an Account of the Life and Writings of the Author."[3] The glaring omission of the nondramatic writing in Rowe's set prompted multiple competing editions of Shakespeare's poetry. In the same year, Bernard Lintott published a single volume entitled *A Collection of Poems* (1709), which contained *Venus and Adonis*, *The Rape of Lucrece*, and *The Passionate Pilgrime*. Just two years later, Lintott added a second volume with the *Sonnets* and "A Lover's Complaint."[4] Meanwhile, between these two editions, Charles Gildon more directly took on Rowe's example, publishing the first complete collection of all the narrative and lyric poems as *The Works of Mr. William Shakespear. Volume the Seventh* (1710).[5]

These proliferating editions speak to a nascent concern with the relation between the literary past and the editorial future of Shakespeare's poetry in the eighteenth century. Lintott was invested in returning to original sources. Following *The Passionate Pilgrime*, he set the sonnets without numbered headings or titles of any sort. But Gildon took a different path. Using Benson's *Poems* as his copy-text, his edition reprinted the conflated sonnet stanzas and thematic titles. Gildon also included an essay on Shakespeare's authorship that lambasted Lintott's *A Collection of Poems* as "a Book lately publish'd containing only some few of his Poems confusedly put together; for what is there called *The Passionate Pilgrim* is no more than a medly of *Shakespear's* thrown into a Heap without any Distinction."[6] Lintott's edition must have seemed a confused "medly" or undistinguished "Heap" because, in following *The Passionate Pilgrime*, it omitted every trace of the organizational framework that readers had come to expect. The titles that, for more than a century, had explained the connections between the short poems vanished without a trace. While Lintott added numbered headings in his second volume, Gildon's edition was the more successful, perhaps, because it was reprinted with John Benson's poem titles and offered more context for reading Shakespeare's compiled work.

Regardless of these distinct approaches to material arrangement, the conceptual framing of both Lintott and Gildon's editions share a striking— and I believe unremarked—similarity: both poetry collections are called "miscellanies." On Gildon's title page, the book is described as "Containing Venus & Adonis, Tarquin & Lucrece and His Miscellany Poems," while Lintott's full title is *A Collection of Poems, In Two Volumes; Being all the Miscellanies of Mr. William Shakespeare* (see Figure 32). This shared vocabulary is a result of the long afterlife of Shakespeare's lyrics within the episteme of authorial collections. "Miscellany" had not previously been used in books of Shakespeare's poetry. When the term appeared in these eighteenth-century editions, it reflected the presumption that textual organization was a natural expression of the life of the poet. Neither Gildon nor Lintott mingled the work of multiple authors, of course, but both did conflate multiple *books*, mixing compilations together to fashion larger, more complete editions. To put it another way, both Gildon and Lintott needed to call attention to the miscellaneous nature of their editions because they were disrupting the material expression of authorship that had become implicit to the design of compiled poetry. The paradox is that, in Shakespeare's case, this authorial arrangement was the result of Benson's anachronistic reading of the 1609 *Sonnets* through the bibliographic and a poetic paradigm of Donne's *Poems, By J. D.*

The centuries-long response to Benson's *Poems* demonstrates how early modern practices of compiling gradually evolved into an editorial apparatus concerned with authorship. The existence of Shakespeare's "miscellanies" seems to have been utterly unremarkable in the eighteenth century, since

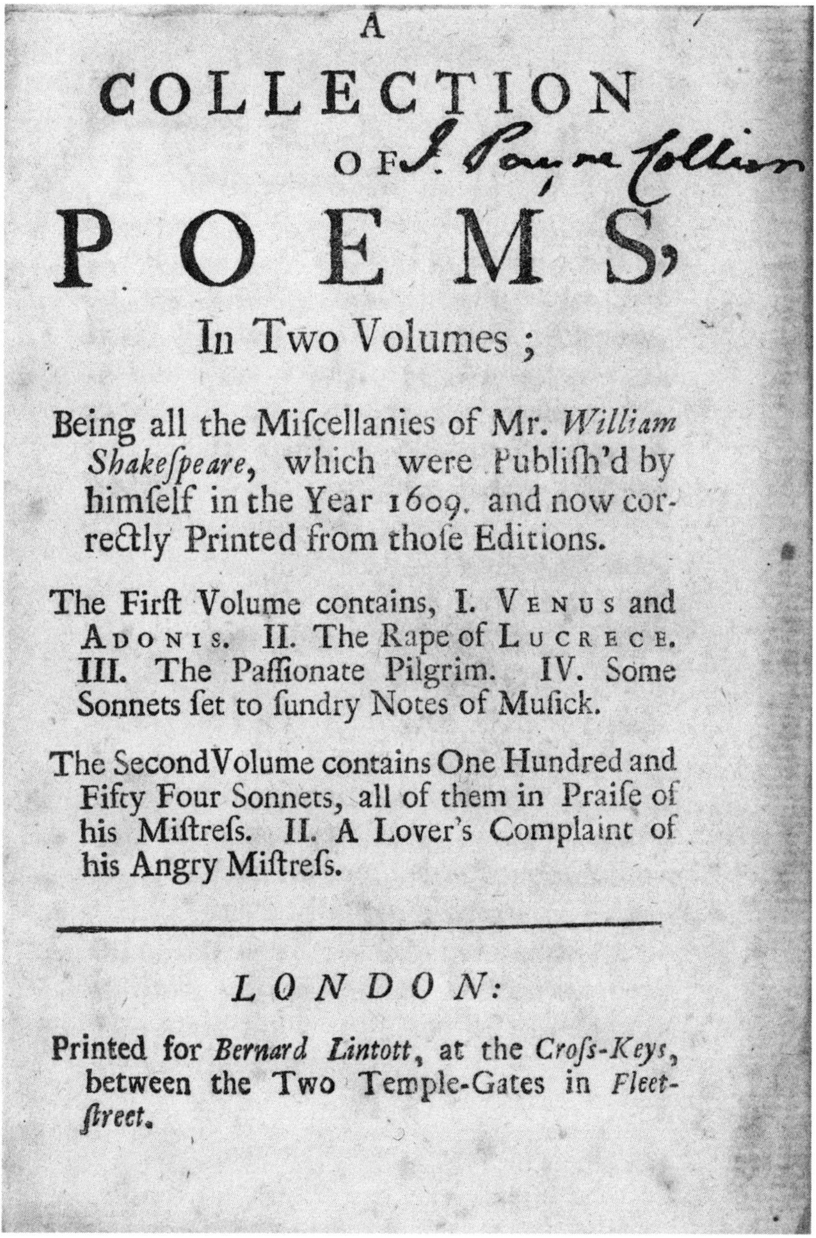

A

COLLECTION

O F *J. Payne Collier*

P O E M S,

In Two Volumes ;

Being all the Miscellanies of Mr. *William Shakespeare*, which were Publish'd by himself in the Year 1609. and now correctly Printed from those Editions.

The First Volume contains, I. VENUS and ADONIS. II. The Rape of LUCRECE. III. The Passionate Pilgrim. IV. Some Sonnets set to sundry Notes of Musick.

The Second Volume contains One Hundred and Fifty Four Sonnets, all of them in Praise of his Mistress. II. A Lover's Complaint of his Angry Mistress.

L O N D O N:

Printed for *Bernard Lintott*, at the *Cross-Keys*, between the Two Temple-Gates in *Fleet-street.*

Figure 32. "All the Miscellanies of Mr. *William Shakespeare*" with John Payne Collier's inscription, from the title page of *A Collection of Poems* (London: Bernard Lintott, 1711), PR2841 .A12c copy 2 Sh. Col. By permission of the Folger Shakespeare Library.

neither Gildon nor Lintott contested the term. The term has likewise escaped the notice of generations of editors, bibliographers, and literary historians who, in studying the poetry of Shakespeare and his contemporaries, have unquestioningly used "miscellany" to refer to printed compilations that never quite align with modern presumptions about the natural division of labor between writers and compilers. *Poems: Written by Wil. Shake-speare, Gent.* was not definitively rejected as a copy-text for new editions until Edmond Malone's 1780 *Supplement to the Edition of Shakspeare's Plays*. Malone's two-volume set added, among other texts, "The Genuine Poems of the Same Author" to the collected drama published by Samuel Johnson and George Steevens in 1778.[7] Malone's innovation was to read Shakespeare's authorial persona through Enlightenment ideals of historical accuracy and individual biography.[8] The anachronism of this identity is a stunning illustration of the fictions written into every dimension of literary history, including the designations of textual genre that we now take as absolute and timeless. It was in fact Benson's unexpected twist in the textual history of the sonnets that made it possible for editors from Malone on to imagine a corpus that could restore an "authentic" expression of Shakespeare that was defined against the miscellany. The 1640 *Poems* was a blatant instance of a corrupt text that had to be corrected by an editorial tradition invested in recovering the personhood of the long dead author. But more fundamentally, Benson was the first to associate Shakespeare's compiled poems with a representation of authorship when he fashioned them after the persona projected by Donne's absent presence.

Shakespeare became the "author" of multiple different "miscellanies" in the eighteenth century through the dynamic interactions between poetic form and the material forms of print. The shifting volume titles of his compiled lyrics—which evolved from *Sonnets*, to *Poems*, to *All the Miscellanies*, to "The Genuine Poems of the Same Author"—reflect how generations of readers refashioned the categories through which we read the past. At the same time, the assumption that these textual formations have been handed down faithfully leads us to disregard the two-way traffic between poetic genre and media change. Shakespeare is such a paradigmatic case that his poetry has often been sidelined in studies of his reception, even though his drama has inspired generations of bibliographers and book historians to rethink the basis of authorship as such.[9] This division between literary genres—and between subfields of literary history—has made it even harder to account for the capaciousness of early modern form as an energy that was materially and aesthetically engaged. By reexamining the categories through which we read the textual past, *Making the Miscellany* has shown the poetry compilation to be an expression of the real-world agency of imaginative writing. Poetry was not confined by the limits of the single poem, nor defined by the interventions of any single textual agent. The physical design of compiled books was itself an aspect of poetic form, and even individual poems carry occluded traces of the complex agencies that come to rest within textual structures.

This survey of how Shakespeare was quite easily incorporated into both authorial and miscellaneous collections offers significant lessons about the media history of early modern poetry in the eighteenth century and beyond. As a conceptual category, the miscellany was an invention of literary history. It was a backward-looking, retrospective designation for a poetic diversity that no longer made sense to modern readers. From the seventeenth century on, an awareness of a prominent mixture of poems and poets was produced by a flourishing tradition of vernacular writing, by the social dynamics of transmission, and—most of all—by the loss of the original context of composition. When later editors and literary historians began to apply the term to early modern poetry books, "miscellany" became a name for compilations that stubbornly resisted attempts to disclose textual origins in the hand of a single author.

Making the Miscellany has offered a double corrective to this normative history. Moving between close literary analysis and a broader attention to material culture, it has drawn out the significant twists and turns, the recursive loops and dead-end forays of textual practices that never fully align with the straightforward chronology of literary periodization. To that extent, this study of the anachronistic development of the miscellany shows that our histories of the book may be impossible to separate from fictions of poetic invention. Whether in sixteenth-century innovations in print or in the experimental remediation of those books in new digital editions, we are always peering at the past through the tangled web of interactions between poems and the compilations in which they travel. Learning to read this dynamic, transtemporal compiling allows us to value the profound influence of poetic form and craft on the textual formations that have been for too long recalcitrant to modern ideals of order.

NOTES

Throughout these notes, the abbreviation "EEBO" refers to Early English Books Online, "OED" to the *Oxford English Dictionary*, and "STC" to *A Short-Title Catalogue of Books Printed in England, Scotland, & Ireland and of English Books Printed Abroad, 1475–1640*, 2nd ed., ed. Katharine F. Pantzer, A. W. Pollard, et al. (London: Bibliographical Society, 1976–91).

INTRODUCTION

Note to epigraph: Robert Herrick, *The Complete Poetry of Robert Herrick*, ed. Tom Cain and Ruth Connolly (Oxford: Oxford University Press, 2013), 1:28.

1. In the sixteenth century, "gallery" referred primarily to a long covered space for walking and only secondarily to a room for displaying visual art (*OED Online*, s.v. "gallery, *n.*," senses 1 and 2).

2. *A gorgious Gallery, of gallant Inventions* (London: Richard Jones, 1578), sig. A1r, Bodleian Mal. 464a.

3. "T. P." was probably Thomas Proctor, who compiled part of the collection, which was then taken over by Richard Williams, and finally by Richard Jones, who likely commissioned the front material. On this extended chain of compilers, see Hyder Rollins, ed., *A Gorgeous Gallery of Gallant Inventions (1578)* (Cambridge, MA: Harvard University Press, 1926), xiv, xx.

4. *A gorgious Gallery, of gallant Inventions*, sig. A1r.

5. Ibid., sig. A2r.

6. Anthony Munday was the son of Christopher Munday, a bookselling draper. Before Munday became a poet and a dramatist, he worked as an apprentice to the printer and bookseller John Allde. See David M. Bergeron, "Munday, Anthony (bap. 1560, d. 1633), playwright and translator," *Oxford Dictionary of National Biography* (2007), online edition.

7. *A gorgious Gallery, of gallant Inventions*, sig. A2r.

8. Ibid.

9. Paul Marquis, ed., *Richard Tottel's "Songes and Sonettes": The Elizabethan Version* (Tempe: Arizona Center for Medieval and Renaissance Studies, 2007), 41.

10. These images were playful responses to the etymology for the "anthology," from the Greek for a gathering of flowers (*OED Online*, s.v. "anthology"). At this moment, "posy" was both a novel term for a bouquet and a more traditional designation for poetry or a poetic composition. As Juliet Fleming observes, "poesie" was used interchangeably with "posy" for a short poem "written in such a way that its material embodiment forms an important part of its meaning" (*Graffiti and the Writing Arts of Early Modern England* [London: Reaktion Books, 2001], 42–43).

11. Jeffrey Todd Knight, *Bound to Read: Compilations, Collections, and the Making of Renaissance Literature* (Philadelphia: University of Pennsylvania Press, 2013), 8.

12. Kirk Melnikoff, *Elizabethan Publishing and the Makings of Literary Culture* (Toronto: University of Toronto Press, 2018), 28.

13. Adam Smyth, *Material Texts in Early Modern England* (Cambridge: Cambridge University Press, 2018), 15, 14.

14. Joshua Eckhardt, *Manuscript Verse Collectors and the Politics of Anti-Courtly Love Poetry* (Oxford: Oxford University Press, 2009), 8, 6.

15. Arthur F. Marotti, *Manuscript, Print, and the English Renaissance Lyric* (Ithaca, NY: Cornell University Press, 1995), 135.

16. Lara M. Crowley, *Manuscript Matters: Reading John Donne's Poetry and Prose in Early Modern England* (Oxford: Oxford University Press, 2018), 10.

17. Ingrid Nelson, *Lyric Tactics: Poetry, Genre, and Practice in Later Medieval England* (Philadelphia: University of Pennsylvania Press, 2017), 13.

18. Colleen Ruth Rosenfeld, *Indecorous Thinking: Figures of Speech in Early Modern Poetics* (New York: Fordham University Press, 2018), 2, 9.

19. M. B. Parkes, "The Influence of the Concepts of *Ordinatio* and *Compilatio* on the Development of the Book," in *The History of the Book in the West*, vol. 1, *400 AD–1455*, ed. Jane Roberts and Pamela Robinson (Farnham, England: Ashgate, 2010), 140, 146.

20. As Arthur Bahr puts it, "compilational reading" is a "mode of perceiving" that "disclose[s] an interpretably meaningful arrangement," often evident in thematic continuities and, perhaps, the sequence of diverse texts (*Fragments and Assemblages: Forming Compilations of Medieval London* [Chicago: University of Chicago Press, 2013], 3).

21. Ralph Hanna III, "Miscellaneity and Vernacularity: Conditions of Literary Production in Late Medieval England," in *The Whole Book: Cultural Perspectives on the Medieval Miscellany*, ed. Stephen G. Nichols and Siegfried Wenzel (Ann Arbor: University of Michigan Press, 1996), 47.

22. Arthur Bahr, "Miscellaneity and Variance in the Medieval Book," in *The Medieval Manuscript Book: Cultural Approaches*, ed. Michael Johnston and Michael Van Dussen (Cambridge: Cambridge University Press, 2015), 181.

23. Angus Vine, *Miscellaneous Order: Manuscript Culture and the Early Modern Organization of Knowledge* (Oxford: Oxford University Press, 2019), 8.

24. Pliny, *The Historie of the World: Commonly Called, the Naturall Historie of C. Plinius Secundus*, trans. Philemon Holland (London: 1601), vol. 2, sig. H5v, Folger STC 20029, copy 1.

25. Ibid.

26. Abraham Holland, *A Continued Inquisition Against Paper-Persecutors* (London: H. Holland and G. Gibbs, 1625), sig. ²A1v, Folger STC 6340, copy 1.

27. The *Greek Anthology* was a collection of some 4,150 epigrams that were most known in selections. On its English translations, see Joshua Scodel, "Lyric," in *The Oxford History of Literary Translation in English*, vol. 2, *1550–1660*, ed. Gordon Braden, Robert Cummings, and Stuart Gillespie (Oxford: Oxford University Press, 2010), 2:233–234. On metaphors of textual digestion in sixteenth-century England, see Mary Thomas Crane, *Framing Authority: Sayings, Self, and Society in Sixteenth-Century England* (Princeton, NJ: Princeton University Press, 1993), 57–60. On the tradition of *florilegia* and cultures of compiling, see Ann Moss, *Printed Commonplace-Books and the Structuring of Renaissance Thought* (Oxford: Clarendon Press, 1996), 24–27.

28. Joshua Eckhardt and Daniel Starza Smith, "Introduction: The Emergence of the English Miscellany," in *Manuscript Miscellanies in Early Modern England*, ed. Joshua Eckhardt and Daniel Starza Smith (Farnham, England: Ashgate, 2014), 1–2.

29. Adam Smyth, *"Profit and Delight": Printed Miscellanies in England, 1640–1682* (Detroit, MI: Wayne State University Press, 2004), 2.

30. Throughout, I have preserved the spellings of early modern book titles, including in the notes and bibliography. At times spellings vary across editions. I give words composed entirely in capitals as words with initial capitals and have made the fonts uniformly italic.

31. Tottel had the resources to speculate on this new kind of collection because he held the lucrative patent for printing law books. See J. Christopher Warner, *The Making and Marketing of Tottel's Miscellany, 1557: "Songs and Sonnets" in the Summer of the Martyrs' Fires* (Farnham, England: Ashgate, 2013), 4–5.

32. For the most up-to-date print history of *Songes and Sonettes*, see Warner, *The Making and Marketing of Tottel's Miscellany*, 11.

33. Thomas Warton, *The History of English Poetry, from the Close of the Eleventh to the Commencement of the Eighteenth Century* (London: J. Dodsley et al., 1774–81), 3:iii.

34. Hyder Rollins, ed., *Tottel's Miscellany (1557–1587)* (Cambridge, MA: Harvard University Press, 1928), 2:4.

35. Elizabeth Pomeroy, *The Elizabethan Miscellanies: Their Development and Conventions* (Berkeley: University of California Press, 1973), 1.

36. Laura Estill, "The Urge to Organize Early Modern Miscellanies: Reading Cotgrave's *The English Treasury of Wit and Language*," *Papers of the Bibliographical Society of America* 112, no. 1 (2018): 66.

37. For an argument about how "the history of reading is also a history of mediating the material world," creating a "narrative" that "pleats the past, present, and future," see Whitney Trettien, "Media, Materiality, and Time in the History of Reading: The Case of the Little Gidding Harmonies," *PMLA* 133, no. 5 (2018): 1138.

38. Herrick, *Complete Poetry*, 1:28 (no. 83), lines 1, 3, 4, 5, 6, 9, 10, 11, 12.

39. Ibid., lines 13–14.

40. George Puttenham, *The Art of English Poesy*, ed. Frank Whigham and Wayne A. Rebhorn (Ithaca, NY: Cornell University Press, 2007), 252.

41. Ibid., 247n3.

42. Ben Burton and Elizabeth Scott-Baumann, "The Work of Form: Poetics and Materiality in Early Modern Culture," in *The Work of Form: Poetics and Materiality in Early Modern Culture*, ed. Ben Burton and Elizabeth Scott-Baumann (Oxford: Oxford University Press, 2014), 2, 5.

43. Ibid., 5.

44. Jenny C. Mann, *Outlaw Rhetoric: Figuring Vernacular Eloquence in Shakespeare's England* (Ithaca, NY: Cornell University Press, 2012), 120.

45. George Gascoigne, *A Hundreth Sundrie Flowres*, ed. G. W. Pigman III (Oxford: Clarendon Press, 2000), 228, from the heading to poem 13.

46. H. C., *The Forrest of Fancy* (London: Thomas Purfoot, 1579), sig. A4v, Bodleian Mal. 283.

47. Henry Lok, *Sundry Christian Passions Contained in two hundred Sonnets* (London: Richard Field, 1593), sigs. A6r, A5v, RB 12519, Huntington Library, San Marino, California.

48. Marquis, *Richard Tottel's "Songes and Sonettes,"* 121.

49. *A Handefull of Pleasant Delites* survives in a full copy from 1584, and there is evidence for earlier editions from 1566 and 1575 in the Stationers' Register and fragmentary sheets now held at the Huntington.

50. J. W. Saunders, "The Stigma of Print: A Note on the Social Bases of Tudor Poetry," *Essays in Criticism* 1, no. 2 (1951): 139–64. For an opposing viewpoint, which identifies this stigma with nineteenth-century editorial regimes, see Steven W. May, "Tudor Aristocrats and the Mythical 'Stigma of Print,'" in *Renaissance Papers, 1980*, ed. A. Leigh DeNeef and M. Thomas Hester (Durham, NC: Southeastern Renaissance Conference, 1981), 11–18.

1. PLAIN PARCELS

1. Warton, *The History of English Poetry*, 3:69.

2. Ibid., 3:iii. Matthew Zarnowiecki has identified Warton as the first to call *Songes and Sonettes* a "miscellany," anticipating the title by which it is commonly known today, *Tottel's Miscellany* (*Fair Copies: Reproducing the English Lyric from Tottel to Shakespeare* [Toronto: University of Toronto Press, 2014], 23).

3. Warton, *The History of English Poetry*, 3:69.

4. Rollins, *Tottel's Miscellany (1557–1587)*, 2:4.

5. The print history of *Songes and Sonettes* is complicated because Tottel repeated dates in his colophons. One edition is dated June 1557, and two are dated July 1557. There are three from 1559, and one each from 1565, 1567, 1574, 1585, and 1587. I take this list of editions from Warner, *The Making and Marketing of Tottel's Miscellany*, 11. The third

edition from 1559 is Warner's recent discovery. See J. Christopher Warner, "'Sonnets en Anglois': A Hitherto Unknown Edition of Tottel's Miscellany," *Notes and Queries* 58, no. 2 (2011): 204–6.

6. C. S. Lewis, *English Literature in the Sixteenth Century, Excluding Drama* (Oxford: Clarendon Press, 1954), 236–37.

7. Marotti, *Manuscript, Print, and the English Renaissance Lyric*, 212.

8. For an argument about how "literary historians" typically "overlook the complexity" and underestimate "the popularity of Tottel's as a collection because, all too often, the anthological context goes unheeded," see Stephen Hamrick's introduction in *Tottel's "Songes and Sonettes" in Context*, ed. Stephen Hamrick (Farnham, England: Ashgate, 2013), 5.

9. The first quarto of *Songes and Sonettes* was published on June 5, 1557, and sold out so quickly that an edition with substantially revised contents, arrangement, and poem texts was set and printed by July 31, 1557. Complicating this history, there are two distinct editions of *Songes and Sonettes* with colophons of July 31, 1557, leading W. W. Greg to conjecture simultaneous setting of duplicate copies, while Rollins showed that the quartos could not have been printed simultaneously because one was set from the other. See W. W. Greg, "Tottel's Miscellany," *The Library*, 2nd ser., 5, no. 18 (1904): 122–23; Rollins, *Tottel's Miscellany (1557–1587)*, 2:19. Paul Marquis supports Rollins's reading with the observation that several of Tottel's other imprints duplicated earlier colophons ("Editing and Unediting Richard Tottel's *Songes and Sonettes*," *Book Collector* 56, no. 3 [2007]: 362–64). While Warner agrees with Marquis's suggestion of a gap of up to eighteen months between the second and third editions, he notes that this practice was not common for Tottel during the late 1550s and posits a special concern with promoting the revised second edition of *Songes and Sonettes* (*The Making and Marketing of Tottel's Miscellany*, 215–19).

10. On the cultural belatedness of this publication of poetry from the 1530s within the religious climate of 1557, see Stephen Hamrick, "*Tottel's Miscellany* and the English Reformation," *Criticism* 44, no. 4 (2002): 329.

11. Steven W. May, "Popularizing Courtly Poetry: Tottel's Miscellany and Its Progeny," in *The Oxford Handbook of Tudor Literature, 1485–1603*, ed. Mike Pincombe and Cathy Shrank (Oxford: Oxford University Press, 2011), 422.

12. As Ingrid Nelson writes of the medieval origins of English compilations, poetry volumes were "ad hoc, improvisatory, and unregulated," more "responsive and adaptive rather than proscribed and determinate" (*Lyric Tactics*, 13).

13. Marquis, *Richard Tottel's "Songes and Sonettes,"* 184. This edition, which takes the second quarto from 1557 as its copy text, is hereafter cited parenthetically in text. Poems are identified with the number assigned by Marquis, and prose (including the headings) is identified by page number.

14. For evidence of the care Tottel showed for setting poetry in his other publications, see May, "Popularizing Courtly Poetry," 425–26.

15. Throughout this chapter, I avoid naming the figures responsible for compiling *Songes and Sonettes* because we lack evidence of who was involved, including the printers

of the early editions. At least since Rollins, the critical tendency was to name Tottel as an "editor" of the compilation, while more recent editions, including Marquis's, have remained agnostic about the extent of the publisher's role. For a summary of these positions, see Jason Powell, "The Network Behind '*Tottel's' Miscellany*," *English Literary Renaissance* 46, no. 2 (2016): 194–95. My thanks to Jason Powell for sharing this research with me prior to publication.

16. Jeffrey Todd Knight, "Organizing Manuscript and Print: From *Compilatio* to Compilation," in *The Medieval Manuscript Book: Cultural Approaches*, ed. Michael Johnston and Michael Van Dussen (Cambridge: Cambridge University Press, 2015), 91.

17. Michelle O'Callaghan, "Textual Gatherings: Print, Community and Verse Miscellanies in Early Modern England," *Early Modern Culture* 8 (2010), para. 2.

18. Powell has uncovered new evidence documenting the sources for Wyatt's poems, arguing persuasively that in *Songes and Sonettes* Tottel was promoting "material that had been authored and collected by someone else" in order "to minimize its association with the Wyatt family" ("The Network Behind '*Tottel's' Miscellany*," 224). In the study of print, Warner replaces "the wide-angle perspective of evolutionary literary history," which was "usually to the Miscellany's detriment," with a study of "its near-contemporary European counterparts and its competition in the London book market." His new approach has shown *Songes and Sonettes* to be "both a pragmatic and an idealistic response to the religious, political, and social upheavals of the English Reformation and Counter-Reformation (Warner, *The Making and Marketing of Tottel's Miscellany*, 2–4).

19. Paul A. Marquis identifies in the revisions between the first and second quartos of *Songes and Sonettes* "emendations to individual poems and to the text as a whole" that demonstrate Tottel's investment in the collection as a carefully planned anthology ("Printing History and Editorial Design in the Elizabethan Version of Tottel's *Songes and Sonettes*," in Hamrick, *Tottel's Songes and Sonettes in Context*, 27; see as well Marquis's "Editing and Unediting Richard Tottel's *Songes and Sonettes*"). Matthew Zarnowiecki has explained the significant "paradox of collecting and preserving occasional, ephemeral poetry" in "Tottel's collection" as an impetus for later authors (*Fair Copies*, 46).

20. See, for instance, Stephen Greenblatt, George Logan, and Katharine Eisaman Maus, eds., *The Norton Anthology of English Literature*, 10th ed., vol. B (New York: W. W. Norton, 2018), 502.

21. William Shakespeare, *The Merry Wives of Windsor*, ed. Giorgio Melchiori (London: Arden Shakespeare, 2000), 1.1.183–84.

22. As Terence Cave writes of this moment, which was characterized by an episteme of Erasmian *copia*, the "categories 'theory' and 'practice' are undermined from the outset," such that the very distinction "is characteristically self-eliminating" (*The Cornucopian Text: Problems of Writing in the French Renaissance* [Oxford: Clarendon Press, 1979], xiv).

23. Tottel's patent was confirmed for life by Elizabeth in 1559. See Peter W. M. Blayney, *The Stationers' Company and the Printers of London, 1501–1557* (Cambridge: Cambridge University Press, 2013), 2:644–646.

24. The text block of the first quarto, which has been cut down, is so small that it has at times been confused for an octavo. See Rollins, *Tottel's Miscellany (1557–1587)*, 2:7–8. There is only one extant copy of the first edition of *Songes and Sonettes*, now held at the Bodleian Library as Arch. G.f. 12 (1).

25. *Songes and Sonettes written by the ryght honorable Lorde Henry Haward late Earle of Surrey, and other* (London: Richard Tottel, June 1557), sig. A1v, Bodleian Library Arch. G.f. 12 (1).

26. Ibid., sig. D4r.

27. Ibid., sigs. M3r, Q1r, Cc3v, Dd2r.

28. On "compiling" as a premodern designation of authorship, see Knight, *Bound to Read*, 9.

29. John Skelton, *Here After Foloweth Certayne Bokes, Co[m]pyled by Mayster Skelton* (London: Henry Tab, 1545?), sigs. A8r, B4v, Early English Books Online (EEBO) copy.

30. Geoffrey Chaucer, *The Workes of Geffray Chaucer Newly Printed* (London: Robert Toye, 1550), sig. A2v, Folger Folio STC 5074 copy 1.

31. Ibid., sig. Qq3v.

32. *OED Online*, s.v. "invention, *n.*" senses 1 and 2. For fuller discussions of poetic invention, see my second and third chapters.

33. John Heywood, *A Fourth Hundred of Epygrams Invented and Made by John Heywood* (London: Thomas Berthelet, 1560), sig. A1v, EEBO copy.

34. *OED Online*, s.v. "poesis, *n.*" On the material dimensions of "poesy" in early modern English, see Fleming, *Graffiti and the Writing Arts*, 42–43.

35. Thomas Tusser, *A Hundreth Good Pointes of Husbandrie* (London: Richard Tottel, 1557), sig. A2r, EEBO copy.

36. For an argument about how Wyatt's poems outperform the eloquence of his models, see Richard Strier, "Paleness Versus Eloquence: The Ideologies of Style in the English Renaissance," *Explorations in Renaissance Culture* 45 (2019): 94–97. My thanks to Richard Strier for sharing this work prior to publication.

37. *Songes and Sonettes* (June 1557), sig. A1v.

38. Ibid.

39. Ibid.

40. Powell, "The Network Behind '*Tottel's*' Miscellany," 224.

41. Hamrick, "*Tottel's Miscellany* and the English Reformation," 329.

42. Warner, *The Making and Marketing of Tottel's Miscellany*, 169.

43. Ibid., 36.

44. *Rime di diversi illustri signori [. . .] Nuovamente raccolte, et con nuova additione ristampate; libro quinto* (Venice: Gabriel Giolito, 1552), sig. O8r, RB 215423, vol. 2, Huntington Library, San Marino, California.

45. The Devonshire manuscript (British Library Add. MS 17492) and the Egerton manuscript (British Library Egerton MS 2711) do not include poem titles.

46. *The Court of Venus* (London: T. Gybson, [1538?]) is extant as a fragment consisting of sigs. E1–F7, now in the Bodleian Library's Douce Collection as Fragm. g.3. *A Boke of*

Balettes [London]: [W. Copland?], [1549?], survives as fragments of folios 44 and 45; the only extant copy was used as end leaves for a copy of the 1551 English translation of Thomas More's *A Fruteful and Pleasaunt Worke of the Beste State of a Publyque Weale, and of the Newe Yle called Utopia*, now held at the Harry Ransom Center as HX 811 1516 E5 1551.

47. May, "Popularizing Courtly Poetry," 430.

48. *Songes and Sonettes* (June 1557), sig. A2r.

49. Ibid., sig. A2v.

50. Ibid.

51. Ibid.

52. Ibid., sigs. B3v, G1r, Aa2r, Cc1v.

53. Burton and Scott-Baumann, "The Work of Form," 2.

54. *Songes and Sonettes* (June 1557), sig. A1v.

55. *Songes and Sonettes* played a significant role in introducing Petrarchan poetry to England. Translations of several Italian sonnets appeared in the compilation, and Catherine Bates has shown that the 1557 title page was the first place the term "sonnet" was printed in an English book ("Profit and Pleasure? The Real Economy of Tottel's *Songes and Sonettes*," in Hamrick, *Tottel's "Songes and Sonettes" in Context*, 40).

56. "Parcel" can accommodate, as Wendy Wall succinctly puts it, "seemingly contradictory formal positions" as "both an assemblage of diverse parts and a constituent portion of a larger whole" (*The Imprint of Gender: Authorship and Publication in the English Renaissance* [Ithaca, NY: Cornell University Press, 1993], 25).

57. *OED Online*, s.v. "parcel, *n.*," 5a. For an argument about Tottel's parcels within an idiom of land use and agriculture, see Seth Lerer, "Cultivation and Inhumation: Some Thoughts on the Cultural Impact of Tottel's *Songes and Sonettes*," in Hamrick, *Tottel's "Songes and Sonettes" in Context*, 152.

58. Andrew Zurcher, "The Printing of the Cantos of Mutabilitie in 1609," in *Celebrating Mutabilitie: Essays on Edmund Spenser's Mutabilitie Cantos*, ed. Jane Grogan (Manchester: Manchester University Press, 2010), 44. See as well, *OED Online*, s.v. "parcel, *n.*," sense 3a.

59. John Calvin, *Sermons of John Calvin, Upon the Songe that Ezechias made after he had bene sicke*, trans. Anne Lock (London: John Day, 1560), sig. ²A1r, Folger STC 4450. The *Meditation* is appended at the end of *Sermons* with a separate register and pagination. I read this note on the divisional title page as an instruction from Day and therefore identify the sonnets that follow as Lock's. For an argument about whether Lock or Day wrote this headnote, see Anne Vaughan Lock, *The Collected Works of Anne Vaughan Lock*, ed. Susan M. Felch (Tempe: Arizona Center for Medieval and Renaissance Studies in conjunction with Renaissance English Text Society, 1999), liv. For a new argument against Lock's authorship, see Steven W. May, "Anne Lock and Thomas Norton's *Meditation of a Penitent Sinner*," *Modern Philology* 114, no. 4 (2017): 793–819.

60. *Songes and Sonettes* (June 1557), sigs. G1v, G2r.

61. Ibid.

62. Ibid., sig. G2r.

63. Ibid.

64. The Egerton manuscript contains fair copies of Wyatt's poems. It was likely transcribed by an amanuensis and corrected by Wyatt between 1526 and 1542. For a description of Egerton, see Richard Harrier, *The Canon of Sir Thomas Wyatt's Poetry* (Cambridge, MA: Harvard University Press, 1975), 1–15.

65. "Who hath herd" ("Of the same" in *Songes and Sonettes*) is on fol. 29v, and "She sat and sowde" ("Of his lover that pricked her finger with a nedle" in *Songes and Sonettes*) is on fol. 37r. British Library MS Egerton 2711, from the Digitized Manuscripts site, http://www.bl.uk/manuscripts/Viewer.aspx?ref=egerton_ms_2711_f500ir.

66. *Songes and Sonettes* (June 1557), sig. G2r.

67. *Songes and Sonettes* (London: Richard Tottel, 1565), sigs. D4r, D4v, RB 31935, Huntington Library, San Marino, California.

68. Burton and Scott-Baumann, "The Work of Form," 5.

69. Ibid., 6.

70. Stephen G. Nichols and Siegfried Wenzel, introduction to Nichols and Wenzel, *The Whole Book*, 1–2.

71. Marquis, "Printing History and Editorial Design," 20, 26, 27.

72. On these changes, see Marquis's introduction in *Richard Tottel's "Songes and Sonettes,"* xx.

73. For this estimate of the number of copies of *Songes and Sonettes*, see Stephen Hamrick, "'Their Gods in Verses': The Popular Reception of *Songes and Sonettes*, 1557–1674," in Hamrick, *Tottel's "Songes and Sonettes" in Context*, 163.

74. Warner astutely observes the signification number of responses in *Songes and Sonettes*, as well as the "circumstance that there are more such poems in the revised second edition" to show that fostering variations "was one of Tottel's goals" (*The Making and Marketing of Tottel's Miscellany*, 95).

75. In the second quarto of *Songes and Sonettes*, these poems run from sig. Bb1v to sig. Cc2r.

76. Henry Williams was the second son of John Williams, a favorite of Henry VIII, and he died before his father in 1551. Verse Miscellanies Online, http://versemiscellanies online.bodleian.ox.ac.uk/glossaries-and-indexes/historicalclassical/#WilliamsHenry.

77. *Songes and Sonettes* (London: Richard Tottel, 1557), sigs. Bb3v–Bb4r, Harry Ransom Center PFORZ 506 PFZ. This is the third edition, which repeats the 1557 colophon.

78. *Songes and Sonettes* (June 1557), sig. Cc2v.

79. Ibid., sig. R1v; Marquis, *Richard Tottel's "Songes and Sonettes,"* 195.

80. *Songs and Sonettes* (June 1557), sigs. O2v and O4r.

81. May argues persuasively that Tottel was appeasing Grimald with these revisions, since the clergyman was the only named poet in *Songes and Sonettes* who was still alive ("Popularizing Courtly Poetry," 424).

82. For an argument about how printers, including Richard Tottel in *Songes and Sonettes*, increasingly regularized poetic meter after the publication of the Sternhold and

Hopkins psalter, see Lucía Martínez Valdivia, "Mere Meter: A Revised History of English Poetry," *ELH* 86, no. 3 (2019): 565–67. For the classic account of the regularization of Wyatt's conversational meter in *Songes and Sonettes*, see John Thompson, *The Founding of English Metre* (New York: Columbia University Press, 1961), 15–29.

83. The Blage manuscript is now held at Trinity College Dublin as D. 27, vols. 2–3. It was owned by George Blage and likely compiled on loose sheets between about 1532 and his death in 1551. For the history of the manuscript, see Kenneth Muir, ed., *Sir Thomas Wyatt and His Circle: Unpublished Poems Edited from the Blage Manuscript* (Liverpool: Liverpool University Press, 1961), ix–xi.

84. Muir, *Sir Thomas Wyatt and His Circle*, poem no. 178, lines 1–4.

85. For Stanhope's history, see Keith Dockray, "Stanhope, Sir Michael (b. before 1508, d. 1552)," *Oxford Dictionary of National Biography*, online edition.

86. On Anne Stanhope's piety, see Dockray, "Stanhope, Sir Michael."

87. *Songes and Sonettes*, 3rd ed. (1557), sig. H1v, Harry Ransom Center PFORZ 506 PFZ.

88. Thompson, *Founding of English Metre*, 18.

89. All three rondeaux appear in the Egerton manuscript, fols. 4r–v and 16v. In *Songes and Sonettes*, they are titled "Request to Cupid for revenge of his unkinde love," "Complaint for true love unrequited," and "The lover sendeth sighes to mone his sute" (pp. 54, 71).

90. Harrier, *Canon*, poem 2, lines 7–9.

91. See, for instance, *Songes and Sonettes* (London: Richard Tottel, 1574), Folger STC 13866, copy 2, which has marginalia that is only evident as very faint traces.

92. *Songes and Sonettes* (London: Robert Robinson, 1587), sig. D3r, Bodleian 8° H 43 Art. Seld. This is the eleventh and final edition. Rollins describes the hands in *Tottel's Miscellany (1557–1587)*, 2:36.

93. Bodleian 8° H 43 Art. Seld., sig. D3r.

94. Ibid., sig. D2r.

95. I follow Rollins's reading of this annotation. There is a single stroke before the "or" that I take as a shortened virgule. See Rollins, *Tottel's Miscellany (1557–1587)*, 2:180n31.

96. Bodleian 8° H 43 Art. Seld., sig. D2r.

97. This reading was created by the setting of the poem in the first edition of *Songes and Sonettes*. Rollins observes "A Mistress Souche (Zouche, Zowche)" was a member of Jane Seymour's court, but that manuscript evidence "shows that Wyatt was not referring to her" (*Tottel's Miscellany (1557–1587)*, 2:180n31).

98. Rollins, *A Gorgeous Gallery*, xiii.

99. Pomeroy, *The Elizabethan Miscellanies*, 1.

100. Even more striking, the first six editions of *Songes and Sonettes* were printed in about three years, between 1557 and 1559. There was then a gap of six years before the seventh edition of *Songes and Sonettes* in 1565.

101. Edward Arber, ed., *A Transcript of the Registers of the Company of Stationers of London, 1554–1640* (London: privately printed, 1875–94), 2:787.

102. *Englands Helicon* (London: John Flasket, 1600), sig. G3r, Folger STC 3191 copy 1.

103. *The Merry Wives of Windsor*, 1.1.183–84.

104. As Adam Zucker observes, "Audiences must either know or be taught through the play's performance itself about the potential powers of Tottel's miscellany for a joke about its inefficiency to have purchase" (*The Places of Wit in Early Modern English Comedy* [Cambridge: Cambridge University Press, 2011], 48).

105. William Shakespeare, *Comedies, Histories, & Tragedies* (London: Isaac Jaggard, and Edward Blount, 1623), sig. pp5r, Free Library of Philadelphia [no shelfmark]. Cited from Claire M. L. Bourne "*Vide Supplementum*: Early Modern Collation as Play-Reading in the First Folio," in *Early Modern Marginalia*, ed. Katherine Acheson (London: Routledge, 2019), 204. This annotator has recently been identified, with some degree of certainty, as John Milton (see Jason Scott-Warren, "Milton's Shakespeare?," *Centre for Materials Texts: A New Forum for the Study of the Word in the World*, September 9, 2019, https://www.english.cam.ac.uk/cmt/?p=5751). Our field owes sincere thanks to Claire Bourne for her consistent generosity in sharing her research findings, as she did with me prior to publication.

106. Bourne has dated this marginalia between 1639 and the second half of the seventeenth century ("*Vide Supplementum*," 207).

107. Ibid., 204.

108. Vaux's poem had a wide circulation, appearing in multiple poetry manuscripts and a broadside ballad. It was identified with Vaux by George Gascoigne in *The Posies* (1575). See Verse Miscellanies Online, http://versemiscellaniesonline.bodleian.ox.ac.uk /texts/tottels-miscellany/tottel-sig-siiiir/.

109. *Songes and Sonettes*, sig. D4r, Harry Ransom Center PFORZ 506 PFZ.

110. Ibid., sigs., D3v, L4r.

111. Ibid., sig. O3v.

112. Ross W. Duffin, *Some Other Note: The Lost Songs of English Renaissance Comedy* (Oxford: Oxford University Press, 2018), 457.

113. Deidre Lynch, *Loving Literature: A Cultural History* (Chicago: University of Chicago Press, 2015), 68.

114. On how Warton's periodization imposed a new distance between eighteenth-century readers and early modern writing, see Jonathan Kramnick, *Making the English Canon: Print-Capitalism and the Cultural Past, 1700–1770* (Cambridge: Cambridge University Press, 1998), 140–41.

115. Warton, *The History of English Poetry*, 3:41.

116. Ibid.

117. Ibid.

118. Joseph Ames, *Typographical Antiquities: Being an Historical Account of Printing in England* (London: J. Robinson, 1749), 288–92.

119. Joseph Ames and William Herbert, *Typographical Antiquities; or, An Historical Account of the Origin and Progress of Printing in Great Britain and Ireland* (London: T. Payne et al., 1785–90), 2:812.

120. The furious response to Collier's tampering with Shakespearean evidence began in 1852 and by 1860 had exposed his responsibility for dozens of forgeries in England's preeminent private and public libraries (Arthur Freeman and Janet Ing Freeman, *John Payne Collier: Scholarship and Forgery in the Nineteenth Century* [New Haven, CT: Yale University Press, 2004], 1:583–640, 718–824).

121. John Payne Collier, *A Bibliographical and Critical Account of the Rarest Books in the English Language* (London: Joseph Lilly, 1865), 1:v.

122. Ibid.

123. George Nott included all of Grimald's poems from the first quarto in an edition of *Songes and Sonettes* that was ready by about 1814, although it never saw publication because it was lost in a fire. Nott then used readings from that source in an edition of Surrey and Wyatt's poems for Longman's in 1815–1816. See Rollins, *Tottel's Miscellany (1557–1587)*, 2:47–52.

124. For these publication dates, see Freeman and Freeman, *John Payne Collier*, 2:1276, 1278.

125. Collier, *A Bibliographical and Critical Account*, 2:406.

126. This "Notice" is bound in with one of the Folger Shakespeare Library's copies of *Tottel's Miscellany*, which also includes Collier's autograph letter to John Shelly about the subscription. *Tottel's Miscellany*, ed. John Payne Collier (London: privately printed, 1865), unpaginated, Folger PR1205.T6 1865 Cage.

127. Folger N.a.52, fols. 33, 42, 25.

128. Collier, *Tottel's Miscellany*, iii.

129. Marquis, *Richard Tottel's "Songes and Sonettes"*; Amanda Holton and Tom Mac-Faul, eds., *Tottel's Miscellany: Songs and Sonnets of Henry Howard, Earl of Surrey, Sir Thomas Wyatt and Others* (New York: Penguin Classics, 2011).

130. *Songes and Sonettes (Tottel's Miscellany), 1557* (Leeds: Scolar Press, 1966).

2. STATIONERS' FIGURES

1. For a discussion of how authorship was understood as the reuse of textual fragments, not "the assimilation and imitation of whole works," see Crane, *Framing Authority*, 4.

2. Rollins, *Tottel's Miscellany (1557–1587)*, 2:4.

3. In Rollins's account, "Rival publishers, naturally enough, imitated Tottel, and in several cases with marked success" (*A Gorgeous Gallery*, xiii).

4. Warton, *The History of English Poetry*, 3:69.

5. Pomeroy, *The Elizabethan Miscellanies*, viii, 116.

6. In the context of early modern drama, Zachary Lesser has demonstrated that, by anticipating how buyers would read plays, the decisions of publishers hold a "history of reading," and "every play publication is already a piece of literary criticism—if only we can learn to read it" (*Renaissance Drama and the Politics of Publication: Readings in the English Book Trade* [Cambridge: Cambridge University Press, 2004], 8).

7. Eleanor Johnson, *Practicing Literary Theory in the Middle Ages: Ethics and the Mixed Form in Chaucer, Gower, Usk, and Hoccleve* (Chicago: University of Chicago Press, 2013), 232.

8. Ibid., 232–33.

9. Dennis Duncan and Adam Smyth, "Introductions," in Duncan and Smyth, eds., *Book Parts* (Oxford: Oxford University Press, 2019), 4.

10. Kirk Melnikoff identifies these frames as one stage in the manifold "processes of compiling" for print, through which "copy was routinely moulded" into "the heterogeneous arrangement that is the Elizabethan book" (*Elizabethan Publishing*, 28–29).

11. As Jessica Rosenberg has observed, the husbandry language that was common in mid-sixteenth-century English poetry was more than a thematic concern; it "carries with it a set of rhetorical patterns and hermeneutic expectations" that supported "aesthetic and stylistic attachments to the density and portability of small forms" ("The Point of the Couplet: Shakespeare's *Sonnets* and Tusser's *A Hundreth Good Pointes of Husbandrie,*" *ELH* 83, no. 1 [2016]: 4).

12. Rosenfeld, *Indecorous Thinking*, 3.

13. On the legacy of the *florilegia* tradition, see Moss, *Printed Commonplace-Books*, 24–27.

14. For a comprehensive survey of the horticultural trope, see Randall L. Anderson, "Metaphors of the Book as Garden in the English Renaissance," *Yearbook of English Studies* 33 (2003): 248–61.

15. Juliet Fleming explains the intersection of writing individual poems and compiling figurative bouquets: "poesie" was used interchangeably with "posy" as a short poem "written in such a way that its material embodiment forms an important part of its meaning" (*Graffiti and the Writing Arts*, 42–43.) See as well *OED Online*, s.v. "poesy, *n.*"

16. As Melnikoff puts it, titles were the "vanguards that contribute[d] to the overall commercial success or failure of a printed book" and "reveal much about these agents' speculative engagement with their copies at hand" (*Elizabethan Publishing*, 36.)

17. Isabella Whitney's collection is something of an outlier in terms of the common syntax, but the unique copy of *A Sweet Nosgay*, now held at the British Library as C.39.b.45, is missing the title page, which may well have carried a more elaborate description.

18. T. S. Eliot, "What Is Minor Poetry?," *Sewanee Review* 54, no. 1 (1946): 2.

19. Rosenfeld, *Indecorous Thinking*, 2, 9.

20. The initials H. C. have been identified as belonging variously to Henry Chettle, Henry Cheeke, and Henry Constable.

21. H. C., *The Forrest of Fancy* (London: Thomas Purfoot, 1579), sig. A2r, Bodleian Mal. 283.

22. On the imagery of the "textual imprint as child" that "recurs in preliminaries to early modern books, putting into play the semantics shared by biological and textual reproduction," see Margreta de Grazia, "Imprints: Shakespeare, Gutenberg, and Descartes," in *Printing and Parenting in Early Modern England*, ed. Douglas Brooks (Aldershot, England: Ashgate, 2005), 35.

23. H. C., *The Forrest of Fancy*, sig. A2r.

24. Ibid.

25. Ibid.

26. Ibid., sig. A2v.

27. Rayna Kalas, *Frame, Glass, Verse: The Technology of Poetic Invention in the English Renaissance* (Ithaca, NY: Cornell University Press, 2007), 105.

28. Ibid., 84.

29. H. C., *The Forrest of Fancy*, sig. A2r.

30. On the significance of "here" as a deictic gesture to scenes of writing and reading, as well as to the book that materially mediates those moments, see Heather Dubrow, *Deixis in the Early Modern English Lyric: Unsettling Spatial Anchors Like "Here," "This," "Come,"* Palgrave Pivot (New York: Palgrave Macmillan, 2015), 33–34.

31. H. C., *The Forrest of Fancy*, sig. A2v.

32. Ibid.

33. Ibid.

34. Ibid., sig. B1r; my emphasis. On publishers' addition of front matter and letters to future readers, see Melnikoff, *Elizabethan Publishing*, 40–44.

35. H. C., *The Forrest of Fancy*, sigs. A4r, A4v.

36. Ibid., sig. A4v.

37. Ibid.

38. Zurcher "Printing of the Cantos of Mutabilitie," 44.

39. Puttenham, *The Art of English Poesy*, 247n3.

40. Ibid., 252.

41. Mann, *Outlaw Rhetoric*, 120.

42. The authorship of *A Smale handfull* is uncertain. Melnikoff ascribes it to Nicholas Breton; see his "Richard Jones (fl. 1564–1613): Elizabethan Printer, Bookseller and Publisher," *Analytical & Enumerative Bibliography* 12 (2001): 178. Hyder Rollins finds it unlikely that Breton would only give his initial here because he used his full name when he published *A Floorish upon Fancy* with Jones just two years later. See Nicholas Breton, *Brittons Bowre of Delights, 1591*, ed. Hyder Edward Rollins (Cambridge, MA: Harvard University Press, 1933), xii.

43. N. B., *A Smale handfull of fragrant Flowers* (London: Richard Jones, 1575), sig. A1v, RB 59551, Huntington Library, San Marino, California.

44. Ibid., sig. A2r.

45. Ibid., sigs. A2r, A2v.

46. Crane, *Framing Authority*, 169. On the apian metaphor more generally, see Crane, 57–60.

47. While the address from the prosopopoeic volume is not signed, in the absence of other letters from the printer, it is possible that Jones wrote or commissioned the treatise that aligns so neatly with his interests. The compiling bookseller was known for an "unabashed underscoring of his own critical agency" in the prefatory addresses that he included more frequently than other publishers (Kirk Melnikoff, "Jones's Pen and

Marlowe's Socks: Richard Jones, Print Culture, and the Beginnings of English Dramatic Literature," *Studies in Philology* 102, no. 2 [2005]: 193).

48. N. B., *A Smale handfull of fragrant Flowers*, sig. A3r.

49. Ibid.

50. Ibid.; my emphasis.

51. *OED Online*, s.v. "peruse, *v.*"

52. *A gorgious Gallery, of gallant Inventions*, sig. N4r. Of particular note in this collection are the songs and ballads that circulated in other publications, including *A Handefull of Pleasant Delites* (1584), which Jones also printed and compiled. On Richard Jones's printing of both ballads and poetry books, see Eric Nebeker, "Broadside Ballads, Miscellanies, and the Lyric in Print," *ELH* 76, no. 4 (2009): 1004–8.

53. *OED Online*, s.v. "gallery, *n.*," senses 1 and 2.

54. Gascoigne, *A Hundreth Sundrie Flowres*, ed. Pigman (2000), 161.

55. *A gorgious Gallery*, sig. A1r.

56. Ibid.

57. Proctor was himself probably continuing the work begun by Owen Roydon, who described his compiling in one of the prefatory addresses, and Roydon seems in turn to have taken over a project started by an R. Williams. *A gorgious Gallery, of gallant Inventions* was entered in the Stationers' Register on June 5, 1577, where it was first called "Delicate Dainties to sweten lovers lips withall" and described as "a handefull of hidden Secretes conteigninge therein certaine Sonnets and other pleasante Devises pickt out of the Closet of sundrie worthie writers and collected together by R Williams" (Arber, *Transcript of the Registers*, 2:313). On this long chain of compilers, see Rollins, *A Gorgeous Gallery*, xiv, xx.

58. *A gorgious Gallery*, sig. K4r. That the "Pretie pamphlets" section does not start on a new sheet suggests that Jones acquired Proctor's compiled poems before he began printing this portion of his book.

59. A pamphlet was a short quarto text that "typically consisted of between one sheet and a maximum of twelve sheets, or between eight and ninety-six pages in quarto" (Joad Raymond, *Pamphlets and Pamphleteering in Early Modern Britain* [Cambridge: Cambridge University Press, 2006], 5). On the likely destruction of pamphlets, see Roger Chartier and Peter Stallybrass, "What Is a Book?," in *The Cambridge Companion to Textual Scholarship*, ed. Neil Fraistat and Julia Flanders (Cambridge: Cambridge University Press, 2013), 196–98.

60. *A gorgious Gallery*, sigs. A2r, A2v.

61. Ibid., sig. A2r.

62. Ibid., sig. A2v.

63. Ibid., sig. A2r.

64. Ibid. On Munday's background, see Rollins, *A Gorgeous Gallery*, xix.

65. *A gorgious Gallery*, sig. A2r.

66. Ibid.

67. Ibid.

68. Ibid. For this dual etymology, see Wall, *The Imprint of Gender*, 103; and *OED Online*, s.v. "invention, *n.*," senses 1 and 2.

69. As John Lennard writes, parentheses were "exploited" to "command attention" for the enclosed material (*But I Digress: The Exploitation of Parentheses in English Printed Verse* [Oxford: Clarendon Press, 1991], 37).

70. Claire M. L. Bourne, "Typography *After* Performance," in *Rethinking Theatrical Documents in Shakespeare's England*, ed. Tiffany Stern (London: Bloomsbury, 2019), 202. My thanks to Claire Bourne for sharing this work with me prior to publication.

71. Zarnowiecki, *Fair Copies*, 8.

72. On this transition, see for instance, G. K. Hunter, "Drab and Golden Lyrics of the Renaissance," in *Forms of Lyric: Selected Papers from the English Institute*, ed. Reuben A. Brower (New York: Columbia University Press, 1970), 1–18.

73. The spelling and capitalization of the title *The Paradyse of dainty devises* varied significantly in each edition. For clarity, I follow the title from 1576 in text.

74. *The Paradyse of daynty devises* was published in 1576, 1577, 1578, 1580, 1585, 1590, 1596, 1600, and 1606. Jones printed at least the 1576 and 1578 editions, and probably the one from 1577 as well. While we have no extant copy of the 1577 *Paradyse*, it was transcribed by William Herbert in a 1777 manuscript that is now held at the Bodleian as MS Douce e.16. Steven May has argued convincingly for reading that transcription as evidence of William Hunnis's involvement in reshaping the collection between the first and second editions ("William Hunnis and the 1577 *Paradise of Dainty Devices*," *Studies in Bibliography* 28 [1975], 63–80).

75. *The Paradyse of daynty devises* (London: Henry Disle, 1576), sig. A1r, RB 13658, Huntington Library, San Marino, California.

76. Ibid., sig. A2r.

77. Disle continued to publish *The Paradyse* until his 1582 death, after which the bookseller Edward White assumed the rights to the book. Additional poems were added: twelve in 1577; one in 1578; seven in 1580; and seven in 1585. Each time new poems were added, nearly the same quantity was cut, such that the 1576 edition contained 99 poems, while there were 105 in the 1585 imprint.

78. Lewis, *English Literature in the Sixteenth Century*, 64. For challenges to Lewis's disparaging view of midcentury verse, see Yvor Winters, "The 16th Century Lyric in England: A Critical and Historical Reinterpretation; Part I," *Poetry* 53, no. 5 (1939): 258–72; and Hunter, "Drab and Golden Lyrics."

79. Lewis, *English Literature in the Sixteenth Century*, 227, 267.

80. Gérard Genette, *Paratexts: Thresholds of Interpretation*, trans. Jane E. Lewin (Cambridge: Cambridge University Press, 1997), 2.

81. Helen Smith and Louise Wilson, "Introduction," in Smith and Wilson, eds., *Renaissance Paratexts* (Cambridge: Cambridge University Press, 2011), 2–3.

82. For this reason, I tend not to use Genette's language of "paratext" in my readings of early printed poetry. The term presumes a hierarchy of textual components that was not yet fully operative in the sixteenth century.

83. *The Paradyse of daynty devises* (1576), sigs. F1v, F2r, F2v. The gloss for the heading of poem 42 comes from its refrain.

84. Ibid., sig. F1v.

85. Ibid., sigs. F2r, F3r.

86. Ibid., sig. ²A1r.

87. *The Paradyse of daynty devises* (London: Henry Disle, 1578), sig. D3r, EEBO copy.

88. *The Paradyse of daynty devises* (London, 1585), sig. M3r, RB 13659, Huntington Library, San Marino, California.

89. Ibid., sig. M3v.

90. *The Paradyse of daynty devises* (1576), sig. ²A1v.

91. Ibid., sig. B4r.

92. Ibid., sig. B4r.

93. Ibid., sig. B4r–B4v.

94. Ibid., sig. E4v.

95. *The Paradyse of daintie Devises* (London: Henry Disle, 1580), sigs. K3v, K4r, K4v, Folger STC 7518.

96. Ibid., sigs. K3v, K4v.

97. The manuscript opens with the translation of St. Bernard's verses in Thomas Tusser's *Five Hundreth Points of Good Husbandry* (1573), Thomas Churchyard's dedicatory verse in praise of learning in *Huloet's Dictionarie* (1572), two poems without identifiable print sources, and the opening address from Barnabe Googe's *A newe Booke called the Shippe of safegarde* (1569). One of the two unknown poems later appeared in *The Trevelyon Miscellany*, a massive and elaborately illustrated manuscript that also copied work from printed books (Thomas Trevilian, *The Trevelyon Miscellany of 1608: A Facsimile of Folger Shakespeare Library MS V.b.232*, ed. Heather Wolfe [Seattle: Folger Shakespeare Library; distributed by University of Washington Press, 2007], fols. 180r-180v).

98. Folger V.a.149, fols. 17v, 22r.

99. Leche may well have been a student practicing his penmanship with the example offered by *The Paradyse* because several initial letterforms are given in a rough emboldened script, perhaps as experiments with how to capture the typography of his source.

100. Folger V.a.149, fol. 21r.

101. *The Paradyse of daynty devises* (1576), sig. C3r.

102. Hyder Rollins, ed., *England's Helicon, 1600, 1614* (Cambridge, MA: Harvard University Press, 1935), 2:3.

103. *The Phoenix Nest* (London: John Jackson, 1593), sig. A1r, Folger STC 21516.

104. O'Callaghan, "Textual Gatherings," para. 8.

105. Ibid., para. 9.

106. On the multiple senses of "rhapsody," see Piers Brown, "Donne, Rhapsody, and Textual Order," in Eckhardt and Smith, *Manuscript Miscellanies*, 41–42.

107. William Scott, *The Model of Poesy*, ed. Gavin Alexander (Cambridge: Cambridge University Press, 2013), 22; on Scott's connections to Sidney, see Alexander's introduction, xix–lxiii.

108. As Gavin Alexander summarizes the fictions of the collection, *Englands Helicon* transformed "a medley of shepherdly voices inspired by Sidney's own pastoral perfor-mances" into a "dialogue with the other poets assembled on its pages" (*Writing After Sidney: The Literary Response to Sir Philip Sidney, 1586–1640* [Oxford: Oxford University Press, 2006], 32).

109. Scott, *The Model of Poesy*, 21–22.

110. On how these publications articulated a new sense of English authority, see Zachary Lesser and Peter Stallybrass, "The First Literary *Hamlet* and the Commonplac-ing of Professional Plays," *Shakespeare Quarterly* 59, no. 4 (2008): 383–87.

111. *Englands Helicon* (London: John Flasket, 1600), sig. A3r, Folger STC 3191, copy 1.

112. Ling wrote the preface for *Politeuphuia* and had connections to several authors in *Englands Helicon*, including Drayton and Munday. See J. William Hebel, "Nicholas Ling and *Englands Helicon*," *The Library*, 4th ser., 5, no. 2 (1924): 153–60; and Rollins, *England's Helicon, 1600, 1614*, 2:60–62.

113. *Englands Helicon*, sig. A4r.

114. Ibid.

115. Ibid., sigs. C1r, C1v.

116. Variants on the attribution "Sheepheard Tonie" appeared on sigs. D4r, F4v, I4r, O3v, Aa3v, and Bb3v. The poem headed "Montana the Sheepheard, his love to Aminta" had first appeared in Munday's translation of *Fedele and Fortunio: The pleasant and fine conceited Comoedie of two Italian Gentlemen* (1585). The poem headed "To Colin Cloute" first appeared in Munday's translation of *The Second book of the Primaleon of Greece* (1596).

117. In addition to Munday's decades-long involvement with compiling stationers like Richard Jones in *A gorgious Gallery, of gallant Inventions*, he was one of the contribu-tors to Bodenham's commonplace book project. See Lesser and Stallybrass, "The First Literary *Hamlet*," 384.

118. It is possible that Ling or Flasket was responding to pressure from the Sidney family. Cancel slips also reassigned a poem attributed to Sidney to Breton, and (most baldly) one from Greville to a blank slip. That the cancels are present in multiple copies suggests they were added before the books were sold. See *Englands Helicon*, sigs. H1r, L3r, N4r, O4r, P1r.

119. *Englands Helicon*, sig. Q2v.

120. Ibid., sig. H2v.

121. Thomas Watson, *The Hekatompathia, or Passionate Centurie of Love* (London: Gabriell Cawood, 1582), sig. ²A4v, Folger STC 25118a, copy 1.

122. Ibid.

123. *The Phoenix Nest*, sig. N1v.

124. *Englands Helicon*, sig. L2v.

125. *The Phoenix Nest*, sig. N2r; *Englands Helicon*, sig. L3r.

126. *Englands Helicon*, sig. L3r.

127. Ibid. Of the three copies of *Englands Helicon* I have checked, this "Ignoto" slip is partially ripped away in Folger Shakespeare Library STC 3191, copy 1; absent in Folger Shakespeare Library STC 3191, copy 2, though the discoloration of the paper reveals its outlines; and present in Newberry Library Case 4A 820.

128. *Englands Helicon*, sig. A4r.

3. GASCOIGNE'S INVENTIONS

1. Gascoigne, *A Hundreth Sundrie Flowres*, ed. Pigman (2000), 1. Pigman's edition includes *A Hundreth sundrie Flowres* as well as the alterations made in *The Posies*. Both are hereafter cited parenthetically in text with reference to page numbers for the prose, including the lengthy poem headings, and to line numbers for the verse.

2. Jane Griffiths, *Diverting Authorities: Experimental Glossing Practices in Manuscript and Print* (Oxford: Oxford University Press, 2014), 155.

3. Rachel Stenner, *The Typographic Imaginary in Early Modern English Literature* (New York: Routledge, 2019), 138.

4. On the work done by initials as the typographic expression of an absent identity, see Marcy North, *The Anonymous Renaissance: Cultures of Discretion in Tudor-Stuart England* (Chicago: University of Chicago Press, 2003), 56–58.

5. On the division of the job, see Adrian Weiss, "Shared Printing, Printer's Copy, and the Text(s) of Gascoigne's *A Hundreth Sundrie Flowres*," *Studies in Bibliography* 45 (1992): 75.

6. We can hear this sense of discovery in the Latin root, *invenire*, literally "to come upon." On how invention was a flexible category for English writers, since grammar schools did not follow a consistent treatment of the topic, see Peter Mack, *Elizabethan Rhetoric: Theory and Practice* (Cambridge: Cambridge University Press, 2002), 46.

7. For the constitutive features of "commonplace book culture," see Adam Smyth, *Autobiography in Early Modern England* (Cambridge: Cambridge University Press, 2010), 126–30.

8. Crane, *Framing Authority*, 175. Roland Greene likewise describes the sixteenth-century fascination with the language of invention as a "palimpsest where several other terms are written beneath the surface" (*Five Words: Critical Semantics in the Age of Shakespeare and Cervantes* [Chicago: University of Chicago Press, 2013], 28).

9. Given the volume's length of fifty-two sheets, it is possible that *A Hundreth sundrie Flowres* was sold bound and likely that it was never read in a provisional or stab-stitched format. For a survey of the frequency at which quartos of various lengths were stab-stitched, see Aaron T. Pratt, "Stab-Stitching and the Status of Early English Playbooks as Literature," *The Library*, 7th ser., 16, no. 3 (2015): 317.

10. Fleming, *Graffiti and the Writing Arts*, 42–43.

11. Crane, *Framing Authority*, 92.

12. Saunders, "The Stigma of Print," 139–40. For an opposing viewpoint, which identifies this stigma with nineteenth-century editorial regimes, see May, "Tudor Aristocrats and the 'Stigma of Print.'"

13. Rosenfeld, *Indecorous Thinking*, 2.

14. These shadowy figures are identified only with initials, even though Smith, the actual publisher, and Bynneman, one of the printers, are named elsewhere in the volume. See George Gascoigne, *A Hundreth sundrie Flowres bounde up in one small Poesie* (London: Richard Smith, 1573), sigs. A1r, X4v, Folger STC 11635, copy 2.

15. Weiss, "Shared Printing," 89, 91.

16. Melnikoff, *Elizabethan Publishing*, 101.

17. Michael Hetherington, "Gascoigne's Accidents: Contingency, Skill, and the Logic of Writing," *English Literary Renaissance* 46, no. 1 (2016): 55.

18. Although these posies are arranged in clusters that are temptingly authorial, Gillian Austen has shown that the posies often contradict other paratexts and undermine any consistency of "biographical identity, mood, or even . . . attitude" (*George Gascoigne* [Woodbridge, England: D. S. Brewer, 2008], 79).

19. Winters, "The 16th Century Lyric," 263.

20. Ibid.

21. Marquis, *Richard Tottel's "Songes and Sonettes,"* 1.

22. For an account of Gascoigne's place in the community of writers at the Inns of Court, see Jessica Winston, "Lyric Poetry at the Early Elizabethan Inns of Court: Forming a Professional Community," in *The Intellectual and Cultural World of the Early Modern Inns of Courts*, ed. Jayne Elisabeth Archer, Elizabeth Goldring, and Sarah Knight (Manchester: Manchester University Press, 2011), 236–39.

23. Laurie Shannon, "Poetic Companies: Musters of Agency in George Gascoigne's 'Friendly Verse,'" *GLQ: A Journal of Lesbian and Gay Studies* 10, no. 3 (2004): 455. Shannon elsewhere notes the significance of the Inns of Court for "an extended network of quasi-corporate authorship" that "arose in the 1560s and beyond" ("Minerva's Men: Horizontal Nationhood and the Literary Production of Googe, Turberville, and Gascoigne," in *The Oxford Handbook of Tudor Literature, 1485–1603*, ed. Mike Pincombe and Cathy Shrank [Oxford: Oxford University Press, 2011], 453).

24. Wall, *The Imprint of Gender*, 25, 244.

25. Alan Stewart, "Gelding Gascoigne," in *Prose Fiction and Early Modern Sexualities in England, 1570–1640*, ed. Constance Relihan and Goran Stanivukovic (New York: Palgrave Macmillan, 2004), 147, 164.

26. Gascoigne, *A Hundreth sundrie Flowres* (1573), sigs. ²D2v–²D3r.

27. Daniel Tiffany, *Infidel Poetics: Riddles, Nightlife, Substance* (Chicago: University of Chicago Press, 2009), 35.

28. Ibid., 35, 39.

29. Humphrey Gifford, *A Posie of Gilloflowers, Eche Differing from Other in Colour and Odour, Yet All Sweete* (London: John Perin, 1580), sig. L2r, EEBO copy.

30. Ibid.

31. Ibid., sig. T4r.

32. Ibid., sig. I1r.

33. Puttenham, *The Art of English Poesy*, 383.

34. Ibid.

35. Ibid.

36. Gifford, *A Posie of Gilloflowers*, sig. I1r.

37. Lorna Hutson, *The Invention of Suspicion: Law and Mimesis in Shakespeare and Renaissance Drama* (Oxford: Oxford University Press, 2007), 130.

38. Ibid., 206.

39. As Pigman points out, *tuli* has an array of meanings: I "carried," "endured," and, perhaps, "related" or "told" (*A Hundreth Sundrie Flowres*, 637).

40. These translations are Pigman's rendering of the heading of poem 61 (ibid., 640).

41. On Gascoigne's innovative ordering of these sonnets, see William O. Harris, "Early Elizabethan Sonnets in Sequence," *Studies in Philology* 68, no. 4 (1971): 465.

42. Gascoigne, *A Hundreth sundrie Flowres* (1573), sigs. ^{2}X1v–^{2}X2r.

43. For an argument about the significance of interruptions in Tusser's calendar, see Jessica Rosenberg, "A Digression to Hospitality: Thrift and Christmastime in Shakespeare and the Literature of Husbandry," in *Shakespeare and Hospitality: Ethics, Politics, and Exchange*, ed. David B. Goldstein and Julia Reinhard Lupton (New York: Routledge, 2016), 48–55. On the paraph as a mark of expressive typography, see Claire M. L. Bourne, "Dramatic Pilcrows," *Papers of the Bibliographical Society of America* 108, no. 4 (2014): 413–52.

44. Thomas Tusser, *A hundreth good pointes of husbandry, lately maried unto a hundreth good poynts of huswifery* (London: Richard Tottel, 1570), sig. L3r, RB 49623, Huntington Library, San Marino, California.

45. Gillian Austen, "The Adventures Passed by Master George Gascoigne: Experiments in Prose," in *The Oxford Handbook of English Prose, 1500–1640*, ed. Andrew Hadfield (Oxford: Oxford University Press, 2013), 159.

46. On the relative lateness of many prose links, see Weiss, "Shared Printing," 96.

47. On the function of "etc." to indicate both incompletion but also a presumption that the reader would understand to complete it, see Laurie E. Maguire, "Typographical Embodiment: The Case of *etcetera*," in *The Oxford Handbook of Shakespeare and Embodiment: Gender, Sexuality, and Race*, ed. Valerie Traub (Oxford: Oxford University Press, 2016), 527–48.

48. On the capacious senses of "compile," see Knight, *Bound to Read*, 8–9.

49. Isabella Whitney, *A Sweet Nosgay, or Pleasant Posye* (London: Richard Jones, 1573), sigs. C5r–v, British Library C.39.b.45.

50. Ibid., sigs. A6v.

51. George Gascoigne, *The Posies of George Gascoigne Esquire* (London: Richard Smith, 1575), sig. T2r. The reader's comments appear in the copy of this book held in the Rare Books and Manuscripts Library, University of Illinois at Urbana-Champaign, as 821 G211575a.

52. On the adoption of *lectio continua* by the English Church, see Susan Wabuda, *Preaching During the English Reformation* (Cambridge: Cambridge University Press, 2002), 27–28.

53. *The Booke of the Common Praier* (London: Richard Grafton, 1549), sigs. ℭ32r–v, Newberry VAULT Case C8726.548.

54. As Maguire observes of this moment, "etc." does not stand in for "a single body part or a sexual act or an omission but all three: a sexual action inflicted on a body, too terrible to be articulated ("Typographical Embodiment," 531).

55. Margaret Simon, "Authorial Feints and Affecting Forms in George Gascoigne's *The Adventures of Master F.J.*," in *Renaissance Papers, 2013*, ed. Jim Pearce and Joanna Kucinski (Rochester, NY: Published for the Southeastern Renaissance Conference by Camden House, 2014), 51.

56. Like *A Hundreth*, the page signatures and pagination are discontinuous in "Hearbes," the section containing the drama.

57. George Whetstone, *A Remembraunce of the wel imployed life, & godly end, of George Gaskoigne Esquire* (London: Edward Aggas, 1577), sig. A2r.

58. Richard Helgerson, *The Elizabethan Prodigals* (Berkeley: University of California Press, 1976), 47–49. See also G. T. Prouty, *George Gascoigne: Elizabethan Courtier, Soldier, and Poet* (New York: Columbia University Press, 1942), 239–41.

59. W. W. Greg and E. Boswell, eds., *Records of the Court of the Stationers' Company, 1576 to 1602, from Register B* (London: Bibliographical Society, 1930), 86–87.

60. Cyndia Clegg, *Press Censorship in Elizabethan England* (Cambridge: Cambridge University Press, 1997), 103–7; Austen, *George Gascoigne*, 85–88.

61. Hutson, *Invention of Suspicion*, 205.

62. John Baker, *The Oxford History of the Laws of England*, vol. 6, *1483–1558* (Oxford: Oxford University Press, 2003), 257.

63. For an account of the centripetal tendencies of sixteenth-century English government, see Steve Hindle, *The State and Social Change in Early Modern England, c. 1550–1640* (New York: St. Martin's Press, 2000), 3–6. For an argument about the influence of this flexible jurisdiction on the English literary imagination, see Bradin Cormack, *A Power to Do Justice: Jurisdiction, English Literature, and the Rise of Common Law, 1509–1625* (Chicago: University of Chicago Press, 2007), 1–2.

64. Charlotte Scott, *Shakespeare and the Idea of the Book* (Oxford: Oxford University Press, 2007), 2; Sarah Wall-Randell, *The Immaterial Book: Reading and Romance in Early Modern England* (Ann Arbor: University of Michigan Press, 2013), 2.

4. THESE ENSUING SONNETS

1. Gascoigne, *A Hundreth Sundrie Flowres*, ed. Pigman (2000), from the heading to poem 13, on p. 228.

2. Philip Sidney, *The Poems of Sir Philip Sidney*, ed. William A. Ringler (Oxford: Clarendon Press, 1962), sonnet 3, line 3, and sonnet 15, lines 2–3. Ringler's edition is here-

after cited parenthetically in text by poem and line number, with arabic numerals for the sonnets and roman numerals for the songs.

3. For representative arguments, see Elizabeth Heale, *Autobiography and Authorship in Renaissance Verse: Chronicles of the Self* (Basingstoke: Palgrave Macmillan, 2002), 144–53; Anne Ferry, *The "Inward" Language: Sonnets of Wyatt, Sidney, Shakespeare, Donne* (Chicago: University of Chicago Press, 1983); and Carol Thomas Neely, "The Structure of English Renaissance Sonnet Sequences," *ELH* 45, no. 3 (1978): 359–89.

4. On the development of the multiple forms of "sonnets," see Cathy Shrank, "'Matters of Love as of Discourse': The English Sonnet, 1560–1580," *Studies in Philology* 105, no. 1 (2008): 31–33.

5. William Shakespeare, *The Complete Sonnets and Poems*, ed. Colin Burrow (Oxford: Oxford University Press, 2002), 381.

6. Henry Constable, *Diana: The praises of his Mistres in certaine sweete Sonnets* (London: Richard Smith, 1592), sig. A4r, RB 58467, Huntington Library, San Marino, California.

7. "Insuing" speaks to a poetic order that was apparently artless, coming into focus without the interventions of compilers. The word was used in the period to refer to a portion of a book or discourse that followed or succeeded another. See *OED Online*, "ensue, v.," sense 5a.

8. While "Astrophil" is the spelling preferred by manuscripts contemporary to Sidney, he was called "Astrophel" in early print, including the volume title *Astrophel and Stella*. Throughout this chapter, the spelling "Astrophil" will be used except for references to those early editions.

9. Scott A. Trudell, *Unwritten Poetry: Song, Performance, and Media in Early Modern England* (Oxford: Oxford University Press, 2019), 64.

10. See my third chapter for the evolving etymology of "invention" at the end of the sixteenth century.

11. *The Poems of Sir Philip Sidney*, 459.

12. On Sidney's rejection of imitative copying, see A. E. B. Coldiron, "Sidney, Watson, and the 'Wrong Ways' to Renaissance Lyric Poetics," *Renaissance Papers, 1997*, ed. T. H. Howard-Hill and Philip Rollinson (Columbia, SC: Published for the Southeastern Renaissance Conference by Camden House, 1997), 49–62.

13. Gavin Alexander, ed., *Sidney's "The Defence of Poesy" and Selected Renaissance Literary Criticism* (London: Penguin Classics, 2004), 10, 9. On Sidney's interest in mental and material expression, see Francis X. Connor, "'Delivering Forth': Philip Sidney's Idea and the Labor of Writing," *Sidney Journal* 31, no. 2 (2013): 53–75. For a comprehensive study of models of imitation, see G. W. Pigman III, "Versions of Imitation in the Renaissance," *Renaissance Quarterly* 33, no. 1 (1980): 1–32.

14. Francesco Petrarca, *Rerum familiarium libri*, trans. Aldo S. Bernardo (Albany: State University of New York Press, 1975), 1:42.

15. Ibid.

16. Rosalie Colie, *The Resources of Kind: Genre-Theory in the Renaissance*, ed. Barbara K. Lewalski (Berkeley: University of California Press, 1973), 14.

17. Margaret Simon, "Refraining Songs: The Dynamics of Form in Sidney's *Astrophil and Stella*," *Studies in Philology* 109, no. 1 (2012): 88.

18. As Joseph J. Scanlon reads *Astrophil and Stella*, "Astrophil fails to fulfill his desires and ends miserably" ("Sidney's *Astrophil and Stella*: 'See What It Is to Love' Sensually!," *SEL: Studies in English Literature, 1500–1900* 16, no. 1 [1976]: 66).

19. Pablo Maurette, "Shakespeare's *Venus and Adonis* and Sixteenth-Century Kiss Poetry," *English Literary Renaissance* 47, no. 3 (2017): 356, 358. My thanks to Pablo Maurette for sharing this work prior to publication.

20. British Library, Add. MS 61822, fol. 96v. Later readers, perhaps perturbed by the apparently unorganized sonnets, supplied two different sets of numeration: arabic numeral headings that give the order of poems in this manuscript and roman numeral marginalia that correspond to the arrangement of the 1598 folio.

21. Mary Sidney Herbert stripped away the work of other poets, corrected multiple errors, integrated the sonnets with the songs, and added a heading above each poem—a simple arabic numeral for the sonnets and ordinal titles for the songs. On the authority of the folio, see Ringler's textual history in *The Poems of Sir Philip Sidney*, 533–34.

22. Alexander, *Writing After Sidney*, 207.

23. Trudell, *Unwritten Poetry*, 78.

24. Ibid., 64.

25. Thomas Newman's second quarto from 1591 dropped the poems from other authors, as well as his preface and another written by Thomas Nashe. Ringler finds that Sidney's heirs forced Newman into this new edition after the first was recalled in September 1591 (*The Poems of Sir Philip Sidney*, 545).

26. Philip Sidney, *Syr P. S. His Astrophel and Stella* (London: Matthew Lownes, [1597?]), sigs. H3r–v, Folger STC 22538.

27. Ibid., K2v.

28. Philip Sidney, *Syr P. S. His Astrophel and Stella* (London: John Charlewood for Thomas Newman, 1591), sig. A2v, EEBO copy.

29. Abraham Fraunce, *The Arcadian Rhetorike* (London: T[homas] Gubbin and T[homas] Newman, 1588), sig. A1r, HathiTrust facsimile of the copy at Columbia University. Thomas Newman and Thomas Gubbyn purchased this license on June 11, 1588 (Arber, *Transcript of the Registers*, 2:492).

30. *Songes and Sonettes* had just been published in an eleventh and final edition in 1587.

31. Philip Sidney, *Sir P. S. His Astrophel and Stella* (London: [John Danter] for Thomas Newman, 1591), sigs. E1v–E2r, Folger STC 22537.

32. Ibid., sig. E1v.

33. *Syr P. S. His Astrophel and Stella* (1597?), sig. F4r.

34. Ibid., sig. H4r.

35. Ibid., sig. K3r.

36. Sonnets were unique, Heather Dubrow explains, because they were "one of the few instances in which a genre is defined in terms of a verse form" ("Lyric Forms," in *The*

Lyric Theory Reader: A Critical Anthology, ed. Virginia Jackson and Yopie Prins [Baltimore, MD: Johns Hopkins University Press, 2014], 122).

37. *The Model of Poesy* develops a history of English poetics that had previously stalled at the wave of rhetorical handbooks published in the 1580s. For the origins of the treatise, see Scott, *The Model of Poesy*, xix–lxiii. On the areas of research opened up by the rediscovery of this manuscript in 2003, see Gavin Alexander and Mary Ellen Lamb, eds., "William Scott's *The Model of Poesy*," special issue, *Sidney Journal* 33, no. 1 (2015).

38. Scott, *The Model of Poesy*, 25.

39. Ibid.

40. Ibid., 28.

41. Ibid., 27–28.

42. Philip Sidney, *The Countesse of Pembrokes Arcadia* (London: William Ponsonby, 1598), sig. ¶4r, Folger STC 22541, copy 1.

43. Ibid., sig. Zz2v.

44. For the classic study of how women are fractured by the male lyric voice, see Nancy J. Vickers, "Diana Described: Scattered Woman and Scattered Rhyme," *Critical Inquiry* 8, no. 2 (1981): 265–79. For arguments that reassess Stella's position as the passive object of Astrophil's passion, see Melissa E. Sanchez, "'In My Selfe the Smart I Try': Female Promiscuity in *Astrophil and Stella*," *ELH* 80, no. 1 (Spring 2013): 1–27; and Laura Kolb, "Stella's Voice: Echo and Collaboration in *Astrophil and Stella* 57 and 58," *Sidney Journal* 30, no. 1 (2012): 79–100.

45. This count excludes sonnets collections within larger composite volumes, like George Gascoigne's "seven Sonets in Sequence" from *A Hundreth sundrie Flowres* (1573) and George Chapman's "A Coronet for his Mistresse Philosophie" from *Ovids Banquet of Sence* (1595), because they are differently fashioned by the design of the physical book.

46. Although Michael Drayton revised *Ideas Mirrour* (1594) multiple times, the later compilations were components of larger books of poems, like *Englands Heroicall Epistles: Newly Enlarged, with Idea* (1599).

47. The relatively few instances of compiled sonnets in manuscript suggest that sonneteers wrote quickly and with print in mind. See Marcy North, "The Sonnets and Book History," in *A Companion to Shakespeare's Sonnets*, ed. Michael Schoenfeldt (Malden, MA: Blackwell, 2010), 208. The only manuscripts with extensive collections of sonnets are work by Sidney and Constable. Sidney's are in British Library Add. MS 15322, British Library Add. MS 61822, and Edinburgh University Library MS De. 5. 96. Constable's appear in Victoria and Albert Museum MS Dyce 25.F.39, British Library Harley MS 7553, Berkeley Castle Select Books 85, Marsh's Library MS Z 3.5.21, and the Arundel Harington Manuscript.

48. Marquis, *Richard Tottel's "Songes and Sonettes,"* 40.

49. As Christopher Warley puts it, the "term 'sonnet sequence' was thought up by Dante Gabriel Rossetti in 1880" (*Sonnet Sequences and Social Distinction in Renaissance England* [Cambridge: Cambridge University Press, 2005], 19).

50. Lewis, *English Literature in the Sixteenth Century*, 327.

51. Thomas P. Roche Jr., *Petrarch and the English Sonnet Sequences* (New York: AMS Press, 1989), xi.

52. Ibid., xii.

53. North, "The Sonnets and Book History," 208.

54. Heather Dubrow, *The Challenges of Orpheus: Lyric Poetry and Early Modern England* (Baltimore, MD: Johns Hopkins University Press, 2008), 179.

55. Gascoigne, *A Hundreth Sundrie Flowres*, ed. Pigman (2000), 227, 256, 278. On Gascoigne's innovative use of the term "sonnet sequence," see Harris, "Early Elizabethan Sonnets in Sequence."

56. Wall, *Imprint of Gender*, 71.

57. Constable, *Diana* (London: Richard Smith, 1592), sig. B2r, RB 58467, Huntington Library, San Marino, California; Constable, *Diana* (London: Richard Smith, 1594), sig. B1v, EEBO copy. On the publication of *Diana*, see the textual history in *The Poems of Henry Constable*, ed. Joan Grundy, Liverpool English Texts and Studies, vol. 6 (Liverpool: Liverpool University Press, 1960), 92–101.

58. *The Paradyse of daynty devises* (London: Henry Disle, 1576), sig. C2v, RB 13658, Huntington Library, San Marino, California.

59. *The Paradyse of daynty devises* (London: Henry Disle, 1578), sigs. I2v–I3r, Bodleian Wood 482 (6).

60. Watson, *The Hekatompathia, or Passionate Centurie of Love* (London: Gabriell Cawood, 1582), sig. C3v, Folger STC 25118a, copy 2.

61. Thomas Lodge, *Scillaes Metamorphosis: Enterlaced with the unfortunate love of Glaucus* (London: Richard Jones, 1589), sigs. F1v–F2r, RB 31529, Huntington Library, San Marino, California.

62. Barnabe Barnes, *Parthenophil and Parthenophe* (London: John Wolfe, 1593), sigs. B2v–B3r, B3v, British Library C.132.i.50.

63. Ibid., sig. D4r.

64. Ibid., sigs. K4r, T3v.

65. Michael Drayton, *The Works of Michael Drayton*, ed. J. William Hebel, Kathleen Tillotson, and Bernard H. Newdigate (Oxford: Shakespeare Head Press, 1961), 1:96.

66. Ibid., "Amour 1," lines 1–4.

67. William Percy, *Sonnets to the Fairest Coelia* (London: W[illiam] P[onsonby?], 1594), sig. A2r, RB 141619, Huntington Library, San Marino, California.

68. Ibid.

69. For an argument about how English sonneteers were "not interested in" the lyric effects of "a whole sequence," see Ferry, *The "Inward" Language*, 125.

70. Samuel Daniel, *Poems and a Defence of Ryme*, ed. Arthur Colby Sprague (Cambridge, MA: Harvard University Press, 1930), 11 ("To Delia," sonnet 1, lines 5–8).

71. For an argument about how account books were themselves performative texts, see Ceri Sullivan, *The Rhetoric of Credit: Merchants in Early Modern Writing* (Madison, NJ: Fairleigh Dickinson University Press, 2002).

72. Samuel Daniel, *Delia: Contayning Certain Sonnets; with the complaint of Rosamund* (London: Simon Waterson, 1592), sig. A2r, Folger STC 6243.2.

73. Robert Tofte, *Laura: The Toyes of a Traveller, or The Feast of Fancie* (London: Valentine Simmes, 1597), sig. E7r, RB 31302, Huntington Library, San Marino, California.

74. Ibid.

75. T. W., *The Tears of Fancie, or Love Disdained* (London: William Barley, 1593), sig. C4v, RB 32085, Huntington Library, San Marino, California.

76. Richard Linche, *Diella, Certaine Sonnets* (London: Henry Olney, 1596), sig. B7v, Folger STC 17091.

77. Ibid., sigs. B7r–v.

78. Constable was a recent Catholic convert who traveled to France with the Essex expedition in the summer of 1591, then stayed on until 1603 in the service of Henri IV and the English Jesuits.

79. Smith had been engaged with the latest trends in printed poetry since the 1570s, when he published Gascoigne's *A Hundreth sundrie Flowres* (1573) and the revised edition of *The Posies of George Gascoigne Esquire* (1575). Charlewood, meanwhile, had within the past year printed the first editions of Sidney's *Astrophel and Stella* and Daniel's *Delia*.

80. *The Poems of Henry Constable*, p. 132, line 5.

81. Ibid., p. 109. In making this case for Smith's control over *Diana*, I am disagreeing with Grundy, who argues that Constable could have sent this introductory sonnet from France with the intent of publishing his gathered work. Grundy does acknowledge that the second and third editions of *Diana* in 1594 and 1595 were probably Smith's doing, since they added forty-one poems that were not Constable's, including eight of Sidney's *Certain Sonnets* first published in *The Countesse of Pembrokes Arcadia* in 1598. Given the lack of evidence for Constable's direct involvement, as well as Smith's history in meeting print conventions for contemporary poetry, I posit the publisher's control over all three editions. See the textual history in *The Poems of Henry Constable*, 93–94.

82. Marsh's Library MS Z3.5.21, fol. 26r. Cited in the online *Catalogue of English Literary Manuscripts, 1450–1700*, https://celm-ms.org.uk/repositories/marshs-library-dublin.html.

83. Ruth Hughey, ed., *The Arundel Harington Manuscript of Tudor Poetry*, 2 vols. (Columbus: Ohio State University Press, 1960), 1:244. María Jesús Pérez-Júaregui describes Constable's poems in the Arundel Harington Manuscript as a "single booklet" that is materially "unrelated to the rest of the contents in the miscellany" ("A Queen in a 'Purple Robe': Henry Constable's Poetic Tribute to Mary, Queen of Scots," *Studies in Philology* 113, no. 3 [2016]: 578n6).

84. On the copying of the Todd manuscript, see Claire Bryony Williams "'This and the Rest Maisters We All May Mende': Reconstructing the Practices and Anxieties of a Manuscript Miscellany's Reader-Compiler," *Huntington Library Quarterly* 80, no. 2 (2017): 284.

85. Victoria and Albert Museum, Dyce 25.F.39, fol. 12.

86. Ibid., fols. 12, 38.

87. Ibid., fol. 12.

88. Ibid., fol. 19v.

89. Constable, *Diana* (London: Richard Smith, 1592), sig. D1r, RB 58467, Huntington Library, San Marino, California.

90. Ibid.

91. Henry Lok, *Ecclesiastes, Otherwise Called the Preacher* (London: Richard Field, 1597), sig. A1r, Folger STC 16696.

92. Lok, *Sundry Christian Passions Contained in two hundred Sonnets* (London: Richard Field, 1593), sigs. ²A1r, D3r, RB 12519, Huntington Library, San Marino, California.

93. Ibid., sig. ²A1v.

94. Ibid., sig. D5r.

95. Ibid., sig. A5v.

96. Ibid.

97. Ibid., sigs. A5v–A6r.

98. Patricia Parker, "Preposterous Events," *Shakespeare Quarterly* 43, no. 2 (1992): 188.

99. Kimberly Anne Coles, *Religion, Reform, and Women's Writing in Early Modern England* (Cambridge: Cambridge University Press, 2008), 147.

100. For a study of the long history of the Sternhold and Hopkins translation, see Hannibal Hamlin, *Psalm Culture and Early Modern English Literature* (Cambridge: Cambridge University Press, 2004), 19–50.

101. *The Booke of the Common Praier* (London: Richard Grafton, 1549), sig. ℭ3r, Newberry VAULT Case C8726.548.

102. On the prominence of the *Miserere* in England, see Hamlin, *Psalm Culture*, 173–74.

103. For a study of Field's career, see A. E. M. Kirwood, "Richard Field, Printer, 1589–1624," *The Library*, 4th ser., 12, no. 1 (1931): 1–39.

104. On Field's work with Harington, see W. W. Greg, "An Elizabethan Printer and His Copy," *The Library*, 4th ser., 4, no. 2 (1923): 102–19.

105. Lok, *Ecclesiastes, Otherwise Called the Preacher*, sig. A5r.

106. Ibid., sig. V7r.

107. Ibid., sig. I7r.

108. Ibid.

109. Lok, *Sundry Christian Passions*, sig. A6r.

110. *The Returne from Pernassus* (London: John Wright, 1606), sig. B2r. Newberry Case 3A 2499.

111. Ibid.

112. *The Returne from Pernassus* had been performed even earlier, prior to 1602 (J. B. Leishman, *The Three Parnassus Plays (1598–1601)* [London: Nicholson & Watson, 1949], 24).

113. Sidney, *The Countesse of Pembrokes Arcadia*, sig. ¶2r.

114. Arthur F. Marotti, "'Love Is Not Love': Elizabethan Sonnet Sequences and the Social Order," *ELH* 49, no. 2 (1982): 396.

115. *A Poetical Rapsody* (London: John Baily, 1602), sig. D2r, Folger STC 6373.

116. I take the order and contents of *The Passionate Pilgrim* from Colin Burrow's educated reconstruction of the first edition, which is extant only in fragments. See his introduction in William Shakespeare, *The Complete Sonnets and Poems*, ed. Colin Burrow (Oxford: Oxford University Press, 2002), 74–82.

117. For an account of the traditional "Delian" structure of *Shake-speares Sonnets*, see Ilona Bell, "'That Which Thou Hast Done': Shakespeare's Sonnets and *A Lover's Complaint*," in *Shakespeare's Sonnets: Critical Essays*, ed. James Schiffer (New York: Garland, 1999), 455, 471. For a counterargument that proposes these conventions were much more standardized, see Heather Dubrow, "'Dressing Old Words New'? Re-evaluating the 'Delian Structure,'" in Schoenfeldt, *A Companion to Shakespeare's Sonnets*, 92–94.

5. BOOKS CALLED *POEMS*

1. Many potential causes for this shift have been posited. Harold Love identified the 1603 ascension of James I as an impetus for restricting potentially controversial writing (*The Culture and Commerce of Texts: Scribal Publication in Seventeenth-Century England* [Amherst: University of Massachusetts Press, 1998], viii). Because manuscript poetry circulation was centered around the universities and Inns of Court, Mary Hobbs proposed that it was "a matter of shared education" that "led to this nostalgia for the past in a climate hostile to the arts" (*Early Seventeenth-Century Verse Miscellany Manuscripts* [Aldershot, England: Scolar Press, 1992], 148, 149).

2. For an account of the "distinctive ability" of manuscript verse collectors to "cultivate relationships between texts," see Eckhardt, *Manuscript Verse Collectors*, 8.

3. Eckhardt and Smith "Introduction," in *Manuscript Miscellanies*, 1–2.

4. As H. R. Woudhuysen has described, there was a tremendous desire for Donne's poetry: compilers "often try to assemble all his known shorter poems" and may have been pursuing the "idea of a collected edition of the poet's work" (*Sir Philip Sidney and the Circulation of Manuscripts, 1558–1640* [Oxford: Clarendon Press, 1996], 158).

5. For the classic account of how an "ambition not only to write great poems but also to fill the role of the great poet" inspired England's first generation of laureate authors, see Richard Helgerson, *Self-Crowned Laureates: Spenser, Jonson, Milton, and the Literary System* (Berkeley: University of California Press, 1983), 2.

6. While Marriot was only one figure in a much broader network of poetic compilers, both in his own bookshop and beyond, I take the success of Donne's printed compilation as a sign of the bookseller's successful investment and name Marriot as the primary agent behind *Poems, By J. D.* For a description of the multiple and, at times unknowable, agents who contributed to the printed *Poems, By J. D.*, see John Donne, *The Variorum Edition of the Poetry of John Donne*, ed. Gary A. Stringer et al. (Bloomington: Indiana University Press, 1995–), 2:lxxvi–lxxxii. On Marriot's positioning of himself as the "printer"

responsible for *Poems, By J. D.*, see David Scott Kastan, "The Body of the Text," *ELH* 81, no. 2 (2014): 466n52.

7. John Donne, *John Donne: Selected Letters*, ed. P. M. Oliver (Manchester: Carcanet Press, 2002), 79–80. For an account of Goodere's important role in collecting and transmitting Donne's poetry, see Daniel Starza Smith, *John Donne and the Conway Papers: Patronage and Manuscript Circulation in the Early Seventeenth Century* (Oxford: Oxford University Press, 2014), 203–8.

8. Circuitously, the *Oxford English Dictionary* uses the evidence of John Donne Jr.'s 1651 printing of this letter to ascribe the origins of the word to Donne in 1614. See *OED Online*, s.v. "valediction, *n.*," senses 1 and 2.

9. *Variorum Edition of the Poetry of John Donne*, 3:lii. The number is even higher, well over five thousand seventeenth-century witnesses, when we include printed sources. For the most up-to-date count, see "Master List of Poems in 17th-Century Sources," *Digital Donne: The Online "Variorum,"* http://donnevariorum.tamu.edu/toolsandresources /master-list-of-poems.

10. On the Westmoreland Manuscript, now in the Berg Collection at the New York Public Library, see *John Donne: Selected Writings*, ed. Janel Mueller (Oxford: Oxford University Press, 2015), xvii–xviii.

11. On the Skipwith Manuscript, now British Library Add. MS 25707, see Arthur F. Marotti, "Neighborhood, Social Networks, and the Making of a Family's Manuscript Poetry Collection: The Case of British Library Additional MS 25707," in *Material Readings of Early Modern Culture: Texts and Social Practices, 1580–1730*, ed. James Daybell and Peter Hinds (Basingstoke: Palgrave Macmillan, 2010), 185–207.

12. On the dates for the circulation of Donne's poetry, see Peter Beal, "Introduction: The Manuscripts of Donne's Verse," *Catalogue of English Literary Manuscripts 1450–1700*, http://www.celm-ms.org.uk/introductions/DonneJohn.html.

13. On the process of collating, correcting, and expanding manuscript collections of Donne's work, see ibid.

14. As Arthur F. Marotti observes, "more poems are misattributed to Donne than to any other English Renaissance poet," (*Manuscript, Print, and the English Renaissance Lyric*, 158). See as well Deborah Aldrich Larson, "Donne's Contemporary Reputation: Evidence from Some Commonplace Books and Manuscript Miscellanies," *John Donne Journal: Studies in the Age of Donne* 12, nos. 1–2 (1993): 115.

15. North, *The Anonymous Renaissance*, 195.

16. The discussion that follows is of Folger V.a.103, a quarto of 169 leaves, including several blanks, that was compiled by the Smith family of Long Aston, Somersetshire, between 1620 and 1665. The primary scribe was also responsible for a related verse collection now held at the University of Nottingham as Pw V 37. For an account of this pair of manuscripts, see Eckhardt, *Manuscript Verse Collectors*, 55–66.

17. Crowley, *Manuscript Matters*, 33.

18. V.a.103, fols. 68v, 69r.

19. V.a.103, fol. 31v.

20. V.a.103, fol. 32r. On the history of this noncanonical poem, see Eckhardt, *Manuscript Verse Collectors*, 56n66.

21. V.a.103, fol. 76r.

22. V.a.103, fol. 76v.

23. Samuel Johnson, *Lives of the English Poets*, ed. George Birkbeck Hill (New York: Octagon Books, 1967) 1:19–20.

24. Ibid., 20

25. T. S. Eliot, *The Varieties of Metaphysical Poetry*, ed. Ronald Schuchard (New York: Harcourt Brace, 1993), 55.

26. John Donne, "A Valediction Forbidding Mourning," lines 21–24, in *The Complete Poems of John Donne*, ed. Robin Robbins (New York: Routledge, 2013), 259.

27. Eliot, *Varieties of Metaphysical Poetry*, 132.

28. *Variorum Edition of the Poetry of John Donne*, 6:179, "Obsequyes upon the Lord Harrington the last that dyed," lines 93–96.

29. Ibid., p. 177, lines 27–28.

30. John Donne, *Devotions Upon Emergent Occasions and Death's Duel* (New York: Vintage Books, 1999), 102.

31. Ibid.

32. For an argument about how "a poem's full significance" arises from the expanded field of "affiliations and resonances that it develops among other texts and in its various contexts, no matter how local or even physical," see Eckhardt, *Manuscript Verse Collectors*, 14.

33. This manuscript is Huntington MS EL 6893. Copied around 1622, it is a quarto of 185 leaves bound in contemporary vellum with watercolor decorations. For a detailed description, see Ted-Larry Pebworth, comp., "First-Line Index to HH1, EL 6893, Henry E. Huntington Library," *Digital Donne: The Online "Variorum,"* http://donnevariorum.tamu.edu/html/resources/fli/gr3assoc-hh1fli.html.

34. EL 6893, fol. 81r.

35. EL 6893, fol. 3r.

36. EL 6893, fol. 81r.

37. EL 6893, fol. 115r.

38. EL 6893, fol. 81v.

39. EL 6893, fol. 115r.

40. Arthur F. Marotti, *John Donne, Coterie Poet* (Madison: University of Wisconsin Press, 1986), 24.

41. John Donne, *Poems, By J. D. with Elegies on the Authors Death* (London: John Marriot, 1633), sig. B1r, Folger STC 7045, copy 2.

42. The satires probably appear last because Marriot had difficulty registering them. He first entered the project in the Stationers' Register on September 13, 1632, when he omitted five elegies and all five satires, which he returned to register on October 31. Donne's elegies would not be printed in full until 1669 (Arber, *Transcript of the Registers of the Company of Stationers of London*, 4:285, 287).

43. On how Marriot made "a volume that more closely resembles a contemporary manuscript compilation than a formal sequence or critical collection," see Erin A. McCarthy, "*Poems, by J. D.* (1635) and the Creation of John Donne's Literary Biography," *John Donne Journal: Studies in the Age of Donne* 32 (2013): 61.

44. *Poems, By J. D.* (1633), sigs. Cc4v–Ddr1.

45. Ibid., sigs. T2v–V3r.

46. Ibid., sig. Gg1v.

47. Ibid., sig. ²A1v, Folger STC 7045.2, copy 1. This introductory statement is on a single sheet that was probably added partway through printing the 1633 *Poems, By J. D.*: it only appears in some copies, and its placement varies.

48. Ibid. McCarthy reads this description as a reference to Orpheus, "whose severed head continued to sing after his limbs' dispersal" ("*Poems, by J. D.* (1635) and the Creation of John Donne's Literary Biography," 61).

49. *Poems, By J. D.* (1633), sig. ²A1v.

50. "The Storm," lines 1–3, in *The Complete Poems of John Donne*, 65–66.

51. Peter Stallybrass, "Books and Scrolls: Navigating the Bible," in *Books and Readers in Early Modern England*, ed. Jennifer Andersen and Elizabeth Sauer (Philadelphia: University of Pennsylvania Press, 2002), 43.

52. Folger Shakespeare Library V.a.245, fol. 44v.

53. This temporary quality makes it a challenge to recount the history of bookmarks, because they were often supplements to bindings that were easily lost over time. We do have visual representations of Bible strings in paintings, as well as descriptions of them in contemporary lexicons, like Richard Perceval's definition of "register" as the "small strings to put betweene the leaves of a booke" in his *A Dictionarie in Spanish and English* (London: Edm[und] Bolifant, 1599), sig. Gg1v, Newberry Case folio X 722.67. For descriptions of extant bookmarks, see Peter Beal, *A Dictionary of English Manuscript Terminology, 1450–2000* (Oxford: Oxford University Press, 2008), 45.

54. The index fills the recto and a little more than half the verso of the leaf after the last printed page in *Poems, By J. D.*, Folger STC 7045, copy 2. The fullest treatment of these annotations appears in Nathanial B. Smith, "The Apparition of a Seventeenth-Century Donne Reader: A Hand-Written Index to *Poems, By J. D.* (1633)," *John Donne Journal: Studies in the Age of Donne* 20 (2001): 161–99.

55. *Poems, By J. D.* (1633), sigs. F3r, H2r, Aa3r, Folger STC 7045, copy 2.

56. Ibid., sig. Ll 4r.

57. Ibid., sigs. M4rv.

58. Ibid.

59. *Poems, By J. D. with Elegies on the Authors Death* was printed seven times in the seventeenth century. Miles Flesher printed the compilation for John Marriot in 1633, 1635, 1639, 1649, and 1650. James Flesher reissued his father's imprint for John Sweeting with a new title page in 1654. Thomas Newcomb printed the compilation one final time for Henry Herringman in 1669.

60. Kastan reads *Poems, By J. D.* as a book "struggl[ing]to constitute" the "aura of authorship" by simultaneously "insisting on poetic presence and physical absence" ("The Body of the Text," 459, 461). See, as well, Stephen B. Dobranski's "The Incomplete *Poems* of John Donne" in his *Readers and Authorship in Early Modern England* (Cambridge: Cambridge University Press, 2005), 119–49.

61. The O'Flahertie manuscript is now held at the Houghton Library as Harvard University Library Eng. 966.5. On the model that this manuscript provided for the 1635 *Poems, By J. D.*, see Dayton Haskin, "The Love Lyric [Songs and Sonets]," in *The Oxford Handbook of John Donne*, ed. Dennis Flynn, M. Thomas Hester, and Jeanne Shami (Oxford: Oxford University Press, 2011), 184.

62. The presumption of a split between the rakish young lover, "Jack Donne," and the mature "Doctor Donne" emerged several centuries after his death. Dayton Haskin has shown how the opposition of Donne's competing authorial personae "was only gradually teased out of the record in the Victorian period, in large measure to account for the fact that what 'Donne' meant to readers of poetry was quite different from what this name meant to readers who were chiefly interested in biographical narratives." See Dayton Haskin, *John Donne in the Nineteenth Century* (Oxford: Oxford University Press, 2007), 12.

63. Adam G. Hooks, *Selling Shakespeare: Biography, Bibliography, and the Book Trade* (Cambridge: Cambridge University Press, 2016), 3. Hooks's focus is the "bio-bibliography" of Shakespeare, the paradigmatic dramatic author, but a similar transformation to the contours of poetic authorship was taking place around Donne's compiled poetry. For an argument about how *Poems, By J. D.* established a legacy of authorship that was taken up in collections by George Herbert, Robert Herrick, and John Milton in the 1630s and 1640s, see Leah S. Marcus, *Unediting the Renaissance: Shakespeare, Marlowe, Milton* (London: Routledge, 1996), 192–98.

64. McCarthy, "*Poems, by J. D.* (1635) and the Creation of John Donne's Literary Biography," 60.

65. John Donne, *Poems, By J. D. with Elegies on the Authors Death* (London: John Marriot, 1635), sigs. B7r, B7v, Newberry Case Y 185.D7172.

66. Francis Davison, *Davisons Poems, or A Poeticall Rapsodie* (London: Roger Jackson, 1621), sig. A2r, Folger STC 6376.

67. Francis Davison, *A Poetical Rapsody* (London: John Baily, 1602), unsigned, Folger STC 6373; *Davisons Poems, or A Poeticall Rapsodie* (1621), sig. A2r.

68. Robert Southwell, *Moeoniae; or, Certaine excellent Poems and spirituall Hymnes* (London: John Busbie, 1595), sig. A1r, EEBO copy.

69. Samuel Daniel, *Certaine Small Poems Lately Printed: With the Tragedie of Philotas* (London: Simon Waterson [and Edward Blount], 1605), sig. A1r, Newberry Case Y 185. D2224. *Certaine Small Poems* was a bibliographic hybrid, with a divisional title page and a separate register for the new play.

70. Drummond put Drayton in touch with his stationer, Andro Hart, to discuss printing the second part of *Poly-Olbion* in Scotland (Bent Juel-Jensen, "Michael Drayton

and William Drummond of Hawthornden: A Lost Autograph Letter Recovered," *The Library*, 5th ser., 21, no. 4 [1966]: 328–30). For an argument about Drummond's *Poems* as a private presentation copy, see H. R Woudhuysen, "The Foundations of Shakespeare's Text," *Proceedings of the British Academy* 125 (2004): 80.

71. During Drayton's life, his *Poems* was published twice by Nicholas Ling, in 1605 and 1606, then taken over by John Smethwick in six further editions, some in multiple states, between 1608 and 1630.

72. Smethwick added this description to his editions of Drayton's *Poems*, perhaps to promote the revisions that would encourage the sale of each successive print run.

73. Robert Gomersall, *Poems* (London: John Marriot, 1633), sig. A3r, Folger STC 11993.

74. Ibid.

75. Ibid., sig. A3v.

76. *Poems, By J. D.* (1635), sigs. A3v–A4r.

77. Ibid., sig. A4r.

78. The spiritually inclined "Anniversaries" on the death of Elizabeth Drury were in a separate section of "Funerall Elegies."

79. *Poems, By J. D.* (1635), sigs. Z4v, Z6r, Z7r.

80. For instance, Richard C. Newton identifies Donne's poetry as a "halfway response" to the new and authorial paradigm established by Ben Jonson, since Donne's posthumous collections "appear to be manuscript miscellanies on the older model" ("Jonson and the (Re-)Invention of the Book," in *Classic and Cavalier: Essays on Jonson and the Sons of Ben*, ed. Claude J. Summers and Ted-Larry Pebworth [Pittsburgh: University of Pittsburgh Press, 1982], 47).

81. John T. Shawcross, "The Arrangement and Order of John Donne's Poems," in *Poems in Their Place: The Intertextuality and Order of Poetic Collections*, ed. Neil Fraistat (Chapel Hill: University of North Carolina Press, 1986), 136.

82. The title first appeared in posthumous compilations of work by Thomas Randolph (1638), William Shakespeare (1640), Thomas Carew (1640), Francis Beaumont (1640), and Thomas Beedome (1641). Heading into the 1640s, *Poems* was increasingly used by living poets including Henry Glapthorne (1639), John Milton (1645), Edmund Waller (1645), James Shirley (1646), Thomas Philipot (1646), and John Hall (1647).

83. Thomas Randolph, *Poems with the Muses Looking-Glasse* (Oxford: Francis Bowman, 1638), sig. *4v, Folger STC 20694, copy 1.

84. Thomas Beedome, *Poems Divine and Humane* (London: John Sweeting, 1641), sig. A2r, EEBO copy.

85. Ibid., sig. G7v.

86. Two folio editions of *Mr. William Shakespeares Comedies, Histories & Tragedies* had been published by William Jaggard, Edward Blount, John Smethwick, and William Aspley in 1623 and 1632. On the growth of Shakespeare's reputation as a playwright across the seventeenth century, see Patrick Cheney's "Afterword" in *Canonising Shakespeare: Stationers and the Book Trade, 1640–1740*, ed. Emma Depledge and Peter Kirwan (Cambridge: Cambridge University Press, 2017), 218–19.

87. William Shakespeare, *Poems: Written by Wil. Shake-speare, Gent.* (London: John Benson, 1640), sig. *3r. Newberry Case YS 8.64. The 1640 publication of Digges's prefatory poem was posthumous. John Freehafer argues that this expanded version, which updated the poem as it was printed in the 1623 First Folio, was intended for publication in the 1632 Second Folio but was not included in that volume because of its harsh attacks on Ben Jonson ("Leonard Digges, Ben Jonson, and the Beginning of Shakespeare Idolatry," *Shakespeare Quarterly* 21, no. 1 [1970]: 64–66).

88. *Poems: Written by Wil. Shake-speare, Gent.*, sigs. D4r–D5r, E4r–v, E4v–E5v, F5r–v.

89. Ibid., sig. *2r.

90. I use the phrase "local order" to designate the arrangement of proximate sonnets and poems, not a totalizing sequence. In Benson's new composite poems, the internal order of sonnets always follows the material organization of the 1609 quarto.

91. *Poems: Written by Wil. Shake-speare, Gent.*, sigs. A2r–A4r.

92. Ibid., sigs. A4r–v.

93. Ibid., sigs. B4v–5v. For a reading of a similar effect in the final stanza of "Injurious Time," a conflation of Sonnets 60 and 63 to 66, where the opening of line 66 contains a deictic that seems both to point back to line 65 and to gesture forward to its own scenario, see Cathy Shrank, "Reading Shakespeare's *Sonnets*: John Benson and the 1640 *Poems*," *Shakespeare* 5, no. 3 (2009): 277.

94. William Shakespeare, *New Variorum Edition of Shakespeare: The Sonnets*, ed. Hyder Edward Rollins (Philadelphia: J. B. Lippincott, 1944), 2:20, 22.

95. Arthur F. Marotti, "Shakespeare's Sonnets as Literary Property," in *Soliciting Interpretation: Literary Theory and Seventeenth-Century English Poetry*, ed. Elizabeth D. Harvey and Katharine Eisaman Maus (Chicago: University of Chicago Press, 1990), 143, 161–62.

96. Margreta de Grazia, "The First Reader of *Shake-speares Sonnets*," in *The Forms of Renaissance Thought: New Essays in Literature and Culture*, ed. Leonard Barkan, Bradin Cormack, and Sean Keilen (Basingstoke: Palgrave Macmillan, 2009), 94.

97. Ibid., 87–88.

98. On the historical formation of Cavalier poetics and Benson's role in that process, see David Baker, "Cavalier Shakespeare: The 1640 *Poems* of John Benson," *Studies in Philology* 95, no. 2 (1998): 152–73.

99. "Magazine of beautie" does not contain any pronouns indicating the beloved's gender. I use male pronouns because Sonnets 4 to 6 fall into the group that, since the eighteenth century, have been considered to be addressed to the young man. Although this decision feels necessary, it obscures the indeterminacy of much of gendering of the beloved in the 1640 *Poems* and the 1609 *Sonnets*.

100. *Poems: Written by Wil. Shake-speare, Gent.*, sig. A7v.

101. Ibid., sig. A8r.

102. Ibid.

103. Ibid.

104. Ibid.

105. On Benson's title of "Magazine of beautie," see Shrank, "Reading Shakespeare's *Sonnets*," 279; and de Grazia, "First Reader," 96.

106. *OED Online*, s.v. "magazine, *n.*," sense 1.

107. *Poems: Written by Wil. Shake-speare, Gent.*, sig. A8r.

108. William Shakespeare, *Shakespeare's Sonnets*, ed. Stephen Booth (New Haven, CT: Yale University Press, 2000), 140–41.

109. *Poems: Written by Wil. Shake-speare, Gent.*, sig. A8r.

110. Ibid., sig. A8r, emphasis added.

111. Ibid., sigs. A8r–v.

112. Ibid., sig. A8r.

113. Ibid., sig. *2v.

114. Marotti rightly notes that Benson was distancing Shakespeare from Donne's difficult and mixed poetry ("Shakespeare's Sonnets as Literary Property," 159–60).

115. Baker, "Cavalier Shakespeare," 156–57.

116. Sasha Roberts observes, "Like Shakespeare's *Poems*, Benson's editions of Jonson attempt to collect and preserve his lyric poems; to do Jonson a service by gathering together his amorous and occasional verse, sonnets, epigrams and elegies, and in so doing provide a worthy supplement to the largely dramatic *Works*" (*Reading Shakespeare's Poems in Early Modern England* [Basingstoke: Palgrave Macmillan, 2003], 160).

117. Joshua Scodel, "Seventeenth-Century English Literary Criticism: Classical Values, English Texts and Contexts," in the *Cambridge History of Literary Criticism*, vol. 3, *The Renaissance*, ed. Glyn Norton (Cambridge: Cambridge University Press, 1999), 545.

118. On how Benson deployed "nearly every popular feature that a desperate young publisher could possibly use to market a mid-seventeenth-century poetry collection," see Faith Acker, "John Benson's 1640 *Poems* and Its Literary Precedents," in Depledge and Kirwan, *Canonising Shakespeare*, 90.

119. On how Digges's poem is "pitched against Jonson from the outset," see Shrank, "Reading Shakespeare's *Sonnets*," 275.

120. *Poems: Written by Wil. Shake-speare, Gent.*, sigs. *3r–*3v.

121. Ibid., K8r–L2r.

122. Baker argues that this image both recalls Jonson's recent status as poet laureate and aligns Shakespeare with Marshall's portrait of Jonson wearing a laurel wreath in his translation of Horace published by Benson in the same year ("Cavalier Shakespeare," 160–61). But since Shakespeare is holding the leaves, not wearing them, the evocative imagery may well have been fused with Donne's example.

123. On the diaeresis in the running head as a classicizing feature, see Shrank, "Reading Shakespeare's *Sonnets*," 275. Although Shrank questions the Jonsonian influence on the 1640 *Poems*, she does not propose an alternative source for this feature.

124. On Benson's use of the novel "valediction" in his title, see de Grazia, "First Reader," 96.

125. On how Benson transformed some of Shakespeare's sonnets into elegies, another verse form often used by Donne, see Robert Matz, "The Scandals of Shakespeare's Sonnets," *ELH* 77, no. 2 (2010): 486–87.

126. "A Valediction: Of Weeping," lines 1–2, in *The Complete Poems of John Donne*, 274.

127. Ibid., lines 26–27 (p. 276).

128. *Poems: Written by Wil. Shake-speare, Gent.*, sig. D2r.

129. Ibid., sig. D2v.

130. Ibid.

131. Ibid. Bradin Cormack shows how bail operates in the *Sonnets* as a legal structure that offers a provisional release ("On Will: Time and Voluntary Action in *Coriolanus* and the *Sonnets*," *Shakespeare* 5, no. 3 [2009]: 260).

132. *Poems: Written by Wil. Shake-speare, Gent.*, sig. D2v.

133. Sonnet 73, lines 1–2, 5–6, 9–10, emphasis added. I here cite Booth's facsimile edition of the quarto (*Shakespeare's Sonnets*, p. 65), but Sonnet 73 does appear later in the 1640 *Poems*, in a conflation of Sonnets 73 and 77 entitled "Sunne Set." This new poem was a notable anomaly in Benson's practice. Although Benson conflated noncontiguous sonnets in five cases, this two-stanza conflation is the only instance in which that gap is not anchored within a longer poem. What is more, this conflation cleverly unites two sonnets on waning youth, juxtaposing the poet's description of his own aging with his prediction of the moment in which the young man will begin to show his: "Thy glasse will shew thee how thy beauties were" (*Poems: Written by Wil. Shake-speare, Gent.*, sig. F6r).

134. *Poems: Written by Wil. Shake-speare, Gent.*, sig. D2r.

135. Sonnet 73, lines 13–14.

136. Lesser and Stallybrass, "The First Literary *Hamlet*," 417, 419.

CODA

1. This focus on drama is often even further restricted to Shakespeare. For representative examples, see David Scott Kastan, *Shakespeare and the Book* (Cambridge: Cambridge University Press, 2001); Laurie E. Maguire, *Shakespearean Suspect Texts: The "Bad" Quartos and Their Contexts* (Cambridge: Cambridge University Press, 1996); and Sonia Massai, *Shakespeare and the Rise of the Editor* (Cambridge: Cambridge University Press, 2007).

2. Lukas Erne, "*Cupids Cabinet Unlock't* (1662), Ostensibly 'By W. Shakespeare,' in Fact Partly by John Milton," in Depledge and Kirwan, *Canonising Shakespeare*, 112.

3. William Shakespeare, *The Works of Mr. William Shakespear*, ed. Nicholas Rowe (London: Jacob Tonson, 1709), vol. 1, unsigned title page, Newberry YS 07.

4. William Shakespeare, *A Collection of Poems* (London: Bernard Lintott, 1711).

5. For this complex print history, see Paul D. Cannan, "The 1709/11 Editions of Shakespeare's Poems," in Depledge and Kirwan, *Canonising Shakespeare*, 171–75.

6. William Shakespeare, *The Works of Mr. William Shakespear. Volume the Seventh* (London: Edmund Curll and Egbert Sanger, 1710), sig. Ff1r, Folger PR2752 1709a copy 5 v.7 Sh.Col.

7. William Shakespeare, *Supplement to the Edition of Shakspeare's Plays Published in 1778 by Samuel Johnson and George Steevens, in Two Volumes*, [ed. Edmond Malone] (London: C. Bathurst et al., 1780), vol. 1, unsigned title page.

8. The classic account of the influence of Malone's editions is Margreta de Grazia, *Shakespeare Verbatim: The Reproduction of Authenticity and the 1790 Apparatus* (Oxford: Clarendon Press, 1991); on the poetry, see her chapter "Individuating Shakespeare's Experience: Biography, Chronology, and the Sonnets," 132–76.

9. For notable exceptions, see de Grazia, *Shakespeare Verbatim*; Hooks, *Selling Shakespeare*; and Roberts, *Reading Shakespeare's Poems*.

SELECTED BIBLIOGRAPHY

PRIMARY SOURCES

Manuscripts

British Library, London
    Add. MS 15322.
    Add. MS 17492.
    Add. MS 61822.
    Egerton MS 2711.
    Harley MS 7553.
Edinburgh University Library, Edinburgh
    MS De. 5. 96.
Folger Shakespeare Library, Washington, DC
    MS N.a.52.
    MS V.a.103.
    MS V.a.149.
    MS V.a.161.
    MS V.a.162.
    MS V.a.245.
    MS V.a.262.
    MS V.a.307.
    MS V.a.322.
    MS V.a.345.
    MS V.a.399.
    MS X.d.580.
Henry E. Huntington Library, San Marino, California
    MS Ellesmere 6871.
    MS Ellesmere 6893.
    MS Ellesmere 11637.
    MS HM 46323.
Marsh's Library, Dublin
    Z 3.5.21.

Victoria and Albert Museum, London
    Dyce 25.F.39.

Printed Books

Barnes, Barnabe. *A Divine Centurie of Spirituall Sonnets*. London: John Windet, 1595.

———. *Parthenophil and Parthenophe*. [London: John Wolfe, 1593.]

Barnfield, Richard. *Cynthia: With Certain Sonnets*. London: Humphrey Lownes, 1595.

Beaumont, Francis. *Poems*. London: W. W[ethred] and Laurence Blaikelocke, 1640.

Beedome, Thomas. *Poems Divine and Humane*. London: John Sweeting, 1641.

Bel-vedére, or The Garden of the Muses. London: Hugh Astley, 1600.

Boccaccio, Giovanni. *A Treatise Excellent and Compe[n]dious, shewing [. . .] The Falles of Sondry Most Notable Princes and Princesses*. Translated by John Lydgate. London: Richard Tottel, 1554.

A Boke of Balettes. London: [W. Copland?], [1549?].

The Booke of the Common Praier. London: Richard Grafton, 1549.

Breton, Nicholas. *The arbor of Amorous Devises*. London: Richard Jones, 1594.

———. *Brittons Bowre of Delights*. London: Richard Jones, 1591.

Calvin, John. *Sermons of John Calvin, Upon the Songe that Ezechias made after he had bene sicke*. Translated by Anne Lock. London: John Day, 1560.

Carew, Thomas. *Poems*. London: Thomas Walkley, 1640.

Certayne Psalmes chosen out of the Psalter of David, and drawen into Englishe Metre. London: Edward Whitchurch, 1549.

Chapman, George. *Ovids Banquet of Sence*. London: Richard Smith, 1595.

Chaucer, Geoffrey. *The Workes of Geffray Chaucer Newly Printed*. London: Robert Toye, 1550.

Constable, Henry. *Diana: The praises of his Mistres in certaine sweete Sonnets*. London: Richard Smith, 1592.

———. *Diana: The praises of his Mistres in certaine sweete Sonnets*. London: Richard Smith, 1594.

The Court of Venus. London: T. Gybson, [1538?].

Craig, Alexander. *The Amorose Songes, Sonets, and Elegies*. London: William White, 1606.

Daniel, Samuel. *Certaine Small Poems Lately Printed: With the Tragedie of Philotas*. London: Simon Waterson [and Edward Blount], 1605.

———. *Delia: Contayning certayne Sonnets; with the complaint of Rosamund*. London: Simon Waterson, 1592.

Davies, John. *Wittes Pilgrimage (by Poeticall Essaies)*. London: John Browne, [1605].

Davison, Francis. *Davisons Poems, or A Poeticall Rapsodie*. London: Roger Jackson, 1621.

———. *A Poetical Rapsody*. London: John Baily, 1602.

Dickenson, John. *The Shepheards Complaint*. London: William Blackwell, 1596.

Donne, John. *Poems, By J. D. with Elegies on the Authors Death*. London: John Marriot, 1633.

————. *Poems, By J. D. with Elegies on the Authors Death*. London: John Marriot, 1635.

————. *Poems, By J. D. with Elegies on the Authors Death*. London: John Marriot, 1639.

————. *Poems, By J. D. with Elegies on the Authors Death*. London: John Marriot, 1649.

————. *Poems, By J. D. with Elegies on the Authors Death*. London: John Marriot, 1650.

————. *Poems, By J. D. with Elegies on the Authors Death*. London: John Sweeting, 1654.

————. *Poems, &c By John Donne, Late Dean of St. Pauls*. London: Henry Herringman, 1669.

Drayton, Michael. *Englands Heroicall Epistles: Newly Enlarged, with Idea*. London: N[icholas] L[ing], 1599.

————. *Ideas Mirrour: Amours in Quatorzains*. London: Nicholas Ling, 1594.

————. *Poemes Lyrick and Pastorall*. London: N[icholas] L[ing] and J[ohn] Flasket, 1606.

————. *Poems: By Michaell Draiton Esquire*. London: N[icholas] Ling, 1605.

————. *Poems: By Michael Drayton Esquire*. London: John Smethwick, 1608.

Drummond, William. *Poems By William Drummond*. [Edinburgh: Andro Hart, 1614].

E. C. *Emaricdulfe: Sonnets Written by E. C. Esquier*. London: Matthew Law, 1595.

Englands Helicon. London: John Flasket, 1600.

Englands Parnassus, or the Choysest Flowers of Our Moderne Poets. London: N[icholas] L[ing,] C[uthbert] B[urby] and T[homas] H[ayes], 1600.

Fedele and Fortunio: The pleasaunt and fine conceited Comoedie of two Italian Gentlemen. Translated by Anthony Munday. London: Thomas Hacket, 1585.

Fletcher, Giles. *Licia, or Poemes of Love*. Cambridge: John Legat, 1593.

Fraunce, Abraham. *The Arcadian Rhetorike*. London: T[homas] Gubbin and T[homas] Newman, 1588.

Gascoigne, George. *A Hundreth sundrie Flowres bounde up in one small Poesie*. London: Richard Smith, 1573.

————. *The Posies of George Gascoigne Esquire*. London: Richard Smith, 1575.

Gifford, Humphrey. *A Posie of Gilloflowers, Eche Differing from Other in Colour and Odour, Yet All Sweete*. London: John Perin, 1580.

Glapthorne, Henry. *Poëms*. London: Daniel Pakeman, 1639.

Gomersall, Robert. *The Levites Revenge*. London: [John Marriot], 1628.

————. *Poems*. London: John Marriot, 1633.

————. *The Tragedie of Lodovick Sforza Duke of Milan*. London: [John Marriot], 1628.

Googe, Barnabe. *Eglogs, Epytaphes, and Sonettes*. London: Raffe Newbery, 1563.

————. *A newe Booke called the Shippe of safegarde*. London: W. Seres, 1569.

A gorgious Gallery, of gallant Inventions. London: Richard Jones, 1578.

Griffin, B[artholomew]. *Fidessa, more chaste then kinde*. London: Matthew Lownes, 1596.

H. C. *The Forrest of Fancy*. London: Thomas Purfoot, 1579.

Hall, John. *Poems*. Cambridge: John Rothwell, 1647.

A Handefull of Pleasant Delites. London: Richard Jones, 1584.

Heywood, John. *A Fourth Hundred of Epygrams Invented and Made by John Heywood*. London: Thomas Berthelet, 1560.

———. *An Hundred of Epigrammes, Invented and Made by John Heywood*. London: Thomas Berthelet, 1550.

Holland, Abraham. *A Continued Inquisition Against Paper-Persecutors*. London: H. Holland and G. Gibbs, 1625.

Horace. *Q. Horatius Flaccus: his Art of Poetry, Englished by Ben Jonson*. London: John Benson, 1640.

Howell, Thomas. *The Arbor of Amitie*. London, 1568.

Huloet, Richard. *Huloet's Dictionarie*. London: Thomas Marsh, 1572.

J. C. *A poore Knight his Pallace of private pleasures*. London: Richard Jones, 1579.

Jonson, Ben. *Ben Jonson's Execration against Vulcan*. London: John Benson, 1640.

Kendall, Timothy. *Flowers of Epigrammes*. London: John Shepherd, 1577.

Linche, Richard. *Diella, Certaine Sonnets*. London: Henry Olney, 1596.

Lodge, Thomas. *Phillis: Honoured with Pastorall Sonnets, Elegies, and amorous delights*. London: John Busbie, 1593.

———. *Scillaes Metamorphosis: Enterlaced with the unfortunate love of Glaucus*. London: Richard Jones, 1589.

Lok, Henry. *Ecclesiastes, Otherwise Called the Preacher*. London: Richard Field, 1597.

———. *Sundry Christian Passions Contained in two hundred Sonnets*. London: Richard Field, 1593.

Meres, Francis. *Palladis Tamia, Wits Treasury*. London: Cuthbert Burbie, 1598.

Milton, John. *Poems*. London: Humphrey Moseley, 1645.

Montemayor, Jorge de. *Diana*. Translated by Bartholomew Yong. London: G[eorge] B[ishop], 1598.

Morley, Thomas. *Madrigalls to Foure Voyces*. London: Thomas East, 1594.

Munday, Anthony. *A Banquet of Daintie Conceits*. London: Edward White, 1588.

N. B. *A Smale handfull of fragrant Flowers*. London: Richard Jones, 1575.

The Paradyse of daynty devises. London: Henry Disle, 1576.

The Paradyse of daynty devises. London: Henry Disle, 1578.

The Paradyse of daintie Devises. London: Henry Disle, 1580.

The Paradyse of daintie Devises. London: Edward White, 1585.

Peele, George. *The Araygnement of Paris*. London: 1584.

Perceval, Richard. *A Dictionarie in Spanish and English*. London: Edm[und] Bolifant, 1599.

Percy, William. *Sonnets to the Fairest Coelia*. London: W[illiam] P[onsonby?], 1594.

Philipot, Thomas. *Poems*. London: John Wilcox, 1646.

The Phoenix Nest. London: John Jackson, 1593.

Plat, Hugh. *The Floures of Philosophie, with the pleasures of poetrie annexed to them*. London: F[rancis] Coldock, 1572.

Pliny. *The Historie of the World: Commonly Called, the Naturall Historie of C. Plinius Secundus*. Translated by Philemon Holland. London: 1601.

Politeuphuia, Wits Commonwealth. London: Nicholas Ling, 1597.

Quarles, Frances. *Divine Poems*. London: John Marriot, 1630.

Randolph, Thomas. *Poems with the Muses Looking-Glasse*. Oxford: Francis Bowman, 1638.

The Returne from Pernassus. London: John Wright, 1606.

Rime di diversi illustri signori [. . .] Nuovamente raccolte, et con nuova additione ristampate; libro quinto. Venice: Gabriel Giolito, 1552.

Rogers, Thomas. *Celestiall Elegies of the Goddesses and the Muses*. London: J[oan] B[roome], 1598.

The Second book of the Primaleon of Greece. Translated by Anthony Munday. London: Cuthbert Burby, 1596.

Shakespeare, William. *A Collection of Poems*. London: Bernard Lintott, 1711.

———. *Mr. William Shakespeares Comedies, Histories & Tragedies*. London: Isaac Jaggard and Edward Blount, 1623.

———. *The Passionate Pilgrime*. London: William Jaggard, 1599.

———. *The Passionate Pilgrime*. London: William Jaggard, 1612.

———. *Poems: Written by Wil. Shake-speare, Gent*. London: John Benson, 1640.

———. *Shake-speares Sonnets*. London: Thomas Thorpe, 1609.

———. *Supplement to the Edition of Shakspeare's Plays Published in 1778 by Samuel Johnson and George Steevens, in Two Volumes*. [Edited by Edmond Malone.] London: C. Bathurst et al., 1780.

———. *The Works of Mr. William Shakespear*. Edited by Nicholas Rowe. London: Jacob Tonson, 1709.

Shirley, James. *Poems &c*. London: Humphrey Moseley, 1646.

Sidney, Philip. *The Countesse of Pembrokes Arcadia*. London: William Ponsonby, 1598.

———. *Sir P. S. His Astrophel and Stella*. London: [John Danter] for Thomas Newman, 1591.

———. *Syr P. S. His Astrophel and Stella*. London: [John Charlewood] for Thomas Newman, 1591.

———. *Syr P. S. His Astrophel and Stella*. London: Matthew Lownes, [1597?].

Skelton, John. *Here After Foloweth Certayne Bokes, Co[m]pyled by Mayster Skelton*. London: Henry Tab, [1545?].

Smith, William. *Chloris, or The Complaint of the passionate despised Shepheard*. London: Edm[und] Bollifant, 1596.

Songes and Sonettes written by the ryght honorable Lorde Henry Haward late Earle of Surrey, and other. London: Richard Tottel, June 5, 1557.

Songes and Sonettes written by the right honorable Lorde Henry Haward late Earle of Surrey, and other. London: Richard Tottel, July 1557.

Songes and Sonettes written by the right honorable Lorde Henry Haward late Earle of Surrey, and other. London: Richard Tottel, 1557.

Songes and Sonettes written by the right honorable Lorde Henry Haward late Earle of Surrey, and other. London: Richard Tottel, 1559.

Songes and Sonettes written by the right honorable Lorde Henry Haward late Earle of Surrey, and other. London: Richard Tottel, 1565.

Songes and Sonets written by the Right honorable Lorde Henry Haward late Earle of Surrey, and other. London: Richard Tottel, 1574.

Songes and Sonnets written by the Right honourable Lord Henry Haward late Earle of Surrey, and others. London: Richard Tottel, 1585.

Songes and Sonnets written by the Right honorable Lord Henrie Haward late Earle of Surrey, and others. London: Richard Tottel, 1587.

Southwell, Robert. *Moeoniae; or, Certaine excellent Poems and spirituall Hymnes.* London: John Busbie, 1595.

Speeches Delivered to Her Majestie this Last Progresse. Oxford: Joseph Barnes, 1592.

Spenser, Edmund. *Amoretti and Epithalamion.* London: William Ponsonby, 1595.

———. *The Shepheardes Calendar.* London: Hugh Singleton, 1579.

T. W. *The Tears of Fancie, or Love Disdained.* London: William Barley, 1593.

Taverner, Richard. *Garden of Wysdom wherin ye maye gather moste pleasaunt flowres.* London: John Haruye, 1539.

T[ofte], R[obert]. *Laura: The Toyes of a Traveller; or The Feast of Fancie.* London: Valentine Simmes, 1597.

Tusser, Thomas. *Five Hundreth Points of Good Husbandry.* London: Richard Tottel, 1573.

———. *A Hundreth Good Pointes of Husbandrie.* London: Richard Tottel, 1557.

———. *A hundreth good pointes of husbandry, lately maried unto a hundreth good poynts of huswifery.* London: Richard Tottel, 1570.

Waller, Ed[mund]. *Poems &c.* London: Hu[mphrey] Mos[e]ley, 1645. Watson, Thomas. *The Hekatompathia, or Passionate Centurie of Love.* London: Gabriell Cawood, 1582.

Whetstone, George. *A Remembraunce of the wel imployed life, & godly end, of George Gaskoigne Esquire.* London: Edward Aggas, 1577.

Whitney, Isabella. *A Sweet Nosgay, or Pleasant Posye.* London: Richard Jones, 1573.

The Whole Booke of Psalmes: Collected into Englysh metre by T. Starnhold, J. Hopkins, & others. London: John Day, 1562.

Wits Theater of the little World. London: Nicholas Ling, 1599.

Yonge, Nicholas. *Musica Transalpina.* London: Thomas East, 1597.

Zepheria. London: N[icholas] L[ing] and John Busbie, 1594.

SECONDARY TEXTS

Acker, Faith. "John Benson's 1640 *Poems* and Its Literary Precedents." *Canonising Shakespeare: Stationers and the Book Trade, 1640–1740*, edited by Emma Depledge and Peter Kirwan, 89–106. Cambridge: Cambridge University Press, 2017.

Alexander, Gavin, ed. *Sidney's "The Defence of Poesy" and Selected Renaissance Literary Criticism.* London: Penguin Classics, 2004.

———. *Writing After Sidney: The Literary Response to Sir Philip Sidney, 1586–1640.* Oxford: Oxford University Press, 2006.

Alexander, Gavin, and Mary Ellen Lamb, eds., "William Scott's *The Model of Poesy*," special issue, *Sidney Journal* 33, no. 1 (2015).

Ames, Joseph. *Typographical Antiquities: Being an Historical Account of Printing in England*. London: J. Robinson, 1749.

Ames, Joseph, and William Herbert. *Typographical Antiquities; or, An Historical Account of the Origin and Progress of Printing in Great Britain and Ireland*. 3 vols. London: T. Payne et al., 1785–90.

Anderson, Randall L. "Metaphors of the Book as Garden in the English Renaissance." *Yearbook of English Studies* 33 (2003): 248–61.

Arber, Edward, ed. *A Transcript of the Registers of the Company of Stationers of London, 1554–1640 A.D.* 5 vols. London: privately printed, 1875–94.

Attié, Katherine Bootle. "Bound to Know, Bound to Love, Bound to Last: Donne's Forms of Containment." *John Donne Journal: Studies in the Age of Donne* 33 (2014): 95–130.

Austen, Gillian. "The Adventures Passed by Master George Gascoigne: Experiments in Prose." In *The Oxford Handbook of English Prose, 1500–1640*, edited by Andrew Hadfield, 156–71. Oxford: Oxford University Press, 2013.

———. *George Gascoigne*. Woodbridge, England: D. S. Brewer, 2008.

Bahr, Arthur. *Fragments and Assemblages: Forming Compilations of Medieval London*. Chicago: University of Chicago Press, 2013.

———. "Miscellaneity and Variance in the Medieval Book." In *The Medieval Manuscript Book: Cultural Approaches*, edited by Michael Johnston and Michael Van Dussen, 181–98. Cambridge: Cambridge University Press, 2015.

Bahr, Arthur, and Alexandra Gillespie. "Medieval English Manuscripts: Form, Aesthetics, and the Literary Text." *Chaucer Review* 47 (2013): 346–60.

Baker, David. "Cavalier Shakespeare: The 1640 Poems of John Benson." *Studies in Philology* 95, no. 2 (1998): 152–73.

Baker, John. *The Oxford History of the Laws of England*. Vol. 6, *1483–1558*. Oxford: Oxford University Press, 2003.

Bates, Catherine. "Profit and Pleasure? The Real Economy of Tottel's *Songes and Sonettes*." In *Tottel's Songes and Sonettes in Context*, edited by Stephen Hamrick, 37–62. Farnham, England: Ashgate, 2013.

Beal, Peter. *A Dictionary of English Manuscript Terminology, 1450–2000*. Oxford: Oxford University Press, 2008.

———. *In Praise of Scribes: Manuscripts and Their Makers in Seventeenth-Century England*. Oxford: Clarendon Press, 1998.

Bell, Ilona. "'That Which Thou Hast Done': Shakespeare's Sonnets and *A Lover's Complaint*." In *Shakespeare's Sonnets: Critical Essays*, edited by James Schiffer, 455–71. New York: Garland, 1999.

Blair, Ann. *Too Much to Know: Managing Scholarly Information Before the Modern Age*. New Haven, CT: Yale University Press, 2010.

Blayney, Peter W. M. *The Stationers' Company and the Printers of London, 1501–1557*. 2 vols. Cambridge: Cambridge University Press, 2013.

Bourne, Claire M. L. "Dramatic Pilcrows." *Papers of the Bibliographical Society of America* 108, no. 4 (2014): 413–52.

———. "Typography *After* Performance." In *Rethinking Theatrical Documents in Shakespeare's England*, edited by Tiffany Stern, 193–215. London: Bloomsbury, 2019.

———. "*Vide Supplementum*: Early Modern Collation as Play-Reading in the First Folio." In *Early Modern Marginalia*, edited by Katherine Acheson, 195–233. London: Routledge, 2019.

Brayman Hackel, Heidi. *Reading Material in Early Modern England: Print, Gender, and Literacy*. Cambridge: Cambridge University Press, 2005.

Breton, Nicholas. *Brittons Bowre of Delights, 1591*. Edited by Hyder Edward Rollins. Cambridge, MA: Harvard University Press, 1933.

Brown, Piers. "Donne, Rhapsody, and Textual Order." In *Manuscript Miscellanies in Early Modern England*, edited by Joshua Eckhardt and Daniel Starza Smith, 39–55. Farnham, England: Ashgate, 2014.

———. "Donne's Texts and Materials." In *John Donne in Context*, edited by Michael Schoenfeldt, 18–29. Cambridge: Cambridge University Press, 2019.

Burton, Ben, and Elizabeth Scott-Baumann. "The Work of Form: Poetics and Materiality in Early Modern Culture." In *The Work of Form: Poetics and Materiality in Early Modern Culture*, edited by Ben Burton and Elizabeth Scott-Baumann, 1–22. Oxford: Oxford University Press, 2014.

Butterfield, Ardis. "Why Medieval Lyric?" *ELH* 82, no. 2 (2015): 319–43.

Cannan, Paul D. "The 1709/11 Editions of Shakespeare's Poems." In *Canonising Shakespeare: Stationers and the Book Trade, 1640–1740*, edited by Emma Depledge and Peter Kirwan, 171–86. Cambridge: Cambridge University Press, 2017.

Cave, Terence. *The Cornucopian Text: Problems of Writing in the French Renaissance*. Oxford: Clarendon Press, 1979.

Chartier, Roger. *The Order of Books: Readers, Authors, and Libraries in Europe Between the Fourteenth and Eighteenth Centuries*. Translated by Lydia G. Cochrane. Stanford, CA: Stanford University Press, 1994.

Chartier, Roger, and Peter Stallybrass. "What Is a Book?" In *The Cambridge Companion to Textual Scholarship*, edited by Neil Fraistat and Julia Flanders, 188–204. Cambridge: Cambridge University Press, 2013.

Cheney, Patrick. "Afterword." In *Canonising Shakespeare: Stationers and the Book Trade, 1640–1740*, edited by Emma Depledge and Peter Kirwan, 216–22. Cambridge: Cambridge University Press, 2017.

Clegg, Cyndia. *Press Censorship in Elizabethan England*. Cambridge: Cambridge University Press, 1997.

Coldiron, A. E. B. "Sidney, Watson, and the 'Wrong Ways' to Renaissance Lyric Poetics." *Renaissance Papers, 1997*, edited by T. H. Howard-Hill and Philip Rollinson, 49–62. Columbia, SC: Published for the Southeastern Renaissance Conference by Camden House, 1997.

Coles, Kimberly Anne. *Religion, Reform, and Women's Writing in Early Modern England*. Cambridge: Cambridge University Press, 2008.

Colie, Rosalie. *The Resources of Kind: Genre-Theory in the Renaissance*. Edited by Barbara K. Lewalski. Berkeley: University of California Press, 1973.

Collier, John Payne. *A Bibliographical and Critical Account of the Rarest Books in the English Language*. 2 vols. London: Joseph Lilly, 1865.

———, ed. *Seven English Poetical Miscellanies, Printed Between 1557 and 1602*. London, 1867.

———, ed. *Tottel's Miscellany*. Privately printed, London, 1865.

Connor, Francis X. "'Delivering Forth': Philip Sidney's Idea and the Labor of Writing." *Sidney Journal* 31, no. 2 (2013): 53–75.

Constable, Henry. *The Poems of Henry Constable*. Edited by Joan Grundy. Liverpool English Texts and Studies, vol. 6. Liverpool: Liverpool University Press, 1960.

Cormack, Bradin. "On Will: Time and Voluntary Action in *Coriolanus* and the *Sonnets*." *Shakespeare* 5, no. 3 (2009): 253–70.

———. *A Power to Do Justice: Jurisdiction, English Literature, and the Rise of Common Law, 1509–1625*. Chicago: University of Chicago Press, 2007.

Cormack, Bradin, and Carla Mazzio. *Book Use, Book Theory: 1500–1700*. Chicago: University of Chicago Library, 2005.

Crane, Mary Thomas. *Framing Authority: Sayings, Self, and Society in Sixteenth-Century England*. Princeton, NJ: Princeton University Press, 1993.

Crowley, Lara M. *Manuscript Matters: Reading John Donne's Poetry and Prose in Early Modern England*. Oxford: Oxford University Press, 2018.

Daniel, Samuel. *Poems and a Defence of Ryme*. Edited by Arthur Colby Sprague. Cambridge, MA: Harvard University Press, 1930.

de Grazia, Margreta. "The First Reader of *Shake-speares Sonnets*." In *The Forms of Renaissance Thought: New Essays in Literature and Culture*, edited by Leonard Barkan, Bradin Cormack, and Sean Keilen, 86–106. Basingstoke: Palgrave Macmillan, 2009.

———. "Imprints: Shakespeare, Gutenberg, and Descartes." In *Printing and Parenting in Early Modern England*, edited by Douglas Brooks, 29–58. Aldershot, England: Ashgate, 2005.

———. *Shakespeare Verbatim: The Reproduction of Authenticity and the 1790 Apparatus*. Oxford: Clarendon Press, 1991.

de Grazia, Margreta, and Peter Stallybrass. "The Materiality of the Shakespearean Text." *Shakespeare Quarterly* 44, no. 3 (1993): 255–83.

Depledge, Emma, and Peter Kirwan, eds. *Canonising Shakespeare: Stationers and the Book Trade, 1640–1740*. Cambridge: Cambridge University Press, 2017.

Deutermann, Allison K., and András Kiséry, eds. *Formal Matters: Reading the Materials of English Renaissance Literature*. Manchester: Manchester University Press, 2013.

DiPasquale, Theresa M. "Donne's Epigrams: A Sequential Reading." *Modern Philology* 104, no. 3 (2007): 329–78.

Dobranski, Stephen B. *Readers and Authorship in Early Modern England*. Cambridge: Cambridge University Press, 2005.

Dolven, Jeff. "Reading Wyatt for the Style." *Modern Philology* 105, no. 1 (2007): 65–86.

Donne, John. *The Complete Poems of John Donne*. Edited by Robin Robbins. New York: Routledge, 2013.

———. *Devotions Upon Emergent Occasions and Death's Duel*. New York: Vintage Books, 1999.

———. *John Donne: Selected Letters*. Edited by P. M. Oliver. Manchester: Carcanet Press, 2002.

———. *John Donne: Selected Writings*. Edited by Janel Mueller. Oxford: Oxford University Press, 2015.

———. *The Variorum Edition of the Poetry of John Donne*. Edited by Gary A. Stringer et al. 7 vols to date. Bloomington: Indiana University Press, 1995–.

Drayton, Michael. *The Works of Michael Drayton*. Edited by J. William Hebel, Kathleen Tillotson, and Bernard H. Newdigate. 5 vols. Oxford: Shakespeare Head Press, 1961.

Driver, Martha. "When Is a Miscellany Not Miscellaneous? Making Sense of the 'Kalender of Shepherds.'" *Yearbook of English Studies* 33 (2003): 199–214.

Dubrow, Heather. *The Challenges of Orpheus: Lyric Poetry and Early Modern England*. Baltimore, MD: Johns Hopkins University Press, 2008.

———. *Deixis in the Early Modern English Lyric: Unsettling Spatial Anchors Like "Here," "This," "Come."* Palgrave Pivot. New York: Palgrave Macmillan, 2015.

———. "'Dressing Old Words New'? Re-evaluating the 'Delian Structure.'" In *A Companion to Shakespeare's Sonnets*, edited by Michael Schoenfeldt, 90–103. Malden, MA: Blackwell, 2010.

———. *Echoes of Desire: English Petrarchism and Its Counterdiscourses*. Ithaca, NY: Cornell University Press, 1995.

———. "Lyric Forms." In *The Lyric Theory Reader: A Critical Anthology*, edited by Virginia Jackson and Yopie Prins, 114–28. Baltimore, MD: Johns Hopkins University Press, 2014.

Duffin, Ross W. *Some Other Note: The Lost Songs of English Renaissance Comedy*. Oxford: Oxford University Press, 2018.

Duncan, Dennis, and Adam Smyth, eds. *Book Parts*. Oxford: Oxford University Press, 2019.

Eckhardt, Joshua. *Manuscript Verse Collectors and the Politics of Anti-Courtly Love Poetry*. Oxford: Oxford University Press, 2009.

Eckhardt, Joshua, and Daniel Starza Smith. "Introduction: The Emergence of the English Miscellany." In *Manuscript Miscellanies in Early Modern England*, edited by Joshua Eckhardt and Daniel Starza Smith, 1–15. Farnham, England: Ashgate, 2014.

———, eds. *Manuscript Miscellanies in Early Modern England*. Farnham, England: Ashgate, 2014.

Eliot, T. S. *The Varieties of Metaphysical Poetry*. Edited by Ronald Schuchard. New York: Harcourt Brace, 1993.

———. "What Is Minor Poetry?" *Sewanee Review* 54, no. 1 (1946): 1–18.

Ellinghausen, Laurie. "Literary Property and the Single Woman in Isabella Whitney's *A Sweet Nosgay*." *SEL: Studies in English Literature, 1500–1900* 45, no. 1 (2005): 1–22.

Erne, Lukas. "*Cupids Cabinet Unlock't* (1662), Ostensibly 'By W. Shakespeare,' in Fact Partly by John Milton." In *Canonising Shakespeare: Stationers and the Book Trade, 1640–1740*, edited by Emma Depledge and Peter Kirwan, 107–29. Cambridge: Cambridge University Press, 2017.

Estill, Laura. "The Urge to Organize Early Modern Miscellanies: Reading Cotgrave's *The English Treasury of Wit and Language*." *Papers of the Bibliographical Society of America* 112, no. 1 (2018): 27–73.

Ferry, Anne. *The "Inward" Language: Sonnets of Wyatt, Sidney, Shakespeare, Donne*. Chicago: University of Chicago Press, 1983.

———. *The Title to the Poem*. Stanford, CA: Stanford University Press, 1996.

———. *Tradition and the Individual Poem: An Inquiry into Anthologies*. Stanford, CA: Stanford University Press, 2001.

Fleming, Juliet. "Changed as Opinions to Flowers." In *Renaissance Paratexts*, edited by Helen Smith and Louise Wilson, 48–64. Cambridge: Cambridge University Press, 2011.

———. *Graffiti and the Writing Arts of Early Modern England*. London: Reaktion Books, 2001.

Fraistat, Neil, ed. *Poems in Their Place: The Intertextuality and Order of Poetic Collections*. Chapel Hill: University of North Carolina Press, 1986.

Freehafer, John. "Leonard Digges, Ben Jonson, and the Beginning of Shakespeare Idolatry." *Shakespeare Quarterly* 21, no. 1 (1970): 63–75.

Freeman, Arthur, and Janet Ing Freeman. *John Payne Collier: Scholarship and Forgery in the Nineteenth Century*. 2 vols. New Haven, CT: Yale University Press, 2004.

Galey, Alan. *The Shakespearean Archive: Experiments in New Media from the Renaissance to Postmodernity*. Cambridge: Cambridge University Press, 2014.

Gascoigne, George. *A Hundreth Sundrie Flowres*. Edited by G. W. Pigman III. Oxford: Clarendon Press, 2000.

Genette, Gérard. *Paratexts: Thresholds of Interpretation*. Translated by Jane E. Lewin. Cambridge: Cambridge University Press, 1997.

Gillespie, Alexandra. "Poets, Printers, and Early English Sammelbände." *Huntington Library Quarterly* 67, no. 2 (2004): 189–214.

Goldring, Elizabeth. "Gascoigne and Kenilworth: The Production, Reception, and Afterlife of *The Princely Pleasures*." *English Literary Renaissance* 44, no. 3 (2014): 363–87.

Greenblatt, Stephen, George Logan, and Katharine Eisaman Maus, eds. *The Norton Anthology of English Literature*. 10th ed. Vol. B. New York: W. W. Norton, 2018.

Greene, Roland. *Five Words: Critical Semantics in the Age of Shakespeare and Cervantes*. Chicago: University of Chicago Press, 2013.

———. *Post-Petrarchism: Origins and Innovations of the Western Lyric Sequence*. Princeton, NJ: Princeton University Press, 1991.

Greene, Thomas. *The Light in Troy: Imitation and Discovery in Renaissance Poetry*. New Haven, CT: Yale University Press, 1982.

Greg, W. W. "An Elizabethan Printer and His Copy." *The Library*, 4th ser., 4, no. 2 (1923): 102–19.

———. "Tottel's Miscellany." *The Library*, 2nd ser., 5, no. 18 (1904): 113–33.

Greg, W. W., and E. Boswell, eds. *Records of the Court of the Stationers' Company, 1576 to 1602, from Register B*. London: Bibliographical Society, 1930.

Griffiths, Jane. *Diverting Authorities: Experimental Glossing Practices in Manuscript and Print*. Oxford: Oxford University Press, 2014

Hamlin, Hannibal. *Psalm Culture and Early Modern English Literature*. Cambridge: Cambridge University Press, 2004.

Hamrick, Stephen. "'Their Gods in Verses': The Popular Reception of *Songes and Sonettes*, 1557–1674." In *Tottel's "Songes and Sonettes" in Context*, edited by Stephen Hamrick, 163–99. Farnham, England: Ashgate, 2013.

———. "*Tottel's Miscellany* and the English Reformation." *Criticism* 44, no. 4 (2002): 329–61.

———, ed. *Tottel's "Songes and Sonettes" in Context*. Farnham, England: Ashgate, 2013.

Hanna, Ralph, III. "Miscellaneity and Vernacularity: Conditions of Literary Production in Late Medieval England." In *The Whole Book: Cultural Perspectives on the Medieval Miscellany*, edited by Stephen G. Nichols and Siegfried Wenzel, 37–51. Ann Arbor: University of Michigan Press, 1996.

Hannay, Margaret P. *Philip's Phoenix: Mary Sidney, Countess of Pembroke*. Oxford: Oxford University Press, 1990.

Harrier, Richard. *The Canon of Sir Thomas Wyatt's Poetry*. Cambridge, MA: Harvard University Press, 1975.

Harris, Jonathan Gil. *Untimely Matter in the Time of Shakespeare*. Philadelphia: University of Pennsylvania Press, 2009.

Harris, William O. "Early Elizabethan Sonnets in Sequence." *Studies in Philology* 68, no. 4 (1971): 451–69.

Haskin, Dayton. *John Donne in the Nineteenth Century*. Oxford: Oxford University Press, 2007.

———. "The Love Lyric [Songs and Sonets]." In *The Oxford Handbook of John Donne*, edited by Dennis Flynn, M. Thomas Hester, and Jeanne Shami, 180–205. Oxford: Oxford University Press, 2011.

Heale, Elizabeth. *Autobiography and Authorship in Renaissance Verse: Chronicles of the Self*. Basingstoke: Palgrave Macmillan, 2002.

Hebel, J. William. "Nicholas Ling and *Englands Helicon*." *The Library*, 4th ser., 5, no. 2 (1924): 153–60.

Helgerson, Richard. *The Elizabethan Prodigals*. Berkeley: University of California Press, 1976.

———. *Self-Crowned Laureates: Spenser, Jonson, Milton, and the Literary System*. Berkeley: University of California Press, 1983.

Heninger, S. K. "Spenser, Sidney, and Poetic Form." *Studies in Philology* 88, no. 2 (1991): 140–52.

Herrick, Robert. *The Complete Poetry of Robert Herrick*. Edited by Tom Cain and Ruth Connolly. 2 vols. Oxford: Oxford University Press, 2013.

Hetherington, Michael. "Gascoigne's Accidents: Contingency, Skill, and the Logic of Writing." *English Literary Renaissance* 46, no. 1 (2016): 29–59.

Hindle, Steve. *The State and Social Change in Early Modern England, c. 1550–1640*. New York: St. Martin's Press, 2000.

Hobbs, Mary. *Early Seventeenth-Century Verse Miscellany Manuscripts*. Aldershot, England: Scolar Press, 1992.

Holton, Amanda, and Tom MacFaul, eds. *Tottel's Miscellany: Songs and Sonnets of Henry Howard, Earl of Surrey, Sir Thomas Wyatt and Others*. New York: Penguin Classics, 2011.

Hooks, Adam G. *Selling Shakespeare: Biography, Bibliography, and the Book Trade*. Cambridge: Cambridge University Press, 2016.

Hughes, Felicity A. "Gascoigne's Poses." *SEL: Studies in English Literature, 1500–1900* 37, no. 1 (1997): 1–19.

Hughey, Ruth, ed. *The Arundel Harington Manuscript of Tudor Poetry*. 2 vols. Columbus: Ohio State University Press, 1960.

Hunter, G. K. "Drab and Golden Lyrics of the Renaissance." In *Forms of Lyric: Selected Papers from the English Institute*, edited by Reuben A. Brower, 1–18. New York: Columbia University Press, 1970.

Hutson, Lorna. *The Invention of Suspicion: Law and Mimesis in Shakespeare and Renaissance Drama*. Oxford: Oxford University Press, 2007.

Hutton, James. *The Greek Anthology in Italy to the Year 1800*. Ithaca, NY: Cornell University Press, 1935.

Ingram, Randall. "Lego Ego: Reading Seventeenth-Century Books of Epigrams." In *Books and Readers in Early Modern England*, edited by Jennifer Andersen and Elizabeth Sauer, 160–76. Philadelphia: University of Pennsylvania Press, 2002.

Jackson, H. J. *Marginalia: Readers Writing in Books*. New Haven, CT: Yale University Press, 2001.

Johnson, Eleanor. *Practicing Literary Theory in the Middle Ages: Ethics and the Mixed Form in Chaucer, Gower, Usk, and Hoccleve*. Chicago: University of Chicago Press, 2013.

Johnson, Samuel. *Lives of the English Poets*. Edited by George Birkbeck Hill. 3 vols. New York: Octagon Books, 1967.

Johnston, Michael, and Michael Van Dussen, eds. *The Medieval Manuscript Book: Cultural Approaches*. Cambridge: Cambridge University Press, 2015.

Juel-Jensen, Bent. "Michael Drayton and William Drummond of Hawthornden: A Lost Autograph Letter Recovered." *The Library*, 5th ser., 21, no. 4 (1966): 328–30.

Kalas, Rayna. *Frame, Glass, Verse: The Technology of Poetic Invention in the English Renaissance*. Ithaca, NY: Cornell University Press, 2007.

Kastan, David Scott. "The Body of the Text." *ELH* 81, no. 2 (2014): 443–67.

———. *Shakespeare and the Book*. Cambridge: Cambridge University Press, 2001.

Kearney, James. *The Incarnate Text: Imagining the Book in Reformation England*. Philadelphia: University of Pennsylvania Press, 2009.

Kirwood, A. E. M. "Richard Field, Printer, 1589–1624." *The Library*, 4th ser., 12, no. 1 (1931): 1–39.

Kiséry, András. "An Author and a Bookshop: Publishing Marlowe's Remains at the Black Bear." *Philological Quarterly* 91, no. 3 (2012): 361–92.

Kneidel, Gregory. "Samuel Daniel and Edification." *SEL: Studies in English Literature, 1500–1900* 44, no. 1 (2004): 59–76.

Knight, Jeffrey Todd. *Bound to Read: Compilations, Collections, and the Making of Renaissance Literature*. Philadelphia: University of Pennsylvania Press, 2013.

———. "Organizing Manuscript and Print: From *Compilatio* to Compilation." In *The Medieval Manuscript Book: Cultural Approaches*, edited by Michael Johnston and Michael Van Dussen, 77–95. Cambridge: Cambridge University Press, 2015.

Kolb, Laura. "Stella's Voice: Echo and Collaboration in *Astrophil and Stella* 57 and 58." *Sidney Journal* 30, no. 1 (2012): 79–100.

Kolkovich, Elizabeth Zeman. *The Elizabethan Country House Entertainment: Print, Performance, and Gender*. Cambridge: Cambridge University Press, 2016.

Kramnick, Jonathan. *Making the English Canon: Print-Capitalism and the Cultural Past, 1700–1770*. Cambridge: Cambridge University Press, 1998.

Kuchar, Gary. "Henry Constable and the Question of Catholic Poetics: Affective Piety and Erotic Identification in the *Spirituall Sonnettes*." *Philological Quarterly* 85, no. 1–2 (2006): 69–90.

Lamb, Mary Ellen. *Gender and Authorship in the Sidney Circle*. Madison: University of Wisconsin Press, 1990.

Laroche, Rebecca. "'O Absent Presence,' Sidney Is Not Here: The Lament for Astrophil and the Stellar Presence of a Woman Writer." *Sidney Journal* 20, no. 2 (2002): 21–44.

Larson, Deborah Aldrich. "Donne's Contemporary Reputation: Evidence from Some Commonplace Books and Manuscript Miscellanies." *John Donne Journal: Studies in the Age of Donne* 12, nos. 1–2 (1993): 115–30.

Leishman, J. B. *The Three Parnassus Plays (1598–1601)*. London: Nicholson & Watson, 1949.

Lennard, John. *But I Digress: The Exploitation of Parentheses in English Printed Verse*. Oxford: Clarendon Press, 1991.

Lerer, Seth. *Courtly Letters in the Age of Henry VIII: Literary Culture and the Arts of Deceit*. Cambridge: Cambridge University Press, 1997.

———. "Cultivation and Inhumation: Some Thoughts on the Cultural Impact of Tottel's *Songes and Sonettes*." In *Tottel's Songes and Sonettes in Context*, edited by Stephen Hamrick, 147–62. Farnham, England: Ashgate, 2013.

———. "Literary Histories." In *Cultural Reformations: Medieval and Renaissance in Literary History*, edited by Brian Cummings and James Simpson, 75–91. Oxford: Oxford University Press, 2010.

———. "Medieval English Literature and the Idea of the Anthology." *PMLA* 118, no. 5 (2003): 1251–67.

Lesser, Zachary. *Renaissance Drama and the Politics of Publication: Readings in the English Book Trade*. Cambridge: Cambridge University Press, 2004.

Lesser, Zachary, and Peter Stallybrass. "The First Literary *Hamlet* and the Commonplacing of Professional Plays." *Shakespeare Quarterly* 59, no. 4 (2008): 371–420.

Lewis, C. S. *English Literature in the Sixteenth Century, Excluding Drama*. Oxford: Clarendon Press, 1954.

Lock, Anne Vaughan. *The Collected Works of Anne Vaughan Lock*. Edited by Susan M. Felch. Medieval & Renaissance Texts and Studies, vol. 185. Tempe: Arizona Center for Medieval and Renaissance Studies in conjunction with Renaissance English Text Society, 1999.

Loewenstein, Joseph. *The Author's Due: Printing and the Prehistory of Copyright*. Chicago: University of Chicago Press, 2002.

Love, Harold. *The Culture and Commerce of Texts: Scribal Publication in Seventeenth-Century England*. Amherst: University of Massachusetts Press, 1998.

Lynch, Deidre. *Loving Literature: A Cultural History*. Chicago: University of Chicago Press, 2015.

Mack, Peter. *Elizabethan Rhetoric: Theory and Practice*. Cambridge: Cambridge University Press, 2002.

Maguire, Laurie E. *Shakespearean Suspect Texts: The "Bad" Quartos and Their Contexts*. Cambridge: Cambridge University Press, 1996.

———. "Typographical Embodiment: The Case of *etcetera*." In *The Oxford Handbook of Shakespeare and Embodiment: Gender, Sexuality, and Race*, edited by Valerie Traub, 527–48. Oxford: Oxford University Press, 2016.

Mann, Jenny C. *Outlaw Rhetoric: Figuring Vernacular Eloquence in Shakespeare's England*. Ithaca, NY: Cornell University Press, 2012.

Marcus, Leah S. *Unediting the Renaissance: Shakespeare, Marlowe, Milton*. London: Routledge, 1996.

Marotti, Arthur F. *John Donne, Coterie Poet*. Madison: University of Wisconsin Press, 1986.

———. "'Love Is Not Love': Elizabethan Sonnet Sequences and the Social Order." *ELH* 49, no. 2 (1982): 396–428.

———. *Manuscript, Print, and the English Renaissance Lyric*. Ithaca, NY: Cornell University Press, 1995.

———. "Neighborhood, Social Networks, and the Making of a Family's Manuscript Poetry Collection: The Case of British Library Additional MS 25707." In *Material Readings of Early Modern Culture: Texts and Social Practices, 1580–1730*, edited by James Daybell and Peter Hinds, 185–207. Basingstoke: Palgrave Macmillan, 2010.

———. "Shakespeare's Sonnets as Literary Property." In *Soliciting Interpretation: Literary Theory and Seventeenth-Century English Poetry*, edited by Elizabeth D. Harvey and Katharine Eisaman Maus, 143–73. Chicago: University of Chicago Press, 1990.

Marquis, Paul A. "Editing and Unediting Richard Tottel's *Songes and Sonettes*." *Book Collector* 56, no. 3 (2007): 353–74.

———. "Politics and Print: The Curious Revisions to Tottel's *Songes and Sonettes*." *Studies in Philology* 97, no. 2 (2000): 145–64.

———. "Printing History and Editorial Design in the Elizabethan Version of Tottel's Songes and Sonettes." In *Tottel's Songes and Sonettes in Context*, edited by Stephen Hamrick, 13–36. Farnham, England: Ashgate, 2013.

———, ed. *Richard Tottel's "Songes and Sonettes": The Elizabethan Version*. Tempe: Arizona Center for Medieval and Renaissance Studies in conjunction with Renaissance English Text Society, 2007.

Martínez Valdivia, Lucía. "Mere Meter: A Revised History of English Poetry." *ELH* 86, no. 3 (2019): 555–85.

Massai, Sonia. *Shakespeare and the Rise of the Editor*. Cambridge: Cambridge University Press, 2007.

Masten, Jeffrey. *Queer Philologies: Sex, Language, and Affect in Shakespeare's Time*. Philadelphia: University of Pennsylvania Press, 2016.

Matz, Robert. "The Scandals of Shakespeare's Sonnets." *ELH* 77, no. 2 (2010): 477–508.

Maurette, Pablo. "Shakespeare's *Venus and Adonis* and Sixteenth-Century Kiss Poetry." *English Literary Renaissance* 47, no. 3 (2017): 355–79.

May, Steven W. "Anne Lock and Thomas Norton's *Meditation of a Penitent Sinner*." *Modern Philology* 114, no. 4 (2017): 793–819.

———. "Popularizing Courtly Poetry: Tottel's Miscellany and Its Progeny." In *The Oxford Handbook of Tudor Literature, 1485–1603*, edited by Mike Pincombe and Cathy Shrank, 418–33. Oxford: Oxford University Press, 2011.

———. "Tudor Aristocrats and the 'Stigma of Print.'" In *Renaissance Papers, 1980*, edited by A. Leigh DeNeef and M. Thomas Hester, 11–18. Durham, NC: Southeastern Renaissance Conference, 1981.

———. "William Hunnis and the 1577 *Paradise of Dainty Devices*." *Studies in Bibliography: Papers of the Bibliographical Society of the University of Virginia* 28 (1975): 63–80.

McCarthy, Erin A. "*Poems, by J. D.* (1635) and the Creation of John Donne's Literary Biography." *John Donne Journal: Studies in the Age of Donne* 32 (2013): 57–85.

McGann, Jerome J. "Literature by Design Since 1790." *Victorian Poetry* 48, no. 1 (Spring 2010): 11–40.

McKenzie, D. F. *Making Meaning: "Printers of the Mind" and Other Essays*. Edited by Peter D. McDonald and Michael F. Suarez. Amherst: University of Massachusetts Press, 2002.

McKitterick, David. *Print, Manuscript and the Search for Order, 1450–1830*. Cambridge: Cambridge University Press, 2003.

Melnikoff, Kirk. *Elizabethan Publishing and the Makings of Literary Culture*. Toronto: University of Toronto Press, 2018.

———. "Jones's Pen and Marlowe's Socks: Richard Jones, Print Culture, and the Beginnings of English Dramatic Literature." *Studies in Philology* 102, no. 2 (2005): 184–209.

———. "Richard Jones (fl. 1564–1613): Elizabethan Printer, Bookseller and Publisher." *Analytical & Enumerative Bibliography* 12 (2001): 153–84.

Moss, Ann. *Printed Commonplace-Books and the Structuring of Renaissance Thought*. Oxford: Clarendon Press, 1996.

Muir, Kenneth, ed. *Sir Thomas Wyatt and His Circle: Unpublished Poems Edited from the Blage Manuscript*. English Reprints Series, no. 18. Liverpool: Liverpool University Press, 1961.

Nebeker, Eric. "Broadside Ballads, Miscellanies, and the Lyric in Print." *ELH* 76, no. 4 (2009): 989–1013.

Neely, Carol Thomas. "The Structure of English Renaissance Sonnet Sequences." *ELH* 45, no. 3 (1978): 359–89.

Nelson, Ingrid. *Lyric Tactics: Poetry, Genre, and Practice in Later Medieval England*. Philadelphia: University of Pennsylvania Press, 2017.

Newton, Richard C. "Jonson and the (Re-)Invention of the Book." In *Classic and Cavalier: Essays on Jonson and the Sons of Ben*, edited by Claude J. Summers and Ted-Larry Pebworth, 31–55. Pittsburgh: University of Pittsburgh Press, 1982.

———. "Making Books from Leaves: Poets Become Editors." In *Print and Culture in the Renaissance: Essays on the Advent of Printing in Europe*, edited by Gerald P. Tyson and Sylvia S. Wagonheim, 246–64. Newark: University of Delaware Press, 1986.

Nichols, Stephen G., and Siegfried Wenzel. Introduction to *The Whole Book: Cultural Perspectives on the Medieval Miscellany*, edited by Stephen G. Nichols and Siegfried Wenzel, 1–6. Ann Arbor: University of Michigan Press, 1996.

———, eds. *The Whole Book: Cultural Perspectives on the Medieval Miscellany*. Ann Arbor: University of Michigan Press, 1996.

North, Marcy. *The Anonymous Renaissance: Cultures of Discretion in Tudor-Stuart England*. Chicago: University of Chicago Press, 2003.

———. "The Sonnets and Book History." In *A Companion to Shakespeare's Sonnets*, edited by Michael Schoenfeldt, 204–21. Malden, MA: Blackwell, 2010.

O'Callaghan, Michelle. "Collecting Verse: 'Significant Shape' and the Paper-Book in the Early Seventeenth Century." *Huntington Library Quarterly* 80, no. 2 (2017): 309–24.

———. "Textual Gatherings: Print, Community and Verse Miscellanies in Early Modern England." *Early Modern Culture* 8 (2010).

Palfrey, Simon, and Tiffany Stern. *Shakespeare in Parts*. Oxford: Oxford University Press, 2007.

Palmer, Philip S. "'The Progress of Thy Glorious Book': Material Reading and the Play of Paratext in *Coryats Crudities* (1611)." *Renaissance Studies: Journal of the Society for Renaissance Studies* 28, no. 3 (2014): 336–55.

Parker, Patricia. "Preposterous Events." *Shakespeare Quarterly* 43, no. 2 (1992): 186–213.

Parkes, M. B. "The Influence of the Concepts of *Ordinatio* and *Compilatio* on the Development of the Book." In *The History of the Book in the West*, vol. 1, *400 AD–1455*, edited by Jane Roberts and Pamela Robinson, 123–58. Farnham, England: Ashgate, 2010.

Pérez-Júaregui, María Jesús. "A Queen in a 'Purple Robe': Henry Constable's Poetic Tribute to Mary, Queen of Scots." *Studies in Philology* 113, no. 3 (2016): 577–94.

Petrarca, Francesco. *Rerum familiarium libri*. Translated by Aldo S. Bernardo. 3 vols. Albany: State University of New York Press, 1975.

Pigman, G. W., III. "Versions of Imitation in the Renaissance." *Renaissance Quarterly* 33, no. 1 (1980): 1–32.

Piper, Andrew. *Dreaming in Books: The Making of the Bibliographic Imagination in the Romantic Age*. Chicago: University of Chicago Press, 2009.

Pitcher, John. "Samuel Daniel's Gifts of Books to Lord Chancellor Egerton." *Medieval and Renaissance Drama in England: An Annual Gathering of Research, Criticism and Reviews* 17 (2005): 216–38.

Pomeroy, Elizabeth. *The Elizabethan Miscellanies: Their Development and Conventions*. Berkeley: University of California Press, 1973.

Powell, Jason. "The Network Behind 'Tottel's' Miscellany." *English Literary Renaissance* 46, no. 2 (2016): 193–224.

Pratt, Aaron T. "Stab-Stitching and the Status of Early English Playbooks as Literature." *The Library*, 7th ser., 16, no. 3 (2015): 304–28.

Price, Leah. "From *The History of a Book* to a 'History of the Book.'" *Representations* 108, no. 1 (2009): 120–38.

Prouty, G. T. *George Gascoigne: Elizabethan Courtier, Soldier, and Poet*. New York: Columbia University Press, 1942.

Puttenham, George. *The Art of English Poesy*. Edited by Frank Whigham and Wayne A. Rebhorn. Ithaca, NY: Cornell University Press, 2007.

Raymond, Joad. *Pamphlets and Pamphleteering in Early Modern Britain*. Cambridge: Cambridge University Press, 2006.

Rienstra, Debra. "'Disorder Best Fit': Henry Lok and Holy Disorder in Devotional Lyric." *Spenser Studies: A Renaissance Poetry Annual* 27 (2012): 249–87.

Roberts, Sasha. *Reading Shakespeare's Poems in Early Modern England*. Basingstoke: Palgrave Macmillan, 2003.

Roche, Thomas P., Jr. *Petrarch and the English Sonnet Sequences*. New York: AMS Press, 1989.

Rollins, Hyder Edward, ed. *England's Helicon, 1600, 1614*. 2 vols. Cambridge, MA: Harvard University Press, 1935.

———, ed. *A Gorgeous Gallery of Gallant Inventions (1578)*. Cambridge, MA: Harvard University Press, 1926.

———, ed. *A Handful of Pleasant Delights (1584)*. Cambridge, MA: Harvard University Press, 1924.

———, ed. *The Phoenix Nest, 1593*. Cambridge, MA: Harvard University Press, 1969.

———, ed. *A Poetical Rhapsody, 1602–1621*. 2 vols. Cambridge, MA: Harvard University Press, 1931.

———, ed. *Tottel's Miscellany (1557–1587)*. 2 vols. Cambridge, MA: Harvard University Press, 1928.

Rosenberg, Jessica. "A Digression to Hospitality: Thrift and Christmastime in Shakespeare and the Literature of Husbandry." In *Shakespeare and Hospitality: Ethics, Politics, and Exchange*, edited by David B. Goldstein and Julia Reinhard Lupton, 39–66. New York: Routledge, 2016.

———. "The Point of the Couplet: Shakespeare's Sonnets and Tusser's *A Hundreth Good Pointes of Husbandrie*." *ELH* 83, no. 1 (2016): 1–41.

Rosenfeld, Colleen Ruth. *Indecorous Thinking: Figures of Speech in Early Modern Poetics*. New York: Fordham University Press, 2018.

Sanchez, Melissa E. "'In My Selfe the Smart I Try': Female Promiscuity in *Astrophil and Stella*." *ELH* 80, no. 1 (2013): 1–27.

Saunders, J. W. "The Stigma of Print: A Note on the Social Bases of Tudor Poetry." *Essays in Criticism* 1, no. 2 (1951): 139–64.

Scanlon, James J. "Sidney's *Astrophil and Stella*: 'See What It Is to Love' Sensually!" *SEL: Studies in English Literature, 1500–1900* 16, no. 1 (1976): 65–74.

Scodel, Joshua. "Lyric." In *The Oxford History of Literary Translation in English*, vol. 2, *1550–1660*, edited by Gordon Braden, Robert Cummings, and Stuart Gillespie, 212–47. Oxford: Oxford University Press, 2010.

———. "Seventeenth-Century English Literary Criticism: Classical Values, English Texts and Contexts." In *The Cambridge History of Literary Criticism*, vol. 3, *The Renaissance*, edited by Glyn Norton, 543–54. Cambridge: Cambridge University Press, 1999.

Scott, Charlotte. *Shakespeare and the Idea of the Book*. Oxford: Oxford University Press, 2007.

Scott, William. *The Model of Poesy*. Edited by Gavin Alexander. Cambridge: Cambridge University Press, 2013.

Shakespeare, William. *The Complete Sonnets and Poems*. Edited by Colin Burrow. Oxford: Oxford University Press, 2002.

———. *Hamlet*. Edited by Ann Thompson and Neil Taylor. London: Arden Shakespeare, 2006.

———. *The Merry Wives of Windsor*. Edited by Giorgio Melchiori. London: Arden Shakespeare, 2000.

———. *New Variorum Edition of Shakespeare: The Sonnets*. Edited by Hyder Edward Rollins. 2 vols. Philadelphia: J. B. Lippincott, 1944.

———. *Shakespeare's Sonnets*. Edited by Stephen Booth. New Haven, CT: Yale University Press, 2000.

Shami, Jeanne, Dennis Flynn, and M. Thomas Hester, eds. *The Oxford Handbook of John Donne*. Oxford: Oxford University Press, 2011.

Shannon, Laurie. "Minerva's Men: Horizontal Nationhood and the Literary Production of Googe, Turberville, and Gascoigne." In *The Oxford Handbook of Tudor Literature, 1485–1603*, edited by Mike Pincombe and Cathy Shrank, 437–54. Oxford: Oxford University Press, 2011.

———. "Poetic Companies: Musters of Agency in George Gascoigne's 'Friendly Verse.'" *GLQ: A Journal of Lesbian and Gay Studies* 10, no. 3 (2004): 453–83.

Shawcross, John T. "The Arrangement and Order of John Donne's Poems." In *Poems in Their Place: The Intertextuality and Order of Poetic Collections*, edited by Neil Fraistat, 119–63. Chapel Hill: University of North Carolina Press, 1986.

Sherman, William H. *Used Books: Marking Readers in Renaissance England*. Philadelphia: University of Pennsylvania Press, 2008.

Shrank, Cathy. "'Matters of Love as of Discourse': The English Sonnet, 1560–1580." *Studies in Philology* 105, no. 1 (2008): 30–49.

———. "Reading Shakespeare's *Sonnets*: John Benson and the 1640 *Poems*." *Shakespeare* 5, no. 3 (2009): 271–91.

Sidney, Philip. *The Poems of Sir Philip Sidney*. Edited by William A. Ringler. Oxford: Clarendon Press, 1962.

Simon, Margaret. "Authorial Feints and Affecting Forms in George Gascoigne's *The Adventures of Master F. J.*" In *Renaissance Papers, 2013*, edited by Jim Pearce and Joanna Kucinski, 43–54. Rochester, NY: Published for the Southeastern Renaissance Conference by Camden House, 2014.

———. "Refraining Songs: The Dynamics of Form in Sidney's *Astrophil and Stella*." *Studies in Philology* 109, no. 1 (2012): 86–102.

Skura, Meredith Anne. *Tudor Autobiography: Listening for Inwardness*. Chicago: University of Chicago Press, 2008.

Smith, Daniel Starza. *John Donne and the Conway Papers: Patronage and Manuscript Circulation in the Early Seventeenth Century*. Oxford: Oxford University Press, 2014.

Smith, Helen, and Louise Wilson, eds. *Renaissance Paratexts*. Cambridge: Cambridge University Press, 2011.

Smith, Nathanial B. "The Apparition of a Seventeenth-Century Donne Reader: A Hand-Written Index to *Poems, By J. D.* (1633)." *John Donne Journal: Studies in the Age of Donne* 20 (2001): 161–99.

Smyth, Adam. *Autobiography in Early Modern England*. Cambridge: Cambridge University Press, 2010.

———. *Material Texts in Early Modern England*. Cambridge: Cambridge University Press, 2018.

———. *"Profit and Delight": Printed Miscellanies in England, 1640–1682*. Detroit, MI: Wayne State University Press, 2004.

Songes and Sonettes (Tottel's Miscellany), 1557. Leeds: Scolar Press, 1966.

Stallybrass, Peter. "Books and Scrolls: Navigating the Bible." In *Books and Readers in Early Modern England*, edited by Jennifer Andersen and Elizabeth Sauer, 42–79. Philadelphia: University of Pennsylvania Press, 2002.

Staub, Susan C. "Dissembling His Art: 'Gascoigne's Gardnings.'" *Renaissance Studies* 25, no. 1 (2011): 95–110.

———. "The Lady Frances Did Watch: Gascoigne's Voyeuristic Narrative." In *Framing Elizabethan Fictions: Contemporary Approaches to Early Modern Narrative Prose*, edited by Constance C. Relihan, 41–54. Kent, OH: Kent State University Press, 1996.

Stenner, Rachel. *The Typographic Imaginary in Early Modern English Literature*. New York: Routledge, 2019.

Stewart, Alan. "Gelding Gascoigne." In *Prose Fiction and Early Modern Sexualities in England, 1570–1640*, edited by Constance Relihan and Goran Stanivukovic, 147–69. New York: Palgrave Macmillan, 2004.

Strier, Richard. "Paleness Versus Eloquence: The Ideologies of Style in the English Renaissance." *Explorations in Renaissance Culture* 45, no. 2 (2019): 91–120.

Sullivan, Ceri. *The Rhetoric of Credit: Merchants in Early Modern Writing*. Madison, NJ: Fairleigh Dickinson University Press, 2002.

Swann, Marjorie. *Curiosities and Texts: The Culture of Collecting in Early Modern England*. Philadelphia: University of Pennsylvania Press, 2001.

Targoff, Ramie. *Common Prayer: The Language of Public Devotion in Early Modern England*. Chicago: University of Chicago Press, 2001.

Thompson, John. *The Founding of English Metre*. New York: Columbia University Press, 1961.

Tiffany, Daniel. *Infidel Poetics: Riddles, Nightlife, Substance*. Chicago: University of Chicago Press, 2009.

Trettien, Whitney. "Media, Materiality, and Time in the History of Reading: The Case of the Little Gidding Harmonies." *PMLA* 133, no. 5 (2018): 1135–51.

Trevilian, Thomas. *The Trevelyon Miscellany of 1608: A Facsimile of Folger Shakespeare Library MS V.b.232*. Edited by Heather Wolfe. Seattle: Folger Shakespeare Library; distributed by University of Washington Press, 2007.

Trudell, Scott A. *Unwritten Poetry: Song, Performance, and Media in Early Modern England*. Oxford: Oxford University Press, 2019.

Vickers, Nancy J. "Diana Described: Scattered Woman and Scattered Rhyme." *Critical Inquiry* 8, no. 2 (1981): 265–79.

Vine, Angus. *Miscellaneous Order: Manuscript Culture and the Early Modern Organization of Knowledge*. Oxford: Oxford University Press, 2019.

Wabuda, Susan. *Preaching During the English Reformation*. Cambridge: Cambridge University Press, 2002.

Wall, Wendy. *The Imprint of Gender: Authorship and Publication in the English Renaissance*. Ithaca, NY: Cornell University Press, 1993.

Wall-Randell, Sarah. *The Immaterial Book: Reading and Romance in Early Modern England*. Ann Arbor: University of Michigan Press, 2013.

Warley, Christopher. *Sonnet Sequences and Social Distinction in Renaissance England*. Cambridge: Cambridge University Press, 2005.

Warner, J. Christopher. *The Making and Marketing of Tottel's Miscellany, 1557: "Songs and Sonnets" in the Summer of the Martyrs' Fires*. Farnham, England: Ashgate, 2013.

———. "'Sonnets en Anglois': A Hitherto Unknown Edition of *Tottel's Miscellany*." *Notes and Queries* 58, no. 2 (2011): 204–6.

Warton, Thomas. *The History of English Poetry, from the Close of the Eleventh Century to the Commencement of the Eighteenth Century*. 3 vols. London: J. Dodsley et al., 1774–81.

Weiss, Adrian. "Shared Printing, Printer's Copy, and the Text(s) of Gascoigne's *A Hundreth Sundrie Flowres*." *Studies in Bibliography* 45 (1992): 71–104.

Williams, Claire Bryony. "'This and the Rest Maisters We All May Mende': Reconstructing the Practices and Anxieties of a Manuscript Miscellany's Reader-Compiler." *Huntington Library Quarterly* 80, no. 2 (2017): 277–92.

Winston, Jessica. "Lyric Poetry at the Early Elizabethan Inns of Court: Forming a Professional Community." In *The Intellectual and Cultural World of the Early Modern Inns of Courts*, edited by Jayne Elisabeth Archer, Elizabeth Goldring, and Sarah Knight, 223–44. Manchester: Manchester University Press, 2011.

Winters, Yvor. "The 16th Century Lyric in England: A Critical and Historical Reinterpretation: Part I." *Poetry* 53, no. 5 (1939): 258–72.

Woudhuysen, H. R. "The Foundations of Shakespeare's Text." *Proceedings of the British Academy* 125 (2004): 69–100.

———. *Sir Philip Sidney and the Circulation of Manuscripts, 1558–1640.* Oxford: Clarendon Press, 1996.

Zarnowiecki, Matthew. *Fair Copies: Reproducing the English Lyric from Tottel to Shakespeare.* Toronto: University of Toronto Press, 2014.

———. "'Nedelesse Singularitie': George Gascoigne's Strategies for Preserving Lyric Delight." *Early Modern Literary Studies: A Journal of Sixteenth- and Seventeenth-Century English Literature* 14, no. 1 (2008): 28 paragraphs.

Zucker, Adam. *The Places of Wit in Early Modern English Comedy.* Cambridge: Cambridge University Press, 2011.

Zurcher, Andrew. "The Printing of the Cantos of Mutabilitie in 1609." In *Celebrating Mutabilitie: Essays on Edmund Spenser's Mutabilitie Cantos*, edited by Jane Grogan, 40–60. Manchester: Manchester University Press, 2010.

INDEX

abstraction, 190, 191, 198; of poem scenarios, 38, 42, 76, 97, 99; in sonnet books, 125, 146, 148

accident, textual, 9, 19, 108, 162

Alexander, Gavin, 134, 236n108

Allde, John, 68, 69

alliteration, 1, 54, 56, 59, 61, 75

Ames, Joseph, *Typographical Antiquities*, 50–51

Amorose Songes, Sonets, and Elegies, The (Craig), 145

anthologies, 6–7, 19, 20, 22, 33, 59, 89, 129

"anthology," 6–7, 8, 22, 57, 220n10

apian metaphor. *See* bee imagery

Araygnement of Paris, The (Peele), 83

Arber, Edward, 51

Arbor of Amitie, The (Howell), 3, 58

Arbor of Amorous Devises, The (Breton), 58

Arcadian Rhetorike, The (Fraunce), 135–36

architectural imagery, 1, 9, 67–68, 69

Art of English Poesy, The (Puttenham), 10, 64, 70, 105, 161

Astrophel and Stella (quartos, Sidney), 83, 126, 134–43, 144, 148, 152, 242n25. See also *Astrophil and Stella* (Sidney); *Countesse of Pembrokes Arcadia, The* (Sidney)

Astrophil and Stella (Sidney), 127–34, 241n8, 242n20. See also *Astrophel and Stella* (quartos, Sidney); *Countesse of Pembrokes Arcadia, The* (Sidney)

attributions, 54, 100; in *Astrophel and Stella*, 135; in Donne, 173–74, 180, 248n14; in *Englands Helicon*, 45, 83–87, 236nn116, 118; in *The Forrest of Fancy* (H. C.), 59, 62; in Gascoigne, 15, 67, 90, 91, 92, 100, 102; in *The Paradyse of daynty devises*, 73, 74, 76–77, 79; in Shakespeare, 197, 205; in *A Smale handfull of fragrant Flowers* (N. B.),

65; in *Songes and Sonetes*, 24–27, 29, 30, 45–46, 50

Austen, Gillian, 119, 238n18

author portraits, 186, 205

authorship, 12, 66, 94, 168–69, 196, 203, 211, 225n28, 230n1, 238n23; and Donne, 169–74, 178–95 passim, 204, 206, 211, 216, 251nn60, 63; and *Englands Helicon*, 86–87; and Gascoigne, 15, 89–92, 100–102, 118, 120, 122–23; modern notions of, 7–8, 12, 14, 23, 49–52, 59, 80, 166–67, 212; and *The Paradyse of daynty devises*, 75; and Shakespeare, 166–67, 170, 200–201, 204, 206, 210–11, 213–16; and Sidney, 127–30, 134–35, 138–42, 164, 166; and *Songes and Sonettes*, 25, 28, 38, 45, 49–52; and sonnet books, 124, 142, 146, 149–53, 157, 164–65, 166–67

Bahr, Arthur, 6, 220n20

Baker, David, 204, 254n122

ballads, 28, 71, 92, 229n108, 233n52

Banquet of Daintie Conceits, A (Munday), 58

Barnes, Barnabe: *A Divine Centurie of Spiritual Sonnets*, 143, 144; *Parthenophil and Parthenophe*, 149–50

Barnes, Joseph, 83

Barnfield, Richard, *Cynthia*, 143, 144

Basse, William, 205

Beaumont, Francis, 205, 252n82

Beedome, Thomas, *Poems Divine and Humane*, 197, 252n82

bee imagery, 65, 68–69, 128–29

Bel-vedére, or The Garden of the Muses, 82

Benson, John, 16, 170–71, 197–211 passim, 212–16, 254nn114, 116, 118, 255n125

Berthelet, Thomas, 25

bibliography, discipline of, 4, 50–51. *See also* history of the book; textual studies

ACKNOWLEDGMENTS

Like a poetry collection, my book speaks to the labors of many hands. I'm happy to have the chance to thank everyone who helped me along the way. This project began at the University of Chicago, where Bradin Cormack, Joshua Scodel, and Richard Strier inspired it and me. Since then, I have been fortunate to have the support of an extraordinary group of colleagues and friends. My heartfelt thanks to Claire Bourne, Adam Hooks, Jeff Knight, Tara Lyons, and Whitney Trettien, who each read nearly everything, often more than once. Piers Brown and Josh Calhoun offered savvy advice at crucial moments. Laura Kolb and Jessica Rosenberg always expanded the horizons of my reading and my thinking.

This book has benefited tremendously from a vibrant group of scholars at work on early modern studies. Faith Acker, Derek Dunne, Lucía Martínez Valdivia, Steve May, Erin McCarthy, Carmen Nocentelli, Joe Ortiz, Jason Powell, Emily Rendek, Debapriya Sarkar, Maggie Simon, Virginia Strain, and Scott Trudell responded to drafts with characteristic energy and grace. My thanks as well to Tamara Atkin, J. K. Barrett, Meaghan Brown, Urvashi Chakravarti, Kim Coles, Megan Cook, Emma Depledge, Lara Dodds, Fran Dolan, Hillary Eklund, Jessica Goethals, Suzanne Gossett, Matthew Harrison, Phebe Jensen, Jim Knapp, Zack Lesser, Erika Lin, Ellen Mackay, Arthur Marotti, Jeffrey Masten, Pablo Maurette, Molly Murray, Vin Nardizzi, Marcy North, Dan Shore, Adam Smyth, Wendy Wall, Sarah Wall-Randell, Thomas Ward, Will West, Mike Witmore, Jessica Wolfe, and Adam Zucker, who all shared their wisdom in conversations that kept me thinking about the broadest reach of the project. Carla Mazzio—ever the most generous—gave me the title.

At DePaul, I have thrived thanks to my colleagues Marcy Dinius, Paula McQuade, Caterina Mongiat-Farina, and Francesca Royster. Multiple deans and research councils supported applications for funding my work, especially when I received an external year of research leave.

My largest debt is to the libraries that have enriched every aspect of my scholarship. This book would not exist without the material support and intellectual community sustained by research centers and archives. The Folger Shakespeare Library made my work possible with both long- and short-term fellowships, as well as an enduring belief in the value of studying the cultural past. Erin Blake, Meg Carafano, Beth DeBold, LuEllen DeHaven, Caroline Duroselle-Melish, Amanda Herbert, Rosalind Larry, Kathleen Lynch, Camille Seerattan, Betsy Walsh, Abbie Weinberg, Owen Williams, and Heather Wolfe all welcomed me into their vast and varied intellectual world. At the Newberry Library, I've had the joy of collaborating with Jill Gage, Lia Markey, and Suzanne Karr Schmidt—Chicago's finest renaissance women. At the Henry E. Huntington Library, Steve Tabor and Vanessa Wilkie literally opened doors for me, taking me to the hidden corners of their vaults and cupboards. At Oxford's Bodleian Library, Sarah Wheale gave me access to the one book that had eluded me for years. At the Harry Ransom Center at the University of Texas, Austin, Aaron Pratt is a dynamic force for good in our field, moving conversations forward with rigor and humor. He was also extremely generous in helping me find resources when I was checking the manuscript during the coronavirus lockdown. (Needless to say, every remaining error is my own.)

This book has been greatly improved by the efforts of everyone at the University of Pennsylvania Press. Jerry Singerman had a sense of what the project could become. I am grateful for the generous scrutiny of Jenny Mann and Joshua Eckhardt, who each sharpened and buoyed my argument. I also want to thank the Folger Institute, which supported the production of my book.

For years now, I've been lucky to have the friendship of Manan Ahmed, Andy Broughton, David Emmanuel, Emily Ponder, Jon Ryan Quinn, Samir Warty, and Stasia Wieckowski. For their love and encouragement, I thank my family: Imogen, Janie, J. T., and Tim Heffernan, Sally Baker, and Ann Marie and Ellen Smith.

Part of Chapter 5 was published in *Shakespeare Quarterly* 64, no. 1 (2013): 71–98, as "Turning Sonnets into Poems: Textual Affect and John Benson's Metaphysical Shakespeare," published by Oxford University Press on behalf of the Folger Shakespeare Library. An earlier version of Chapter 3 was originally published in *Modern Language Quarterly* 76, no. 4 (2015): 413–45, published by Duke University Press.